little ◄······

# free

······► library

### NORTHERN LIGHTS LIBRARY SYSTEM

Scan me

D0442710

# Gail Vaz-Oxlade

# A Woman of Independent Means

## A WOMAN'S GUIDE TO FULL FINANCIAL SECURITY

Stoddart

Published in 1999 by Stoddart Publishing Co. Limited
34 Lesmill Road, Toronto, Canada M3B 2T6
180 Varick Street, 9th Floor, New York, New York 10014

*Distributed in Canada by:*
General Distribution Services Ltd.
325 Humber College Boulevard, Toronto, Ontario M9W 7C3
Tel. (416) 213-1919    Fax (416) 213-1917
Email customer.service@ccmailgw.genpub.com

*Distributed in the United States by:*
General Distribution Services Inc.
85 River Rock Drive, Suite 202, Buffalo, New York 14207
Toll-free Tel. 1-800-805-1083    Toll-free Fax 1-800-481-6207
Email gdsinc@genpub.com

03  02  01  00  99  1  2  3  4  5

**Canadian Cataloguing in Publication Data**
Vaz-Oxlade, Gail E., 1959–
A woman of independent means: a woman's guide to full financial security

Includes bibliographical references and index.
ISBN 0-7737-3181-4

1. Women — Finance, Personal.
I. Title.

HG179.V393 1999    332.024'042    C98-933091-5

Jacket Design: Angel Guerra
Text Design: Tannice Goddard

Printed and bound in Canada

*Stoddart Publishing gratefully acknowledges the Canada Council for the Arts and the Ontario Arts Council for their support of its publishing program.*

*To my husband, Ken, who taught me that the pursuit of fortune is a fool's game, that love is the root of happiness, and that happy is the richest a woman can be.*

*I am the richest woman in the world. Thank you.*

# Contents

# Thank You

The past two years have been very interesting. Why stop at two? The past five years have been mind-blowing. The most significant events were certainly the births of my two children, but running a close second is the work I have been doing trying to help people come to terms with money and the role it plays in their lives. From the self-publication of my first book, *The RRSP Answer Book*, now published annually by Stoddart, through my run at the magazine industry with *FinancialXPress*, through to the co-operative effort it took to get this book to the shelves, the entire experience has been fantastic. I have been especially energized by the willingness of individuals to give of their time and knowledge, of themselves in so many ways, in order to further the cause. There are a lot of people to thank.

To my dear friend Victoria Ryce, who listened when I had to work things out, read my drafts, and gave me balanced and invaluable comments. Thank you for always being on the other end of the phone and listening to my endless ideas. I value your advice and your friendship more than I can say.

To my husband, Ken, who listened as I worked through my battles with this book, encouraged me, and helped me sort the wheat from the chaff. Again, thank you for your soft honesty and enduring patience.

Thank you Gwin Gill. It was kind of you to let me into your busy day to listen to my plan and give advice. Your questions changed the direction of this book and made it the work I am so proud of now.

Thank you to Bruce Cohen, Ellen Roseman, and Tessa Wilmot for pointing me to some of the women who would become my friends in the writing of this book. Tessa, a special thanks to you for all the extra gabbing we've done.

Thank you to all the women who shared their stories with me — many of whom are not directly identified. You have been kind in letting me into your lives and sharing many difficult memories and experiences with me.

And to the women who shared their knowledge, advice, and experience with me, thank you. You were terrific. And smart too!

Finally, to Marnie Kramarich, thank you for your patience, wisdom, and stick-to-it-iveness in editing this book. Boy, are you tenacious!

# Introduction

*Our pursuit of money, or any enduring association with it, is capable of inducing not only bizarre, but ripely perverse, behaviour.*

JOHN KENNETH GALBRAITH

*The greatest crimes are caused by excess and not by necessity. Men do not become tyrants in order that they may not suffer cold.*

ARISTOTLE

When I set out to write this book, one of my main objectives was to help women put money in perspective. It seems money has become far more important than it should be, and it makes us behave in unhealthy ways, whether that means single-mindedly pursuing wealth for its own sake, blindly spending beyond our means, or enduring sleepless nights over the possibility of a bounced cheque.

On September 3, 1997, *USA Today* published a bar graph that described what people worry about in terms of their money. When divided by gender, the results were very telling. An overwhelming 70% of women feared not having enough money when they were old. They wanted safer or insured investment products (73% women, 56% male), they were unnerved by stock fluctuations (50% women, 33% male), and they tended to avoid making decisions for fear of making a mistake (33% women, 22% male). This bears out other research that shows women are more risk-averse and afraid of being poor in old age. And so we should be.

When Statistics Canada released its report "Growing Old in Canada," an alarming 40% of women over the age of 75 who were living on their own had incomes below the poverty line. And since a woman 75 or older has a greater chance of being disabled than her male counterpart, this can paint a grey picture of the future. But we have the ability to brighten that picture, by taking charge of our present financial situation and making plans for the future. We just have to understand how money works to do it.

Unfortunately, many people have an irrational fear of what is a very basic economic tool. If we can forget, just for a moment, the more complex issues — investing, retirement planning, writing a business plan — and look to the simple tasks, we can see the extremes to which some people will go to avoid taking care of their finances. They would rather buy overdraft protection, one of the most expensive forms of credit, or keep a float of money in their accounts earning next to no return, than reconcile their cheque books. They don't save. Using credit cards, they spend their yet-to-be-earned income without much thought to future implications. They don't have enough or the right kind of insurance. They don't have wills. They just don't want to think about it.

*The Wealthy Barber* sold millions of copies by delivering a simple set of messages in a simple way. David Chilton successfully opened people's eyes to the most basic steps of money management, including the importance of saving and accepting personal responsibility for retirement planning, home ownership, and risk management. In *Balancing Act*, Joanne Thomas Yaccato delivered the message that anyone can do it. Using her own experiences in coming to terms with the role money plays in her life — and with the mistakes she had made — Joanne went a long way toward demystifying money and showing how it can be controlled.

But despite the best efforts of many financial writers to put money in perspective, the language of money remains extreme. We talk about "worshipping money" and about being "money crazy." We consider money to be dirty: "filthy" rich, "stinking" rich, "money laundering," "dirt cheap." We worry about being "ripped off" or "taken to the cleaners." We are loath to the idea of talking to our children about money, fearing we will imbue them with an immoral love (or is it lust?) for money.

Most financial discussions fail to help people understand how they feel about money. While they may demonstrate how to budget, stress the importance of saving, and describe the various investments available, they seem incapable of motivating people to put these simple ideas into practice. What little that has been written on the psychology of money often doesn't integrate the practical information.

This book has been designed to deal with both the psychological and the practical. And rather than providing all the information in one voice, which is also traditional for books on personal finance, this book will offer the perspective of a dozen women who have expertise in money management. Each of these women has been carefully selected not only for her expertise and knowledge, but for her integrity.

This book will not solve your financial problems. I know that is the implicit promise of most books on money, but that promise is unrealistic. Just as money — or more money — is not the solution to most people's needs for love, security, power, freedom, status, or comfort, so this book cannot miraculously take you from where you are now to where you want to be. Only you can do that.

What this book will do, if you are a willing participant in the process, is help you uncover your personal feelings and attitudes toward money. It will provide you with information and proven techniques for positive money management. It will be a guide to what you must think about to stay on an even keel and keep money in perspective. It will ask you many questions that prompt you to find out for yourself how to achieve financial health. By answering these questions, you will find that money management is easy. You will learn new ways of dealing with money. And you will achieve the results you want.


## LIFE-CYCLE FINANCIAL PLANNING

In addition to helping you understand *who* you are when it comes to money, this book emphasizes the importance of *where* you are on the road of your life. Life-cycle issues have been used for years to help manufacturers and retailers decide how to target their customers. If you're a single woman without children, you probably read a different magazine, eat different food, and wear different clothes than a woman who is mired in rug-rats. When I was single, I ate out more often, I wore high-heeled shoes, and I hardly ever thought about spot removers for my carpet, my couch, or my clothes.

Just as where we are in our life cycle influences the commodities we buy, so too does it affect which financial products we should own. As I've moved through my life cycle, I've gone from shopping for GICs to shopping for mutual funds. I've had to think about divorce, stepchildren, and financial commitments to ex-spouses. And I've been forced to face my own mortality and make a will.

Perhaps the single change in my life that has most affected me is the birth of my children. I had no idea that it would be such an all-consuming, over-the-top, fantabulous experience. I've found in talking with women that I'm not the only one completely blown away by motherhood. In fact, one of the questions I'm most often asked is, "How can I stay home with my baby and still help make ends meet?" This is just one example of how a change in life cycle can throw a spanner in the works of the best-laid plans.

It is also one of those issues that's so new that women haven't had any long-term practice dealing with it. Our liberation has given us many new opportunities, and with those opportunities has come the need to make choices. I often suggest to new preggies, for example, that they try living on one income while they are pregnant to see how the family copes, should the sweet smell of baby addle their brains and leave them longing to remain prisoners of their love. It would be a dry run at living on one income, just in case one income is all there will be in the future. And it's a great way to actively pay down debt and build up reserves for emergencies, even if they do decide to return to work after the baby is born.

The life-cycle issue has become increasingly complicated as our norms have changed. In her book *New Passages*, Gail Sheehy says that until recently, "Chronological age has served as a uniform criterion for normalizing the roles and responsibilities that individuals assume over a lifetime . . . age norms have shifted and are no longer normative." In today's fast-moving, ever-changing, nothing's-the-same-as-it-was world, age has little to do with stage, and it's less clear where we should be when. While only one in 10 people lived to age 65 for most of human history, eight in 10 people in North America today will see their sixty-fifth birthday. No longer are 40-somethings delivering their 60-something parents into the care of old-age homes; now it is the 70-something delivering her

90-something mother. And the old demarcations we've grown used to — adulthood at 21, retirement at 65 — have no place in our current reality.

The traditional life sequence — school, job, marriage, child-rearing, empty-nesting, widowhood — has become jumbled. Many women complete their degrees well after the traditional school age. Many delay having children until their careers are well established. And divorce has changed the family structure so that many women now must raise children on their own, or help to raise stepchildren when they may never have expected to be parents at all. Just thinking about the various forms a family can take is enough to boggle the mind. And with these new social structures come new financial considerations.

Since there is no such thing as a normal life cycle anymore, does that mean we have to throw out the concept of life-cycle planning? I don't believe it does. After all, whether you are 20 or 40 and having your first child, the issue of educational savings becomes important. And whether you are widowed at 55 or divorced at 30, you'd better have your own credit history established if you want to be able to function within the financial world.

Think about financial planning as a trip through the supermarket. First there are the essentials you must have to keep body and soul together. What you put in your basket will be a direct reflection of your needs and the needs of those around you. If you are single, your essentials may be few and your fridge quite empty. If you're married with children, you'll need a larger larder. Once you're stocked with the core stuff, then you have to look at changes in the normal weekly routine that will affect what you're buying. If you're planning to have the folks over for turkey dinner, you'll be adding cranberry jelly and stuffing to your basket. If you're throwing a birthday party, oooh, now we're getting to the good stuff: ice cream and cake.

Then there's the shopping you do just in case . . . just in case friends drop in and you need pâté and crackers for a light nosh, or just in case you get a cold and need a steaming bowl of chicken soup.

The financial life cycle is similar. First there's the core stuff, the basics of your financial larder. Just about everyone needs a chequing account and a banking card. Everyone needs to establish a credit history. And everyone should begin investing as soon as they have an extra $25. (Yes, that's all it takes to get started, and the longer you wait the harder it is to convince yourself you can live without spending that 25 bucks.)

As you move through your life cycle, you'll need to add or delete from your financial basket. Early on, you'll be adding. As soon as you have some assets, you'll need a will. As soon as you have dependents, you'll need insurance. And as you increase your income, you'll need to buy more and different types of investments to meet your long-term goals. Later, you'll be deleting. Once you've established a good asset base and most of your dependents have gone their own ways, you can get rid of most, if not all, of your life insurance. As you move closer to retirement, you will consolidate your retirement savings for convenience and ease of conversion. You may even shift some of your assets to your children's hands, or to a trust, to reduce your estate and the taxes payable on death.

Finally, there are the financial precautions you take just in case . . . just in case you lose your job; just in case you become disabled; just in case you suddenly find yourself the primary breadwinner in your family.

## WHY A BOOK ABOUT WOMEN AND MONEY?

This is the question I heard most when people asked me what my next book would be about. After all, money can't tell the difference between X and Y chromosomes. That's true, but apparently society, our work environment, our legal system — just about every social construct you can imagine — has yet to catch up. If you don't believe me, ask yourself these questions:

- Why do women still make less than men for work of equal value? Yes, the gap has closed, but why are we still not equal?
- Why are elderly women and women with children the poorest members of our society?
- Why is it that when a couple divorces, a woman's income goes down and a man's goes up?
- Why did a vice-president at a mutual-fund company once tell me that "women are not our market"?

*This book isn't just about money. If it were, then the advice would be gender neutral. This book is about women taking control of a part of life that until now they may have wished away or ignored.*

Most financial planning books assume a person will continue to earn an income, without snags, for the majority of her life. They seem to abandon women who must deal with significant changes like motherhood, divorce, widowhood, disability, and the like. Yet, it is at these very moments that we need guidance, support, and information. It is then, when our life plan changes, that we must make adjustments to our financial plan so we remain proactive in managing this thing called money.

That's why we need a book for women specifically. And that's why I wrote this book. I hope that you will be able to take from it the information you need as you move through your life, adjusting your plan for significant changes, tweaking it for small ones. You can look to Part I for a general exploration of what money means to you; to Part II for the solid goods on all the basic aspects of financial planning and management; to Part III for the details on how to adapt financially to the events that most of us encounter in life, such as parenthood, partnering, and retirement; and to Part IV to learn how to handle those just-in-case scenarios that tend to send our finances on a detour.

The other reason I wrote this book is that I sometimes despair at women's unwillingness to be authors of their own fate. More often than not, the reason given for not taking control of the money is, "I just can't." Yes, you can. If you choose not to take control, that's your choice. If you choose to write your own script and direct your own future, read on.

## Some Definitions

When I use the term "marriage," I mean it in the broadest sense: your desire to have a continuing relationship, regardless of your specific family structure. When I use the terms "spouse" and "partner," again, it's in the broadest sense. This is the person with whom you have, and want to continue to have, a relationship. Recognizing that families have changed — having lived in just about all kinds, I'm a first-hand witness — my definition of a family is *everyone* you love who loves you back (even if they also hate you periodically), and with whom you have to relate for the common good of all.

# 1

# WOMAN,
# KNOW THYSELF

*Money is both real and not real, like a spook.
We invented money and we use it, yet we
cannot either understand its laws or control
its actions. It has a life of its own which it
properly should not have.*
LIONEL TRILLING

*O*ne of the very first questions I was asked when I set out to write this book significantly changed my approach and focus. The question was, "Why do some women do absolutely nothing to take care of their finances, despite the fact that they know better?" For several weeks I rolled the idea around in my head. Why are some women good at planning for the future, while others are not? Why do some people save, while others spend every cent they make, and then some? Why is it easier for some to defer gratification, while others must immediately have it . . . whatever "it" is?

Most financial planning books tell you what you need to know to achieve the results you want. And if you look at the financial planning section in most bookstores, you'll be amazed at the way the shelves sag with advice. But what good is it to know what you should do if you don't do it? We say we want to be secure, but we do little to take care of the what-ifs. We think we'd like to own a home of our own, but we never save a cent for the downpayment. We say we know it's silly to pay loads of interest on a credit card, but we continue to carry a balance.

The next few chapters are about sorting out these contradictions. While subsequent parts of this book will explore the practical details of personal finance — details you may be anxious to get to so you can fix what's wrong with your current financial picture — I recommend that you spend some time thinking through the issues we're about to explore. It is an exercise that may have a profound and lasting impact on the way you look at money.

# 1

# The Importance of Money

*Money means in a thousand minds a thousand subtly different, roughly similar, systems of images, associations, suggestions, and impulses.*

H. G. WELLS

Everyone's seeking financial freedom. But ask 50 people what constitutes financial freedom and you can expect 50 different definitions. Often it's associated with having enough money to never worry again. But that raises the question, "How much is enough?" The fact is, financial freedom has absolutely nothing to do with how much money you have. Read that last sentence again. Financial freedom comes when you have control — when money anxieties and fears no longer creep into your thoughts as you lie in bed late at night. We can all have financial freedom, regardless of how much we make, if we put money in its proper perspective.

Unfortunately, some people fail to recognize that they are worth more than the car they drive, the home they live in, or the clothes they wear. They use money to create the image they want others to see. Then they spend all their energy maintaining the image. Perhaps they want to be seen as generous, and spend lavishly on children, lovers, and friends. Perhaps it's the desire to be seen as successful that drives them to spend more than they make. Some even work to cultivate a negative image without realizing it. Rather than accepting responsibility for their lives and their money, they continue to play the role of victim, battered by their circumstances.

In researching this book, I heard and read many stories about the influence of childhood experiences on our money values. One of the saddest was the story Suze Orman told in her book, *The 9 Steps to Financial Freedom*.[1] She tells of arriving at her dad's restaurant with her mother just in time to watch flames engulf the building. Her father had escaped unscathed when, realizing that all his money was in the metal cash register inside the building, he ran back in to retrieve it. "He literally picked up the scalding metal box and carried it outside. When he threw the register on the ground, the skin on his arms and chest came with it." Orman relates the experience to the early money values she developed: "That was when I learned that money is obviously more important than life itself. From that point on, earning money, lots of money, not only became what drove me professionally, but also became my emotional priority."

Financial freedom doesn't begin with making more money. It doesn't start in a financial planner's office. And it doesn't begin with investing to earn a return of 32%. *Financial freedom begins in your head.* It begins with understanding what money is, what it means to you, and how you developed the feelings you have about money.

## WHAT IS MONEY ANYWAY?

*"Papa! what's money?"*

*The abrupt question had such immediate reference to the subject of Mr Dombey's thoughts, that Mr Dombey was quite disconcerted.*

*"What is money, Paul?" he answered. "Money?"*

*"Yes," said the child, laying his hands upon the elbows of his little chair, and turning the old face up towards Mr Dombey's; "what is money?"*

*Mr Dombey was in a difficulty. He would have liked to give him some explanation involving the terms circulating-medium, currency, depreciation of currency, paper, bullion, rates of exchange, value of precious metals in the market, and so forth; but looking down at the little chair, and*

---

1   Suze Orman, *The 9 Steps to Financial Freedom* (Random House Inc., 1997), p. 3.

*seeing what a long way down it was, he answered: "Gold, and silver, and copper. Guineas, shillings, half-pence. You know what they are?"*

*"Oh yes, I know what they are," said Paul. "I don't mean that, Papa. I mean what's money after all?"*

CHARLES DICKENS, *DOMBEY AND SON*

Apparently it is easier to use money than it is to define it. Money has as many meanings as there are people and their personal perceptions. As British economist Sir Ralph Hawtrey once said, "Money is one of those concepts which, like a teaspoon or an umbrella, but unlike an earthquake or buttercup, are definable primarily by the use or purpose they serve." Marshall McLuhan said, "Money is a language for translating the work of the farmer into the work of the barber, doctor, engineer, or plumber . . . Money is the store of other people's time and effort." Aristotle said, "Money has been introduced by convention as a kind of substitute for need or demand . . . its value is derived, not from nature, but from law, and can be altered or abolished at will."

Trying to define money is as difficult as trying to define love. Yes, it is the paper and coin of which it is made, and it represents value. But currency itself has no intrinsic value. You can't eat it, wear it, or hold it close late at night. And there are parts of the world where you can't even use it to buy what you need.

At its most basic level, money is a means of completing financial transactions. It is a measure of value that can be traded for goods or services. Most financial planning books try to deal with this aspect of money: how to get it, how to use it, how to keep it. And most promote the belief that more is better. Seldom do they ask you to quantify the cost of attaining more.

*Thanks to the natural resources of the country, every American, until quite recently, could reasonably look forward to making more money than his father, so that, if he made less, the fault must be his; he was either lazy or inefficient. What an American values, therefore, is not the possession of money as such, but his power to make it as proof of his manhood.*

W. H. AUDEN

But the emotional and psychological costs of making money are as important as the pedestrian what-to-dos. Money causes confusion. It has a special meaning to each of us based on our childhood experiences. We all have our own money myths — it may represent security, power, acceptance, love, evil — which we then wear like hair shirts.

As a culture, we recognize that money is the basis of our economy and our means for survival and growth. We read about the monster "inflation" and worry about outliving our money. We watch as our cost of living increases and immediately feel poorer. We worry about whether we are in a depression or a recession. We personalize those economic indicators without really understanding them.

Let's take the Consumer Price Index (CPI) as a case in point. No matter how often it is referred to as a measure of your cost of living, it isn't, and here's why. It is calculated based on a sample of prices of goods and services that people tend to buy regularly; however, it doesn't account for the fact that you do not buy a new car every month or every year, or the fact that today's car is much more energy-efficient than previous years' cars. It also doesn't account for changing buying habits after the base period it uses as a comparator. After all, the price of everyday items such as orange juice, coffee, and gas fluctuate based on a variety of factors, but the CPI does not. As Andrew Hacker puts it:

> If wages seemed to go further in 1970, one reason is that shopping lists were simpler. Those were the days of Keds and typewriters and turntables. Today, the Index includes Nikes, laser printers, and multiple-CD changers that cost more because they do more. Even bread has been upgraded: croissants and exotic grains have replaced blander white loaves; Starbucks costs more than Maxwell House. Since cars have so much high-tech gear, a new one costs about half a young couple's income, visibly up from 38 percent in 1970.[2]

That's not to say that economic indicators are invalid and should be ignored. We need to understand them so we can put them in context. What we should not do is panic about economic statistics that have little bearing on our day-to-day lives. Yes, inflation, the CPI, and our gross national product all affect our money and its worth, but it's more important to ask how they affect you personally. If they don't, chill out.

---

2   Andrew Hacker, *Money: Who Has How Much and Why* (Scribner, 1997), p. 61.

Stop worrying. Relax. If they will have an impact on you, stop worrying and do something about it. It's all in your hands. You have the control, and with this book, you'll have the know-how.

Human beings are motivated by strong social drives. Just ask any teenager to name the most important thing in her life, and she'll say it's her friends. Ask her what the second most important thing is, and she'll say it's money. Why money? Because it lets her be with her friends.

As long as we recognize that money is a tool — a means of acquiring the things we need — we've got money in perspective. The problem comes when we see it as the source of all the other things in our lives, such as love, happiness, control, or security.

## Beyond Skill

If managing money were only a skill, we could learn it and be done with it. But there's more to it than that. After all, some of the most skillful money managers in business are pathetic when it comes to managing their personal finances. Years ago I worked with a woman who was a credit-card maniac. As the office manager, she was wonderful at keeping the books, keeping the spending in check, keeping the bank at bay. At home, her personal finances were a disaster. I remember sitting at her kitchen table watching her play what she called "credit-card roulette." This was a monthly game where she decided who would get their minimum monthly payment. Every card she had — there were more than 40 cards in her wallet — was run up to the limit. Her decisions about who to pay were based on which card she would need to use during the upcoming month.

This was a dreadful place to be. She ached physically from the stress. She couldn't see any way to clear her debts so she resolved to live month to month until the whole thing just caved in. She had new living room furniture, a new stereo, and heaps of other stuff. She also had headaches, backaches, and a short temper.

The cards were taken away, one by one, sometimes at the bank, where the teller would simply keep the card with little explanation. She really didn't need an explanation. Sometimes her plastic was repossessed in stores where she was mortified to find the store clerk instructed by the card company to cut up the card right in front of her. I was with her on one such occasion and she was a wreck. Whenever she was sent a new card — credit-card companies are notorious for lending to people they shouldn't — she would sign the back and spend herself out of her blues.

Eventually she took control of the situation and started using the skills she had all along but just wasn't using. She dumped the cards, got a consolidation loan, and paid off her debts. It took years, but she got better.

This story may seem extreme or all too familiar. It illustrates the point that women often feel incompetent and inadequate in managing their money, often in sharp contrast to their competence in other areas. And some women feel guilty and ashamed around money, or resentful of their inability to get more and keep it.

## How Do *You* Feel About Money?

Your attitudes toward money speak volumes about how you have dealt with this part of your life so far. For all the savers I have met, there have been as many spenders. For all those who have worried about money, there are those who avoid dealing with it completely. For all the risk-takers, there are those who are terrified of losing. For as many people who believe that money is the key to happiness, there are just as many who think it leads to misery and corruption.

I have met a lot of these people as I have travelled the country promoting *The Money Tree Myth: A Parents' Guide to Helping Kids Unravel the Mysteries of Money*. One of the most oft-asked questions is, "But what about the morality of money?" Does a car have morality, or is it the person behind the wheel who decides not to drive drunk? Can any inanimate object have a morality or is it the onus we put on that object that gives it such human characteristics? We have to separate the emotional from the practical when we set about teaching our kids about money. If we send our children messages that imply that money has power beyond its role as a means of exchange, we do them a disservice.

Regardless of the impressions you have grown up with, *money does not have a morality*. Money is paper and coin, nothing more.

The best way to develop a healthy attitude toward money is to understand why you have the attitudes you do and then find ways to build on your strengths and minimize your weaknesses. That usually involves taking an inventory and thinking some deep thoughts.

Identify the following statements as true or false based on your first reaction to them:

True    False    I have a good relationship with money.

True    False    If I had more money, I wouldn't have to think about it as much.

True    False    When I feel low I buy myself something nice. Even if I have to charge it, I feel much better.

True    False    Whoever has the most money has the most power.

True    False    It's irresponsible to spend money frivolously. Saving is the key to security.

True    False    I'd rather go shopping than save money.

True    False    My retirement is taken care of, so I don't have to worry about it.

True    False    I'd bet $20 for a 1-in-100,000 chance to win $1 million.

Okay, done? Good. Now answer the questions in *italics*:

True    False    I have a good relationship with money. *Can you have a relationship with an inanimate object?*

True    False    If I had more money, I wouldn't have to think about it as much. *How much money is enough to eliminate your concerns?*

True    False    When I feel low I buy myself something nice. Even if I have to charge it, I feel much better. *How do you feel when the bill comes in?*

True    False    Whoever has the most money has the most power. *In what areas of your life do you feel powerful?*

True    False    It's irresponsible to spend frivolously. Saving is the key to security. *Saving is more important than . . . (what?) What are your priorities for* spending?

True    False    I'd rather go shopping than save money. *Do you have a financial safety net? If not, how will you deal with an emergency?*

True    False    My retirement is taken care of, so I don't have to worry about it. *If your external supports (marriage, job, government support) changed, would you still be all right in retirement? What are you doing to take care of yourself?*

True   False   I'd bet $20 for a 1-in-100,000 chance to win $1 million. *What if the odds were 1 in 1,000,000? What if the odds were 1 in 10? Is it your chance of winning or the cost of participating that influences your decision?*

It is by challenging your own attitudes in this way that you can take control of how you feel about and deal with money.

## WHERE DID YOUR ATTITUDES COME FROM?

Who we are with money is a direct result of what we learned as children. Answer the following questions to see what pictures emerge for you. It might be helpful to jot down some notes as you think about these questions:

- What are your impressions of how your mother dealt with money? How did she feel about her work inside and/or outside the home? What did she explicitly teach you about money? How did you feel about those money lessons?
- What are your impressions of how your father dealt with money? How did he feel about his work inside and/or outside the home? What did he explicitly teach you about money? How did you feel about those money lessons?
- How did your parents relate to each other when it came to financial matters? What did they feel about each other's money habits? Did they fight about money?
- If you have siblings, did your parents treat you all similarly when it came to money? If not, what were the differences? How do your siblings deal with money now?
- Did anyone else — a teacher, religious leader, grandparent, or other relative — influence the way you think about money today? What messages did you get from them?
- Did your friends have things you didn't? Did you get more or less allowance than your peers? Did you live in a nicer home? Did they

have nicer clothes? What was cool to have back then, and did you have it?

- Did you have to be good to receive special treats? Did you receive money as gifts?
- Did you feel ashamed of having more or less than your friends?
- Did you steal from the corner store, your mother's purse, your father's pocket, your sister's piggy-bank?
- Was your family rich or poor? Why do you feel you were either rich or poor?

Most children feel powerless. Someone else decides when they will eat, sleep, and play. Someone else decides what they will wear and what they will watch on TV. All too often, people carry that sense of powerlessness into their adulthood, even though they manage to take on jobs, raise families, and meet their commitments. The lessons they learned about money run like tapes in their heads, controlling their financial behaviour. Or worse, there were no childhood money lessons, and they feel helpless and scared to death of making a mistake. Money means many things to many people. What does it mean to you?

## Money Means Power

*They who are of the opinion that Money will do every thing, may very well be suspected to do every thing for Money.*

GEORGE SAVILE

"I don't care, as long as you're under my roof, we'll do things my way." That's one of the most familiar power plays. It means, "Since I have the money, I make the rules." But there are other things parents do that send the power message just as clearly. Allowances or support cheques that are promised but rarely delivered without a reminder; constant financial bail-outs with verbal reminders of how lucky you are to have been saved; regular lectures on the respect, duty, or gratitude you owe for having been cared for.

Of course, as with any myth, there's always a grain of truth that allows the myth to survive. The fact is that money does represent power for many people. After all, who among us has a boss who makes less than we do? Most supervisory power comes from the fact that the boss can take your money away. Within families, the spouse who makes the money often feels the right to choose how that money is handled.

Having more money also often leads to more choices: a better education, the opportunity to start and support a new business, the freedom to pursue creative outlets. Money can buy you better health care, a better table in a restaurant, and more acquaintances.

### Money Means Love

*Love buyers love to play Santa Claus. Money and gifts are to them the means of making others happy and thus winning their friendship and affection . . .*

*In the final analysis, love buyers get what they pay for — a substitute.*
HERB GOLDBERG AND ROBERT T. LEWIS

Turn on your television and you'll be faced with myriad commercials trying to convince you that by spending your money to buy long-distance gift certificates, a new car, or the latest brand of toothpaste, you'll be better loved. If you go shopping when you're lonely or unhappy, if you buy things for others that you can ill afford, or if you shop regardless of your ability to pay for those items, the likelihood is you've got the money-equals-love virus. Women who shower their mates with expensive presents are often using money as a symbol of love. People who lend money to friends may be giving to secure their friendships. Listen to the words of anger often spoken when a love or friendship is betrayed — "you owe me," "I gave you everything," "you stole the best years of my life" — and you'll recognize the language of money.

If you don't believe that people equate love with money, just look at what happens when love disappears from a relationship — especially when divorce isn't a joint decision — and all that's left is to work out the financial dissolution. The communication can get downright ugly. And look at the way we relate to our children: "If you're good, I'll buy you a toy." Will those children then form the habit of rewarding themselves with material things when they feel down or stressed out? Or will they choose to reject money because they see it as a means of control?

## Money Means Security

*If a person's attitude toward money is essentially a defense against poverty, then this person may never truly experience wealth. The experience of wealth is, after all, a subjective thing.*

THOMAS MOORE

For many people, money represents security. These people place great emphasis on preparing for the future and their money management style is cautious and well planned. However, when faced with a threat to that security, these people can panic, or become depressed or angry. While they seldom spend capriciously, they also seldom enjoy what they have. They are constantly squirrelling away a little more, denying today's wants in favour of tomorrow's needs. For them, money offers no pleasure, other than in its acquisition. Each dollar spent represents a dollar they will not have in the future. Women often make this link, partly because of their socialization. Since women have traditionally been dependent on men — fathers, husbands, male bosses — for their security, they have learned to prize that security greatly. They anticipate desertion and disaster and try to prepare for it. On the flip side, of course, are the women who still believe these "heroes" will provide them with security for the rest of their lives. By being good little daughters, wives, and employees, they hope to keep the income streams to which they have become accustomed. Witness the number of women who remain in abusive relationships (marital, familial, or work-related) because they believe they have no other way to support themselves.

Take the case of Yvonne, who quit her job after 20 years. She wasn't independently wealthy. She wasn't anywhere near retirement age. She was just fed up. Having worked at a hospital where constant financial cutbacks had resulted in a significant change in the emotional atmosphere, she was worn out and angry. She watched people with whom she had worked for decades be laid off. She felt they had been shafted, shuffled off, and sideswiped by "the new economic reality." The expectations for those who remained were enormous: more hours, less room for promotion; more productivity, less socializing; more input, less corporate loyalty. Even after she left she continued to hear from old friends about the horrors of the new work environment. Women who were dependent on their jobs to support themselves and their children were being bullied into doing more, staying later, working harder. The general response to the unfairness of it all was that because of the huge labour market, and shrinking job market, if you didn't like it, there were plenty of people who would be happy with the job.

This kind of emotional abuse is pervasive in today's corporate culture and it's a shame. Ultimately, money becomes the means by which we can escape. If we just had more money, we could tell the boss just what to do with the job. Once again, money becomes the answer.

## Money Means Happiness

*Money is human happiness in the abstract; and so the man who is no longer capable of enjoying such happiness in the concrete, sets his whole heart on money.*

ARTHUR SCHOPENHAUER

When we equate money with happiness we put too much stock in what money can do for us. When what you want (more money) is different from what you need (a sense of safety, a pat on the back, a sense of personal accomplishment), you will never feel satisfied. It's like trying to eat carrot sticks when all you really want is a big bowl of ice cream. No matter how much of the good orange stuff you eat, you can't fill the hole and the hunger drives you to seek another substitute; in the end, you'll have your spoon in the ice-cream container — exactly where you wanted to be all along.

If happiness is elusive, money isn't the answer. Perhaps you should look at what your spirit is seeking. In *Happy People*, Jonathan Freedman reports that material wealth has little bearing on a person's sense of happiness.[3] We are fooling ourselves when we use money to try to replace the things we feel are missing from our lives, such as family, meaningful work, a sense of community, and creative play. In *The Poverty of Affluence*, Paul Wachtel says:

> Our economic system and our relation with nature have gone haywire because we have lost track of what we really need. Increasing numbers of middle-class Americans are feeling pressed and deprived not because of their economic situation per se — we

---

3   Jonathan Freedman, *Happy People* (Harcourt Brace Jovanovich, 1978), p. 136.

remain an extraordinarily affluent society — but because we have placed an impossible burden on the economic dimension of our lives.[4]

## HOW IMPORTANT IS YOUR STUFF?

For over six months I lived without furniture in my living room. I swore I'd never spend another cent to put furniture in until our children, Alex and Malcolm, were of an age when the couches wouldn't be at constant risk. Then, of course, I envisioned the animal tracks the dog and two cats would make when they decided to get comfortable in the cushions, on the cushions, and behind the cushions. I was quite happy offering family and friends the floor, although Ken, my husband, was distressed. But he was brave. He understood my reluctance to spend money we didn't really have since I was on maternity leave and the cash wasn't exactly overflowing.

After six months and a short consulting project I changed my mind. With some money in the bank, the room seemed a little emptier. When I had no money, it had been easy to justify not spending any. Now that we were flush again, it was harder to see Ken try to deal with my frugality. So I acquiesced and we bought two love seats just in time for Malcolm's first birthday party. Imagine the surprised looks on the family's faces when they saw a place to sit! Ken was pleased. I was happy.

This story has three morals (a lot for such a short story, don't you think?). The first is, I've reached the stage in my life when acquiring stuff just doesn't do it for me anymore. There was a time when I would have had to have those couches immediately. That time has passed as my life has filled with other things that have more meaning. The second moral is, spending money you don't have is dumb. You can always go a few weeks, months, even years, putting a little aside each week, until you have the money. The third moral is that we don't live in isolation and we have to consider the other people we affect with our decisions.

How important are things to you? Do you often spend money you don't have acquiring things you feel you must have? Perhaps it's a new suit, or a new pair of shoes. Perhaps it's a new car. Maybe it's new living

---

4   Paul Wachtel, *The Poverty of Affluence* (New Society Publishers, 1989), p. 2.

room furniture. Why do you have to have it? What will happen if you don't acquire it immediately?

I remember when we moved my son Malcolm from his crib into a big bed. We didn't have anywhere to store his toys, and I wanted to buy the shelves I'd chosen. But money was tight that month. I pondered the idea of charging the shelves on my card — I wanted my son's room to be beautiful — feeling sure I would have the money the following month when the bill came in. Ken, whom I'd always considered much more of a spender, was the voice of reason. "His room looks fine," he said. "Let's wait." Since by nature I'm a debt-avoider, it didn't take a lot to convince me. But for a few moments there, my desire to give my son what I thought he should have was way ahead of my good sense. It happens to the best of us.

Research shows that our possessions say a lot about how we feel about ourselves.[5] They help us define who we are and make statements about how we wish to be perceived by others. Most of us are quite skilled at reading the meaning of objects. We make judgments about people based on what they are wearing, what kind of car they drive, and where they live.

People who lose their possessions — those who are forced to flee their country of birth, or who face physical disasters such as earthquakes and fires — often feel they have lost something of themselves. To see how important your stuff is to you, take some time to think about the following question: If a fire threatened to destroy all your personal possessions, and you could save only three things, what would they be, and why?

I'm not sure why, but I've asked myself this question many times over the years and it's interesting how my answers have changed. Now, I'd have to save Beri-Bear, my daughter's favourite plush toy. I'd want my memories boxes that have mementos from my husband and many photos from my life. What else? I'm not sure. At one time I would have included my hippo collection (I've been collecting hippos for years). At another, it was my poetry book, which recorded all the angst I'd felt through my youth. The pillow I've had since childhood always made the list. Not anymore. As life has changed, so have my priorities.

---

5  Peter Lunt and Sonia Livingstone, *Mass Consumption and Personal Identity* (Open University Press, 1992), p. 59–85.

The close connection between who we are and what we own carries over to money. Since money is our means for acquiring what we then use to define ourselves, the money itself becomes a part of our definition of self. Here are some more questions to ponder:

- How important is your stuff to you?
- If you could have another person's stuff, whose would you choose?
- How many things do you currently have on your "I wish I could have" list?
- How much money would you need to acquire the things to make your life perfect?
- How much of what you have would you sell to help someone else buy food or shelter?

## WHERE TO GO FROM HERE

So, what have you learned so far? Do you have more of a sense of why you feel as you do about money? Do you have the skills, but not the emotional competence? If you don't have the skills, the rest of this book will help you. If you don't have the emotional competence, you're going to have to do some soul searching to come to peace with how you feel about money. You may want to see a psychologist who deals with money issues. You may want to talk more about it with friends and family. The very fact that you are reading this book means you want something to change. But you're the only person who can make that change.

Next we'll look more closely at how being a woman can and should affect how you deal with your money. Guess what? We have special obstacles to overcome. But guess what else? We are uniquely equipped to overcome them.

# 2

# Women and Money

*Moreover, it is equally useless to ask what might have happened if
Mrs. Seton and her mother and her mother before her had amassed great
wealth and laid it under the foundations of college and library, because, in
the first place, to earn money was impossible for them, and in the second,
had it been possible, the law denied them the right to possess what money
they earned. It is only for the last forty-eight years that Mrs. Seton has had
a penny of her own. For all the centuries before that, it would have been
her husband's property — a thought which perhaps may have its share in
keeping Mrs. Seton and her mother off the Stock Exchange.*

VIRGINIA WOOLF, *A ROOM OF ONE'S OWN*

Women and men relate to money differently. We have different fears,
different concerns, and different perspectives. Is this news to you?
It probably isn't. But do you know why?

## Women are comfortable expressing their feelings
and their vulnerability.

That's because women are traditionally raised in an atmosphere of accom-
modation and co-operation. While men have been socialized to hunt,
women were the gatherers. We are much more open to communication,
to sharing ideas, to asking questions. We are less afraid of appearing

foolish. We would rather ask the question and get an answer than sit quietly in ignorance forever. It may take a while to work up the gumption to interrupt, ask, inquire, find out, but women want knowledge and they'll take it from any number of sources. This all bodes well for women increasing their financial know-how.

**Many women still believe that dealing with finances is a man's job.** Even as I write this I can hardly believe it myself. Just how far have we come, baby? Time and again I speak with women who have completely relinquished financial control to their husbands, fathers, or sons. I continue to be astounded. You might think that this is a characteristic of older women — women who haven't been educated in the finer points of feminism. You'd be dead wrong.

Who's in a better position to have a handle on personal finances than an accountant or a financial planner? Yet, I have a story for you that clearly demonstrates that "knowing" and "doing" are two distinctly different things. My girlfriend Marla, a financial adviser, had been married for several years when she and her accountant husband separated. At that point Marla decided to take a long, hard look at the money situation. She was surprised to discover that despite the fact that both she and her husband had been saving and investing aggressively, their portfolio had not done much in the past few years. Marla had left all the investing up to her husband, who, as it turned out, had chosen financial products that performed badly. Marla ended up paying for her husband's mistakes. Now, you might ask, what would motivate a well-educated, professional money manager to leave the decision making to someone else? The answer is all too familiar to many women. First, if money creates a conflict, and you want to avoid conflict, you choose the route of least resistance and let him do it all. If you have different investment strategies, and you've been convinced that doing it your way will take too long, you let him have his way. If you trust him implicitly, you let him make the decisions and live with the consequences, good or bad. No one is always right, after all. If you don't have the time, don't have the energy, don't have the desire to do it for yourself, it's easy to give the responsibility to someone else.

If money is so important in terms of keeping a roof over our heads and food in our children's tummies, then why are so many of us still willing to let our partners do the "dirty work"? And how are we going to cope when he goes away?

The incidence of divorce has increased dramatically since the late 1960s, mostly because legislation has made it easier to get divorced. The first time I divorced, I had to wait for three years to pass before I could file. The second time, a one-year separation was all it took.

Out of a population of approximately 30 million, just over 1.4 million Canadians are divorced, with the numbers skewing higher for women than for men (800,000 to 625,000, respectively). That seems like a small number when compared with the population at large, but consider the fact that only 17 million people have entered a communal state at all (that is, they have been married, widowed, or divorced). When the number of divorced Canadians is expressed as a percentage of this 17 million (we've eliminated all the die-hard singles and the children), we see that almost 8.25% of the once-married population are wed no more. As a population, we stand a 1-in-12 chance of divorce. And as women we're more likely to stay divorced.

The difference between the life expectancies of women and men also means women tend to be left on their own. Girls born in 1991 can expect to live to a ripe old age of 81, while their brothers born the same year will likely live to age 75. The older we get, the longer we can expect to live, and the smaller the gap between us and our brothers. So if you were 65 in 1991, you can expect to live to 85, and your male counterpart can expect to live to 81.

The incidence of women heading a single-parent family in Canada has risen dramatically since 1971. Then it was only 10%. By 1991, 16% of all families with children were headed by a woman alone, and 80% of all single-parent families were headed by women.

So, what's the point of all these statistics? Well, we patter around the concept of taking personal responsibility by talking about the "divorce rate" and "life expectancies." But to be perfectly blunt, if you think you'll always have someone to take care of your money for you, you're wrong. He may die. He may leave you. Ultimately, you'll have to do it for yourself. You might as well start now.

**Other people believe that dealing with finances is a man's job.**
How better to illustrate this point than with a story about shopping for a car? Barb Godin, a former senior vice-president of credit for the Bank of

Nova Scotia, remembers going to the dealership to buy a new car. She began by warning her husband, on pain of death, not to open his mouth. In they went.

"Immediately, they greeted my husband. He said, 'My wife is here,' and they said, 'Oh hello, how are you?' I was looking at several cars and as I was off looking, they were selling to him. No one was paying any attention to me. He said, 'I think you want to speak to my wife, not to me.' So they came to me, but the look on their faces said, 'We really don't want to speak to you because you don't know anything about cars,' not knowing that I look after the automotive finance portfolio so I know a tad about them. They paid me no respect. They talked down to me. They treated me as if this was something I would have to seek the counsel of my husband on before I could make the purchase. I was incensed and ended up walking out of three dealerships. Finally I walked into a dealership where I dealt with a female salesperson. We had a wonderful time."

This kind of treatment is not restricted to car dealerships. Women constantly complain about not being taken seriously, not being treated with respect, and not being seen as able and competent. So while the times are changing, it may not be happening quickly enough for some women.

**Women are less likely to take credit for their successes, but are completely willing to accept all responsibility for their mistakes.**
This goes back, once again, to our socialization: to the fact that men want to *win* and women want to *win together*. Our very language demonstrates our commitment to keeping the field even so that everyone saves face. While a man might say, "Sit down and have a cup of coffee," a woman would say, "Let's sit down and have a cup of coffee." This socialization toward the group, the team, the together approach means women seldom see themselves as the driving force behind a "win."

According to Olivia Mellan,

When men make money in the stock market . . . they tend to take the credit, attributing the successful outcome to their own cleverness and financial acumen. Where they lose money on their investments, they tend to put the blame on their advisers. When women make money in the stock market, they credit outside influences, such as their advisers, or sheer good fortune. When they lose money, they tend to blame themselves. Since men are raised to be competitive "winners" and to hide their vulnerability, it is easy to see why they project their blame on others. And since women are raised to be accommodators, and to accept a stance of vulnerability and dependency, it is understandable that their first impulse is to swallow blame and to deflect credit.[6]

**Women earn less.**

For a wide variety of reasons, women have less money than do men. First, they earn less. According to Statistics Canada, in 1993, the average annual pretax income for all women was just $16,500, a whopping 42% less than for men. This is a reflection of the fact that women not only earn less than men, but that many women have no income at all. In 1993, 12% of all women had no income at all, compared with only 5% of men. In 1994, 42% of women did not participate in the labour force. So any income they derived was in the form of earnings from investments, pensions, or government support. Of the 58% of women who earned an income, 26% did so on a part-time basis. In the prime earning years, far more women than men work part-time. While 20% of women aged 25 to 44 worked part-time, in the same age group only about 4% of men were employed part-time. Of women 45 to 54, 24% worked part-time, while only 6% of men worked part-time in this age group. Needless to say, less time on the job means less income, so it's not surprising that women continue to make less than men. Part-timers also have little or no access to company benefits. In 1989, only 26% of part-time employees in the service sector were covered by company medical insurance plans. And only 22% had company pension plans. These exclusions are significant for women's present and future economic security.

If you think women choose to work part-time, you may be surprised. When you look at the reasons why women work part-time, the picture is startling. Of the part-timers between the ages of 25 and 44, 40% of the women (compared with 18% of the men) said they worked part-time because that was the only type of work they could find. For those 45 and over, 32% of women could only find part-time work (compared with

---

6   Olivia Mellan, *Money Harmony* (Walker and Company, 1994), p. 122.

men whose numbers register as too small to be expressed). Personal and family responsibilities also play a big part in women's decisions to work part-time. Of women aged 25 to 44, almost 23% work part-time because of personal and family responsibilities — a category where again, the numbers for men are too small to be reported.

Of those women who were employed on a full-time, full-year basis, women's average income was $28,400, or just 72% of their male counterparts' salaries. But not all the news is bad. For the next generation, things are looking up. Women who are 24 and younger, working full-time, earned 91% of the average male salary for that age group. The wage gap may be narrowing, but we still have a long way to go in equalizing incomes, particularly for older women.

As we progress up the age scale, women regress in terms of their ability to cope financially. Fifty-six percent of women 65 and older who were not living with their families had low incomes (see the following table). Imagine it. More than half of all women who are retired and alone are in the low-income category.

## What Is Low Income?

*Statistics Canada's definition of low income is based on the number of people in a family and the size of the population.*

| No. of People in Family | Size of Population | | | | |
|---|---|---|---|---|---|
| | 500,000+ | 100,000–499,999 | 30,000–99,999 | <30,000 | Rural |
| 1 | 16,482 | 14,187 | 14,039 | 13,063 | 11,390 |
| 2 | 20,603 | 17,671 | 17,549 | 16,329 | 14,238 |
| 3 | 25,623 | 21,978 | 21,825 | 20,308 | 17,708 |
| 4 | 31,013 | 26,604 | 26,419 | 24,583 | 21,435 |
| 5 | 34,671 | 29,739 | 29,532 | 27,479 | 23,961 |

**Women leave the workforce sooner and more often.**

Sad to say, our greatest gift is also a major contributor to our economic insecurity. Our desire to nurture gets in the way of our ability to build our wealth. Whether we are taking time off to have and raise our children, to care for our elders, or to accompany our spouses into retirement, women spend far less time in the workforce than do men.

Having and raising children is one of life's great joys. The birth and care of my children changed me dramatically. I went from a 17-hour-a-day, seven-day-a-week worker to a woman who cannot bear to be away from her kids. I still work — from home. And I choose my work carefully so that I don't have to be away from the kids for too long. It has affected my income stream dramatically. I earn about 70% less now than I used to. And I've had to restructure my priorities in order to manage. But I manage. Other women are far less fortunate.

One of the issues I had to deal with was the interruption in my income stream while I was pregnant, and during my "maternity leave." Having two pregnancies-from-hell gave me a whole new appreciation for women who work through their pregnancies. But I found I was not alone. In sharing my horror stories with other women, I found many who barely dragged themselves through their pregnancies, and whose work and careers had to be put on hold temporarily. Since I have always been self-employed, I also had no maternity benefits during my time off with the babies. Here, again, I was not alone. While 89% of mothers on maternity leave received some form of monetary compensation, 77% of women received only EI (employment insurance) benefits. In spite of the fact that most parents receive less than 57% of their regular earnings during their leave, parents choose to take the time off. That commitment to the family is in direct conflict with a woman's desire to be financially independent. The way things are now, it's a choice. And unfortunately, it is our financial security that suffers when we put the family first.

Work absences due to personal or family-related responsibilities rose from 1.9 to 5.2 days a year between 1977 and 1990. That figure may seem low until you consider that parents use their own vacation or sick days to care for kids. Employed mothers surveyed by the Conference Board of Canada in 1989 were four times more likely than fathers to report that they stayed home from work when their children were ill. And according to Donna S. Lero's "Canadian National Child Care Study," child-care problems were three times more likely to affect a mother's productivity or involvement in the workforce than a father's. The most common effect of child-care problems reported included:

- not being able to work overtime when requested or desired
- worrying about children's care while at work
- reduction in commitment to job due to child-care problems

- reduction in work hours
- turning down job offers
- leaving a job because of child-care problems

As our parents age, elder care becomes more of an issue. And since the responsibility for elder care has traditionally fallen on the shoulders of women, we can expect even more interruptions in income. Only a small number of employers surveyed by the Conference Board of Canada provided benefits to employees to assist with the care of elderly or disabled family members. Only 10% offered information on care for family members with disabilities, and only 6% offered elder-care information or referral services.

**Women are chronically afraid because of their lack of economic security.**
Even women who are well heeled have fears of losing everything and ending up on the street. This is known as the "bag-lady syndrome," and it stems from women's deep-set insecurity about their ability to support themselves and their children in times of trouble. And there are good reasons for women's sense of financial insecurity that go beyond their lower salaries and more sporadic workforce participation patterns.

One factor affecting women's income is their family status. As we've seen, women make up the large majority of single parents in Canada. And single-parent households headed by women have by far the lowest incomes of all. This is reflected in the number of children living in low-income households. While 13.7% of all Canadian children lived in low-income households in 1993, 41% of those low-income kids lived in single-parent families headed by women. It's no wonder we fear for our children and ourselves.

Divorce treats women and men very differently. Typically, a man's income rises after divorce, while a woman's usually falls. For many women, alimony and child support form a significant part of their family income. According to the 1990 General Social Survey, in that year support payments (for single-parent households headed by women) accounted for 18% of the family income. The most alarming statistic of all is the fact that in 1994, of all the support orders in Ontario, only 24% were in full compliance with no arrears. So, not only do women have to face the full emotional responsibility of raising their children, but they often receive little consistent financial support from their children's fathers. Compounding the problem that women have less money to deal with challenges and crises is the fact that we are more likely than men to encounter these challenges. Because women live longer than men, we have to cope for more years on less money, and we are more vulnerable to disabilities, since disabilities increase with age. In 1991, 48% of women 65 and older had disabilities. My husband was absolutely right when he summed up the statistics this way: "Men die, women get sick." In 1991, 36% of women over 65 had severe disabilities, compared with 27% of men. Disability in later years puts more pressure on financial resources. At a younger age, a disability can completely wipe us out because it eliminates or severely hampers our ability to earn an income. Even here, men and women play on different fields. While 11% of men aged 55 to 64 with disabilities were unemployed, 18.4% of women of the same age with disabilities were unemployed. Of all disabled men and women with an income, while men's average income was $20,625, women's average income was only $14,365.

**Women seem less willing than men to take risks with their money.** There is a debate raging about whether or not women are naturally more risk-averse than men. Some say yes, as witnessed by women's reluctance to take chances, go for the gold, shoot the hoop. The investment statistics bear out this reluctance to take risk. According to research published by the Toronto Stock Exchange in 1996, women are almost twice as likely to think the stock market is too risky. Men, on the other hand, seem to revel in taking chances.

The proponents in the "no" camp believe that women have been socialized, rather than born, to engage in different risk-taking behaviour. Since they have traditionally been less financially secure, they are less willing to take a risk with what they do have. Since they have always earned less, lived longer, been dependent, they want to shore up the resources they have, and keep them safe.

In his book *Galen's Prophecy*, Jerome Kagan provides research to support both positions. In his studies, Kagan found a greater female susceptibility to a fear state. He also cites epidemiological surveys revealing that extreme fearfulness is less frequent in boys. Kagan suggests that because men have been socialized over the centuries to face fear regularly through hunting and combat, their negative reaction to fear has been biologically reduced. Women, on the other hand, who were socialized as gatherers, had less exposure to the fear factor and, therefore, continue to react more strongly to fear. In other words, because men are more accustomed to dealing with fear, they have adapted biologically to deal with fear. Women didn't need to make the same adaptations. The result: girls are more fearful than boys at every age. In fact, according to Kagan's studies, "among the distressed infants who showed high fear at both fourteen and twenty-one months, 86 percent were girls." [7]

As women we can accept the fact that we are biologically less willing to take risk. However, when that unwillingness creates its own risk — the risk of not having enough money to meet our needs when we no longer have a steady income — it becomes clear that we need to get beyond our biology. Perhaps it is time for us to begin reconditioning ourselves so that we accept the fear we feel and move beyond it to achieve the goals we seek. We need to do this not only for ourselves, but also for our children.

In *The Money Tree Myth*, I suggest that parents introduce their children to the world of investing early. One way is to track the performance of a group of stocks chosen for their interest to children — McDonald's, Nike, Disney, Coke — over the long term. Children who are socialized to the ups and downs of the market, who have the opportunity to watch stock prices as they move through their natural rise-and-fall cycles, will be less concerned with short-term volatility when they become adult investors.

**Women choose advisers differently.**
If you look at financial decision making as having two parts — the thinking (logical) part and the feeling (intuitive) part — then women lean toward the feeling side, while men tend to lean toward the thinking side. The mistake many women make is that they choose to deal with an adviser because they feel comfortable with that person, rather than looking at the individual's track record and experience. Men, on the other hand, seldom ask themselves how they feel about a person. They are more likely to make a decision based on the company's reputation and the adviser's past performance.

---

7   Jerome Kagan, *Galen's Prophecy* (WestviewPress, 1994), p. 195.

**Women live longer than men.**
While the statistics speak for themselves, we seem unwilling to hear what they have to say.

Intellectually, we know that we will outlive our husbands. Emotionally, we're not willing to face it. Intellectually, we know we have to be able to take care of ourselves. Emotionally, we avoid the subject entirely. It seems to take a major event in our lives to bring the significance of the statistics home to our own reality.

After Kathy Farrell's mother died in 1996, she and her husband were walking through Mount Pleasant cemetery. "I was looking at the grave markers when I noticed that on family plots the date the male died was say, 1850, and the date his female partner died was some 15 or 20 years later. It was such a punctuation of something I had just experienced personally.

"The most profound thing for me was my mother's death. Through that, I got a whole new perspective on financial planning. Her situation was so typical of most. While we know statistically that women live longer than men, until you experience this in your life, you don't really understand what the implications are.

"In my case, my father died about 10 years before my mother. He, like many men, did not believe in life insurance because he believed the insurance company always won. He was well-off relative to most people and he felt there was plenty of money. But after he had been dead for several years my mother started to feel very poor. She needed to take a lot of drugs, and the drug costs were exceeding her income so she began eating into capital.

"The house was paid for, but there were still the basic costs such as taxes and upkeep. I see it time and again. People think that once the house is paid for, it's an expense-free item. It's not. My mother was no longer able to do the gardening. If she wanted to make a capital improvement, that was a separate cost. Even with help from myself and my sister, my mother got to the point where she stopped buying things such as clothes for herself because she simply didn't feel she could afford it.

"The process of my mother's financial deterioration started well before she began to die. When she did become very ill, it went on and on.

"In the movies, people die. But that's just true for men. I used to think how lucky my father was to have just died. No pain, no struggle. My mother had to deal with the loss of dignity. After about a year and a half, I was so drained emotionally."

When Kathy spoke of the strain of her mother's ordeal on both her mother and the rest of the family, there was a sadness in the realization that, at the very least, all the financial stress could have been avoided. The idea of financial planning took on a whole new meaning for Kathy. It isn't about acquiring the most, or having the most. It's about taking care of the details so that the financial issues don't come as a shock. It's taking care of the day-to-day so the tomorrow isn't a horror. As Kathy says, "Life's difficult enough — you experience so many stresses psychologically and emotionally." If you have your financial act together it's one less thing to worry about. Kathy is right when she says, "A lot of the other things you can't do anything about. They just happen. You might as well do something about the things you can control."

**It's a woman's world.**
Thankfully, women are becoming so much more powerful as an economic force that our special needs are being recognized. And our unique approaches — our desire to be fully informed, our team-oriented styles, our cautious optimism — prepare us to move forward, building on our strengths. Since we are so willing to look at both our skills and our emotional baggage when it comes to money, we are well positioned to learn, develop confidence, and take control. So are you convinced and ready to take charge of your financial well-being? Because now we'll go through the steps you need to take to do just that. You'll be surprised at just how un-money-related they actually are.

# 3

# Seven Steps to Financial Well-Being

*You are responsible, forever, for what you have tamed.*

ANTOINE DE SAINT-EXUPÉRY

Financial freedom is a state of being that has far more to do with attitude and approach than quantity. That's what this chapter is about: understanding your attitudes and qualifying your approach so no matter how much money you have, you can view it and use it positively. By taking steps to come to terms with money's role in your life and by committing to change, you can figure out what your personal barriers have been and vault them. You can face your fears, get back in touch with money as it really exists, and take responsibility so you can be free from worry. Ultimately, to change, you've got to *do something differently.*

It's strange, but money is one of our deepest, darkest secrets. While we may feel comfortable talking about many intimate and personal issues — our marital problems, our sex lives, health issues — we are hugely resistant to talking about money truthfully and openly. In the most profound sense, money says absolutely nothing about us, yet we hold our money secrets closest to our hearts.

If you're interested in how you perceive money, and in how to put money in perspective so you can understand your own reactions, you'll find the next exercise interesting.

## STEP ONE: FIND OUT WHAT INFLUENCES YOU

The first step toward financial freedom involves determining your "financial style." Read through the following categories and see how many you rate as true for yourself. Remember, styles may not be exclusive. And you may have shifted styles as you moved through the different stages in your life. What's your predominant style now? To which group of questions did you most often answer "True"? Do you see yourself the way others see you?

### Are You a Miser?

| | | |
|---|---|---|
| True | False | I enjoy holding on to my money. |
| True | False | I find it difficult to spend on myself. |
| True | False | I find it difficult to give to others. |
| True | False | I seldom give to charity. |
| True | False | I'm always on the lookout for the least expensive gift. |
| True | False | I'm afraid I won't have enough money. |
| True | False | I often put off buying because I'm sure I can get it cheaper elsewhere. |
| True | False | My family often gets angry with me because I refuse to spend money. |
| True | False | I could never trust anyone else with my money. |
| True | False | I often say, "I can't afford it." |

What drives the Miser? It's not really meanness, although it may appear that way to others. It's fear: fear of not having enough, fear of being poor, fear of catastrophe. In order to protect themselves, misers make sure they never run out of money. The best way to have money is to not spend any. These people have no confidence in their ability to make more money. They think the gravy train is about to end and they'll be left destitute.

What the Miser has to learn is that money is just a symbol of security. And she has to learn to stop imagining all those worst-case scenarios that make her feel even more fearful.

If you fear poverty so much that you create poverty in your daily life, you are living your worst nightmare. Stop. Instead of focusing so much on the future, live each day as if you have enough money. Remember, it's not money that makes you rich. It is what you choose to do with your money that will determine the richness of your life.

### Help Yourself

- Make a list of five things you would like to buy for yourself: flowers, books, a new blouse, candles, hippos. Ask a friend or family member to look at your list and add two things she has heard you say you want. For each of the next seven weeks, buy one item on your list.
- Make a list of the people closest to you. Beside each name, write one item you know that person wants to buy, or that she or he would enjoy receiving. If you can't think of anything, write in "a card and some flowers." Then, each week for the next few weeks, buy one of the items on the list and present it to your loved one.
- Each time a catastrophic image comes into your mind, write it down on a piece of paper. Put it in a box created specifically for this purpose. At the end of each week, take those bits of paper and tear them up, burn them, or bury them in the garden. Do one piece at a time, reminding yourself with each that you will not give up control of your happiness to this Demon Worry.

### Are You a Spender?

| | | |
|---|---|---|
| True | False | I love to shop. |
| True | False | I have a hard time saving. |
| True | False | I find it difficult to defer gratification. |
| True | False | I am not working toward any long-term financial goals. |
| True | False | I never seem to have enough to pay my bills. |
| True | False | My credit cards are maxed out. |
| True | False | I often pay for dinner and buy gifts for friends. |
| True | False | I cannot go into a store without buying something. |
| True | False | I can't resist a bargain. |
| True | False | I get angry if confronted about my spending. |

What drives the Spender? The first type of Spender is the person who spends to create an image and has an enormous desire to be noticed. She buys designer clothes, jewelry, expensive cars, luxury items. She needs to be noticed to feel validated or approved of. She wants to impress. She craves preferential treatment and is vulnerable to any pitch that treats her as special. And she likes to shock people by being outrageous. Success is important to the image spender and she is easily impressed by power and fame. She wants to be a part of the "in group," and is prepared to spend her way in. And she wants to be perceived as generous. She competitively races for the bill, buys the most expensive present, and does anything to maintain the facade.

The second type of spender is the bargain seeker. She's in it for the hunt. When she finds a bargain, she feels victorious. While she can often afford to pay full price, the satisfaction comes from adding up how much she has saved. Often bargain hunters buy things they don't need simply because the deal was too good to pass up.

Then there's the compulsive shopper. Whether she has five dollars or $500 in her wallet, she has to spend it as quickly as possible. Often after spending, she feels guilty or ashamed that she didn't handle her money better. She hits the shopper's low and feels anxious. But she shops again, just as wildly. She shops to hide from her misery. She shops for the excitement. She shops to escape loneliness. She shops to enrich her life. She absolutely itches to shop. And because the buying is more important than the having, she may have clothing with the tags still on hanging in the closet, or household items still in their original boxes stacked in the cupboard. She buys not because she needs the item, but to satisfy her urge to shop.

**Help Yourself**
- Admit that your shopping is having a negative effect on your life. Don't beat yourself up, just recognize that you have to take the problem seriously.
- Keep a journal of your spending. Write down every item you buy, the amount you spent, and how you felt. Don't "forget" your ledger and don't leave anything out. *This is a tough job*. Don't judge your spending, just note your purchases. At the end of the week, total up how much you've spent.
- Shift your source of enrichment from "getting" to "doing." Look for activities you really enjoy and spend more time doing them: potluck dinners with friends, long walks in the early evening with your partner, going to the park with your son.
- The next time you want to buy something, write it on your list and write the current date beside it. Tell yourself you will buy the item

in two weeks if you still need or want it.

- Stay out of the mall. Turn off the shopping channel. Throw out the catalogues *before* you browse through them. Leave your credit cards at home. Carry only a small amount of cash with you.
- Do your shopping like a purchasing department. Usually before a purchasing department will buy an item, it must be convinced that the item to be bought is of benefit to the company, that it is of good value, and that there is money available to pay for it. Before you buy anything, make sure the item meets these criteria.
- Switch from buying consumable items to buying investments. Buy some stock. Buy an RRSP. Buy a mutual fund. Shop around, compare rates, bargain hunt. Make sure you get yourself an adviser to ensure you aren't just buying — but buying wisely. You'll be spending money to increase, instead of deplete, your net worth.

**Are You an Avoider?**

| True | False | I don't reconcile my statement and cheque book. |
| True | False | I don't look at my financial statements when they arrive, I just stick them in a drawer for another time. |
| True | False | I don't know how much money I have in my wallet. |
| True | False | I don't know how much money I have in my bank account. |
| True | False | I don't pay my bills on time. |
| True | False | I don't have a will. |
| True | False | I don't read the financial press. |
| True | False | I don't feel very competent about handling my money. |
| True | False | I don't know how much I owe on my credit cards. |
| True | False | I don't do my taxes until the very last minute. |

Women avoid handling their personal finances for all sorts of reasons. They feel overwhelmed by the prospect of managing their money. They may feel ashamed because of their lack of skill. But in almost all cases, the longer they avoid dealing with their money issues, the lower their self-respect. One way of overcoming this sense of dread is to hand the responsibility over to a financial planner. Unfortunately, giving over responsibility for your money is a dangerous game. It's one thing to seek advice, and another to give up all control.

An Avoider who is married will often leave all the money management to her spouse. He'll take care of everything. These Avoiders are often unaware of the family's assets and shocked to find out how well-off or destitute they are when forced by divorce or death to face the realities of their financial lives.

### Help Yourself

- Once a week, do something to deal with your money such as balancing your cheque book. Set up a filing system for your financial statements and sort them out.
- Stop procrastinating. Pay your bills as they come in. Sit down and do your taxes before the deadline.
- If your spouse handles all the money issues, start communicating about what you have and which responsibilities you can assume. Don't be surprised if he is hesitant to give up control. You have empowered him and he may feel at risk by divulging financial information. Be firm and persistent, but gentle.
- If you do not have one, establish your own financial identity. Open up a bank account in your name. Establish credit in your name. Get yourself an adviser — a broker, financial planner, or accountant — that is yours alone (as opposed to yours and your mate's).

### Are You an Acquirer?

True    False    I love having lots of money at my disposal.

True    False    I'm very focused on increasing my net worth.

True    False    I often compare the amount of assets I have with others.

True    False    I feel in greater control when I have more money.

True    False    I often take a flyer to try to get ahead financially.

True    False    People who have less than me are lazy or stupid.

True    False    I spend a great deal of my time working.

True    False    Money is power.

True    False    Time is money.

True    False    I feel in greater control when I have more money.

While a healthy attitude toward money means you will use it to experience life and to enrich the lives of those around you, an Acquirer relates to money as if the acquisition is the ultimate goal. She believes it's not what you do with your money, it's how much you have. And since greed makes people vulnerable to dubious get-rich-quick schemes, the desire to acquire doesn't always translate into wealth.

The desire does, however, translate into effort. Acquirers are notorious workaholics. Their motto is "time is money." Spouses and children are ignored, and evenings and weekends are spent on the phone doing deals or managing projects. And their perception of money becomes distorted: no amount is ever enough.

Hard-core Acquirers will go to any lengths to increase their net worth. They will take from others. They will cheat, steal, or involve themselves in shady schemes. The end justifies the means. The goal is to get as much as possible, in any way possible. All that matters is money.

### Help Yourself

- Look beyond your financial assets to the other "assets" in your life: spouse, children, friends, personal time, self-development, gratifying work, creative release, spirituality, relaxation, community. Are you expending as much effort to increase your net worth in those areas? List the things that you consider to be "assets" in your life. How can you increase those assets?
- Look realistically at the role money plays in your life. How does your acquisitional behaviour work against your personal well-being? Long commutes, long workdays, lost vacations, few interactions with your loved ones are all costs associated with your drive to acquire. Today, decide you will spend one hour with a child, mate, or friend, just shooting the breeze. Talk about life, dreams, loves, adventures, a good book, a fine meal. Don't mention money.
- What skills do you have that could benefit your community? Choose a community project and volunteer. Keep your commitments to the group.

### Are You a Depriver?

True    False    I am always broke.

True    False    I feel unworthy if given a promotion or other form of recognition.

True    False    Even though I have a low-paying job, I often take work home or put in lots of unpaid overtime.

| | | |
|---|---|---|
| True | False | I often dream about ways to make more money. |
| True | False | I lose valuable items. |
| True | False | Each time I feel as if I'm getting ahead, something happens to put me back at square one. |
| True | False | If I enjoy what I do, like fixing cars, sewing, or painting, I can't charge for it. |
| True | False | I do not feel capable of handling my money. |
| True | False | I'm not willing to buy into the system and give up my freedom. |
| True | False | Money just isn't important. |

Why does the Depriver constantly sabotage her efforts to get ahead financially? She may feel undeserving. She may prefer that people not expect too much from her. She may not know a lot about finances, and she may be unwilling to learn. To her, money is incomprehensible. Or perhaps it is dirty. To some, having money will make them spiritually bankrupt or politically incorrect. They think it is virtuous to be broke. Or perhaps they simply want to stay within their peer group, believing that rich people are greedy, arrogant, power-mad, and selfish. To want money is to want all those other characteristics.

Some Deprivers seem to want to achieve financial security. They are dreamers, thinking of ways to get money, working out elaborate schemes to make their fortunes. Unfortunately, they never quite get the plane off the ground. They procrastinate or sabotage themselves. Or perhaps they fail in order to reject their parents' obsession with money.

Another reason for depriving is to avoid the grief of loss that will accompany failure. Remaining poor feels safer. By not drawing attention to themselves, they can avoid being hurt. If they achieve success, others will envy them and want to hurt them.

**Help Yourself**

- Just for today, don't deprive yourself. Pat yourself on the back for a job well done. Treat yourself to a nice lunch.
- Set some goals. What do you like to do? How can you use your skills to improve your financial picture?
- Stop thinking and speaking about money as if it were evil or dirty. Money is paper and metal. What you decide it represents is a

reflection of your morals — not of the morals of money itself. Remember, an inanimate object can't have a morality.

- Find a money mentor, someone knowledgeable and experienced who doesn't share your dread of money. Look for someone who will share your successes joyfully.

### Are You a Debtor?

| | | |
|---|---|---|
| True | False | I get a thrill out of using my credit cards. |
| True | False | I like having access to credit — the more I have, the happier I am. |
| True | False | You don't have to have money to spend money. |
| True | False | I only pay the minimum amounts on my credit-card balances, and my cards are usually maxed out. |
| True | False | Creditors are always overreacting. |
| True | False | My cheques often bounce. |
| True | False | I don't pay bills on time, even when I have the money. |
| True | False | I feel uneasy just walking into a bank. |
| True | False | When I divvy up the dinner bill with friends, I put the bill on my charge card and pocket the cash. |
| True | False | I've taken a consolidation loan and then run my cards right back up again. |

Debtors dig themselves into a hole by borrowing excessively and misusing credit. Regardless of whether they can afford to or not, Debtors borrow, mainly because they can't face the limitations of their budget. They find it easy to delay paying bills, and often blame others when the natural consequences occur: "How dare my bank bounce this cheque."

While consolidation loans often work for people who get into debt solely as a result of a change in their personal and economic circumstances — for example, people who are laid off, become disabled, or face sudden, unforeseen expenses — they seldom work for the chronic debtor. Instead of offering a way to get out of the abyss, the loan frees up other credit that is then immediately used up again. And since Debtors traditionally set unrealistic expectations for themselves when they do try to eliminate their debt, they often rein themselves in too tightly. They are then forced to use credit just to make ends meet.

**Help Yourself**

- Admit to yourself, and to someone else, that you have a problem. Recognize that you cannot get out of debt by taking on new debt. More credit just exacerbates the problem. Become a critic of debt. Do you really want to pay interest on that dress, stereo, or dinner for the next three years? If you only pay the minimum amount each month, you could end up paying twice as much as the original cost for the item.
- Decide that you will not take on any new debt today. By going one day at a time, you'll move closer to freeing yourself from the Debtor's cycle. Join a support group such as Debtors Anonymous.
- Cut up your credit cards and close the accounts. Paying cash ensures you won't take on new debt and makes you more conscious of what you are spending.
- Don't spend more than you make. Make a spending plan that shows how you intend to use your money (as opposed to a budget that is restrictive and constraining). Include a few of the frills that make life more bearable: an occasional meal out, fresh flowers, a movie, a new book. If you do not enjoy the quality of your life, you won't stick to your spending plan.
- Accept responsibility for your debts. That doesn't mean being harsh with yourself. Accept that what is done is done and get on with life. Call your creditors and work out a repayment schedule you can live with. Pay off your most expensive debt first, then apply more money to the next most expensive as it becomes available.

## STEP TWO: MAKE PEACE

We would all do well to heed this ancient Chinese proverb: "He who knows he has enough is rich." The second step in achieving financial freedom is to make peace with how much you have.

Whether you make $20,000, $60,000, or $200,000 a year, few people can say honestly that they're happy with their financial lot. Witness all the people who never have time for a holiday, who miss school pageants, or who never take the day off in the middle of the week. It seems we always want more.

A few years ago, after my daughter was born and I started to pull back from corporate consulting, my accountant asked me how concerned I was about lower billings. He was trying to help me plan my income for the future. As I tried to explain to him that my life was changing, I suddenly realized that I was no longer prepared to do the things I had done in the past just for the money.

During my second pregnancy, these feelings grew even stronger. During one particularly tedious project where the client was being petulant, my mind drifted to my daughter at home and I realized my priorities had shifted and I wasn't prepared to put up with the corporate nonsense anymore. I still enjoy working on fast-paced projects where my expertise is valued. But I won't take just any job. I have to trust the client, and the client has to trust me. If not, I've found no amount of money compensates for the aggravation. I realize this is a luxury I've worked for and a choice I make to have less.

To free yourself of the self-doubt and the need to keep up with the Joneses, accept your current situation and set a realistic goal for when enough is enough.

John Stuart Mill once said, "Men do not desire to be rich, only to be richer than other men." To cut through the Gordian knot of debt, quantify for yourself how much is enough. In their book *Your Money or Your Life*, Joe Dominguez and Vicki Robin have charted what they refer to as the "Fulfillment Curve":

At the peak of the Fulfillment Curve we have enough. Enough for our survival. Enough comforts. And even enough little "luxuries." We have everything we need; there's nothing extra to weigh us down, distract or distress us, nothing we've bought on time, have never used and are slaving to pay off. Enough is a fearless place. A trusting place. An honest and self-observant place. It's appreciating and fully enjoying what money brings into your life and yet never purchasing anything that isn't needed . . . [8]

Which brings us to the question of what a "need" is. In my book *The Money Tree Myth*, I describe the various types of needs and how important it is to distinguish between them.

---

8   Joe Dominguez and Vicki Robin, *Your Money or Your Life* (Penguin Books, 1992), p. 25.

First there are the wants, which come about because you simply don't have something right now. It's the need to remedy the lack of a specific item or a state. I want a new dress. I want a new set of dishes. I want to be left alone. Next there are the concerns. These relate to things we worry about. I'm concerned about keeping my money safe, so I need a bank account. I'm worried about how my friends will see me, so I need the latest fashion item. I'm worried I won't be loved, so I buy my children plenty of presents. Then there are the problems. Something has happened that has created a need. My house is too small, so I need a new one. My car just died, so I need a loan to buy a new car. I can't make ends meet so I need to make more money. Finally, there are the desires. These are the "I wish I had" or "I wish I could have" statements. I wish I could take the kids to Disney World. I wish I could buy a new coat. I wish you would listen to me.

The distinctions between these types of needs are not always easy to see. Even professional salespeople have difficulty distinguishing between a want, concern, problem, or desire. But there are differences, and the differences relate to value.

Don't get me wrong. Sometimes it's perfectly appropriate to get something just because you want it. I collect hippos. I buy them because I want them. They don't satisfy any concern or problem and it's not a matter of desire. It's straight out want. I have no goal in buying a hippo, except for the gratification it brings. I have quite the hippo collection, but if I see another one I like, I'll probably buy it just because I want it.

Understanding the motivation to buy goes a long way toward determining the value of the purchase. Without this understanding, people will inappropriately place the same value on one purchase as on another. That hinders their ability to judge the appropriateness of the buying decision.

There are three questions you can ask yourself whenever you find you need something. The first relates to your level of fulfillment. How will the satisfaction of this need make me feel more fulfilled? The second relates to your purpose — your goals, your image of your life, what you want to accomplish. How will the satisfaction of this need move me closer to my purpose? The final question relates to responsibility, and a sense of how your life fits in with those around you. How will the satisfaction of this need affect those around me?

### STEP THREE: FIND YOUR MONEY SET-POINT

Dietitians know that people who use only a diet to change their weight usually return to the same weight because we each have a preset internal metabolic rate. The only way to truly change our weight is to reset our internal thermostat by increasing that metabolic rate. Consider the fact that we may also each have an internal thermostat that measures our comfort level with our savings and net worth. When we seem to be moving above this point, we do whatever is necessary to return to equilibrium: go shopping, change jobs, leave the workforce, acquire some debt. I have a girlfriend who can't sleep at night if her savings account drops below $1,800. It's a marker she has set for herself based on absolutely nothing. But no matter how much she and I have talked about the importance of setting up an emergency fund, she can't get her savings *beyond* the $1,800 level. Each time the account rises above her marker, off she goes on a holiday, or there's a new painting, or there's a spiffy new outfit.

If you allow your set-point to be determined by some illogical internal gremlin, *you* are not in charge. If you want to take control, you must either evict the gremlin and reset your set-point, or trick her. If you plan to evict, know the task won't be easy. To begin, sit down and determine what your set-point is. Next, figure out if it works for you. Is it livable? If not, what should it be?

If you can't evict the gremlin then you'll have to trick her. There are all sorts of ways to do this. For example, I know one woman who has four or five bank accounts. Each time she gets to her set-point, she walks away from the bank account and opens another. It's not a very convenient or efficient system, but it works for her. A friend of mine reset her set-point by convincing her gremlin that it was appropriate to have a different set-point for each of her objectives. The more objectives she had, the higher her overall set-point. At last count, she was saving for retirement, a return to school, a downpayment for a second home, her three children's educations (separately), and a fund to care for her parents should the need arise later in life.

### STEP FOUR: FACE THE FEAR

Yes, we're all very busy. We're running the kids to day care, running to work, running to our next appointment. No matter what job you have, whether you are selling real estate or coffee, working as a vice-president or a secretary, focusing on your career or on your family, you manage to make time for the things that are important to you. As a wise man once said to me, "If I spent as much time taking care of my money as I do others', I'd be rich." Time, or a lack of it, doesn't prevent you from dealing with your money. Fear does.

As a young adult, I remember reading a book entitled *Feel the Fear and Do It Anyway*, by Susan Jeffers. The premise of the book was that we all carry fears that stop us from doing what we want. As children, we are constantly faced with fear: "Be careful!" "Don't run into the street, you'll be squashed like a bug-a-bug!" These messages stay with us, heightening our anxiety and creating barriers to our achievement. The only way around them is to face them head on and get over them. If we do not, those fears will grow like weeds, suffocating our ability to achieve peace.

What are your fears? Do you worry that you won't have enough when you grow old and will end up a bag lady? Even the very rich describe this fear, so it isn't related to how much money you have in the bank. Do you lose sleep worrying about whether your children will be okay, should something happen to you? Do you think about what you'd have to do to keep a roof over your head and food in your children's stomachs if something happened to your husband? Do you worry that you just can't keep up, or that there's no other job you could ever do?

We all have fears that creep into our minds and steal away our serenity. But if you don't know what you're afraid of, you can't come to terms with it. So, if you're prepared to try dealing with your fears, begin by asking yourself, "What am I afraid of?" If nothing comes to mind immediately, give it time. Make sure you write down your fears. Looking back at the questions on pages 12–13, can you see a connection between your fears and the messages you received as a child? If you don't immediately see a connection, that's not unusual, since many of our earliest memories are deeply buried. Just keep thinking about it, and I'm sure the picture will become clear for you.

## STEP FIVE: GET BACK IN TOUCH WITH MONEY

Go into your wallet and take out a five-dollar bill. Now tear it up. Could you do it? Most people can't. Yet every day we toss money in the garbage:

the books we buy but never read; the leftovers we scrape into the garbage can; the dress we get for a steal but wear only twice. We can fool ourselves in dozens of ways when it comes to "stuff," but it's a lot harder when it comes to the actual money. That's why it's important to start touching the real stuff again.

If you feel a little divorced from money, it's not really surprising. Each technological advance has distanced us from our money, making it more convenient for us to spend. Cheques, for example, are a representation of money: a promise to pay. But if you've ever written a cheque you knew would bounce (or written one that bounced unexpectedly), you know that a cheque and money are two separate animals. Another technological advance is the credit card. Looking back over the purchases you made in the past month, how many fewer would you have made if you didn't have your credit card with you? Sometimes we don't even call it a credit card; instead we refer to it as plastic, distancing ourselves even further from what it actually represents: money. The same holds true for debit cards, except in this case, the money actually has to be there. But a debit card gives us easy access to our cash, and that convenience has made the system successful beyond all expectations. On May 15, 1997, *The Financial Post* reported that in just over two years, since the national launch of the debit system, 50% of Canadians were using their bank cards to pay for groceries, gas, retail purchases, and most other products and services. In fact, direct debit achieved in five years what it took credit cards 25 years to do in terms of broad consumer acceptance. Why? Simple. Debit cards make it easier to spend money. They are faster and more convenient than writing cheques. They are more widely accepted than are credit cards. And they are one of the cheapest ways to pay. (Nothing beats cash for minimizing transaction costs.)

Auto debits, direct payments, telephone banking, on-line banking — these conveniences all stand between you and the actual paper and coin that is money. To get back in touch with your money, for the next month or so, spend nothing except cash. At the end of the month, compare your expenditures with those of the previous month. Is there a difference? How inconvenient was it for you? How did you feel about spending each time you took cash from your wallet? How much money do you have in your wallet now?

## STEP SIX: BE RESPONSIBLE

"I *am* responsible," you say vehemently. Great. So you have a will and a power of attorney. And you have enough insurance so your family will manage if your income is suddenly gone. And you've taken precautions in case you become disabled. And you have a retirement plan so your children won't have to support you. And you have six months' savings put aside so if the unexpected occurs, your kids can sleep peacefully in their own beds. You also have a pay-yourself-first plan because you know the importance of investing.

A big part of financial freedom is having all the i's dotted and t's crossed so you can free yourself from worrying about the what-ifs of life. Saying you'll get to it isn't enough. Merely knowing you've taken care of your loved ones will move you a long way along the path to financial freedom. If you really love your spouse and your children, you must do more than say you love them. You must act as if you love them. And if you truly love yourself, you must prove it by doing the responsible thing. When you use money to take care of those around you, you have your priorities straight: people first, then money. If you fail to take care of your responsibilities, how much happiness, love, laughter, and joy will the money bring?

## STEP SEVEN: DO IT!

To be financially free, you can't just think about it, you've got to act. And while people are more important than money, the money won't take care of itself. That's your job. It's not up to your accountant, broker, banker, lawyer, husband, son, financial planner, or mother. If you don't respect and tend to your money, you'll find little available when you need it. So take control — and find the financial freedom you're seeking.

Taking action is precisely what we're going to talk about next: doing the things you can — the things you must — in order to have the control you need to achieve financial freedom. See you in Part II.

# II

# TELESIS

*The business of life is to go forward.*
SAMUEL JOHNSON

*Where I am today has everything to do with the
years I spent hanging on by my fingernails.*
BARBARA ARONSTEIN

*E*ach *year as I do the media rounds for RRSP season I am asked, "When should I start contributing to my RRSP?" For young people, the question implies they have lots of time and can wait. For older individuals, the question should really be, "Is it too late for me?"*

*It is never too soon or too late to begin taking care of your money, no matter how your bottom line reads today. If you find you are in debt and see no way of getting out, take heart and take control, starting today. If you've been busy paying your mortgage, paying for your children, paying for your lifestyle and haven't managed to build yourself a nest egg, you can take control, starting today. If you feel overwhelmed, inexperienced, inept, you can take control, starting today. You just have to understand* telesis.

*Telesis is defined as the "deliberate, purposeful utilization of the process of nature and society to obtain particular goals."⁹ It is progress that is intelligently planned and directed. It is what you must do to get to where you want to be. Instead of planning to save, you save. Instead of planning to pay off those debts, you simply start paying them off. It doesn't mean you will achieve all ends immediately. It does mean you will no longer delay starting. You won't wait until your next raise to open up your pay-yourself-first monthly savings plan. You'll do it immediately. And you won't wait until you have a "decent" contribution to begin using an RRSP; you'll start with that $50 you managed to squirrel away.*

*I started contributing to an RRSP when I was 22. I wasn't prescient. I didn't know back then that there would be controversy surrounding government pensions, or that I would never benefit from a corporate pension plan. I just knew that I was supposed to save. So save I did. And I used an RRSP because I just couldn't believe the tax man would give me his money to do with as I wished, simply for choosing an RRSP over another savings vehicle. I had been saving since I was a little girl when my dad had offered the incentive of a savings-matching program. Seems the government had a similar deal going, so I took it. And in doing so, I implemented telesis and formed a habit I never intend to lose.*

*Telesis and* inertia *go hand in hand. Most people associate inertia with an inability to move. But, in fact, inertia is "a property of matter by which it*

---

9  *The Random House College Dictionary, Revised Edition*, 1975.

*remains at rest* or in uniform motion *in the same straight line unless acted upon by some external force."*[10]

Now, *think about inertia as it applies to the theory of* telesis. *Once you're moving, it'll take a 10-foot-wide brick wall to stop you. Having established your pay-yourself-first plan, you will keep saving and investing every month for the rest of your life. A comrade-in-writing of mine, Victoria Ryce, refers to it as "painless portfolio building." As she says, "You only miss the money in the first month. By the second month, the pain is gone." That's the beauty of inertia. Once on a roll, you'll continue to roll unless some remarkable force gets in your way. Another Victoria-ism: "Getting rich is boring." Since you don't have to think about it, you can just keep investing monthly — same-old, same-old — until you are rich. That's* telesis *at work!*

The best way to get *telesis working for you is to put in place your financial basics: the strategies and habits you'll need to keep your financial body and soul together. Where to start? First you need a plan . . . a spending plan.*

---

10 *Merriam-Webster Collegiate Dictionary, Tenth Edition,* 1996.

# 4

# Establish a Spending Plan

*If hippos are on sale, two for a dollar, that's a bargain . . . but only if you have a dollar and need two hippos!*

WHO KNOWS

*The best things in life are free, but the next best things are expensive.*

ME

*Every mickle makes a muckle.*

OLD JAMAICAN SAYING

I remember a time when I thought that if I could just make $30,000 a year, I'd be set. Since I was only making $10,000 a year at the time, I couldn't imagine what I'd do with all that money. The reality was that by the time I was earning $30,000 I had higher expenses. I had to pay more tax, buy a new car, dress in more expensive business attire.

It's easy to spend money once you get used to having it. And it doesn't take long to get used to it. Like a gas expanding to fill a container, your expenses grow in proportion to your new income. And if you're not careful, you may find your spending plan popping like a balloon.

A spending plan is a way of keeping track of the money you get and the money you spend. The best thing about a spending plan is that it gives you a very clear picture of your financial reality. Many people cringe when I talk about the need for a spending plan. They relate being proactive about what they're spending with having to give up things they enjoy. In reality, a spending plan gives you the freedom to enjoy yourself, because you don't have to worry about how you'll pay the bill when it comes in. You'll know right from the start whether you can afford the purchase or not.

How does a spending plan differ from a budget? Budgets feel restrictive and are often set unrealistically so, like diets, they seldom work. With a spending plan, you decide how to spend your money so it does you the most good.

One of the truths of money is that the more you have, the more you'll spend. People who let the spending just happen inevitably end up drowning in a sea of debt. Exhausted from bailing to try and get back into the black, they finally give up and sink into credit oblivion.

The trick with any spending plan is to not let it be the tail that wags the dog. Without a keen sense of where you're going, and what you want to achieve, it's very easy to fall into the trap of spending more and more. As Mr. Micawber says in Charles Dickens's *David Copperfield*, "Annual income twenty pounds, annual expenditure nineteen six, result happiness. Annual income twenty pounds, annual expenditure twenty pounds ought and six, result misery." What most people don't know is that this is a version of something Charles Dickens's daddy said to him from debtors' prison.

Have you ever made a large cash withdrawal from a banking machine, only to wonder a few days later where all the money went? Where did the last $100 you withdrew go? Stop for a minute and write it down. Chances are you can account for most of it, but there may be five, 10, or 20 dollars missing from your list.

What does it cost you to live each month? Most people underestimate their expenses because they forget the things that don't occur every month. Did you include your gym costs even though you pay them once a year? How about your house or car insurance? Did you include the cost of your haircuts, your contact lenses, or your vacation? Do you pay someone to shovel your snow, clean your windows and carpets, or do your taxes? Did you buy one or two cords of wood last winter? Did your kids go to camp? What about your vet bills, the flowers for your garden or

patio, your coworker's going-away present? Or how about those magazines you picked up at the supermarket checkout, the batteries for
Tickle-me-Elmo, or the charcoal for the barbecue? And what about the
bottle of wine you gave your friends when they had you over for dinner,
or the five dollars here and 10 dollars there your son or daughter hit you
up for?

When you do all your money management in your head, it's very easy
to forget things — sometimes important things — that will have an
impact on your overall financial life. If you write cheques without record-
ing what you've paid for, it's easy to forget how much you've spent. You're
always guessing how much you have left. And you shouldn't really be
surprised when your account is overdrawn. After all, if you don't know
how much you have, how can you know how much you can spend?

People who barely make it from one paycheque to the next are often
surprised when they take the time to do a spending plan. They may not
have realized just how much they spend on impulse purchases, lunches or
drinks with friends, parking tickets, candy bars, or lottery tickets. Just as
importantly, they usually find it much easier to reach their goals when
they have a plan to work with. One of the best ways to gain a perspective
on your spending habits is to keep a log of everything you spend, each
time you do the transaction. Now, hold on a second. Don't go all cross-
eyed on me. The idea is to figure out where you're spending all those
five-, 10-, and 20-dollar bills that seem to go missing each month. It's also
about learning more about yourself and where you place your priorities.
This isn't about shame, blame, or deprivation. You don't have to change
anything you don't want to change. But you should at least know. By
keeping a spending log, you will have a clear picture of your expenses so
you can see what you're getting for your money.

Another important concept that is often drowned out by the sound of
the credit card swishing through the machine is that of relative value.
Relative value refers to the relationship between what an item costs and
what you have to do to pay for it. It's not a new concept. Adam Smith
talked about it in *The Wealth of Nations* in 1776 when he wrote, "The real
price of everything, what everything really costs to the man who wants to
acquire it, is the toil and trouble of acquiring it."

What does it cost to buy that new coat? The absolute cost relates to
how long you have to work to come up with the cash. If it costs $260 and

your *disposable hourly income* is $4.25, you'll have to work for about 61.5 hours to earn enough money. That can put a whole new perspective on the real cost of the coat.

The idea of a disposable hourly income is not one most people are familiar with. It is your gross income less your fixed total expenses (including income tax) divided by the number of hours you work. Let's say you make $30,000 a year, have two weeks' vacation, and work a 45-hour week. Assuming your average tax rate is 29%, you'll net $21,300. Let's also say that your fixed monthly expenses (things like rent, mortgage, loan payments, food, utilities, phone, drugs, transportation) total $1,500 a month, or $18,000 a year. Your disposable hourly income would be $1.47:

$$\frac{21,300 - 18,000}{45 \text{ (hours)} \times 50 \text{ (weeks)}} \quad \begin{array}{l} = \\ = \end{array} \quad \frac{3,300}{2,250} \quad = \$1.47 \text{ / hour}$$

Yeech! You probably don't even want to do this exercise, right? It looks pretty depressing. But if you don't do it, you won't see how hard you have to work to pay for the item you're thinking about buying.

Many people who make what seems to be an extremely good living get themselves into holes precisely because they are not aware of their disposable hourly income and their spending patterns. Let's take the case of Margaret and her husband, Frank. Frank is an executive who makes $180,000 a year. That's a lot of money, right? So Margaret could never figure out why they never had any money. After taxes, Frank's income dropped to $96,000 a year. But as Margaret saw it, that was still $8,000 a month. What was the problem? When they did their spending plan, they discovered that their monthly expenses were very high: a $2,000-a-month mortgage, a huge food bill to feed themselves and four kids, clothing, school fees — it all added up to about $6,000 a month. Then, of course, there was Frank's penchant for buying whatever took his fancy. And Margaret, though she considered herself a smart shopper, found that she loved to shop and would use any excuse to buy: new drapes, new clothes for the kids, and fresh flowers for the house. It all added up. After keeping track of their spending patterns for three months, they became far more aware of where their money was going. Then Margaret calculated Frank's disposable hourly income. Since he travelled quite a bit and worked hard, she tracked his hours for three months and came up with a weekly average of 57 hours. It turned out that Frank's disposable hourly income was just $8.42.

You might find it useful to go through the exercise yourself. As Joe Dominguez and Vicki Robin say in *Your Money or Your Life:*

> Money is something we choose to trade our life energy for . . . When we go to our jobs we are trading our life energy for money. This truth, while simple, is profound . . . While money has no intrinsic reality, our life energy does . . . Life energy is all we have. It is precious because it is limited and irretrievable and because our choices about how we use it express the meaning and purpose of our time here on earth.

Think of a spending plan as an architectural drawing. Without one, you may build too big a bathroom and end up not having enough space for all the bedrooms you need. Or you might put the staircase in the wrong place. Maybe you won't remember to put in enough windows. Your rooms will be dark and you'll have to spend more money on lighting. With a spending plan, as with an architectural drawing, the first thing you do is think about all the must-haves. Then you have the flexibility to build in the want-to-haves. You'll know your rent is covered each month, so you won't be evicted and have to spend extra money moving. You'll know just how much you can afford for food, so you won't eat steak for the first three days of the month and then live on macaroni and tuna for the remainder. You'll know just how much you can afford to spend on transportation, so you can decide whether you can afford to indulge in a cab ride without having to walk to work for the next four days. Once you make a spending plan, you will feel better for knowing the truth about where your money is going. And you will be in control of the money that's controlled you for too long.

## COMING OUT EVEN

A spending plan is made up of two parts: income and expenses. *Income* is the money that comes in. It's your salary or commission, dividend or interest income, alimony, child support, pension, or disability income. It is all the money you receive, whether it comes in monthly, quarterly, or in some other time frame. It does not include money you think you *might* get. So, if your bonus is not guaranteed, then don't include it in your spending plan. After all, if it doesn't flow in when you expect it to, and you've already planned to spend it, you'll be up the creek. Better to not include it, and then use it to boost your savings or cover a long-wished-for treat.

The term *expenses* refers to money going out. Expenses represent your monthly costs in after-tax dollars. When you pay amounts annually — insurance, camp fees, tuition — divide these amounts by 12 to come up with a monthly amount so you can work these expenses into your plan.

The best way to figure out your expenses is to gather all your bank statements, credit-card bills, and whatever other records you have of how you spent your money for the past two years. (If you do it only for one year, your figures may be skewed by unusually high or low bills in that particular year.) Make a category for each bill: telephone, food, vet bills, gym fees, child care, health, gifts — *everything*. Total each category and divide by 24; that's your monthly average. Now add all the category averages together. This is the amount you spend each month.

Are you surprised? Is it more or less than you thought? Chances are it's more, since most people underestimate. Are you spending more than you are bringing in? Well, if you have a negative gap, there are two things you can do about it: make more or spend less. Look back over your categories and think about how much you *want* to spend for each. Notice that I used the word "want." *You're* in charge of this. *You* say how much you will or will not spend. You can keep right on digging a hole, or you can decide to take control.

The thing about a spending plan is that it isn't carved in stone. It would be nice if life were predictable, but it isn't. Here's just one example of how the unpredictability of life can make your knees weak and your temper flare. One winter, it seemed as though every heat-producing appliance in our house went kaput. First it was the furnace. Imagine two days with no heat. Then the dryer blew, just when I had the biggest, wettest load of towels (could that have been it?). Then the microwave. I prayed that the gremlins would find a new place to live, checked with my Feng Shui book to see if things were in the wrong place, and started sprinkling the house with lavender. The VCR blew next.

Since we could never have predicted that these appliances would all give up the ghost in the same month, there was no way to plan for their repair or replacement. Not in the traditional sense, anyway. But a smart spending plan makes allowances for the unexpected. Spending plans should have a repairs-and-maintenance or supplies-and-services category that accounts for these kinds of expenses and ours did. We call ours "unusual expenses."

Once you've done all the work to come up with the numbers for your spending plan, get ready for the really tough part: the discipline of using it. A spending plan has three columns:

- "Planned" is the money you expect to spend on each of these areas. You may plan to spend $25 a month on prescription drugs, $150 on food, and $10 on books and magazines.
- "Actual" will show the amount you had to lay out. Your spending plan may call for you to put aside $200 a month for children's clothes. It's unlikely you'll spend $200 each and every month. However, in September as you ready the kids for school, you may find you spend considerably more than $200. If you spend $375, this is the figure that would go in the actual column.
- "Difference" is the difference between what was planned and the actual amount spent. If you intended to spend $5 a day on lunch but brown-bagged it three days each week because your horrendous workload meant you couldn't leave your desk, your "planned" would be $100, your "actual" would be $40 (for the two days each week that you escaped from the office), and the "difference" would be $60 followed by a plus (+) sign to show you've spent less than you planned. On the other hand, if you planned to spend $25 on a gift for a friend, but spent $40 (which would go under "actual"), the "difference" would be $15 followed by a minus (–) sign to indicate you exceeded your spending plan.

If you go off track in a particular category one month, don't panic and think you've blown the whole deal. Look at other categories and see where you can adjust to make up the difference. If you planned to spend $3,000 a year on clothes, but blew your budget by September, you could either stop buying clothes, or you could steal the money from your vacation category. It's your choice.

If you're saying to yourself, "Get real, there's no way I can keep up this record-keeping stuff" or "I'd rather be poor than be a slave to this stupid form," I understand completely. The idea is not to become a slave to the plan. It's to go through the process so you can see on paper where your money is coming from and where it's going. It's to get it out of the nebulous grey zone of "I think I spend . . ." to the black-and-white facts.

If you don't believe a spending plan can make a significant difference in your life, I challenge you to use one for just three months and prove me wrong. Then write me and tell me how little use it was. I believe that once you do the plan and use it for three months, you'll find real value in having gone through the exercise.

If you don't believe you can find the time to do this for even three months, I've heard this before too. It is a sad statistic that shows that Canadians, on average, spend 10 hours a year taking care of their money and 1,000+ hours a year watching TV. You'll have to decide where your priorities lie.

## LOOKING AT AVERAGES

While averages don't mean a hoot to some people, others want a benchmark against which to measure their financial dealings. For those who like to know what the rest of Canada is doing, here are some numbers you may find interesting. These numbers are all based on the 1992 year, the last year for which data was available at the time of writing.

The average family income before tax in Canada is $46,076 and, on average, Canadians manage to spend 98.85% of that income on household expenditures. Shelter costs about $8,102 a year — or about 17.6% of the average income. Food runs at about $5,686 — about 12.3%. Transportation is a whopping $5,640, with the cost of private transportation ($5,198) far outstripping public transportation ($442). Household costs, including utilities, furnishings, and equipment, are about $4,779. Clothing comes in at $2,222; personal care is about $844 and health-care costs are approximately $867. And despite all that's written about the need for Canadians to take responsibility for their financial futures, the amount spent on financial security — pensions, life insurance, and employment insurance — is a measly $2,289, or 5% of the average income. Compare that with the $2,300 spent on recreation. While Canadians spend about $1,400 a year on tobacco and alcohol, they spend less than half of that — only $678 — on reading and education. Of course, as you probably already expected, the biggest part of our expenses is the whopping tax bill each year — an average of $9,378, or 20% of our average income.

Of course, the numbers vary significantly from one province to the next and from one income group to the next. And averages are just averages. But it is interesting to look at where we place our priorities. If you want the latest numbers, look for Statistics Canada, Catalogue No. 62-555. The data are nicely presented at the Statistics Canada website.

## TRIMMING EXPENSES

Many categories of your spending plan will have fixed amounts, but many others can be fiddled. If you buy lunch at work every day, you could decide to skip the lunch out twice a week and save. If you get a haircut every eight weeks, schedule it for every 10 weeks instead and save yourself some money. If you buy magazines off the rack, you could subscribe and save 50% or more. Or go to your local library every second week and binge in the periodical section. Decide to trim, a little here and a little there, until what you spend matches with what you want to spend.

Here are 9,999,999,999 ways to save. Just kidding!

- If you smoke, quit. If you smoke a pack of cigarettes a day at $3.50 a pack, you'll save $1,277.50 a year. If you put $600 of that in an RRSP for the next 15 years and earn an average return of just 7%, you'll end up with $15,500. Put it all away and you'll have $34,394.49. Another reason to quit: If you don't smoke you'll pay 10% to 15% less in premiums on most life insurance and disability insurance policies. That's like getting a month of coverage free each year.
- Take your lunch to work, at least some of the time. If you save $15 a week on lunch, in a year you'll save $780. Invest half that in an RRSP and earn 7% on it, and in 15 years you'll have $9,000.
- Share newspapers with coworkers. If you buy a paper twice a week, instead of five times, you'll save $117 a year.

- Subscribe to magazines. If you buy a monthly magazine costing $3.50 at the newsstand, it'll cost you $42 a year. Buy it by subscription, and you'll pay only $21. Even better: share subscriptions with friends.
- Use the library. Check out books, magazines, tapes, and CDs instead of buying them.
- Buy your phone. Pick one up at a garage sale and save the monthly cost of renting.
- Use a long-distance package. Do the research and choose the package that saves you the most. If your phone habits change (when your daughter goes off to university in another city), check to make sure your plan still works for you.
- Pay your life insurance premiums a year in advance if the company offers a one-month discount.
- When it comes time to renew your mortgage, negotiate. If you can shave just a half-percent off your mortgage, you'll save $500 a year on a $100,000 mortgage.
- Accelerate your mortgage payments. Paying your mortgage on an accelerated basis means an extra payment every year that goes directly to your principal. On a $100,000 mortgage at 11%, amortized over 25 years, you'll save $62,486 in interest over the life of the mortgage.
- Check the blue-book value of your car to determine whether you should still be insuring for comprehensive and collision.
- Are you insuring heirlooms that you could never replace even if they were lost or stolen? Weed out the things you don't need covered anymore.
- Ask your insurance agent for the various discounts available: claims-free policyholders, those who insure both home and car in the same place, and people with security systems all get a break on their rates.
- Increasing the deductibles on your home and car insurance can save you big bucks. You have to be sure you'll have the money to pay the deductible yourself. Sticking it on your credit card and carrying it for months defeats the purpose. But if you don't intend to make a claim for under $500 or $1,000 because you're concerned about how it'll affect your premiums, then you might as well raise your deductible and save.

- Don't buy extended warranties on household appliances. Instead, use a credit card that automatically extends the warranty.
- Set up a co-op baby-sitting service with other parents in your neighbourhood. You take care of three kids once a week, and you'll have two days off.
- Grocery shop with a list and stick to it. If you run out, wait until your next planned shop. Buy in bulk, if you'll use the items, and buy generic (at least try the generic alternative). Buy in bulk with friends and split the savings.
- Buy off-season, providing you can reasonably estimate your child's next size. Your son's next winter wardrobe will be considerably cheaper at the end of this winter.
- Don't even go into convenience stores. Almost everything is more expensive.
- Buy gifts when they are on sale and put them away for birthdays, anniversaries, and other special holidays.
- If you're carrying a balance on a credit card, switch to a card that charges lower interest. On a $3,600 balance, switching from a 17% card to a 9.9% card will save you over $250 a year in interest. Dump the cards from which you've transferred the balance. If you give in to temptation and run those balances up again, you'll be in even worse shape.
- Review your bank statements to see how much you pay per month in service charges. Would you be better off with an all-inclusive monthly fee? Do you have the option of free transactions if you maintain a minimum monthly balance? Shop around for the right account.
- Don't bounce cheques. A friend of mine regularly bounces cheques and each time she does it costs her $19.95 in service fees — never mind what she's doing to her credit rating. And it's not that she doesn't make enough money. She's just a bad money manager.
- At the grocery store, comparison shop and buy on sale. And buy seasonal items in season; what is plentiful will be cheaper.
- Check unit prices to see what it actually costs. Those little calculators on the grocery store shelves serve a purpose. I've often been surprised to find that the bulk items are sometimes more expensive than the regular items on sale. When your favourite products go on

sale, buy enough to last until the next sale.

- Buy second hand. It's amazing what you can get in a garage sale or thrift shop: good quality at a great price. My stepdaughter once outfitted herself for an entire season at the Goodwill store for $35. And I've scored big at garage sales and second-hand shops: beautiful baby clothes for a fraction of their original cost; a mountain of Duplo for $30; lovely books that my children and I still enjoy together.
- Leave your credit cards at home except when you plan to spend. Taking them with you leaves you open to impulse purchases.
- Use public transportation. Figure out what it's costing for the convenience of having a car and decide if it's worth it. Here's a case in point. Julie owns a car. Her loan payment is $236 a month and her insurance payment is $416 a month for a total of $652, which is exactly one-third of her take-home pay. She doesn't live in the car. She doesn't use the car for work. She has the car in case she needs it. Wow!
- Go to the movies on Cheap Tuesdays or when matinees are less costly. Or wait for the film to move to a second-run house and see it there for half the price.
- Write letters instead of making long-distance telephone calls. Or get on the Internet and e-mail. My cousin Van and I discovered e-mail. She's in Florida and I'm in Toronto. Boy, what a difference that has made to our telephone bills. We could spend up to an hour on the phone talking about the kids. Now we e-mail and it takes less than a minute to send the same message. We "talk" more often too.

Look at your spending at least once a year to see where you may have formed some habits you no longer need or want. Think back to a few years ago and ask yourself if you ate out as often, went to as many movies, spent as much on clothes. What's changed? Would it make sense to return to your previous standard, or is your new standard of spending right for the time?

The whole idea is to make sure your needs, wants, and desires are in the right perspective and that you're fully aware of where your money is going. After all, if you feel it is your right to go to that concert, lease a new car, or eat out a couple of nights a week because you work so hard, just remember that because you work so hard you also have the right to be debt-free, well balanced in terms of saving and spending, and on your way to achieving your financial and life goals. It's your money. It's your life. It's your peace of mind.

## SETTING GOALS

Whatever money represents for us, it should never become the centre of our lives. But the management of money should become one of the tactics we use to achieve our goals. Whether we want to buy a home, provide for our children's schooling, or retire to a small island in the South Pacific, money is one of the means we will need to achieve our ends.

Life is full of choices. We make them every day. Monday we had the choice of going to work or staying home. Most of us went to work. Tuesday we chose to see a movie. And Friday, we'll either go dancing or put some music on the stereo and catch up on that John Grisham novel.

How we choose to use our money is, in large part, dependent on what we envision for ourselves. However, if you feel it's the money that's giving the orders, you may not be able to see beyond your immediate circumstances to the dreams you want to achieve.

### A dream is a gift we give ourselves

Had any good dreams lately? What's stopping you? Maybe you can't remember how. Ask yourself, "If I could have anything I wanted — no holds barred — what would it be?" Grab a pencil and paper and write them down. And don't just limit yourself to financial goals. Remember, no holds barred. Keep going. Think! Absolutely anything you want. How's your list coming? You should have 10, 27, 50 things by now.

Having listed all your dreams, now categorize them as short-, medium-, and long-term:

- If you want to realize your dream within the next year, write "ST" beside it.
- If you expect your dream to be realized in the medium term (two to five years), write "MT" beside it.
- If your dream will take longer than five years to happen, write "LT" beside it.

The next step is to prioritize your dreams. Start by creating a shortlist of six dreams that are most important to you. Even within your shortlist you will have priorities. To decide which goals are most important, weigh them against each other. Is having a home more important than taking that trip to the other end of the country to see your ailing grandmother? Is buying a car more important than paying off your credit-card debt? Is taking a trip to see your grandmother more important than paying off your credit card? What's your priority? Reorder and number your dreams 1 through 6 in order of priority.

**Goals are dreams with a deadline**

Now it's time to set a date for achieving your dreams. This doesn't mean that the date won't change. That's just a tad too optimistic. But without a date there is no sense of urgency and no commitment to moving forward. Go ahead, set your dates.

Now you know where you want to go and you have an ETA. That's the hard part. The rest is easy. It just takes a plan, a commitment, and, perhaps, a guide to help you through the maze of alternatives and information. Use all the resources at your disposal: books, seminars, friends. Talk to your banker, your broker, your financial planner — whomever you trust to act as a guide. And remember, you won't get there just by dreaming about it. *Telesis* will take you there.

# 5

# Establish an Emergency Fund

*A gem is not polished without friction, nor a person perfected without trials.*

Chinese Proverb

*When written in Chinese, the word crisis is composed of two characters. One represents danger and the other represents opportunity.*

John F. Kennedy

A n emergency fund is used to meet unexpected expenses. (If you're in debt now this may sound unrealistic to you, but read on to see why you need an emergency fund and how to get one.) Financial media often talk about emergency funds in the context of unforeseen unemployment, that is, you need an emergency fund just in case you are "outplaced" and it takes more than a day to get another job. This is true, but it doesn't matter if you're self-employed, working for the greatest company in the world, or have the most airtight employment contract ever seen. Everyone needs an emergency fund. Unforeseen medical expenses not covered by insurance or a new roof can put a serious crimp in your budget, even when you're fully employed.

The size of your emergency fund will depend on your financial commitments. If your spending plan is tight, you'll need to establish a fairly significant emergency fund. One rule of thumb is that you have the equivalent of six months' income set aside for emergencies.

Of course, to set up an emergency fund, you have to save. Some people find it easy to save, many others don't. Think about how much you have saved right now. Do you think it is enough? Do you feel safe? How do you feel about saving? Are you for it or against it? Why? What did you learn about saving as a child? From your parents? From your spouse? Does saving seem like an impossible dream because of your current financial circumstances? How do your religious beliefs affect your savings habits? If you got a $100-a-week raise today, how much of it would you save?

If you've never been a saver, you'll need to figure out your attitude toward saving before you can change your habits. If you don't believe savings are important, you won't save. It's that simple. Unfortunately, the other reality is that not saving can have some nasty repercussions.

The reason most people don't bother with an emergency fund is that they figure nothing terrible is ever going to happen to them. Optimism is fine to a point, but not when it puts you and your family in jeopardy. Here's a scary story.

Madelaine found herself unable to work. She was experiencing a variety of weird physical symptoms and was severely depressed. She had a disability plan at work and, under the instructions of her psychiatrist, decided the pressure and stress of the job were too much and stayed home. She claimed her disability benefits, only to find that she was declined because the insurance company's representatives felt she could work — if not at her present job, then somewhere else. She had no diagnosis to support her physical complaints. Madelaine went through hell. With no emergency fund, she found herself even more stressed out and, worse, feeling like she was nuts. It took almost 10 months for the doctors to locate the problem. And it was a serious one too. In the meantime, Madelaine had no recourse. Luckily, her husband was able to fill the gap. But the strain on the relationship was obvious. And the strain on Madelaine only made her physical condition worse.

If you don't think bad things can happen to you, here's a statistic to wake you up: Regardless of your current age, there's a one-in-three chance that you'll become disabled before you turn 65. If it happens, you'll probably experience a cash-flow crunch — either you'll receive less money than you are accustomed to or you'll have to live through the wait period before your benefits kick in. Disability isn't the only potential problem we face. There's the car that dies at the most inopportune moment or the emergency trip you must take to deal with a family crisis. It's all the what-ifs you've imagined, and their potential cost. If you don't have an emergency fund, you may get through the crunch, but you'll probably use a very expensive form of credit to do so. And you'll end up paying heavily for not having been prepared.

Once you have your emergency fund set up, keep it in conservative, highly liquid assets. There's no point in having an emergency fund in a five-year GIC where you can't get at it. A money-market fund is a safe bet. If the idea of having $10,000 sitting in a money-market fund earning a low rate of interest makes your blood run cold, the following strategy may be for you. First, apply for a personal line of credit equal to your emergency fund. Next, invest your emergency fund as you would any other investment dollars. (Okay, okay, perhaps with a little less risk.) In the best-case scenario, should you need to access your emergency fund, your investments will be at their all-time high and you can sell them, reap a nice capital gain, and cover your emergency. However, should the timing be all wrong for liquidating your investment, you could buy yourself the time to let your investment do its thing by first calling on your personal line of credit.

Whichever route you choose, make sure you build an emergency fund for unforeseen expenses into your spending plan. Make like a boy scout: Be prepared.

## SAVING VERSUS INVESTING

I can't believe there was ever a debate about the difference between "saving" and "investing," but there was. At one point, I had to write an educational piece for a financial institution describing the difference. Unfortunately, some of the mist is still swirling. Here are my definitions.

Saving is the act of accumulating money by setting aside a portion of your income. Saving is what you do when you take cash out of your cash flow and set it aside. Let's say you have an automatic savings plan that deducts $50 from your chequing account and puts it into an investment for you. Let's also say you go out and charge $50 on your credit card that you can't afford to pay off this month. Have you saved anything? NO. Since you didn't take the money out of your cash flow (you used your credit card to put it back into your cash flow once it was deducted from your chequing account), you haven't saved a thing. Don't fool yourself. If you have "savings" and "debt," you've got less than you think.

Investing is what you do to earn a return on the money you've saved. So if you have $500 in a savings account earning .25%, it's invested — not particularly well, but it's invested. And if you have $500 in mutual funds, GICs, bonds, debentures, stock, or anything else of a financial nature, it's invested too. As long as it's potentially earning a return, it's invested.


## SAVING STRATEGIES

Do I have to say that saving regularly is an important part of your overall financial strategy? Unfortunately, for many people, saving doesn't come naturally. According to an Angus Reid Group survey published in July 1997, almost one-third of Canadians do not save. The theory is, and statistics bear out, that a person's stage of life is pivotal in determining her savings goals. If you're under 35, there's a 41% chance that you are not saving. There's also a 58% chance that you make less than $30,000 a year. With as little as $100 a month, or $23.08 a week, you would be right on track with your savings. If you're over 35 and you're not saving, you're in the minority. Seventy-two percent of people aged 35 to 54 have accumulated some investments, while 77% of those over 55 are taking care of themselves. With homes to buy, children to raise, and expenses at their peak, the under-35 set just doesn't have the money to save.

Hogwash! If you don't save, it's because you don't want to save. After all, I'm not talking about hundreds of dollars a month. Take $5 from your cash flow for savings and you're doing better than you were in terms of taking care of yourself. And since Canadians feel travel is more important than an emergency fund,[11] I don't think I'm being harsh.

If you don't save, you're asking for trouble. The goal should be 10% a year. That's 10% of your gross family income. That may not always be achievable. Some years, you may come up short. But if you never put anything away for the future — just in case, for your children's education,

---

11 "Investment Issues," Angus Reid, Ernst & Young, July 1997.

for your own retirement — then you're not taking care of yourself. And if you delay starting until you'll have more disposable income, the cost to your cash flow will be enormous.

Here are some ideas that may help:

- Open up a pay-yourself-first plan that deducts money from your chequing account each month and automatically invests it for you. You'll be surprised how quickly you get used to living without that money.
- To avoid impulse spending, move your savings to a money-market fund. You'll need 24 hours' notice to transfer the money back to your chequing account. Don't use a savings account (see pages 76–77).
- Purchase CSBs through a payroll deduction plan.
- Invest part or all of any windfall such as tax refunds or gifts you receive.
- Find out about any deferred profit-sharing or share-purchase plans offered by your employer.
- Practise being thrifty. When you save money on an item, immediately put the savings in your money-market fund. If you save on an item and then just spend that money on something else, you haven't saved a thing.
- When a regular expense such as a loan payment or tax installment is eliminated from your budget, continue putting that amount into savings.
- When you get a raise, save half your increased earnings.
- If you have consumer loans or credit-card debt, make paying off those debts a priority. Take the amount you would have spent on interest and save it.
- Contribute to an RRSP and use your tax refund to increase your next RRSP contribution or to start an unregistered investment account for a downpayment on a home, for your children's education, or some other goal.

Saving doesn't come naturally to a large percentage of the population. If you're not turned on by watching your money grow in a savings or investment account, you'll have to find some other motivation for saving.

How about this: You're supposed to do it, and if you don't do it you'll have no one but yourself to blame when you find yourself up to your armpits in alligators. Just for one moment, be a pessimist. Yes, you could lose your job, get sick, smash up your car, have a tree fall on your house. Those are good reasons to save. A more important reason is because taking care of yourself and those you care for is your responsibility. Saving should be a part of life. It's necessary to save if you want to be financially healthy. Remember *telesis*? *Do it!*

# 6

# Cash Management

*It is better that a man tyrannize over his bank balance than over his fellow-citizens.*

JOHN MAYNARD KEYNES

Most people find that their financial lives revolve around their bank. They have a chequing account and a savings account. When they buy a house, their bank provides the mortgage. When they apply for a credit card, it's their bank's version of MasterCard or Visa. And when they begin investing, they often start with the GICs, mutual funds, and other investments offered at their local branch. For the purpose of this section, it doesn't matter whether you deal with a bank, trust company, credit union, or caisse populaire — we're talking about the place where you do your banking.

## ALMOST EVERYONE NEEDS A CHEQUING ACCOUNT

Choosing the right chequing account can be a real test in today's complicated banking world. And the banks haven't made it any easier for us. With the introduction of new-and-improved-this and better-than-ever-that, we now have an overwhelming variety of account features from which to choose.

In the past, the main consideration in choosing a bank was convenience. We chose a branch that was close to home or close to work. But you don't have to buy from the bank on the corner anymore. Telephone banking and banking machines are making it easier to choose a bank based on the products it offers and the service you get for the money you pay.

Start by looking at the services you are now using to make sure you aren't paying for things you don't need. Make a list of the services you use regularly and not-so-regularly so you aren't paying for services you won't use or use only once in a blue moon. Then shop around to see who has the best package for you. Review brochures in the sanity of your home and at your own pace. Once you've identified the accounts and services you like, make a list of questions to ask the banker to make sure the package does what you expect. And make sure there aren't any hidden costs. Take the time to read the fine print.

Many banks offer no-charge chequing and no-charge use of banking machines (usually referred to as ABMs or ATMs) if you maintain a specific minimum balance. Consolidate your existing accounts to get to the minimum. If you wish to keep your accounts separate, ask your bank to link the accounts so you meet the minimum balance requirement and only pay one set of fees. Many institutions also offer a package of services with a single monthly fee. Compare the individual fees with the cost of the package. If you use quite a number of services, you may be able to save by buying a packaged account. My account allows me to do almost everything for $14 a month. My accounts are all linked, so I pay only one fee. And I can even do two transactions at another bank's ABM at no cost each month. It also includes my telephone banking.

Compare the interest you're earning with the cost of running the account. There's no point in earning minimal interest if the service charges on that account are more than you would pay on another non-interest-bearing account. And there's no point in keeping scads of cash earning little or no interest just to minimize fees. You could be better off paying a fixed monthly fee and investing that chunk of cash.

Use the banking machine to do your routine transactions since this can save you the cost of individual fees. Deposits, withdrawals, and bill payments made at your bank's ABM are often cheaper than those done at a teller's wicket. Plan for your cash needs and make your withdrawals from your own bank's network. Each time you withdraw cash from an ABM belonging to another financial institution, you may be charged a fee, which can be as high as $1 per withdrawal for machines in Canada and $2 or more for withdrawals in the U.S. You would think that such a high charge would be an automatic deterrent. Not so. In a recent two-year study of women's banking habits, up to 25% of women regularly used an ABM from another financial institution.[12]

Another alternative is to use your banking card as a debit card since, most often, the transaction fees are less than the cost of writing a cheque. This is a popular option, with almost 31% of women using debit cards. And the convenience is undeniable: In 1997 alone, Canadians swiped their debit cards more than one billion times.

Do not use the ABM to keep track of your account balance. If you do, you may find yourself counting on a balance that isn't really there because a cheque you've written has still to clear. Use your cheque-book register to keep track of your account — regardless of whether those transactions are cheques, debit-card transactions, cash withdrawals, or credit-card charges — and reconcile it monthly against your bank statement to make sure you're working with an accurate balance.

If you run your account to the limit each month, consider overdraft protection. This is an automatic loan that kicks in when you don't have enough in your account to cover a cheque. The interest rate is high, however, so you should only use it for emergency shortfalls — not as a line of credit. Not having overdraft protection can be expensive too. At one bank, the cost of an NSF (not sufficient funds) cheque is $19.25. And that doesn't include the cost of having an NSF show up on your credit bureau report.

Check your statement when you receive it each month. I can't tell you how many times I've found extra fees on my statement that, with a single call, I've had removed. If you aren't watching the pennies, the dollars can go missing pretty quickly.

If you travel to the U.S. regularly, consider opening a U.S.-dollar account. Keeping your funds in U.S. dollars, as opposed to switching back and forth, can save you money on the exchange fees.

If you find that your cheques are being held for several days after you

---

12 "1997 PMB Two-Year Readership Study," Print Measurement Bureau.

deposit them, go in and tell the bank manager you want *the hold* removed. Banks hold cheques for as long as seven business days — longer if the cheque is drawn on a foreign account — to ensure the cheque clears before the funds are released. If you're a good customer, you shouldn't have to wait.

If you have a mortgage, an RRSP, and other investments at several institutions, consider consolidating so you can throw your weight around. Banks love to have all your business and you can use the economic power of consolidation to lower your mortgage rate, earn higher interest on investments, and reduce service charges. Shopping for a bank is like shopping for anything else. If you want to get the best deal going, you have to compare and you have to negotiate. Above all, you should only buy what you need.

If you have money on deposit at a bank that also happens to be your credit-card issuer, the bank can go into your account and take those funds if you become delinquent on your credit card. Avoid this by keeping your deposit accounts at an institution other than the one that issued your credit card.

Finally, if you're charged for something that you think is unfair, complain. You'd be amazed at how many times fees will be waived because of your relationship with a branch staff member or because you have a big mouth.

## ALMOST NO ONE SHOULD HAVE A SAVINGS ACCOUNT

There's an interesting expression in the financial services industry that was around long before *Jurassic Park* and *The Land Before Time*. When a product or service is no longer for sale, it's referred to as a dinosaur. While accounts come and go almost as quickly as the seasons, one type of account should be extinct: the savings account.

Canadians have millions of dollars sitting in savings accounts earning a pittance in interest. Most haven't even considered the options. With today's low interest rates, if you have money sitting in a savings account, your money is idling. It's probably not even earning enough to offset the service fees you pay for your overall banking needs. There are alternatives.

The most obvious options are money-market funds or Treasury-bill (T-bill) funds. Both these alternatives offer most of the benefits of a savings account. Since unit values are managed to remain stable, there is little or no risk. You can access your money with as little as 24 hours' notice. And the increased return means your money is working considerably harder to offset those bank fees and help make ends meet. Money-market funds sometimes even beat short- and medium-term guaranteed investment certificates (GICs) without the restriction of locking up your money for a specific term. In fact, you can earn 3% or 4% more on a money-market fund if you shop carefully. Check the mutual-fund listings in the newspaper to see where you'll get the best deal and then weigh the return against the convenience of being able to access your funds quickly at your local financial institution.

Some people think the process of getting into and out of a money-market or T-bill fund is complicated. A money-market transaction can take less time than lining up at a teller to make a deposit. What about access to your money? Most financial institutions will allow you to transfer funds from your money-market fund to your chequing account with a signed request by fax. That means you can have your chequing account credited without going into the bank. Others give you access through their telephone banking service.

You might think that for an investment that pays better than a GIC, you would need a mountain of money. Not so. With as little as $500, you can move your savings (and short-term deposits) into a money-market or T-bill fund and earn more. You'll also have the added convenience of receiving your statements at home so you don't have to line up to get your passbook updated with a disappointing amount of interest.

## VIRTUAL BANKING

Virtually everyone is talking about it, and if you're not already doing it, might I suggest it's only a matter of time. Whether you bank through the ABM network, by telephone, or by using your computer, you're participating in the world of virtual banking.

My girlfriend Cookie is a perfect example of how virtual banking is changing the way Canadians get at their money. When she moved, she chose to keep her account at her original branch and bank in new ways. She liked the people there and she really liked the service they gave. How astute of her to realize that you don't get the same service at every branch.

So she maintained her relationship with the branch even though the location was no longer convenient.

If you can order a pizza, you can bank by phone. Telephone banking is easy and convenient, and if you do it often enough, you can hit the buttons pretty quickly so you don't have to listen to the irritating instructions. Using telephone banking, I've transferred money from one account to another, paid all my monthly bills, checked my balances, and transferred money to my mutual-fund account. And I can do it all at three in the morning. Telephone banking is immediate, and you're given a transaction number to confirm what you've done. You can do it from any touch-tone telephone, so you can even cover your bills when you're on holiday.

The attraction of virtual banking is that it makes your life easier. With more demanding schedules and the ever-increasing challenge of balancing home and work, people who don't have the time to run to a branch to apply for a mortgage, pay bills, or make routine transactions can do their banking on their own terms. And they can save money too.

The field is virtually exploding as people seek easier access to their accounts, more control, and up-to-the-minute information. Here are a few questions to ask so you choose the service and the bank that's right for you:

- What transactions can I make? Services differ by bank. Figure out what you're looking for, what stage you are at, and what services you need. How much of your information can you access? How many different types of transactions can you make? What are the limitations?
- Which bills can I pay? When I first started banking by telephone, I was frustrated when I tried to pay my realty tax bill at the Bank of Montreal and they couldn't accept it. I had to make a special trip to the ABM. Some banks are more aggressive than others in arranging to handle the payment transactions of creditors.
- Do I want to be able to see my account information? Cookie chose computer banking because, as she says, "I can see it in front of me. Right away my account balances change. That's why I like it. I feel more secure that it's been done and is registered."
- Is the system available 24 hours a day, seven days a week? Nothing can be more frustrating than finally finding the time to do your

banking only to be greeted with a message that says the system is down.

- When I access my accounts, is the information up-to-date? It's no good working with an old balance. That's why we're into technology, right?
- From where will I want access? If you're on the road without a laptop or access to a computer, the telephone service may make more sense.
- Will I want to download financial information into a software package that lets me track my spending and manage my finances? Some banks provide software so there's no need to export information to a separate financial planning package such as Quicken.
- Can I use my existing account number and access this information from my branch as well as by virtual banking? If it's simplification you're after, the last thing you need is a whole new set of account numbers and passwords.
- Can I do everything from one place? If the bank's systems don't all talk to each other (and sometimes they don't), you may end up reentering information.
- Does the service allow me to use my equipment? Every existing dial-up system is compatible with Windows 3.1 or 95. Few are able to interface with Macintosh. Check before you sign up.
- What's the cost and how much can I save? The costs and potential savings are all over the map. Do a little telephone shopping before you start virtual banking.

## HOW SAFE IS VIRTUALLY SAFE?

Information is transferred to and from a banking network in two ways: through a direct dial-up to your bank's network, or via the Internet. While many people worry about the security of information transferred via the Internet, sophisticated encryption procedures mean the information is scrambled so it's virtually impossible for someone else to get at the private details of your life. And someone would have to tap your private phone line to get the information sent via direct dial-up. Want to protect yourself further? Here are some do's and don'ts:

- Do keep a back-up of your information.
- Do keep a record of transaction numbers given at the completion of each activity in case there's a mix-up.
- Don't access your personal information via your company's intranet (the company's internal computer network) without completely erasing your records from the caching.
- Don't give your access code to anyone else.
- If you complete a transaction at a call centre, don't assume the transaction has been completed. When I transferred money from my money-market fund to my chequing account through a call centre, the human factor came into play. The transaction was never processed. I had to call my branch to get the job done right.

It makes sense to look over your financial services from time to time to see if the products you're using still match your needs. The banking world is constantly changing and the banks are very competitive. But don't think that just because the service is offered, you need to have it. Review how you use your bank account so you only buy based on what you're actually using. Don't be lured into buying a product just for the prestige. Shopping for financial services is like shopping for anything else. If you want to get the best deal going, you have to compare and you have to negotiate. Above all, you should only buy what you need. All that shopping around and comparing can get mighty confusing (and many of the features offered may seem pretty attractive) so you must be careful not to buy bells and whistles you don't need.

### FINANCIAL RECORD KEEPING

Staying in control of your financial life is infinitely easier if you're organized. Whether you invest in a software program such as Quicken or do it all on paper, knowing where everything is will make it easier to keep a handle on your money.

To keep your paperwork organized, you need a place to put all that paper that comes pouring in through the mail: bank statements, bills, credit-card statements, warranties, investment records, and the like. Organize it by category so that should you need to find something you won't have to go wading through reams of paper looking for a single item.

Set aside a filing drawer or get a filing box for keeping your financial stuff. Make up as many file folders as you need to organize your information. If you have three separate bank accounts, it's a good idea to set up a folder for each. Some typical folder headings are Automobile, Bank Statements, Credit Card, Home Purchase, Home Improvements, Household Bills, Income (tax, salary stubs, bonus statements), Insurance (separate files for house, life, disability), Investments, Mortgage, Pension, Personal Papers (birth certificates, marriage and divorce documents, wills, powers of attorney, passport, SIN, etc.), RRSP, Warranties/Equipment Booklets, Work (performance reviews, memos on job performance). An alternative to file folders is to use a three-ring binder with tabs. My husband likes this much better. He's a minimalist and keeps just the important stuff. I use a drawer, folders, and save *everything*.

If you're a pack rat like me, you'll have to cull your files from time to time so you aren't overwhelmed. Hold on to receipts for anything that's tax deductible or required for a warranty. Keep receipts for anything you'll need for insurance purposes. Hold on to your bank statements and cheque stubs for at least three years in case you're audited.

Financial record keeping also involves monitoring your accounts. If you aren't balancing your cheque book against your statement each month, you're not paying enough attention. For some reason, people hate this job, even though it isn't particularly difficult. But unless you're wealthy enough to keep so much cash in your account that you never have to worry about covering all your cheques, you've got to reconcile your cheque book.

It helps if you carry your cheque-book register around with you and write in everything you spend as you spend it, including your debit-card and credit-card transactions. Then, when your statement comes in, you can quickly check all the transactions because they are all in the register. And when your credit-card bill comes in, there are no surprises. Simply write the cheque number for all the transactions on the bill beside the transactions in the register. You won't be tempted to spend money you don't have — even if those transactions haven't come in on the latest bill — because the money has already been deducted from your register.

One good habit I picked up from business is to record my cheque number and date on the bills that I'm paying. When I pay my bills by telephone banking, I write the date of payment and confirmation number on my bill. It's dead easy to find stuff when I must.

Financial record keeping, like most money management, isn't hard. But it does require discipline. If you skip an entry, toss an important piece of paper, misplace a warranty, it'll cost you. It's a pain in the derrière finding the time to file those little pieces of paper, reconcile those statements, check those credit-card bills before you write the cheque, but you have to do it if you want to be financially healthy. So *do it!*

# 7

# Putting a Roof Over
# Your Head

*I want a house that has got over all its troubles; I don't want to spend the
rest of my life bringing up a young and inexperienced house.*

JEROME K. JEROME

Shelter is one of life's basic necessities and it takes a variety of forms:
apartments, town houses, basement flats, houses, condominiums.
Most people start off by renting. If you're at this point in your life, make
sure you read your lease. Yes, I know that most of it sounds like
gobbledygook, but if you don't read the fine print you may be in for a
shock.

If you have roommates, make sure they are all listed on the lease and
have them all sign the lease. This ensures you will all share legal responsibility in case of a problem. It also protects you if a roommate suddenly
changes her mind and decides to move out.

If a security deposit is required, find out how it works. Landlords
sometimes ask for a sum of money up front to protect themselves from
the cost of repairing any damage you might do. However, the security
deposit should not be used to pay for basic maintenance on the unit. Get
a receipt for the security deposit, and ask for a letter stipulating what the
money will be used for. And find out whether or not you will be paid
interest on the money while it remains unused. When your lease is up and

you move out, the landlord should refund your deposit if you did not cause any damage. Take pictures of how you got the unit and how you left it so you have some physical proof should there be a dispute with your landlord.

Other key things to watch for in a lease:

• Can you have pets?
• What are the rules regarding noise?
• What happens in the case of non-payment of rent?
• What rights of entry does the landlord or his representative have?
• What are the rules for rent increases?
• What about upkeep; who's responsible for what?
• Can you have roommates? Do they have to sign the lease?

Know your rights. The law protects renters in many ways. But if you don't know your rights, you won't know when someone is taking advantage of you.

## THE RENT-VERSUS-OWN QUESTION

At some point the rent-versus-own question may come up. The considerations are not all financial, so the decision will involve more than just comparing your monthly rent with the monthly mortgage you would pay.

Home ownership requires a certain commitment and responsibility not only in terms of money, but also in terms of time, and not everyone is up to the challenge. Once you own your first home, you'll quickly realize that there is always something that needs to be fixed: the roof, the wiring, the plumbing, the eavestroughs, the furnace. If it's not the inside of the house, it's the outside. A couple who live in my neighbourhood bought a home with a pool. First they had a termite problem. Then the skylights had to be fixed. The pool lining went. There seemed to be a constant onslaught of things needing repair.

Then, of course, there are the lifestyle issues. Some people are just too busy living to be bothered with the ongoing maintenance of a home. Painting, caulking, trimming, mowing, and shovelling are furthermost from their minds. Avid travellers who find themselves away from home for long spells may have problems with security issues. People who move often because of work may find their equity eaten up by real estate and legal fees. If you find yourself selling your existing home in a down market and buying in an up market in your new location, you may have less than you need for the downpayment that would make it an even trade.

If you like the idea of having your own place to do with as you wish, ownership might be right up your alley. If you're handy around the house and like puttering about, go for it. If you want to put down roots, if you want to become part of a community, owning your own home could be a very rewarding experience.

Often when people start thinking about buying a home, their focus shifts from simply providing shelter to making a profit. One home-ownership myth is that a house is a good investment. This isn't always so. Witness all those people who bought into the market during the boom of the 1980s and then saw their equity evaporate as the real estate market took a dive. Many were left owing more than their homes were worth.

While conventional wisdom says that renting is throwing your money away because you're developing no equity, renters don't have to worry about taxes or major home repairs. And if you have the discipline to invest the extra you would have had to pay if you owned, you could end up ahead. On the flip side, no matter how small the principal portion of your mortgage payment (and it's incredibly small in the early years), as long as the market is stable or rising, every month you will be building equity and increasing your net worth. A short-term view often makes the owning picture appear somewhat bleak. But as you pay off more of your mort-gage, more of your payments will go toward building equity.

If you're doing a calculation to determine which route — renting or buying — would put you further ahead financially, let me warn you that there is a lot to consider. First, you'll need a crystal ball to see where the housing market will be in five, 10, or 25 years. As I write this, the housing market has been brisk and has been termed a "seller's market," but the reality is that a home I bought in 1989 is still worth only 84% of my purchase price. It may be a seller's market, but only if the price is exactly what the buyer is prepared to pay. The standard calculation used for illustrative purposes usually compares the amount the home has appreciated over the years with the growth in assets that would have been realized had the homeowner invested in the equities market instead, but the answer is often misleading. There are a number of factors to be taken into account to make the calculation truly realistic. Consider the costs associated with home improvements and maintenance. When my good friend Victoria bought her new home in the Gatineau, she had to hire no less than eight repair people for plumbing, painting, heating, chimney cleaning, appliance repair, carpet cleaning, wiring, and floor replacement. A house is a constant source of expenditure. Also take into account the property tax you must pay, as well as things such as the real estate commission due if you sell the home (and the capital gains if the home is a second property).

This might sound like I am against home ownership. I'm not. But for almost everyone I've spoken with, the decision to buy or rent has had as much to do with emotion as with money. It is a decision based on a desire to put down roots, to have a place to call one's own. If you do not take these important elements into consideration, the cold hard figures can lead you astray. You might end up ahead financially, but with significantly less personal satisfaction than if you had a home to call your own.

## A HOUSE OF YOUR OWN

Owning a home is not an impossible dream. If you're just toying with the idea of buying your own home, you may feel fear, or even dread, at the idea of making such a huge commitment.

There are two things you have to think about when you decide you want to buy property: First, how much can you afford to spend? Second, how large a mortgage payment can you handle?

A starting point in figuring out how much you can afford is to multiply your gross annual income (your income before taxes) by 2.5. Include only income you're sure you will receive, and if you and your spouse both have incomes, add them together. This is referred to as your household income. Let's say your gross salary is $32,000. Your honey makes $26,000 a year gross. You could afford to buy a house with a price tag of $145,000 ($32,000 + $26,000 = $58,000 x 2.5) or less. Remember, however, this is only an estimate. Not only do you have to think about the price of house you can afford, you must also consider how you will work those mortgage payments into your spending plan.

Financial institutions use a calculation called "debt service ratio" to determine how much they'll lend you based on how much you can afford to repay each month. Your debt service ratio is your before-tax income divided by the necessary monthly payment. From the bank's perspective, 30% is the upper limit. You, too, can use this as a starting point to determine how much you can afford. Of course, to calculate the total amount you'll be spending, you have to figure in the downpayment you'll need to get into the house.

So let's see how it would work. Let's say you and your partner make $6,000 a month before taxes. Thirty percent of that would be $1,800 a month, which is what the bank will say you can afford in mortgage payments. At a rate of 10%, according to the mortgage amortization tables, that means you could afford a mortgage of $200,000. Add on your downpayment and voilà . . . you've got the total cost of the house you can afford.

The amount you can afford to spend each month will also depend on whether you have other debts such as a car loan, credit-card balances, a student loan, or alimony and child-support payments. The amount you spend on items such as clothing, transportation, food, entertainment, and so on would also have to be considered. Add up how much you spend, except for housing, and deduct the total from your monthly take-home pay.

Next, consider what it will cost to live in your new home. Ask friends or family what their heating, electricity, water, insurance, repair, and maintenance bills are like for similar homes.

The safest way to find out exactly how much you can afford to spend and what your payments will be is to be pre-approved for a mortgage. Have a lender work out all the figures to tell you how much you will be able to afford to spend on a house, and how much your monthly mortgage payments will be.

When interest rates are rising, most people also want some way of protecting their interest rate. Most mortgage pre-approvals offer an interest rate guarantee for anywhere from 30 to 90 days. To get the guaranteed rate, you must complete the transaction (i.e., close the house and have the mortgage funds disbursed) within the guaranteed period. If the period expires, the guarantee is gone. If interest rates are lower at closing than the rate guaranteed, make sure you get the lower rate.

With pre-approved financing, your offer to purchase may be more attractive to the seller. But despite the implication, just because you're *pre-approved* doesn't mean you're *guaranteed* financing, so make your offer conditional on financing. Your pre-approval is based on your credit-worthiness, downpayment, and ability to service the debt. However, since you haven't chosen the house you're going to buy yet, the mortgage is only approved in principle. Final approval is subject to the property qualifying. An appraisal is needed to determine this. Once you have located the house you want to buy, the normal mortgage application procedure is followed, but with much of the qualifying information already on hand, your application should move quickly.

Just because you've been pre-approved by one lender doesn't mean you have to borrow from that company. You should still shop around even if it is easier to be pre-approved by your existing financial institution. Lenders are constantly coming up with new and improved product features as a way to lure you into their stores. Make sure you know what you want, and shop till you find it.

## THE LANGUAGE OF MORTGAGES

Mortgages come with a language all their own, and to the uninitiated it can be quite confusing. Here are some of the most common terms you'll meet when you go shopping for a mortgage:

- *Amortization* refers to the number of years it will take to repay the entire amount of the mortgage based on a set of fixed payments. The *term* is the amount of time that the mortgage agreement covers, usually anywhere from six months to five years.
- A *first mortgage* is a debt registered against a property that is secured by a first call on the property. If you don't make the required payments — referred to as *defaulting* — the first lender has first right to the property. A *second mortgage* comes next in line and carries a higher interest rate, reflecting the increased risk to the lender.
- An *open mortgage* allows you to repay the loan on any payment date without penalty. A *closed mortgage* cannot be pre-paid in total or renegotiated prior to the end of the term.
- A *fixed-rate mortgage* has an interest rate that remains the same throughout the term, regardless of whether rates move up or down. A *variable-rate* (also called *floating-* or *adjustable-rate*) *mortgage's* rate is based on the prime lending rate and can be adjusted monthly to

reflect changes in current rates.

- A downpayment of 25% or more qualifies you for a *conventional mortgage*. With between 5% and 25%, you'll be dealing with a *high-ratio mortgage*.

## COMING UP WITH THE DOWNPAYMENT

Once you get over being a scaredy-cat and decide you want to own a home, the next question you'll ask is, "How am I ever going to save enough for a downpayment?" The answer is simple: *telesis*.

It's easy to look at the real estate market and be overwhelmed by the size of the downpayment you'll need. Don't be put off. With a sound plan and a commitment to making your dreams a reality, you can put yourself in a home of your own.

First, decide how much you are prepared to spend and how large a mortgage payment you can handle. Next, figure out your expected downpayment and how long you're prepared to wait before you jump into the market. The longer you can wait, the more you can accumulate. The less time you have, the more you'll have to put aside each month to meet your goal. Finally, get saving.

The best way to build your downpayment? Sign up for a periodic investment plan. Offered through most financial institutions, these plans make setting aside a specific amount each month very convenient. Once you've determined how much you want to invest, each month you can have that amount automatically transferred from your account to purchase the investment of your choice, be it a mutual fund, term deposit, or what have you. Over time you accumulate a substantial nest egg while minimizing the pinch; after all, your money is taken before you can even think about how to spend it.

Of course, you have to find the money before you can put it aside or allow it to be whisked into a periodic investment plan. While most of us live up to our means — we spend almost every cent we make — if you're determined to find the money for a downpayment, you will. It may mean tightening your belt or, at the very least, reviewing how you spend your money to see where you can cut corners. Track your spending for a couple of months. You may be pleasantly surprised at how much you can set aside once you eliminate all the little frivolities that, in the long run, add very little to your life. There are dozens of things you can do to save money (see the suggestions in Chapters 4 and 5), but if you can't seem to find a place to cut, show your budget to your mother. In minutes she'll find a dozen places where you are wasting money. In lieu of your mom, turn to a close friend for help.

When it comes to deciding how to invest the money you're accumulating for a downpayment, depending on your time frame, you may want to be somewhat aggressive. After all, if you rely on a GIC paying 4% interest, following the Rule of 72 (which says that you divide the interest rate into 72 for the number of years it will take to double the investment) it'll take 18 years for your money to double. If you invest in a balanced mutual fund and manage an average return of 9%, you'll shorten your doubling time to just eight years. Look to an aggressive-growth mutual fund and you may see your return jump to 12%, and your money double in six years.

If you've been paying premiums on a whole life insurance policy, you've probably accumulated a cash value against which you can borrow. Check it out with your insurance company. Some people turn to parents, grandparents, or other relatives to help if they are able. In the U.S., in 1991, almost a quarter of all first-time home buyers relied on loans and gifts from relatives to make up their downpayments. Note well: Your financial institution will want to know where the money came from (they'll check your bank records to see if it was really yours), so you'll need a letter from your benefactor explicitly stating that the money is a gift and that there is no expectation of repayment.

Planning to get married? Ask for cash in lieu of yet another small appliance. Explain that this will help you into your first home, and be explicit about how important it is that this dream come true. If you are buying a new home because you are divorcing, consider asking for your alimony payments as one lump-sum amount to be paid from the proceeds of the sale of your principal residence. This will get you back into the housing market as fast as possible — and maximize the real value of every dollar you receive.

Don't forget about the RRSP Home Buyers' Plan. Under this plan you can withdraw up to $20,000 from your RRSP as a tax-free loan toward a downpayment on a home. The loan must be repaid in annual installments or the amount not repaid will be included in your income for that year and taxed! My *RRSP Answer Book* has all the details of how this plan works.

Consider a partner. Can you find a friend or relative who would also like to get into the housing market, and with whose help you can manage the downpayment? Alternatively, if your partner has the cash and you don't, you can assume a larger percentage of the mortgage as your responsibility. Treat this transaction as a business arrangement, and take the appropriate legal steps to ensure you are both well protected.

## WHAT FLAVOUR IS YOUR MORTGAGE?

The size of your downpayment will dictate the type of mortgage for which you will qualify. With 25% or more of the purchase price down, you can finance your new home using a fixed-rate conventional mortgage. This is the vanilla type of mortgage, which charges a fixed amount of interest for a specific period of time and is restricted to a maximum of 75% of the loan-to-value ratio.

Loan-to-value ratio is exactly what it sounds like: the ratio between the loan amount and the value of the property. So a 75% loan-to-value ratio means that 75% of the value of the property can be financed, while the other 25% must come from your resources. The value is usually defined as the lesser of the appraisal value and the purchase price.

For uninsured variable-rate mortgages (VRMs), financing is restricted to a maximum of 70% of the loan-to-value ratio, so you'll have to come up with at least 30% of the purchase price as your downpayment. For insured VRMs, financing is restricted to a maximum of 85% of the loan-to-value ratio, so the minimum downpayment required is 15%.

If you can only arrange a downpayment of between 10% and 24% of the purchase price of the property, then you'll need a high-ratio mortgage. These mortgages are insured through the Canada Mortgage and Housing Corporation, or CMHC, and are usually restricted to a maximum of 90% of the first $180,000, and 80% of the balance of the loan-to-value ratio. So a minimum of 10% of the equity must come from your own resources. You should also note that an application fee and insurance premium are applicable for high-ratio mortgages. This insurance premium is calculated as a percentage of the loan amount, and the percentage depends on the loan-to-value ratio. The higher the loan-to-value ratio, the higher the premium cost. This premium may be paid in cash or added to the mortgage amount. The following table shows examples of the insurance premium that is usually added to the mortgage:

| LOAN-TO-VALUE RATIO | COST |
| --- | --- |
| 0.0% to 65% | 0.50% of loan amount |
| 65.1% to 75% | 0.75% of loan amount |
| 75.1% to 80% | 1.25% of loan amount |
| 80.1% to 85% | 2.00% of loan amount |
| 85.1% to 90% | 2.50% of loan amount |

In 1992, CMHC introduced "First Home Loan Insurance," designed to assist first-time home buyers. In 1998, the program was broadened to include all home buyers. This program requires a minimum downpayment of only 5%. The maximum loan amount is calculated as 95% of the lesser of the sale price, the appraised value, or the maximum house price.

## HOUSE HUNTING

When it comes to buying a house, do-it-yourselfers may think they can save a ton of cash handling the details on their own and negotiating away the commission the seller would have paid, but it ain't necessarily so. Home buying is a complicated legal and financial business. A guide who has been around the block a few times can help substantially in assuaging your fears, calming your nerves, and keeping you on the straight and narrow in terms of your home-ownership priorities.

"The first thing you have to do is choose an agent and a mortgage person to work with," says Karen Bryce, a real estate agent with Sutton Group. Ask friends and family who they've dealt with, what they liked, and whom they think would be a good fit for you. You should get great service from both these individuals as you go through this exciting and somewhat frightening experience. "That means you get callbacks and lots of information. I have clients come in for a three-hour appointment before we start looking at houses," Karen says. "They have to feel comfortable with me. And after 15 years of doing business, I've only had two people not prepared to work exclusively with me.

"I like to get everything on the table before I start. I explain that I only work on commission and that I don't get paid until the house closes. Some people have no idea how this works so it's best to talk about it.

I need to know how much they are qualified for — how much mortgage they will get, what downpayment they have, and, by extension, how much they can spend — so I don't even take them to see a house until they have been to the bank and pre-qualified. Of course, just because you're pre-qualified for a mortgage doesn't mean you can just go out and buy a house. You still have to fulfill certain conditions.

"Ninety-nine percent of people have never seen an offer before," says Karen. "So in my first meeting with a client, I explain about agent relationships — the relationship between the buyer and her agent and the seller and her agent — and how I'm compensated. The contract clients sign is usually for a two-month term." According to Karen, if the agent is listening and the buyer's requests aren't outrageous, it should take between two and three weeks to find the house.

That's exactly how it happened to me. When I was shopping for my semi-detached home, I was prospected by an agent who said she was willing to work with me. I told her that I was just looking around, getting familiar with the market in the neighbourhoods I was interested in, and wouldn't be ready to buy until the summer (it was early February). She said that was fine and that she would help me look around. We looked at lots of houses, just to get a good idea of which of my must-haves and which of my want-to-haves were likely to show up together. Then we found it. It was the perfect little house. I fell in love. We put in an offer and it was accepted to close in April. "Whew," I said. "That was fast!" While I was happy with my new house, I was breathless with the speed of it all. The lesson here: Don't go shopping before you're ready to sign an offer.

"The next thing we talk about," says Karen, "is location. Location and price are the two most important factors." You have to decide where you

*The top producer in her office in her first year in real estate, Karen Bryce has been managing her clients' expectations and fulfilling their dreams since 1985. As associate broker with Sutton Group–Bayview Realty Inc., Karen sold more than 40 homes in 1998. Karen believes there's usually no reason people should be helping pay their landlords' mortgages because "you could be investing that money in your own home." Real estate is a seven-day-a-week job, but Karen and her husband like to take time out to go to the movies or vacation abroad — when they aren't jumping through hoops for their two grown children.*

want to live and how much you're willing to pay. "More than once I've asked clients if they are going to change the amount they'll spend, or change the location in which they look."

People always have priorities in terms of what they're looking for in a house. They usually write down a wish list. But they often don't have a specific mental picture of what the house should look like. That's for the best, since Karen suggests that buyers should not be too tied to many of the things people typically put on their lists: air conditioning, central vacuum, finished basement. You can always rig in these types of extras. Even an open-concept feeling can be created post-purchase. It is more important when you go house shopping to be clear on the elements that *can't* be changed. Don't be unduly influenced by the nice-to-haves. They can become the conditions, in your own mind, that will affect which house you choose over another, and how much you pay.

"Even if you fall in love with the first house you walk into," says Karen, "I'd still want you to look at 10 to 12 other houses so you can see what else you can get for the same money." The kitchen in the first house might be the best, but the second house may have a perfectly finished basement. You then have to ask yourself: What's more important, the kitchen or the basement, and what will it cost to remedy what's lacking? If it costs twice as much to get the kitchen you want than the basement you want, then buying the perfect kitchen and doing the basement later probably makes the most sense.

The other important thing to talk about is the offer. "When you do an offer, the agents do not read you the clauses that are standard — the fine print. So you should go over the offer and make sure you understand it before the time comes to sign," says Karen.

At the offer stage Karen explains the waivers and the fact that in most cases there will be two conditions present: inspection and financing. "If there are any structural problems with the house, if the roof is about to go or termites have invaded, then an inspection will tell you that." The other thing the inspection will do is highlight all the little things you'll need to fix. "You will never get a perfect house," says Karen, "not even if you buy brand new." And she's right. By its very nature, home ownership means you'll always be fixing something.

As a first-time home buyer, you might think that you would somehow be involved in the offer process. Perhaps you've imagined negotiating with the vendor. Even if you expected simply to be present when the offer was presented, you'd be wrong. "I review the offer with my clients who wish to buy, and then I alone take that offer to the vendor's agent and the vendor. If there is negotiating to be done, I move between the seller and the buyer. When the offer is accepted by the vendor, the property is sold except for any outstanding conditions." Assuming all goes well, your agent will have you sign waivers for all the conditions of the offer.

"The closing date also has to be negotiated," says Karen. Flexibility is often the key to working this issue out quickly. Sometimes a vendor has no choice on the closing date, so the purchaser may have to be flexible. I remember when we were buying our house on Carlaw, in Toronto, I was pregnant and expanding quickly. I was determined to be in my new home before I was too big to walk up the stairs under my own power. And since we needed to have access to the house for a couple of weeks before we moved in so we could paint, an early closing date was important. But as Karen points out, "as first-time buyers, if you can give multiple closing dates, you have a better chance when there are a number of people making offers."

What else gives you an edge in the multiple-offer situation? Ultimately, the only way to win this game is to pick the right price. "Lots of people say they don't want to get into a multiple-offer situation," says Karen. In reality, it's not that big a deal. Go with your best shot and resolve yourself to the outcome. You'll be no further behind than having made no offer at all.

## PREPARING FOR THE MORTGAGE INTERVIEW

Once you've found the perfect house, it's time to nail down your mortgage. To do so, you'll have to go to your preferred financial institution for an interview.

There's a great deal that goes into being prepared for the mortgage interview. My book *Shopping for Money* includes everything you need to know about all types of credit, and it tells you what lenders look for. When applying for a mortgage, you have to provide specific information about your financial circumstances. Take the following documentation with you to the interview:

- personal identification, such as your driver's licence or social insurance card, as well as a list of personal information, including your address, the name of your landlord or present mortgage holder, and the amount you are now paying in rent or for your mortgage
- a list of all your assets and liabilities, with a realistic value set for each; also a list of all your credit cards, as you'll probably be asked for the numbers (to check your credit history)
- written confirmation of employment income from your employer, and confirmation in writing of income from any other sources, showing a consistent amount from year to year; take your notices of assessment from Revenue Canada as proof of your income history
- for self-employed people, the last three years' income-tax returns and/or financial statements
- a copy of the accepted purchase agreement, along with a statement regarding urea formaldehyde foam insulation (this statement is normally included on the standard offer-of-purchase forms used by real estate brokers) and a photograph of the house or a copy of the listing
- your lawyer's name, full address, and telephone number
- the name, address, and telephone number of someone who can provide access to the property for the appraisal (this may be the realtor or the vendor)
- heating cost estimate and property tax estimate (usually found on the listing) and condominium fees, if applicable
- for properties that do not have municipal services, well and/or septic tank certificates
- confirmation of downpayment. If it is a gift, a letter confirming that it is a gift with no repayment terms is needed. If the downpayment is to come from a second mortgage, a written confirmation of the terms and conditions of this mortgage must be provided by the second mortgagor.

## CHOOSING A TERM YOU CAN LIVE WITH

What term should you take? That's a good question. Before you look at the issue of term specifically, there are things you should consider so you can manage your mortgage to your best advantage.

When you're looking at term and interest rates, you also need to look at payment amounts and amortization. Interest rate, payment amount, and amortization period are directly related. If you take a $100,000 mortgage at 10% with a 20-year amortization period, your monthly payment would be $951.67. If the rate was 11%, your monthly payment would be higher, at $1,015.64. If the rate was 9%, your monthly payment would be $889.19. So the lower your interest rate, the lower your payment amount.

Now let's look at how the amortization period affects your payment. A $100,000 mortgage at 10% with a 20-year amortization period has monthly payments of $951.67. Choose a 25-year amortization period, and your payments would be $894.49. A 15-year amortization period would give you payments of $1,062.27. So the longer your amortization period, the lower your payment amount, and the shorter the amortization period, the higher your payment amount.

Putting these two factors together will help you figure out what you can live with. The first place to start is to figure out the payment amount with which you'll be comfortable over the long term. Since interest rates are beyond your control, you only have the option of playing with the amortization period to get the payment amount you want. Having done that, you have to consider what will happen if rates go up or down. Since the "up" is the one we all hate, let's look at it first.

If rates go up, you have two choices. First, you can work the increased payment amount into your budget. Second, you can increase your amortization to bring your payment amount back in line. Now, that may mean moving your mortgage to another financial institution, so be prepared for the cost of writing a new mortgage.

What if rates go down? Great! Now you could benefit from a lower payment amount. But think about this a minute. You've already worked the payment into your budget. If you keep your payment amount the same, you'll be paying off your mortgage a lot faster. So don't pocket the difference. Keep applying it to your mortgage.

One final point on managing your mortgage: Rather than locking yourself into a high payment amount that you have to struggle to make each month, do yourself a favour. If you can, choose a payment amount you find easier to live with. Then make sure you have pre-payment options that allow you to make additional payments when you have the cash available. That way, you'll have a payment amount you can manage comfortably, and you can still aggressively pay down your mortgage.

Now, back to the term. You still have to decide what term is best for you. Here are some questions to ask yourself:

- *Where are rates now and where are they going?*
Trying to predict where rates are going is a tough job. You can twist yourself into knots worrying about what will happen. At the end of 1992, we saw interest rates fall to their lowest point in 35 years. No one ever thought they'd get that low again. Wrong! 1997 brought even lower rates. It would be equally wrong to assume that rates can't skyrocket again. I know it's bad economics, but if anyone had told us in the seventies that interest rates would be in the upper teens in the eighties, we'd have said they were crazy.

    If you feel rates are at a point you can live with and you want to guarantee that rate for as long as possible, you'd choose a long term; this is referred to as "going long." This is a good strategy if rates appear to be rising.

    But what if rates are falling? You may want to remain flexible to take advantage of future lower rates. One way is to choose a short term — referred to as "going short." Then, when your term is up, you can renew at the lower rate. Another option is to go for an open mortgage. You'll pay a higher rate of interest, but you'll have the flexibility to pre-pay or renew at any time. You could also choose a variable-rate mortgage so that as rates come down you benefit from the lower rate. Or you could choose a convertible mortgage, which lets you take advantage of lower rates and then lock in when you feel the rates have bottomed out.

- *Do you want a fixed payment amount?*
Some people choose a long-term mortgage to ensure they'll have a fixed payment amount they can live with for as long as possible. This makes it much easier to plan for your mortgage payments and everything else in your life — particularly when your cash flow is tight and even a small upward movement in interest rates would be disastrous.

- *Are you a gambler?*
Some people don't mind the stomach turning associated with fluc-

tuations in rates. Others can't stand the stress. If you're not comfortable with the game, pick a payment amount you can live with and lock in.

- *Are you prepared to keep a close eye on the market?*
  If you're going to choose a short-term, open, variable-rate, or convertible mortgage, then be prepared to keep a careful watch on what interest rates are doing so you can lock in when rates bottom out. If you're not prepared to do this, go with a mid- to long-term rate.

## PAYMENT FREQUENCIES

Financial institutions offer a variety of payment frequencies so you can choose when and how often you wish to make your regular payments. The traditional monthly payment amount is calculated using the amortization tables available in libraries and most bookstores. However, if you're paid semimonthly, biweekly, or weekly, you may wish to use a payment frequency that matches your cash flow.

Some people want to take advantage of the savings made available by using a faster-pay or accelerated frequency. With this, you make extra payments against your mortgage, but in such small amounts that those extra payments fit easily into your cash flow. With accelerated payments, in one year you make the equivalent of 13 months of payments in the space of 12 months. That extra payment reduces your principal, so you save on your interest costs in the long term. Based on a mortgage of $100,000 at a rate of 11% amortized over 25 years, you would save $62,486 in interest over the life of the mortgage using a faster-pay biweekly or weekly frequency.

Many financial institutions allow you to change your payment frequency as your needs change. Be aware that there may be a charge for interest adjustment from your current payment due date to the revised date.

## MAKING EXTRA PAYMENTS AGAINST YOUR PRINCIPAL

The best way to pay your mortgage off fast is to pour any extra money you have into the mortgage whenever you can. However, this is one area in which all mortgages are not created equal. While some banks offer very flexible options, others still think you should fit with their schedules. If extra payments are a priority for you, shop carefully for the mortgage that offers you the level of flexibility you're looking for.

At least one bank offers an option that will let you make an additional payment up to 12 times a year (or once a month) up to your normal payment amount. If your regular monthly payment amount is $900, you could make an additional payment of anywhere from $100 to $900 every month and that money would go directly to your principal. Back when I was consulting on a regular basis, I found this feature extremely useful. In those months when billings were good, I could double my regular monthly payment and pay down my mortgage while saving bags and bags of interest. An additional feature that came attached to this one was the fact that each time I doubled, I had the right to skip a future payment. What's the point? Well, in those months when the projects weren't coming fast and furiously, I could take pressure off my cash flow by skipping a monthly payment. Yes, I effectively negated the time and interest savings, but boy did that flexibility ever give me peace of mind. I still believe the options of doubling up and skipping are the best features in the marketplace.

While this next feature isn't as flexible as the first, it has its benefits. Some institutions let you increase your monthly payment up to double the original amount. So, if your regular monthly payment is $1,200, you could increase it to as much as $2,400. The drawback with this alternative is that with some financial institutions, once you raise your repayment amount, you can't go back.

Almost every lender lets you make a lump-sum payment of 10% to 20% of your original principal once a year. While some institutions want it on your anniversary date, others will let you do it on any payment date.

### BALANCING MORTGAGE PAYDOWN WITH OTHER GOALS

Did you know that 58% of Canadians with a mortgage don't have an RRSP? It seems that once that mortgage note is signed, getting rid of what can be the single largest debt we ever take on becomes of paramount importance. But the building of retirement assets is just as important. It all comes down to time. The longer you have your mortgage, the more interest you'll pay. And the earlier you begin saving for retirement, the more money you'll have accumulated through tax-deferred compound growth.

There are other parts of your financial life that also need to be managed. In coming up with a downpayment for a home, many people tap all their available resources. They even dip into their emergency fund (if they have one at all) to minimize the amount of mortgage they have to take, or to qualify. But an emergency fund is an important part of the plan, and without it you leave yourself open to all sorts of dire consequences.

Doing anything to the exclusion of everything else is not healthy. You need an emergency fund for the near future. And you need to sock away money regularly for your long-term future needs. So, if you're asking yourself whether you should contribute to an RRSP or pay down your mortgage, here are some factors to consider.

If your income is particularly high one year, then your marginal tax rate will also be high, and a contribution to an RRSP may significantly reduce your tax liability. But if your income is low one year, the tax savings from a small contribution limit and lower marginal tax rate might be outweighed by the interest savings from paying down your mortgage. Remember, too, that the further you are from retirement, the more valuable are contributions to an RRSP, since the money has a longer period to benefit from compounding. The closer retirement is, the less impact an RRSP contribution will have in terms of compounding, and the more important it is to get rid of your debt.

The amount of time left on your mortgage amortization schedule is also important. The faster you repay your principal, the more interest you save in the long run. So, you'll save more interest by paying down a mortgage with a 20-year amortization remaining than one with a 5-year amortization remaining.

Avoid falling into the RRSP carry-forward trap. You may be tempted to carry forward your unused deduction room indefinitely for use in later years, but remember that delaying contributions means your RRSP won't have had the time to do greatest justice to your contributions in terms of compounded return. One $5,000 contribution delayed for just five years will cost your RRSP over $16,000, assuming a rate of return of just 8% — another good reason to reflect carefully on the decision.

Of course, there will always be circumstances when you'll want to swing your decision in favour of a mortgage paydown. If the interest paid on the mortgage is significantly higher than the return being earned on an RRSP, paying down the mortgage may be appropriate.

The answer to the RRSP-versus-mortgage paydown question does not have to be either/or. You can make your maximum RRSP contribution and use the proceeds from your tax refund to pay down your mortgage. Let's say you decided to contribute $8,000 a year to your RRSP. With a marginal tax rate of 45%, you would receive a tax refund of $3,600 each year. Let's also say you apply that refund against your $100,000 mortgage (with an interest rate of 10%). Assuming an average return of 10% each year on your RRSP portfolio, in 30 years your retirement savings will have grown to about $1.4 million. And by applying your refund to your mortgage, you will save almost $89,000 in interest and have your mortgage paid off in 12 years instead of 25. This strategy lets you save for retirement and secure your future, earn tax-sheltered income, reduce the amount of current income tax paid, and reduce the amount of interest to be paid on the mortgage, not to mention the amortization. Many financial institutions have software programs that can show you how much you will save by applying your tax refund as a payment against your mortgage principal. Ask for some examples to see how much you can save. It makes a lot more sense to work toward both objectives than to grapple with the issue of which should be a priority. With the right balance, you can have it all!

## MOVIN' ON UP

If you're considering upgrading to a new house, you may also be considering one or more of the following questions:

- How do I get the same great rate on my new mortgage as I have on my existing mortgage?
- Should I discharge the mortgage and take out a new mortgage? What will that cost me in penalty interest?
- Should I let the purchaser assume the mortgage and take out a new mortgage on the new house?

If you decide you want to take your mortgage with you when you move, then it's time to learn all about the portability option on your mortgage. By porting your mortgage, you can continue taking advantage of your existing mortgage rate. If you find you need additional financing, you can blend your existing mortgage with a new one, eliminating the need for a much costlier second mortgage.

The biggest benefit of porting your mortgage is that it eliminates the interest penalties that apply to a straight early discharge of an existing mortgage. This can mean major savings, particularly when the interest rate on your existing mortgage is higher than the rate currently available for a new mortgage.

You can port your mortgage in one of three ways:

1. If you're taking your remaining mortgage term, interest rate, and principal balance to your new property without increasing or decreasing the principal, that's called a straight port.
2. If you're an empty nester, or simply downgrading to a less expensive home, you'll be interested in porting and decreasing. The mortgage is ported, but the principal is reduced. A penalty for lost interest, also referred to as an interest-rate differential, or IRD, may be payable when a smaller loan amount is requested.
3. If you're upgrading and need more financing on your new home than originally existed on the home being sold, then you'll port and increase. The mortgage is ported, the principal is increased, and your interest rate is blended so that you still have the advantage of the original rate on at least a portion of the mortgage.

If you plan to port your mortgage, both you and the new property will still have to meet normal lending guidelines, so a full mortgage application and property appraisal will be completed. And you can only execute your portability option if your existing mortgage is in good standing. Since a new mortgage document must be drawn and registered on title, normal appraisal charges, legal fees, and an administration fee may apply.

**Setting the price on your existing home**
Once you decide to put your house on the market, one of the first things you'll have to think about is where you'll set your asking price. This is

probably the most crucial issue when it comes to listing your home. It entails a financial strategy, along with all the emotion that accompanies selling — and buying — a home. Price is the primary motivation for long hours of negotiation and for the eventual decision to buy or not to buy.

House prices are closely tied to fluctuations in our economy. Prices soar and plummet on a variety of factors including inflation, where interest rates are, where they are going and, of course, demand and supply. And price has two sides in dire opposition. Buyers always want to know if the market has reached the bottom. Sellers want to know if prices are going up.

So, where do you start if you're planning to sell your home and have to set a price? Begin by checking the market value of your property. Ask at least two real estate agents for appraisals. Check the multiple listings for prices of similar homes in your area. Carefully assess how market conditions have changed in the last six months and how they may affect your asking price. Then set your price within 3% to 5% of the average price you've come up with. If the market indicates that your home is worth about $189,000, set your price no higher than about $198,450. Of course, you could set your price at the bottom end of the scale — $179,500 — if you want to get lots of offers and close quickly. You might even benefit from a bidding war that drives up the price slightly.

If you set your price high because you *feel* your house is worth more, don't be surprised if it takes a while for an offer to come in, or if you then have to drop your price once, twice, or even several times in order to interest buyers. Don't be insulted by low-ball offers. And don't think that just because you need the money to get you into a more expensive home that buyers will be willing to fund your dreams. In a buyer's market — one where buyers set the tone for sales because there are fewer of them — buyers are much more likely to win in negotiations because there's so much available, and they usually have time on their side. In a seller's market — one where sellers write the ticket and buyers often bid it up — buyers will go to lengths to make their offer attractive.

Setting the right price may just be the most important aspect of selling your home. Even with the ideal location, the perfect features, and the home in tiptop condition, the price has to be right for buyers to bite. And since most purchasers already have a price in mind when they set about house hunting, pricing too high could take your home right out of their "viewing" range. Also keep in mind that the right price means your house will spend less time on the market, so you'll have to spend less time keeping it in "show" condition and negotiating.

When the time comes to sell, resist the urge to overprice your house. Setting a reasonable price that intrigues potential buyers into your home will, over the long run, save you money, disappointment, and time.

# 8

# Establish Your Credit Identity

*The human species, according to the best theory I can form of it, is composed of two distinct races, the men who borrow, and the men who lend.*

CHARLES LAMB

*A money lender. He services you in the present tense; he lends you in the conditional mood; keeps you in the subjunctive; and ruins you in the future.*

JOSEPH ADDISON

Lots of books have been written about the evils of borrowing (never borrow), how to get out of debt (stop borrowing), and how to stay out of debt (never ever borrow again). I've even written one myself: *Shopping for Money*. In it, I explain how credit works and how to make it work better. It has been the least popular of the five books I've written so far. Yet, clearly people have a problem with borrowing. In 1997, bankruptcies in Canada were at their highest level ever, with a total of 97,497 bankruptcies (that's 2.9 bankruptcies for every thousand Canadians). In fact, the bankruptcy rate has more than quadrupled since 1984.[13]

The fact is, credit is a way of life and if we try to live without it, it becomes very hard to accomplish our goals. After all, does anyone you

---

13 "The Credit Line," Credit Counselling Service of Metropolitan Toronto, June 1997.

know have the cash to buy their first home without borrowing? Credit isn't bad. How we use credit is the problem.

Priorities have shifted dramatically over the past several decades. People who grew up during the thirties, forties, or fifties believed that they had to save. They paid cash for almost everything they bought. They were willing to wait until they were well established and had all the necessities before splurging on the extras.

Barbara Godin talks about growing up in a strict European home. She says, "We saved all of our milk bottles. My father made his own wine and beer at home. We even churned our own butter. We learned the value of every single cent. And when we did spend money, it wasn't on candy or pop, the non-necessities of life. It was on a good, sturdy pair of shoes." When she wanted a new bicycle, her dad said, "You can't afford the bicycle until you have the good shoes."

The lesson was well learned. Barb and her husband worked hard to buy their first car. "We worked every day in the office until 6:00 p.m. Then we travelled for two hours by bus to a factory and cleaned toilets. We did 200 toilets each night. We'd get home at 1:00 a.m. We did this seven days a week. We saved every single dollar. When we went into the dealership, we paid for the car in cash. We were just kids, in our early twenties. I'll never forget that. That to me was a much better experience than saying, 'Oh, put it on a charge card or I'll pay for it over time.'"

*A recognized leader in the field of credit risk management, Barb Godin spent 14 years with the Bank of Nova Scotia, where her most recent position was senior vice-president responsible for retail lending and automotive finance. Previously Barb was a member of the Management Advisory Board for the Office of the Superintendent of Bankruptcies and two-term president of the Canadian Credit Risk Management Association. In 1998 Barb moved her model cars, husband, and kids to the United States, where she is now executive vice-president and chief credit risk management officer for KeyBank USA.*

The sixties, seventies, and eighties saw a significant shift in people's attitudes toward borrowing. Then it was considered the only way to get ahead. People leveraged investments. They took on huge debt loads. They wanted it all — immediately. The idea of working, saving, and then buying was a thing of the past; the new approach was to charge the purchase and pay it off over time. The result: huge debt loads that have kept growing year after year, resulting in phenomenal levels of personal bankruptcy.

There's a balance that has to be struck between the I-want-it-now camp and the I-need-to-save-for-it camp. "That's where the credit trade-off comes in," says Barb. "It's very difficult to say to someone applying for credit, 'Why are you trying to get a loan for a $20,000 entertainment cen-tre when you haven't bought a home yet and you haven't built up any assets? Where are your priorities?'" But even if the lender isn't saying it aloud to you, rest assured that he or she is thinking it. It's all part of the credit analysis that allows lenders to determine whether you're a good risk. As Bulwer Lytton wrote in 1864, "There is no test of a man's char-acter more generally adopted than the way in which his money is managed. Money is a terrible blab; she will betray the secrets of her owner whatever he do to gag her. His virtues will creep out in her whis-per — his vices she will cry aloud at the top of her tongue."

"The privacy issue," says Barb, "is a big deal. People don't want to be counselled anymore. While previously I might have asked, 'Are you sure this is what you want?' now it's simply a matter of do they qualify." On the credit side, lenders have lost their advisory role. "Credit has become a commodity," says Barb. "When I grew up, credit was not a commodity. It was something you sought advice on. Today people say, 'What's your price. I demand it. I expect it. Give it to me.' Now investments are the strong advisory product."

While the installment loan used to be the credit of choice for most people, the focus has shifted to revolving credit — credit cards and per-sonal lines of credit. Unfortunately, if you choose to use revolving credit, you miss the checks and balances that lenders typically use to validate your reason for borrowing. Instead, because the credit is readily available, it's easy to use without thought of the other aspects of your financial life.

Most people don't understand how to use credit to their advantage. They react to their circumstances, and they keep reacting, as they get fur-ther and further into debt. When the debt becomes unmanageable, they throw up their arms in despair and say that credit is evil. Well, it's not. Well-planned borrowing can be a useful way to realize dreams and achieve financial goals. Well-planned borrowing can get you where you want to be. But it takes a good understanding of how credit works, when to use credit, and which type of credit will make borrowing work for you.

## ESTABLISHING A CREDIT RATING

If you are a good risk and have qualified to use it, it's credit. If you've used it, it's debt. It's funny how a single concept can have such different meanings depending on which end of the stick you're holding. If you've got credit, you're great. You're responsible. You're worthy. You're an up-and-comer. If you've got debt, exactly the opposite is true. Yet we're talking about the same thing: your ability to use someone else's money to achieve your goals.

You can't develop a credit rating until you have paid back a loan. A credit rating is your reputation in terms of your ability to pay back money you've borrowed in a responsible and timely way. If you've been consistently late in making your payments, you'll have a bad credit reputation. If you've ever missed a payment completely, you'll have an even worse rep. If you've always made your payments on time, you will have a great credit rating and just about anyone will be willing to lend to you under the right circumstances.

One way to start building a credit reputation is to borrow some money to contribute to an RRSP. You can pay back the loan over a five- or six-month period and you'll have started saving for the future. And you don't have to worry about whether or not they'll give you the loan. As long as you take the RRSP out with that lending institution, you'll get the loan.

Barb Godin talks about the process of lenders granting credit. "When you sign a credit application form, you give the lender permission to check your credit rating. If you have no credit history, we don't know if you would be a good credit risk or not. So immediately, you become an unknown commodity and that's harder to deal with."

A credit card is one of the easiest ways to establish a credit rating. Apply for a card with a low limit, make small purchases, pay off the card each month, and become a credit star. Another way to establish a credit rating is to take out a loan. If you are a first-time borrower, you may need a guarantor to get the loan (the guarantor is a person who has established a credit reputation and who guarantees to repay the loan if you don't). When you pay back that money promptly, you establish your credit rating. If you have assets such as a car, investments, or a home to use as collateral, you can use that collateral to secure the loan. If you don't repay the loan, the financial institution will seize the asset pledged as collateral and sell it or cash it in order to collect its money.

Some people have difficulty establishing that they even exist when it comes to getting credit. If you are a married woman and all the cards are in your husband's name, even if you make the payments on the card, you're contributing to his credit rating, not your own. The card company doesn't care who signed the cheques. They base their reports to the credit bureau on who holds the card. Women who are recently divorced or widowed often face the shock that they don't exist in the world of credit, simply because all the credit reporting was done in their husbands' names. If you are a married woman, make sure you have at least one credit card in your own name. And use it. You'll have to apply for it and qualify for it on your own. Initially, you may have to use a secured credit card. A secured credit card is one that is fully secured, meaning there's no risk to the credit card company because you provide the company with enough cash to cover your balance. Financial institutions typically want twice the amount of credit you're asking for. So if you want a credit card with a $500 balance, you must put up $1,000 in cash. After you've made regular payments for about a year or so, the financial institution will drop the security requirement and return your deposit.

Barb Godin says that prior to the early 1990s all reporting for a couple was done in the man's name. Now, however, credit bureaus have separated the reporting for men and women. To make sure you establish a credit history, she suggests that when you go to borrow money, make sure you borrow it in your own name. And if you do borrow with your husband, insist that the credit granter report the information to the credit bureau in your name. Typically, credit granters report only in the name of the first person who signed on the credit application. If that happens to be the man — and typically, men are handed the paperwork first — all the credit history for that loan is reported in his name. So if you want the credit history for the loan, insist on signing first.

## CHOOSING THE RIGHT CREDIT CARD

To know which credit card is best for you, you'll first have to decide how you plan to use the card. If you usually carry a balance from one month to the next, then a low-interest card is your best bet. If you pay your card off in full every month, look for a card that doesn't charge an annual fee and provides the longest grace period. If you want to take advantage of some of the "rewards" available, you'll have a lot to choose from, but you'll end up paying for the privilege.

Every specialty credit card has a list of features as long as your arm. Wading through the options — points for travel or gift selections, cash rebates, and myriad insurance coverages — can bewitch even the most cautious shoppers into believing they are getting good value. Some cards give you points toward the purchase or lease of a new car, assuming you already know you want to drive that kind of car. I have a girlfriend who continued to carry a balance on her Visa card because she'd accumulated so many points toward the purchase of a new truck she couldn't see giving up the card. If she'd saved the interest in a separate account, she'd have the truck by now. Some cards provide cash back on travel arrangements, providing you use their travel service. Or you can use your credit card to work toward a rebate on the purchase of your first home, which is a terrific head start as long as you're sure that institution will have the best mortgage deal when the time comes to sign the offer.

The real test of the value of a credit card is in what it does for you. Collision damage waiver on car rentals saves about $12 a day. Trip cancellation or interruption insurance, baggage insurance, and emergency travel or medical assistance provide you with peace of mind as you set off. Free traveller's cheques eliminate the usual 1% fee. And medical insurance benefits can look pretty attractive to holiday travellers. If you don't travel enough for these features to at least cover the cost of your card, you'll have to take a good look at the other bells and whistles that are meant to justify the fee.

Most specialty cards offer to extend for an additional 12 months the manufacturer's warranty on items purchased with the card. Some let you replace items bought on your credit card if they are lost or damaged within 90 days of purchase. Both these insurance features are a good deal, if you use them. If the only reason you have your card is to take advantage of the rewards (the banks' term for accumulating points to buy merchandise from a catalogue), make sure you claim your points and that you're not paying more for the merchandise from a catalogue than you would in a store. If you're looking for a card that will pay for itself, look for a card that will give you a cash rebate.

If you think you have to pay more for a snazzy credit card just to get a higher limit, save yourself some money. With a good credit history, you can simply write to your card issuer and ask for a credit increase. And it won't cost you a cent more in annual fees.

Whether you are a binge shopper or a model of self-control, limiting your access to credit is a smart move. No one needs more than two credit cards: one Visa, one MasterCard. Make one a no-frills, no-fee card and pack as many special features on the other as you'll use. If you carry a balance, make sure it's on the cheaper card.

While most credit cards allow you to take cash advances, don't. Advances accrue interest the moment they are taken.

## TO BORROW OR NOT TO BORROW

Credit is a part of life. Whether you are financing the purchase of new appliances, replacing your furnace, or financing your children's education, borrowing can offer real benefits. After all, it'd be tough on the family to have to wait out a winter while you save the money you needed to buy a new furnace. Borrowing money, putting in the furnace, and paying off the loan in easily manageable payments makes a lot more sense. The question isn't simply whether or not to borrow. Sometimes we have to. Instead, ask yourself:

- Do I really need it?
- What's the mark-up?
- What's this going to cost me in total, including all the interest I'll have paid?
- What else do I have to give up to buy this?

If you need a car to keep your job, my best guess is that your answer to the first question is a resounding yes. The next question is a very important one. The cost of borrowing can vary significantly. The higher the interest rate you pay, the greater the cost. So are you going to buy a new car or a used one? Will you use bank financing, dealer financing, or will you lease? Also, the longer the term of the loan, the greater the cost to you. And what could be worse than having your loan outlive the item you borrowed to buy? By negotiating the lowest possible rate and taking the shortest possible term, you can pay off the loan faster while reducing the overall costs.

This leads to the third question. Since the longer you take to pay off the debt and the higher the mark-up, the more you'll pay, it's a worthwhile exercise figuring out what that item will cost you in total. Let's say you buy a new car for $23,000, and your loan is for five years at 6%. That car will have cost you approximately $27,000. Do the same calculation on your credit-card purchases and you may not be quite so willing to charge ahead with your purchase. If you buy $2,500 worth of new furniture on a credit card that charges 17% interest, and you pay the minimum requirement of 5% per month, it'll take you almost two years to pay off the charge, and that furniture will end up costing you almost $3,000.

Don't overlook the last question. The more the payments restrict your cash flow, the greater the cost to you in terms of stress and having to go without other things you feel contribute to a comfortable lifestyle. If you choose to make higher payments over a shorter term, you have to be sure your other important living needs can still be met. Resist the urge to steal from Peter to pay Paul. Paying off your loan quickly won't do you any good if you run up your credit cards during the process. If you choose instead to take a slightly longer term so that your payments are lower and fit more comfortably into your cash flow, remember this will mean a longer commitment and more interest over the full term of the loan. Weigh the answers to each of these questions carefully in deciding how you'll manage your credit needs.

Whether or not you qualify for a loan, you should question your borrowing motivation and rationale if:

1. You aren't sure the usefulness of a purchase will outlast the repayment period. It's bad enough when we spend cash on impulsive purchases, but when we have to pay for those impulsive actions way beyond the item's life, that can be really hard to take. Ask yourself, and answer honestly, "Will I be severely handicapped without the item?"
2. An installment plan makes it seem too good to pass up. That's not the right place to start. Begin by deciding whether you need the item at all, and then calculate how much you'll be paying in interest.
3. You're adding more debt to your already high debt load. Piling new debt on top of old is dangerous. It can lead you to the point where all your discretionary income is spent making loan payments. Avoid

this scenario by setting priorities before borrowing.

4. You haven't told anyone you intend to borrow. Making unilateral decisions about financing is a great way to put a strain on your relationships. And if you haven't worked up the guts to tell the most trusted people in your life, maybe it's because you know you won't be able to justify the decision to them. Perhaps you'd like to reconsider?

5. You're buying something to cheer yourself up. Lots of people go shopping to lift their spirits. Unfortunately, shopping, like drinking, can create a hangover. Ask yourself how you'll feel when the bill comes in. Adjust your perspective. Maybe a smaller, less-expensive treat will make you feel just as good.

6. You're trying to impress others. Some people need to keep up an image of success. Others shop together to build or strengthen their relationships — my stepdaughter, Amanda, refers to it humorously as "female bonding." But when it comes to paying off the card or repaying the loan, it isn't so funny. Ask yourself if it's really worth it.

### KNOW THE COST OF BORROWING

People with credit cards fall into one of two categories: those who pay off their balances in full every month, and those who don't. If you're in the former category, you're using your credit card as a convenience and a short-term borrowing opportunity (because of the time between when you charge and when you have to pay). You're smart. It costs you little or nothing for the convenience (depending on the type of card you have) and you can accumulate all sorts of extra benefits by using your card — things like travel miles, extra purchase insurance, and the like. If you're in the second category, you have plenty of company. It's been estimated that approximately 60% of Canadian women carry a balance on their cards. Unfortunately, you are paying heavily for the privilege.

If you don't pay your balance off completely and on time, you'll be charged interest which is typically calculated on a daily basis. Interest calculations begin on the day the transaction is posted to your account, usually within a few days of having made the purchase. So, if you charged $1,000 last month and made a partial payment of $400 on the due date, you will still be charged interest on the full $1,000 up to the day the

$400 was credited, since you didn't pay off your balance completely. The remaining balance of $600 will become the "retail revolving balance," which will continue to accrue interest until it is repaid.

Financial institutions have done research showing that most people will go out of their way to earn .5% to .75% more on a GIC. Yet they will pay 7% to 14% more interest than necessary, just because it's a credit card. If you have an outstanding balance of $1,000 on which you're paying 17%, that's costing you more than $14 a month, or almost $169 a year. And that's after-tax dollars! You'd have to have a $1,000 GIC paying better than 24% to break even. If you can find a GIC paying 24%, let me know!

Instead of carrying a balance on your credit card, you'd be better off using an installment loan or personal line of credit to pay off your credit card. If you'd go out of your way to earn .5% more in interest, how far out of your way would you go to save 7% in interest costs? Fact is, you don't have to go far — just to your nearest financial institution. What are you waiting for?

The other thing to know about collecting credit cards and higher credit limits is that it can affect your ability to borrow money when you really do need it. If you're applying for a mortgage, the amount of credit you already have access to will be taken into account when deciding how much more you can borrow. Even if your cards are completely paid off, because you have those seven cards, each with a $3,000 credit limit, you have already been granted $21,000 in credit. Should you choose to, you could run all those cards to the limit, severely affecting your ability to repay your mortgage. So don't accumulate cards indiscriminately. Instead, choose the cards that do you the most service, and stick with one or two. You don't need store cards. They charge the highest interest. Go into your wallet now and cut them up. Everyone accepts Visa or MasterCard.

Did you know that when you borrow money to make an investment, the interest on that money is tax deductible? Let's say you sold some stock to pay off a $2,500 debt at 17%. You'd be saving $450 a year in interest costs. If you borrowed $2,500 to buy back that stock and paid 10% interest on the loan, that loan would cost you about $250 a year. And since the interest on a loan for investment purposes is tax deductible, you'd actually end up paying far less — up to 50% less — in after-tax dollars. Assuming a marginal tax rate of 40%, you could pay off your high-cost debt, have your stock, and still save $300 in interest.

Don't be so concerned about having a security net that you fail to use your resources to your best advantage. Start thinking about your money in terms of your overall net worth, rather than just two categories: how much you owe and how much you've saved. Get rid of that high-cost debt in small steps or large, and then you can reallocate the money you would have paid in interest to asset accumulation. Look at the big picture and then make the decisions necessary to paint that big picture black.

It's not unusual for people to borrow for what they feel are good reasons, only to find that over time they have grown a nasty amount of debt they find hard to cope with.

*If your debt is costing you more than your savings are earning, cash out and pay off.* If it sounds like I'm repeating myself, that's because I am. This is a crucial point. I do not mean to say that you should use your RRSP savings to pay off your debt, since the tax bite to cash out would make the whole exercise far too expensive. However, if you have unregistered savings such as a savings account, GIC, Canada Savings Bonds, or mutual funds that you've been putting aside, pay off your debt and start saving again. If you're still not convinced, here's my last shot at getting you to see your assets and your debts as belonging in the same pot.

Let's say you have a $5,000 loan and $5,000 in a GIC. The loan has an annual interest rate of 9%, and you're earning 4% on the GIC. If you keep the GIC for a year, you'll earn $200 in interest. But you'll have to pay tax on that money. Assuming your average tax rate is 30%, you'll pay $60 in tax so you'll end up with $140 in your pocket. The loan will cost you $450 this year, so you'll end up paying more than three times more in interest on the loan than you earned on your GIC. But if you used the $5,000 GIC to pay off your $5,000 loan, while you'll earn no interest, you'll also pay no interest and you'll end up ahead by $310. Got it?

Another way to reduce the cost of your debt is to *transfer your high-cost debt to a lower-rate loan.* This is called refinancing, and there are many ways to do it. You can take a consolidation loan and pay off all your existing loans so you have a single monthly payment each month. You can refinance by renegotiating an existing loan to a lower rate. Or you can apply for a lower-interest-rate credit card and transfer the balance on an existing card to the new card. It doesn't matter how you do it, just *do it!* It is obviously better to pay 10% on a loan than 17%. Yet so many people carry high-cost debt. Take the case of Paula. When she came to me to ask for advice, she had a $3,000 Visa balance, on which she was paying about 17%. She wasn't even aware that other cards charged as little as 9.9%. I told her to apply for a Canada Trust MasterCard and transfer her balance. She did and now she's working on becoming debt-free. Of course, this strategy only works to your advantage if you put those credit cards on ice until the loan is repaid. If you go out merrily charging away, in no time at all you'll find yourself in an even deeper hole with both a loan and a balance on your cards.

### HAVING TROUBLE MAKING PAYMENTS?

Personal debt is an enormous problem in North America, and the level of debt continues to grow dramatically. In the U.S., the outstanding amount of installment credit in 1945 was $3 billion. By 1959, it had risen to $39 billion, and by 1973 it was $148 billion. By 1989, personal debt in the U.S. was at $674 billion. But that's the U.S., right? Canadians aren't nearly as debt-oriented as Americans, right?

In 1971, the per capita personal debt in Canada was $2,205. By 1990 it had risen to a whopping $15,467 — an increase of over 700%. In 1995 Visa and MasterCard balances rose 13% over the previous year to $17.4 billion.[14] Clearly, Canadians are in much the same boat as our American cousins when it comes to accumulating debt.

Laurie Campbell of the Credit Counselling Service in Toronto says it is a myth that low-income earners are the ones spiralling out of control financially. "It is Canadians as a whole," she says. "We're neck and neck with the U.S. in terms of bankruptcies." Even more startling is that "104% of Canadians' [net] income is going toward paying off debt. We're in a credit crisis." And since Statistics Canada says that about 50% of people pay off their credit cards each month, those who don't must have huge credit balances to produce such high average levels of debt. Laurie says there is a direct correlation between the number of credit cards a person has and the amount of debt being carried. "The more credit cards, the more debt. It's obvious. Very few of us can walk around with 10 credit cards in our pockets and have them all at zero balances."

---

14 Angus Reid, *Shakedown* (Doubleday Canada Limited, 1997), p. 207.

*Laurie Campbell is the program manager of the Credit Counselling Service of Toronto. Laurie has been with the agency for eight years and speaks often on the issues of credit and debt. She was involved extensively in the development of the education department within the agency and recently helped in the publication of* How Chuck Taylor Got What He Wanted, *a credit primer geared to high school students. Laurie is on the board and a vice-president of the International Credit Association. She, her husband, and their two babies live in Toronto and love walking Chloe, their big, wonderful mutt.*

It's far easier to get into debt than to get out of debt. Consider how you think about your debt. When your credit-card statements come in, are you more concerned about how much you owe in total on all your credit cards, or how much your monthly payments will be each month? Do you even know how much you owe on all your credit cards? Here's an interesting observation made by David Benner in his book *Money Madness and Financial Freedom* about the level of control debtors feel:

The more a person owes, the more they tend to believe that the events in their life depend on external circumstances rather than on their own efforts and abilities. This means that their financial affairs are experienced as beyond their control. Those more in debt also tend to not manage well under stress. They report a corresponding lack of confidence in their ability to manage their affairs.[15]

Clearly, financial freedom means being in control. Financial freedom also means freedom from financial stress. But to achieve this when it comes to debt, you must understand the difference between being reactive — waiting for the worst to happen — and being proactive — taking control of the situation and getting on with life.

If you run into trouble making your credit-card (or any type of credit) payments, *you can get out.* It may take some time, but you can do it.

Begin by calling the credit company and explaining the problem. If you've lost your job, or become ill and are not working, tell the credit

---

15 David Benner, *Money Madness and Financial Freedom* (Detselig Enterprises Ltd., 1996), p. 133.

company. If you are simply in over your head, tell the credit company. The important thing is to *tell the credit company*. They would much rather talk to you than send you nasty letters and wonder if they will ever be paid. You will probably be able to work out a repayment plan. You may even be able to negotiate with them to reduce the total amount you owe if you make a full payment. So here are the steps:

1. Contact your creditors and tell them what's happening.
2. Try to work out a payment plan that fits with your cash flow.
3. See if the creditor will take less if you agree to make a single repayment.
4. See if your bank will agree to give you a consolidation loan. By doing this you can save a good deal of interest.
5. Put yourself on a spending plan.

Whenever you fall off track, your credit rating gets bruised. If you want to be considered a good risk, you have to work at reestablishing your credit rating. One way is to get a secured credit card and make your payments faithfully.

**What happens if you don't deal with the problem?**
Debt collection practices vary from one creditor to another. Legal steps that can be taken are regulated by provincial law. As a general rule, repossession (seizure) of goods, garnishment, and other court actions are covered under provincial law, while bankruptcy is covered by federal legislation.

If you default and have offered collateral, creditors have the right to seize the goods and sell them to try to recoup their losses. Even if you haven't offered collateral, creditors may be allowed to seize other goods in order to recover the debt. You usually have plenty of notice and are given one last chance to clear up the debt.

A creditor may also apply for a court order to garnishee your wages or bank accounts. If a garnishment is issued, the creditor claims the money you owe directly from your employer or from the financial institution where your accounts are held. You may also be required to pay any court costs.

If the amount owed is quite small, the creditor may choose to sue you in small claims court to recover the debt. Larger amounts usually mean the lender may have to go to a higher court.

If you simply cannot carry on, you may have to declare bankruptcy, or you may be forced to do so by your creditors (see Chapter 24).

## PAY OFF YOUR STUDENT LOAN

On the day that I spoke with Barb Godin, she had spent the morning looking over the bankruptcy numbers. She says that a lot of the bankruptcies today are the result of student loan problems. "I don't believe that our youth today really understand what they are doing to themselves. They have a live-for-today attitude and believe that student loans are funny money and that you really don't have to repay them."

My husband, Ken, tells the story of repaying his student loan. The bank manager expressed surprise that he had bothered. He said, among his peers, practically no one repaid a student loan, so he was an anomaly. But Barb warns, "The rules of the game have changed. It really does matter. By defaulting — not paying — they take themselves out of the credit arena for up to seven years."

Aileen has experienced what Barb is talking about. When she and her husband married, she didn't give much thought to the $48,000 in debt he had coming out of dental school. He was a great guy and she loved him. When he defaulted on the loan and declared personal bankruptcy to get rid of the debt, she understood. She had watched him agonize about how he was ever going to be able to afford his own practice with this debt hanging over him. Five years later, life looked good. He was working as an associate at a walk-in clinic, she was well established in her marketing career and three months pregnant. They decided to buy a home. He would convert the ground floor to a dental office and set up on his own. She would go back to work after her maternity leave and everything would go on as usual. Aileen was stunned when she and her husband were declined for a mortgage. When they inquired as to the reason, the bankruptcy was raised. But that was five years ago, she said. Yes, but it stays in the record for seven years and it's out of our hands, they said. No one would touch them.

Barb believes that part of the debt-load problem stems from the fact that people aren't aware of just how much of an impact a default has on their financial life. Another contributing factor: the cost of going to school has increased so dramatically that young adults are leaving school with enormous financial burdens. Yet another contributor to the problem relates to personal responsibility. "Young adults are not understanding or accepting the responsibility that comes with borrowing — the explicit promise of repayment," says Barb. And as if all that wasn't wreaking enough havoc, banks jump into the fray. "If you are a student doing undergraduate or postgraduate work, everyone wants to give you credit. No one knows if you're going to repay or not, but everyone assumes that because you have this long work life ahead of you, you will continue to deal with the person who first granted you credit. So, without asking, you're inundated with credit offers. Or you fill out this credit form on campus and you check 12 boxes for 12 different credit cards and you get them all. And you think, 'My goodness, this is easy.' Everyone has the best intentions; everyone thinks he can handle it. Slowly the credit balances rise. It's easy to say, 'Well, the minimum payment is only $50 and I know I owe $100, but I'll catch up next month.' Next month never comes. And you get used to that. While you're in school you don't have to make any payments against your student loan either." So there it is, a pattern that begins to set: credit is easy. Repayment can be postponed.

"Then you graduate," says Barb, "and no one wants to give you credit. You've turned into a pariah because you only have a month or two on the job. And look at how much debt you're carrying." And remember you have to start repaying your student loans. And get that Visa bill paid down. So now you've finally entered the working world, and the bottom falls out. On top of rent, food, and all the other life-sustaining bills, there's a horrendous debt to repay.

There's no easy answer to this problem. Part of the responsibility clearly lies with the credit grantors in preparing students for their future need to repay. Barb says that lenders are now sitting down with students and their parents to "make it a three-way obligation." By having parents also sign, it increases the pressure on the young adult to repay the loan or, by default, the parents will be on the hook.

That may be the answer for the banks, but it certainly doesn't give parents or students any great sense of peace. Really, the question of whether or not to use credit — and how best to manage that credit — are the keys to staying financially healthy. Yes, it may be difficult to work and go to school at the same time. But will it be any more difficult than graduating $20,000, $30,000, or $40,000 in debt? How will a newly employed graduate deal with life's costs, which stubbornly continue to rise, and repay such a heavy financial burden? And we can expect the burden to grow even heavier. While the Association of Universities and Community Colleges reported that the average debt load for students who graduated in 1996 was $22,000, as tuition and other costs increase, that debt will increase. According to Statistics Canada, between 1985 and 1995, university tuition increased 134%. If costs continue to rise at the same rate, the current cost of about $9,000 a year is expected to spiral to a whopping $16,000 a year by 2005. That's almost $65,000 for a four-year degree. Then, of course, there are the costs of keeping body and soul together while your child is expanding his mind. We'd better start teaching our children about credit, how it works, and what it costs if we expect them to be able to use it successfully.

## A FINAL WORD ON USING CREDIT WISELY

Sometimes it's easy to forget that you have to pay for what you buy, particularly when you use credit cards for the majority of your purchases. If you want to stay in control of your finances and use credit wisely, here are some guidelines:

- Make a spending plan and stick to it. Make sure you know how much is coming in and how much is going out each month. Remember to include items that are paid less frequently (such as car and house insurance) or irregularly (such as dental bills).
- Get rid of extra credit cards. Everyone needs a credit card or two. No one needs three, four, seven, nine, or 12. If you have a department store credit card — approximately 52% of Canadians do, and women are more likely to than men[16] — cut it up. The interest rate is staggering, and you don't need the extra temptation.
- Avoid impulse shopping. If you had to use cash to buy the item, would you still buy it? Will you still want it tomorrow? Next week? Next month? Next year?
- Comparison shop for both the items you're buying and the financing

---

16 "Canadians and Credit," Ernst & Young, May 1996.

you're using. Never buy anything without comparing costs and value.

- Always read and understand any financing arrangements you are signing, particularly store financing arrangements. Understand how much the financing will cost, any fees attached, and any penalties you'll have to pay. Know how much interest you'll be paying in dollars.

- Be wary about co-signing or guaranteeing a loan for someone else. If that person defaults, you will be called upon to pay off the loan. Lenders are supposed to advise you of the risks involved in a separate meeting, but ultimately you are responsible for where you put your signature.

- Keep track of all your credit purchases. Save your receipts or keep a written record of credit-card purchases so you can compare them with your statement. Never just pay the statement off without checking it carefully. Mistakes can be made and you may be double-charged, or charged for items you did not buy.

# 9

# Establish a Pay-Yourself-First Investment Plan

*If a person was wholly rational there would be no drive to wealth, only a drive to meet the requirements for living.*

OTTO FENICHEL

*Men do not desire to be rich, but to be richer than other men.*

JOHN STUART MILL

*Money is one of the most useful contrivances ever invented; it is not its fault that some people are foolish enough or miserly enough to be fonder of it than of their own souls.*

GEORGE BERNARD SHAW

The single best investment you'll ever make is in yourself. It doesn't matter how much money you make in your lifetime, how much stuff you accumulate, how rich you *feel*, if you don't have some money put away for the future, you'll be in a pickle when it comes time to retire. That's where the pay-yourself-first investment plan comes in. Maybe you've already established one. It's either in your RRSP (my favourite; see the last section of this chapter) or in an unregistered investment account.

Now, I know that everyone likens a pay-yourself-first plan to a periodic investment plan that's invested in mutual funds of some kind. When I talk about a pay-yourself-first (PYF) plan, I'm talking about taking money out of your cash flow (to create savings) and putting it somewhere it can work for you (investing). That "somewhere" doesn't have to be a mutual fund. It can be a CSB. It can be a GIC. It can be an individual stock or bond. *It has to be something you are knowledgeable about and comfortable with.*

One of the biggest complaints I hear about the world of investing is that the jargon is stifling. Strips aren't malls. Convertibles aren't cars. TIGRs aren't wild animals. Why the whole different language? Two reasons: first, most professions use jargon to make life easier for the players in the game. Abbreviations are the main offenders in this department. It's easier to say MBS than mortgage-backed security, GIC than guaranteed investment certificate, and TIPS than Toronto 35 Index Participation Units. Some of the abbreviations, like GIC and DRIPs (Dividend Reinvestment Plans), have become pretty well known so most people aren't baffled. Others, like ADR (American depository receipt), PEAC (payment-enhanced capital security), and SPEC (special capital-gains security), are still used only within the industry and are sure to boggle the minds of "outsiders." And new shortforms are coming along all the time as new investment alternatives are created. Do you know what a BOOM is? How about WEBS, RTUs, or REITs? Take heart. Even the people closest to the products find it hard to keep up sometimes. That's one of the reasons you need a really good investment adviser by your side as you wade through the jargon and the proliferation of products available for investing your money.

To understand even the basics, you must take the responsibility to educate yourself. This is one of my biggies when it comes to taking control of your financial life. If you don't know what you're doing, the answer isn't to do nothing — or worse still, to give the control to someone else. The answer is to find out, get educated, read and learn, and then read and learn some more. You can't expect someone else to take care of your money as well as you would yourself. And you can't blame someone else when your investments go awry. *It's your money, so it's your job.*

After years of emphasizing that RRSPs are a form of registration, not an actual investment, I still have people telling me they *invested* in an RRSP. You can *contribute* to an RRSP, but since an RRSP is not a financial instrument, you can't invest in one. An RRSP is simply a form of registration. It's like having a big umbrella labelled "RRSP," under which you put all the financial instruments (stocks, bonds, mutual funds, GICs) that you're buying to make your retirement savings grow.

Why are people still confused? After all, each RRSP season we are absolutely deluged with RRSP information. Magazines, newspapers, radio, and television cover the topic in great detail, and we swim in advertisements and promotions from financial institutions that are scrambling to win our RRSP dollars. There are also dozens of good books explaining how RRSPs work and why you should have one, the best of which is *The RRSP Answer Book* written by . . . ME! So if there's so much "education" out there, why are there still so many questions?

While banks, insurance companies, and mutual-fund companies have paid great lip service to educating consumers, that education has been neither broad enough nor deep enough. Most educational material is presented in a highly promotional context, leaving out the issues or concepts that are perceived to be — and I quote one bank executive — "too complicated for the unsophisticated investor" — doublespeak for "they don't need to know that" or worse, "they just won't get it." Apparently, as consumers, we have more money than brains!

Advertisements are misleading, delivering only part of the information needed to make an informed decision. When the strategy of taking a large, long-term loan to catch up unused RRSP contribution room was initially being flogged, none of the advertisements addressed the difference between the interest costs on a single 10-year loan for $50,000 and several one-year loans for $7,000 each. As consumers, we're expected to be sophisticated enough to figure that out for ourselves. How about the cost to our cash flow and its impact on our ability to make current contributions to our RRSPs? Why bother? After 10 years, you could just borrow again and spend another $16,000 in interest catching up for the contributions you didn't make because you were busy paying off the first loan.

Everyone has to take some responsibility for Canadians' lack of education on money matters. Consumers aren't allowed to say "It's the banks' fault" because heaven knows you just have to visit the library and you'll find dozens of books on the financial topic you're interested in. But we also can't say that the financial services sector is totally without blame. After all, the rapidity with which new financial instruments are being launched, and the media blitz used to entice us into these derivative and often very complicated products is unprecedented in terms of dollars spent and influence on consumers. If consumers are going to be bombarded with BOOMs and intrigued by IPOs, these great new, wonderfully improved, fabulously whiter-than-white investments had better be accompanied by some clear, complete, and concise communication designed to educate consumers.

In some ways things are getting better. With the growth in mutual-fund sales, more people are beginning to understand what mutual funds are and how they work. And they are becoming less concerned about short-term volatility and more focused on long-term returns. This was clearly seen in the October 1997 slide and rebound in the market. Spurred by a fall in Hong Kong, markets in North America, Europe, and Australia took a nosedive. The following day, while Hong Kong continued to plummet, the other markets recovered quickly. No panic. No pain. When I asked my stock broker, Ann Richards, how much her phone had rung, she said, "Only about three times." Mind you, she was busy calling her clients to make sure they were okay. "Even those who were retired and living on a fixed income," she said, "seemed fine. They said, 'Ann, I'm not worried about this. Markets go up and down. I'm in it with a plan.'"

Ann is a really good broker and her clients' lack of panic is a testament to the time she takes to make sure she understands their objectives. And it's a testament to the time she takes to ensure her clients understand what they're investing in, what ups and downs they can expect, and how to stay on track to meet their objectives.

Thankfully, there are lots of good people out there willing to help you with your money. Your job is to find yourself a financial adviser who brings to the client/adviser relationship the experience and expertise, kindness and care, and thoughtfulness and thoroughness you need. (See Chapter 13 for more on how to establish financial relationships.) Thankfully, too, there are many investment options out there that even the most inexperienced consumers can grasp with just a minimum commitment of time and energy.

There's absolutely nothing wrong with starting out with the safe, tried-and-true investments that you're already familiar with. But don't stop there. Branch out. Ask questions of your banker, your broker, your personal adviser, your father, your daughter, anyone who can give you more information and help you spread your investment wings. In this respect, women

*Gerry Merkley has worked in the financial services sector for over 17 years, in roles ranging from financial counselling to investment product management, from retirement planning and education to vice-president of mutual funds for Canada's largest trust company. The mom of two young boys, Gerry knows first-hand that financial solutions must be both convenient and flexible. Gerry's work on developing risk-profiling programs gives her keen insight into the emotional barriers women face. "It's okay to be intimidated or over-whelmed by the choices, but it's not okay to let those emotions stop you from planning for your financial future."*

have it over men, hands down. We're more willing to ask for advice. We're more willing to question, to think about how we feel about something, and to want to know more.

## WHERE DO I START?

Having decided to take the plunge and invest, if you're not sure where to start, you're in good company. Gerry Merkley says, "It's very confusing for people. It's very confusing even for people in the business. With so many options, the first question inevitably is, 'How do you begin?'"

## PURPOSE

Gerry says your launching point should be to ask yourself, "What am I saving this money for?" Are you planning a holiday, planning to take time off work for school or to raise your family, planning to make sure you have money for retirement? People say one thing, but do another. Take the example of Alison, who religiously put money into an RRSP every year because she said she was planning for her long-term future. But each time Alison had an emergency, the first place she turned to was her RRSP. Out came some cash. So Alison wasn't using the RRSP as long-term savings for the future; instead, she was using it as an emergency fund. Alison told me how frustrated she was that no matter how diligent she was, her long-term savings weren't growing fast enough. She figured she was investing in the wrong things and needed to be more aggressive. She needed one of those mutual funds that would get her a zillion percent a year.

I asked her to show me her statements for the previous six years. There, in black and white, were all those small cash withdrawals Alison had made. The problem wasn't what Alison was investing in, the problem was that she wasn't leaving the money invested at all. She kept dipping in. She hadn't firmly decided what this money was for, or worse, she had decided that it was for emergencies.

To rectify the problem, I suggested that Alison put half her normal contribution into her RRSP, and contribute the other half to her newly established emergency fund, until she built up the emergency fund that she felt comfortable with. Now, Alison has an emergency fund that she keeps at about $3,500 (less than recommended but in keeping with her personal money set-point), and is back to making full contributions to her RRSP. Interestingly, since she established her emergency fund, Alison hasn't dipped into her RRSP once.

### Commitment to purpose

Gerry says the next question to ask is, "Is the investment touchable or untouchable?" This goes back, in part, to the purpose of the money (as in Alison's case). "The answer to this question will depend on your personality," says Gerry. Let's take saving for a child's education as an example. Some people may say it's touchable while others do not. "You really have to be truthful with yourself," says Gerry. When I asked if that's one of the areas where people often fall short — they're not as honest with themselves as they could and should be — Gerry replied quite tactfully and with a smile, "I would say so."

## TIME HORIZON

Time frame is also very important. If you're saving for a child's post-secondary education, whether your child is two or 12 will have an impact on the investments you choose. The longer you have until you will need to use the money — the longer your time horizon — the more time your investment has to even out its return. So you have to match your time horizon to the investment you are choosing.

What does the time horizon of your investment have to do with what investment you choose? GICs have no volatility and the return is guaranteed. You can't lose your principal and you know exactly what you'll earn in interest on the day your GIC matures. The same holds true for a bond or mortgage investment. So it doesn't matter whether you go long or short, you're guaranteed your return as long as you hold to the end of the term you choose. Equity mutual funds and direct investment in equities are a whole different kettle of fish. They can be quite volatile, with some offering more price stability and others offering more opportunity for growth. Either way, they don't work as short-term investments since they may be at a low just when you need the money and must sell them. They work as medium- and long-term investments, where you have time to ride out the highs and lows and average out your return.

Less than three years is considered a *short-term* investment horizon. Three to seven years is considered *medium term*, and seven years or beyond is considered *long term*. I tend to agree with those people, like James P. O'Shaughnessy, author of *What Works on Wall Street*, who see 10 years as the marker for long-term investments. That would make a seven-, eight-, or nine-year investment medium term and anything over 10 years long term.

Short-term investors should avoid putting the majority of their money in equity investments where the risk of losing that money is greater. Choosing fixed-income investments that generate a steady return while offering a higher level of security is a better idea. Medium-term investors can balance their investment portfolios by using both equity and fixed-income alternatives. Long-term investors have the luxury of time and can therefore choose an asset mix that is weighted more heavily with stocks and stock-based mutual funds. They have the time to ride out the natural volatility associated with the equities market.

Since no single investment offers the perfect opportunity for a high return, liquidity, security, tax advantages, income generation, and convenience, keep your specific goals and investment objectives clearly in mind. And as you get older, or as your personal circumstances or economic conditions change and your investment horizon shortens, you'll need to rebalance your portfolio's asset mix.

### RISK PROFILING

The proviso to all this is that you have to buy investments with which you're comfortable. You may have a long-term investment horizon, but if you're uncomfortable with the thought of your investment fluctuating in value, you may not be an equity investor.

"Once you decide your purpose — 'what am I trying to achieve here? what is my goal?'" says Gerry, "then it's a matter of doing a needs analysis [Gerry's term for what others in the industry refer to as risk profiling]. You have to find an analysis that's comprehensive, because what happens, and I'll use myself as an example, is that what you think you are, you aren't really. When I've gone through a superficial risk profile I've come out high on the tolerance scale. Like I'm a cowboy. But I'm not. I'm quite conservative, based on my detailed needs analysis."

Those quickie, four-question profiles that are administered by some financial institutions don't really help you to better understand yourself. After all, if a financial service's profiler tells you that you're growth-oriented and quite aggressive, you believe, right? You want to believe. But what happens when you're challenged by a slip-sliding market or a change in personal circumstances?

Gerry talks about the work done at Canada Trust in developing their needs analysis. "When we did the archetype on risk, we made it difficult. We insist people make choices. Some get fed up with these types of questionnaires because they say, 'Well, I can't answer these questions. They are too hard.' But you have to make choices. Six questions that rank you high, medium, or low risk aren't enough because if things don't go the way you expected them to, chances are you'll be extremely uncomfortable. If you don't have confidence in the [risk-profiling] exercise you went through, you won't stay the course. You'll do exactly the wrong thing at the wrong time. You'll panic and you'll bail out. If you're comfortable with your risk profile, you don't even look at the market. You're comfortable with your choices. So, find a needs analysis that takes you the extra step so that you are completely comfortable."

Remember, too, that everyone is a "person" first — even brokers. While we believe that those who we think are better educated, more in tune, or anesthetized to the volatility of the market should know better, they are people first and so they may act emotionally. I remember speaking with an investment adviser in late 1997 about how gold was doing. "It's in the toilet," she replied. I suggested that meant it was a good time to buy. (Remember the old adage, "Buy low, sell high.") Her response: "But it's in the toilet." She couldn't get past her own personal bias — her emotional baggage — to look at the opportunity a low gold price offered.

As Gerry puts it, "The logic and the emotion just don't come together."

## THE RELATIONSHIP BETWEEN RISK AND RETURN

I'm often asked to recommend investments — I never do this, because there is no way to follow up when investments or the person's circumstances change — and the request is always for something that pays a huge return with no risk. There is an old investment saying: "The greater the risk, the higher the potential return; the lower the risk, the lower the potential return." And there is no such thing as a risk-free investment. It's really all a matter of degree.

### What is risk?

Understanding risks and how to come to terms with them will take you a long way toward being a smart investor. Here are some examples of the risks associated with some pretty traditional investments:

- Stocks and stock-based investments like equity mutual funds can be volatile. *Volatility* is the investment's penchant for fluctuating in value over the short term. High-flying equity investments are typically associated with volatility, though you may be surprised at where volatility raises its ugly head. Industry-specific mutual funds, such as mining or technology, or funds that invest in small-capitalization companies can be very volatile. And even bonds can be volatile investments if interest rates start to swing up and down.
- All equity investments have some capital risk associated with them. *Capital risk* is the potential for losing some or all of the original capital investment.
- GICs and other fixed-income investments such as bonds and mortgages seem relatively risk-free, right? Think again. Interest-bearing investments suffer *interest-rate risk*. One risk is that interest rates will rise and you will be locked in to a lower rate (or that you'll have to sell your bond at a capital loss). Another is that if you've invested at a high rate, interest rates may be significantly lower when it comes time to renew.
- Well, at least there's your risk-free savings account. Wrong again! If

your investment's rate of return is the same as or lower than the current rate of inflation, this is called *inflation risk*, and the end result is that your investment will lose value year after year. Your money will be worth less.

Everyone measures risk differently since it is relative to our personal circumstances. While one woman may think investing $5,000 in a stock is an okay thing to do, another may balk. If $5,000 represents the second woman's total savings, or if it represents a substantial portion of her annual disposable income, she will be less willing to throw caution to the wind. On the other hand, if that $5,000 represents only 5% of an overall investment portfolio, the risks can seem a lot less serious.

When a loss would be deeply felt financially, the level of risk is much higher. Interestingly, however, the sense of risk decreases as the pot grows bigger and the odds improve. Would you invest $50 if you had the chance of winning $5,000? What if the jackpot were $500,000? Or $5,000,000? See what I mean? The bigger the pot, the more willing most people are to take the shot. Now, what about the odds? Would you invest $50 to win $5,000,000 if your odds were 100 to 1? If your odds were 10 to 1? What about 2 to 1? Most people would have no problem investing $50 for a 50% chance of winning $5,000,000. What would you do?

It's human nature to measure risk against the opportunity to win. The bigger the risk or potential downside, the bigger the opportunity for return needed to persuade us to go for the gusto. But we've seen that risk has another face that is not widely understood. What's the risk to you personally in not taking any chances, in always playing it safe? What's the risk in being so conservative that you end up losing ground year after year in terms of the real value of your money?

## DIVERSIFICATION

The key to building a healthy investment portfolio that gives a good return while minimizing risk is *diversification*: a little of this, and a little of that. Some stocks, some bonds, some GICs. A touch of foreign investment, a little tucked away in a money-market fund where it is easily accessible. By hedging your bets you'll protect yourself from negative swings in any one type of investment. When the stock market dumps and bonds glow, your bond portfolio will pull you along. When bonds dive and the market soars, your equity investments will save the day. And when Canada spirals while Europe, South America, or Asia skyrockets, you'll have enough invested internationally to keep your return balanced.

Whether you call it "asset mix," "investment mix," or "asset allocation," it's the same thing. It means diversifying by dividing your money among a variety of different types of investments. Asset mix usually falls into one of three groups: conservative, balanced, or growth-oriented. But within each of those three groups, there are many different sub-groups defined by very subjective criteria.

To illustrate my point: I consider myself to be fairly conservative. I'm more likely to buy blue-chip stock or a large-cap mutual fund than a mutual fund that focuses on emerging industries. Yet, if you put me beside a woman who wouldn't dream of investing in anything but GICs, I look pretty risk-tolerant. Stick me beside Gerry Merkley, who considers herself to be somewhat conservative but who believes small-cap U.S. is the way to go, and you have to ask, "What does conservative actually mean?"

It's also interesting to think about the fact that men and women do not benefit from the same asset allocation models in the same ways. While these models typically lump men and women together, our needs are different, so our models should also be different. Because women are more at risk for becoming principal providers of elder care and child care, because women live longer on a fixed income during retirement, and because women usually do not have the income expectations of their male counterparts, we *must* be more growth-oriented right off the bat. And we have to maintain a growth orientation for as long as possible. Equally as important is that we continue to save throughout our lives using new savings to rebalance our asset allocation as we age.

One misconception about asset allocation is that if you buy stock in several different companies, you will automatically be well diversified. This ain't necessarily so. To effectively diversify, not only do you have to buy stocks of different companies, those companies should be in different industries and in different countries. Here are five ways to diversify a portfolio:

- by the types of investments — using bonds, deposits, stocks, mutual funds, and real estate

- by the quality of the investments — the lower the quality, as rated by the industry (e.g., A bonds versus AAA bonds), the higher the return offered to offset the higher potential for loss
- by region (in Canada, North America, or global markets)
- by currency
- by levels of liquidity — holding some long-term deposits such as strip bonds or equity funds, along with some shorter-term investments such as Treasury bills

An illustration that is widely used to help investors visualize the relationship between the risk an investment holds and the return it generates is called the investment pyramid. Rather than use the pyramid, however, I'd like to present you with the following chart that more clearly shows the relationship between risk and return.

## RISK VERSUS RETURN

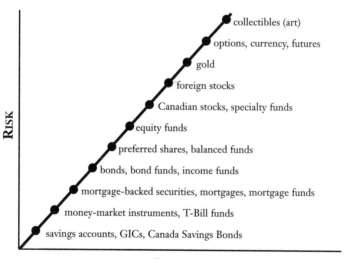

As you can see, most of the investment options that are traditionally used, such as savings accounts, GICs, and CSBs, are really low on the risk scale, and equally low on the return scale. Increasingly, investors are coming to understand that safety of capital should not be their only objective since the potential that the assets will not grow sufficiently to keep pace with inflation is as significant a risk. Assuming you invest $100,000 at 4%, you'll earn about $4,000 in interest a year. At an average tax rate of 30%, you'll end up with only $2,800. Your return would fall from 4% to 2.8%. In 10 years' time, at an average inflation rate of 4%, that $2,800 will be worth only $1,900. And inflation will eat away at the principal too — $100,000 will be worth only $68,000 in 10 years, and only $46,000 in 20 years.

As you move up the scale, the investments take on a higher risk profile, but also offer opportunity to enjoy higher returns. At the top of the scale are the most risky, with the highest potential return. Only the most astute and experienced investors, those with cast-iron stomachs, should play in this arena. But there is plenty in the middle for us common folk.

The asset mix you choose will have a direct impact on the return you earn on your portfolio. The more risk you are willing to take, the more return your portfolio may potentially generate. A typical conservative investment portfolio might hold 20% in cash, 60% in fixed-income investments such as bonds or mortgages, and 20% in equities. It's a portfolio that is geared more toward capital preservation and income than it is toward growth. A balanced portfolio would hold 10% in cash, and 45% each in fixed income and equities. Investors who want both income and growth, and split their portfolios 50–50 between fixed income and equities, are balanced in their asset mix. A typical growth portfolio would hold 10% in cash, 30% in bonds, and 60% in equities. Investors with this kind of portfolio are not as interested in generating income and are willing to risk far more in capital in order to potentially earn a much higher return.

Here are some figures to help put the whole thing in perspective. If you had $10,000 to invest from January 1970 until June 1995, here's how much you would have earned[17] if:

• you were a conservative investor, and went the route of complete capital safety with a high level of liquidity: $69,815.

---

17 Indices used — for cash: 90-day Canada Treasury bills; for bonds/fixed income: Scotia McLeod Long-Term Bond Index; for stocks/equities: Toronto Stock Exchange 300 Total Return Index; for foreign: The Centre for Research in Security Prices (USA) total return index in Canadian dollars. Source: 1995 Andex Chart.

- you were willing to take a little more risk and went the route of a balanced portfolio: $89,082.
- you picked the growth portfolio: $100,263.
- 20% of the equities in your growth portfolio were in foreign investments: $110,510.

The perceived level of risk associated with an investment depends on your personal ability to handle risk. Since risk is a trade-off for good return, you have to ask yourself how much sleep you are prepared to lose for the opportunity to wake up richer. Of course, there are some who choose to stay at the bottom of the scale, never venturing into alternatives such as fixed-income mutual funds, individual corporate bonds, or equity mutual funds. If you're one of these people, and you're doing it for the right reason — you have no stomach for volatility or for the potential capital loss, and you aren't concerned about inflation — then you should stay just where you are. As Gerry points out, most tools for risk profiling will emphasize the need for you to diversify, but there are always some investors who "need GICs because [they] just don't have the stomach for anything else, even though there is risk associated with that choice." For these investors, the risk that their return may be less than needed is a risk they can bear. What they can't bear is the idea of losing any of their money. These people, and those who are not aware of what they are investing in, don't understand the associated risks, or have good reason to avoid the risks we've been talking about, should stay out of investments such as equities. The lure of the potential return shouldn't be the focus of the decision. Remember what Gerry said right off the bat: Know your purpose in investing, understand your commitment to your purpose, know your time horizon, and perhaps most importantly, know yourself (your investment personality).

After a media blitz during the 1996 RRSP season, I received a call from a woman who wanted some advice. She had seen me on TVO's Studio 2, where I had been answering caller questions about mutual funds. She thought I was down to earth and wanted the real scoop on mutual funds. "Should I be investing in mutual funds?" she asked.

"Tell me about your situation," I responded.

"I'm retired," she said, "living on a fixed income. I have no dependents, no family at all. I'm getting about 2.5% on my money right now, and I'm not very happy with that."

"How much do you have to invest?"

"$400,000."

Wow, I thought. "How much are you falling short in terms of meeting your day-to-day needs?"

"Oh, I'm all right," she said. "I'd like more of a cushion, but I'm not touching my capital."

Again, wow. "Have you ever invested in mutual funds before?" I asked.

"No," she said.

"Why do you want to invest in mutual funds?" I asked.

"My friends are all into mutual funds. They think I'm stupid to be stuck in GICs at 2.5% when they're getting 15% or 20% in [equity] mutual funds. And my insurance adviser says that he can double my money in six years. He's recommending mutual funds really strongly. But I'm not sure about this at all. I need some help. Will you tell me what to do?"

"How old are you?" I asked.

"Eighty-seven," she replied.

I was stunned. She was 87 with $400,000 in capital and enough income to meet her normal needs. Before I even realized what I had said I asked, "And how rich do you want to be when you die?"

Looking back, it was a pretty blunt question. But she'd already heard me being pretty blunt for an hour on TVO so I guess she wasn't surprised. She laughed. "I knew you'd cut right to the chase," she said. "I guess I shouldn't bother with the mutual funds."

"Stay out of mutual funds," I said. "They are not for you. At your age, with your circumstances, all you need to do is get a slightly better return. You can get 5.5% on a CMHC bond. Would 5.5% be enough?"

"That would be perfect."

This conversation was interesting for a few reasons. First, she was thinking about investing in mutual funds without knowing what they are or how they work. The recent popularity of mutual funds has meant that more of our investment dollars have flooded into these investment vehicles. However, many people know little about how mutual funds operate. They don't understand the basic premise of mutual funds, or the types of investments different mutual funds hold. And they don't understand how changes in market or economic conditions will affect their mutual-fund holdings. They do know the results can be spectacular. They do know their brother, cousin, best friend, and next-door neighbour are buying them. They don't know that some of these people have no idea what they are doing. The result is that many people rush into investments and then rush out when the investment doesn't perform to their expectations, not realizing that mutual funds usually perform best in the long term.

## ECONOMICS 101

Whether you're thinking about investing or trying to decide if this is the right time to go shopping for a house, a basic understanding of economics will help in your decision making. According to a study done by the Canadian Bankers Association, approximately 67% of Canadians feel that if they knew more about the economy, they'd make better financial decisions.[18]

Patti Croft, vice-president of Sceptre Investment Counsel Limited, says investors "don't need to fixate on indicators such as quarterly growth rates, but should understand how those economic factors affect things like inflation, interest rates, foreign exchange rates and the Canadian dollar, and financial markets."

Economics seems to be a big mystery for most. I may go into the bank and hear that mortgage rates have just increased. They tell me that's because they're worried about inflation. But how are all these ideas linked and what do they mean to me?

As Patti says, "The beauty of economics is in its sheer logic." That logic isn't immediately apparent to those who are not initiated in economic theory. Patti draws a distinction between predictability and logic, which in part explains why no one ever seems to be able to say what will happen next. And Patti likes to talk about global economics because "Canada represents only about 3% of the global economy. The reality today is that what happens in Frankfurt, Tokyo, or Thailand affects us in Canada."

Inflation is one of the economic indicators that most worry investors. "Inflation is simply a measure of how fast the prices of goods or services that we buy are rising," says Patti. So when you hear on the radio or read

---

18 "The Economy and You," Canadian Bankers Association, 1998.

*Patti Croft was ranked #2 economist in Canada in a 1995 survey and was the youngest ever female economist of a major financial institution. In 1997, she joined Sceptre, where she wears two hats: chief economist and portfolio manager for over 100 high-net-worth clients. Patti appears frequently in the media as an economic commentator, and is on the board of Women in Capital Markets, which helps women network and become more aware of the opportunities in capital markets. Patti is a single mom of two boys and a girl, ages 15, 11, and seven. She enjoys all kinds of activities — aerobics, boxing, and Ashtanga yoga — but says, "The reality is, beyond work and the kids, there isn't much time left!"*

in the newspaper that the inflation rate this month is 1.8%, that means the cost of a basket of goods and services as selected by Statistics Canada is 1.8% higher than it was a year ago. Of course, not everyone buys the goods in that basket. And a big change in one item in the basket can take the average up or down without actually affecting consumers' budgets. Take, for example, what happened to the Consumer Price Index (CPI) when the heavy taxes on cigarettes were removed. We actually experienced a period of disinflation — inflation was negative for that period of time — because the price to consumers went down. However, if you did not smoke, you would have experienced no drop in the cost of your own personal basket of goods and services.

For those living on a fixed income, inflation means a reduction in your ability to meet your needs over time. A dollar worth 100 cents in 1971 saw its purchasing power fall to less than 25 cents by 1991. Increases in inflation often also signal increases in interest rates because lenders don't want to be left out of the loop when it comes to collecting rent on the money you've borrowed. But inflation can be battled, and your chief weapon is diversification. With a mix of investments, you can reduce your exposure to inflation risk by focusing on your real return.

Real return is the return you earn on an investment after you've accounted for taxes and inflation. Let's say you invested $10,000 in a GIC paying 4.25%. During the second year of your five-year term, inflation rose to 5%. While your certificate will earn $425 in interest each year (assuming it isn't compounding), your net return would be less than you would need to keep pace with inflation. To be able to have the same purchasing power, you would have had to earn $500. Now we have to figure in the taxes. With a tax rate as low as 20%, you would need a return of 6.25% on your certificate just to keep pace with inflation ($10,000 x 6.25% = $625 in interest – 20% for tax = $500). If you earned a return of 7.25%, your real return would be only 1%.

There's no point in patting yourself on the back for earning 12% if inflation is running at 10%, because your real return is only 2%. On the other hand, if inflation is only running at 2% and you have an investment paying a measly 6%, you're cool because although at first glance your return looks pathetic, your real rate of return is higher than in the first example.

People are also in the dark about interest rates and why they go up and down. As savers, we want to earn the highest possible interest. As borrowers we want to pay the lowest. High interest rates are good for people living on a fixed income. Low interest rates are good for businesses. Whether you're shopping for a loan or trying to decide where to invest, you need to consider not only the current rate, but also the direction in which rates are headed. That's demonstrated through what is called the yield curve.

"Yield curve is another thing that scares people," says Patti. The yield curve is a graphic representation of interest rates, at a certain point in time, for various financial instruments with different terms, from three-month Treasury bills to 30-year Government of Canada bonds. When long-term rates are higher than short-term rates, this is referred to as a *normal* yield curve. When long-term rates are lower than short-term rates, the yield is referred to as *inverted*. And when there's little difference, economists refer to that as a *flat* yield curve.

Where we are in the yield curve — normal, inverted, or flat — has implications for making our money grow through investing and managing our debt, as well as for the economy as a whole. For example, when interest rates are falling (when the yield curve is inverted), bond prices will rise, which is great for bond investors. An inverted curve means that money is in short supply, that there is great short-term demand, but that there is also a fear of assuming long-term commitments. "If you're shopping for a mortgage and the yield curve is steep, there will be a big difference between what you pay for a six-month mortgage and a five-year mortgage. That's how it affects people in their day-to-day lives," says Patti.

In late 1997, Canada was experiencing a steep normal yield curve. Three-month rates were under 3% and long bonds — those with terms of 10 years or higher — were at about 6.5%. So there were 350 basis points (100 basis points equals 1%) between short and long rates. "Historically that's a very steep yield curve," says Patti. "A steep yield curve usually indicates that with short-term rates low, the economy will grow fast down the road. We don't have to worry unless the curve flattens or inverts."

Canadian rates have wobbled from a high of over 21% in 1981 to a low of 3.25% in 1997. Why all the variability? Several factors affect rates, including global market forces, inflation, and monetary policy. From a market forces perspective, when more people want to lend than to borrow, the price of money falls. This drop in rates makes it less attractive to save and more attractive to spend. When more people want to borrow than to lend, then the price of renting someone else's money goes up. That makes it more attractive to save and far less attractive to spend, particularly if purchases are being financed.

Current rate and direction also influence how people invest their money. When rates are low, GICs, term deposits, and savings bonds are much less attractive, driving people to look for returns other than interest. The result: people turn to the market for capital gains and dividends. When rates skyrocket, people are less willing to assume the risk associated with equities because they feel they can get a comparable return on a completely secure interest-based investment.

Which brings us to another interesting question: Who the dickens are the "central bankers" we hear so much about, and do they have a purpose other than to make life miserable for investors? A central bank, like the Bank of Canada, is responsible for setting interest rates and controlling the money supply. When the bank tightens the money supply by raising rates, it wants to slow down the economy. When it relaxes the money supply by lowering rates, it is trying to stimulate the economy.

The bank rate is the lowest rate at which the Bank of Canada lends money to members of the Canadian Payments Association — our six major chartered banks and four other financial institutions. This rate sets the tone for all other short-term interest rates such as the rates your bank charges for things like your mortgage, your car loan, or your personal line of credit. The central bank monitors the state of the Canadian economy through numerous market indicators, including inflation, the exchange rate for the Canadian dollar, and employment figures, and decides when conditions warrant a change. In response to a change in the bank rate, the major banks usually alter their prime rate — the rate they charge their most creditworthy customers — which in turn affects the rate they offer everyone else for loans and fixed-term investments.

How does a change in the bank rate affect the economy? Well, when it costs more to borrow money, that cost at once slows spending and is a major factor in the increase in the price of goods. Consumers spend less because it costs more to buy the item on credit. Big-ticket items like cars are a perfect example of how even a small increase in interest rates can significantly affect the price. Manufacturers have to pay more interest on their credit facilities to carry on manufacturing and they pass that increased cost on through the increase in the price of their products. That increase in the price of the widget increases the price of the doodads being built with those widgets, which in turn increases the price of the whatchamacallits being manufactured from those doodads. Then consumers make the decision not to buy that whatchamacallit because they don't want to spend that much more on it. "Consumer spending is two-thirds of economic activity," says Patti. "If that slows, it means much more moderate economic activity." Let's follow the whatchamacallits a little further to see how this works. Okay, no one's buying whatchamacallits, so the people who make them decide to slow production, cut a line, lay off some workers. That means the people who make the doodads end up in the same position. Ditto the people making the widgets. Then, with scads of people out of work, there's not enough money going around to buy even the few whatchamacallits being made. Eventually, the whole economy slooows dooown too.

"As an economist," smiles Patti, "you have to combine psychology with science." The economics textbooks will tell you that the economy is $c + i + g + (x - m)$. The "c" represents consumer spending. In theory, consumers have jobs, they get income, they spend. "The psychology is the unquantifiable element: why they buy what they buy." Historically, consumer spending has been a key driver of the economy. That's why in the 1970s and 1980s when boomers were young and buying houses — and just about everything else in sight — they drove inflation up.

The "i" in the economic formula is investment spending — primarily

business investment spending on things like machinery and equipment —
that increases the productive capacity of the economy. The "g" is government spending. "While government spending used to make up quite a
large percentage of the economy, in the past few years we've seen a down-
sizing of our government at all levels. If government spending is in
decline, the economy goes with it." And Patti believes that "government
spending isn't coming back any time soon." The last part of the formula,
"(x − m)," stands for exports minus imports. That's our net trade.
"Exports are critical for Canada," says Patti. "We're called an 'open
economy' because so much of our economic activity is export-related. But
while we're exporting we're also importing the many things we don't
produce in this country." In the best of worlds, we'd have a trade surplus,
meaning we'd export more than we import. Trade surpluses and deficits
have an impact on the currency values of different countries.

Currency issues also have a tremendous impact on our economy.
There is no predetermined value for the loonie, so it is simply one more
commodity that can be bought or sold. If more people want to buy it than
sell it, the dollar goes up. If more people want to sell, it goes down.

Economists use something called purchasing power parity (PPP) to
help determine what the value of a currency is. "PPP looks at two countries and asks, 'At what exchange rate could I buy a Big Mac in the United
States and a Big Mac in Canada and have those expenditures be equal
given the current rate of inflation in both countries?'" Patti explains.
However, the perceived value of the currency doesn't always bear any
resemblance to the actual value in real life. Let's take the example of the
Canadian dollar. In September 1997, the Canadian dollar was perceived
to be undervalued. While most people believed, based on PPP, that the
Canadian dollar was worth about 80 cents, it was trading at only 72 cents.
The outlook: a higher Canadian dollar, just about anytime soon. But it
wasn't to be. By June 1998, the dollar had dropped even further, into the
68-cent range, and was still headed south. It would hit the very low 60s
before heading up again. "While we uniformly predict that the dollar is
undervalued," said Patti, "no one can predict when it will go back to the
neutral value" — the point at which it is neither under- nor overvalued.
Periods of undervaluation and overvaluation can last for many years
because currencies are affected by psychology. If the rest of the world
senses any instability in Canadian politics or the economy — as when

there's talk about Quebec separation — the dollar takes a beating. The other things that affect the value of our dollar include our trade balance, government policies, unemployment rate, national debt, and level of productivity, to name just a few.

In our yakety-yak about the value of the Canadian dollar, we're always comparing it with the U.S. dollar. Economists also closely watch the difference between the two countries' inflation rates. In September 1997, inflation in the U.S. was at about 2% to 2.5%, while in Canada we were under 2%. "We had been below the U.S. for about seven years. Historically, it is extremely unusual for us to maintain an inflation rate below the U.S.," says Patti. At the same time, interest rates in Canada were below U.S. rates right out to the 30-year area of the yield curve. "Implicit in the fact that interest rates are below the U.S. is a call on the Canadian dollar," says Patti. That "call" comes from the expectation that the value of our dollar would rise.

Another factor that determines exchange rate is based on the trade situation. The "capital account" is an estimate of how much interest and dividends we owe the rest of the world. Canada's large budgetary deficit of the past has been significantly reduced. But we still have a lot of foreign-held debt. "Every month we owe foreign investors the interest on the debt so we end up exporting capital." There is also something called the "current account," which includes the trade and the capital account flows. "The current account for Canada had been, until recently, in surplus. A current account surplus is usually associated with a strong currency."

To tie up some loose ends, let's look at how the central bank uses currency rates and interest rates to guide the economy. First, it is important to note that the central bank does not control where 10-year bond rates trade. Long-term interest rates are primarily a reflection of where investors believe inflation is going. If they think inflation is rising, they will demand a higher return on their fixed-term investments to compensate for inflation's erosion of their return and that, in turn, will push up long-term rates. But the central bank does "control call money rates and very short-term interest rates," says Patti.

"The head of the central bank worries when the Canadian dollar gets too weak, because it increases import price inflation, and gives too much juice to the export side of the economy." Exporters love a cheap currency because it drives up their business. But from a central banker's perspective it could make the economy overheat too fast, which could drive up inflation down the road. So when the Canadian dollar gets too weak, historically the Bank of Canada has stepped in and raised short-term interest rates in an effort to support the dollar.

So what economic factors specifically affect stock market investors? "The stock market is affected by growth of the economy. And by interest rates: with their decline they have really helped improve corporate earnings. But the other factors are more company-specific or industry-specific," says Patti. "If oil prices are weak and going lower, then you'll see the oil and gas sector being hit. If high technology is the flavour of the week, as we've seen in the United States, then that sector will do particularly well."

We often wonder what on earth is happening when we see a period of escalation in prices followed by corrections or falls in prices. "What's probably changed," says Patti, "is the expectation for the outlook for that sector or something that we call valuation: is the stock cheap or is it expensive?" According to Patti, the fundamental measurements we have used to say whether a market is overheated or not didn't apply to the market boom in the late 1990s simply because there had been fundamental changes in the economy. While many people have expounded on the overvaluation of stocks based on their high P/E ratios, Patti counters that "during periods of low inflation, the P/E ratio can rise very rapidly and still represent good value." The P/E ratio, or price-to-earnings ratio, is the relationship between the price of a stock and the company's earnings. Patti continues, "So when you hear that the market looks rich, it's expensive so you shouldn't get in, it's not just the market that's the issue." You have to look at industries individually, and then companies within the industry. You could have an industry that's flatlined — the sector as a whole isn't growing — but within that industry one or two companies are skyrocketing based on their individual financial pictures.

Looking at the details of the industry and company is essential, but you also need to take a macro perspective by watching the global economy. What happens in Japan, Europe, and elsewhere is reflected in the direction taken in New York. While countries once employed a certain amount of protectionism — supporting their own economies first — most of those protections are gone. Patti cites the currency problems in Southeast Asia as an example of how globalization comes into play. "Those are competitive devaluations. The Southeast Asian economies could no longer operate in the old regimes so their currencies had to fall in order for things to be balanced and for the countries to compete." The world truly is a global market and as investors we have to take that into account.

Since the market as a whole is not a good indicator of where money can be made, and unless you're buying an index you're not buying the market as a whole anyway, then how do you decide where to invest? Because no single investment offers the perfect opportunity for the highest return, full liquidity, and most security, we have diversification.

Remember diversification? One misconception people often hold is that if they buy several different companies' stock or several mutual funds, they will automatically be well diversified. This isn't necessarily so. To effectively diversify, you have to invest not only in different companies, but also in different industries and different countries. The same theory holds true for mutual funds. If you don't, you could suffer "deworsification" — an errant sense that you are diversified if you hold lots of different stocks but you haven't been judicious about spreading your assets over several industries, types of investments, or economies. All you have done is rendered your portfolio unmanageable.

## GAIL VAZ-OXLADE'S DOZEN GOLDEN RULES OF INVESTING

There are hundreds of different investment options from which you can choose when starting an investment portfolio. I've come up with twelve rules to help you decide among all these financial products. I'll begin at the beginning, with the most important rule of all:

GVO Golden Rule #1: *Know what you're investing in.* If you want to expand your investment horizons, learn all about the investments you're interested in before you buy them. That means you also have to understand the factors that affect your investments. Invest your time before you invest your money and you're more likely to be successful.

GVO Golden Rule #2: *Know yourself.* If you want to be able to buy the right types of investments for your specific needs, you must also understand your personal comfort level with regard to both risk and volatility. If you don't know who you are, the stock market can be an expensive place to find out!

GVO Golden Rule #3: *What you don't know can be just as important as what you do know.* But how do you know what you don't know? Good question. That's the Catch-22 most investors face when they are entering a new investment arena. The answer is simple: Ask tons of questions and read masses of information. Unfortunately, investing isn't the breeze most people would like to believe it is. If it were that easy, all the people working in the investment world would be stinking rich and living in Bora Bora.

GVO Golden GVO Golden Rule #4: *Accept the responsibility for your decisions.* If you can't live with a trade gone bad, don't make it. And be prepared to put a little work into the decision. You can't expect other people to take care of your money as well as you would. Remember, it's your money. And you shouldn't blame others for decisions you make — because ultimately, they are your decisions. So, follow the first three rules carefully, and make this rule the cornerstone of your relationship with all your advisers.

GVO Golden Rule #5: *Have a plan.* It's surprising how many people invest by the seat of their pants. Perhaps they rely on a broker's advice. Maybe they follow the financial press and buy what's hot. Unfortunately, without a specific plan many people may find themselves playing it safe or putting too much money in high-risk investments. Without a specific plan, achieving any goal at all is a hit-or-miss proposition.

You don't have to be a financial whiz to develop a plan. What you have to do is take a good look at what your priorities are, and then make some decisions about what you'll have to do to meet those priorities. If you don't have gobs of money to invest, a plan is even more important.

Planning begins with setting some goals. This may seem like an obvious first step. But do you have a written set of goals for your investment portfolio? If you don't, you should. Once you've set your goals, the next step is to develop an action plan to meet those goals.

GVO Golden Rule #6: *Invest monthly.* It's much easier to find $25 a month than it is to find $400 all at once. So let's say you're determined to make your maximum RRSP contribution of $6,000. Instead of borrowing from the bank at the last minute because you just couldn't save it all up, and then paying it back monthly with interest, pay yourself first. Open up a monthly contribution plan and slide money away in smaller increments that you won't miss quite so much.

Most monthly investment programs will allow you to contribute as little as $25 a month. My friend Victoria Ryce says that when she used to ask people if they could find just $25 in their spending plan that they could recycle to their "painless portfolio building," there were always lots of nods in her audience. In the case of the objective "to invest $1,200 in equities this year," you might choose to put yourself on an investment plan where you contribute $100 a month so that, at the end of the year, you will have accumulated your $1,200 almost painlessly.

GVO Golden Rule #7: *Make sure your objectives are realistic.* There's a great saying on Wall Street: Both bulls and bears can make money in the market, but hogs get slaughtered. While most people get excited when they see returns of 18%, 24%, or 36%, and the media love to highlight the 66% or 130% returns, expecting to achieve those kinds of returns year after year is unrealistic. If your objectives aren't realistic, you'll never be satisfied. Part of making peace with money is setting realistic objectives that are attainable, so you can pat yourself on the back. A realistic objective for investing is to earn an average of 12% over the long term. That's not 12% every year — it's an average return of 12%. If you beat yourself up over a couple of bad years, or raise your expectations after a couple of stellar years, you're not being realistic. Nor are you being kind to yourself. Remember, balance is the keyword of achieving financial freedom.

Investing is hard work. To be good at it you have to learn a lot of stuff, keep up to date with changes in products and economic trends, and have a strategy. By working hard, anyone can become relatively good at investing. And by setting realistic objectives, anyone can feel good about investing.

GVO Golden Rule #8: *Don't do it just because everyone else says you should.* If you follow the herd you're sure to step in a lot of cowpies. If you make an investment simply because it seems like the right thing to do, you're making the wrong decision. If you make an investment just because people say you should, you're making the wrong decision. If you ask plenty of questions and listen carefully to the answers, understand the investment well, understand your priorities, and weigh them carefully against the information you're getting, and make a decision that fits with your overall strategy, chances are you'll make the right decision. Remember the 87-year-old woman whose friends were cajoling her into investing in mutual funds? They had her fully prepared to make an investment that wasn't right for her, but with a little research (she called me!) and resistance to peer pressure, she avoided making the wrong decision.

GVO Golden Rule #9: *Don't try to time the market.* Yes, there can be a right and a wrong time to buy most types of investments. Buying equity-based investments after the market has been steadily rising for some time may not be prudent. Similarly, when interest rates are poised to go up, that's not the time to buy bonds. But market timing is a risky business and far too sophisticated and time consuming for us regular folk. Far better you invest regularly and average out the market swings. You can do that by dollar-cost averaging.

Dollar-cost averaging is a complex name for a simple investment technique. Rather than accumulating a large sum of money before making an investment, it is wiser to invest small amounts at regular intervals. Dollar-cost averaging means you don't have to worry about investing at the right time. However, for it to work effectively, you should use it as a long-term strategy — and stick with it! Don't let market performance shake your trust. It's a great system.

GVO Golden Rule #10: *Diversify.* Don't put all your eggs in one basket. Heavens, how sick are you of this saying? But it's true. If you spread the money around, you don't have to worry about losing it all in one fell swoop. And don't invest all your money in the Canadian economy. Investment in the world economy will help to reduce your dependence on our economic growth and a sometimes volatile Canadian dollar. It'll also allow you to benefit from strong economic growth in other countries or regions. By purchasing several different investments, you can build a well-diversified portfolio to reduce exposure to investment risk; if one investment doesn't do particularly well, the others may make up the difference.

GVO Golden Rule #11: *Stay the course.* If you find you are a little shy of the stock market, or you rank as conservative but decide to go into the market anyway, get yourself a buddy (preferably a financial adviser) who can hold your hand through the rough spots. A knowledgeable adviser will be able to remind you of your initial objectives and reassure you of what is happening so you don't make the fatal leap out of the market at just the wrong time.

And now, the final and most important rule of all.

GVO Golden Rule #12: *Keep a level head.* It's easy to get carried away, to forget the plan, to launch into an investment you don't really understand because someone else has made a killing. And it's easy to get scared, to want to run when everything seems to be turned the wrong way. It's good to keep reminding ourselves that the things we feel aren't real; they are just feelings. If you think your plan's gone awry, then sit down and review it logically. If you wish you were doing a little better, look at investments that might get you there: learn all about them, know the upsides and the downsides, and then make a levelheaded decision.

During one RRSP portfolio review, Ann Richards pointed out that while the market was up significantly, my portfolio had grown a measly 1%. Easy to get upset about, right? I didn't. I had a plan and I was sticking to it. I was holding Korea, which had gone right into the tank, and I wasn't about to sell. So I suffered a much lower average return than I normally would have. We did a four-year review to see how the plan was doing overall, and the figures showed I was earning about 12% on average over the last four years. That was my goal, so there was no reason to panic. Keeping a cool head let me look beyond the immediate circumstances of my portfolio. Looking at my long-term plan made it easy to see that I wasn't off by a mile. Looking beyond the immediate results, sticking with the plan, and keeping a cool head would all allow me to profit nicely as Korea recovered.

## RETIRE RICHER SOONER PLAN (RRSP)

One of the best vehicles for long-term savings is an RRSP. An RRSP is a tax-deferral plan registered with Revenue Canada. With an RRSP, you can deposit a portion of your earned income and claim the contribution as a tax deduction. Not only are the contributions made to an RRSP tax deductible, but the income generated by the investments inside an RRSP is not taxed until withdrawn from the plan. This means you can accumulate a much larger investment for your retirement than you could by investing outside an RRSP.

When you make an RRSP contribution, you receive a tax receipt to be filed with your tax return in order to claim your deduction.

Many people think an RRSP is an investment. It isn't. It is simply a way of registering your investments so they receive preferential tax treatment. Think of an RRSP like an umbrella. The investments you buy with your RRSP dollars — whether they are guaranteed investment certificates, mutual funds, stocks, bonds, or Treasury bills — are all held under this umbrella. As long as they remain under this RRSP umbrella, they continue to be treated in a special way. However, if you take these investments or cash out from under the umbrella — if you deregister them — they no longer benefit from this special tax treatment.

Anyone 69 or younger at the end of the year who has earned income may contribute to an RRSP. There is no minimum age restriction for establishing an RRSP, which means that even children may have RRSPs as long as they have earned income. If you are over 69 but still have earned income for RRSP purposes, remember you can contribute to a spousal RRSP up to the end of the year in which your spouse turns 69.

Contributions to an RRSP may be made at any time during the year, or within the first 60 days of the following calendar year. However, if you're turning 69, you must contribute before December 31, since your RRSP must be matured before year-end. Your RRSP contribution limit is the lesser of 18% of your previous year's earned income and the current year's RRSP dollar limit (set by the government). If you belong to a company pension plan or deferred profit-sharing plan (DPSP), your contribution limit may be reduced by your Pension Adjustment (PA) and, possibly, your Past Service Pension Adjustment (PSPA).

The notice of assessment you receive from Revenue Canada after you file your tax return shows your RRSP limit. If you can't find your notice of assessment, call Revenue Canada's computerized TIPS service. The telephone number is listed in the blue pages of the phone book.

If you decide to take the money out of your RRSP, you will have to pay tax on both the initial contribution and the income earned. Financial institutions are required to withhold tax. Outside Quebec, the rate is 10%

on the first $5,000, 20% on withdrawal amounts between $5,000 and $15,000, and 30% for amounts over $15,000. You'll have to include any amounts withdrawn in your income for the year withdrawn. The tax withheld is remitted to Revenue Canada and you will receive a T4RSP slip that you must file with your tax return showing the total amount of the withdrawal and the tax withheld. Once you file your tax return, the true taxes owing based on your marginal tax rate will be calculated, so consider yourself warned: you may end up owing more tax.

### What is a locked-in RRSP?

When an employee leaves an employer, taking accumulated pension benefits from the ex-employer's plan before retirement, those funds are usually transferred to a locked-in RRSP (also referred to as a "locked-in retirement account"or "LIRA"). This type of RRSP has limiting provisions attached to it. For example, locked-in RRSP funds cannot be withdrawn all at once. These funds can only be used to purchase a life annuity, Life Income Fund (LIF), or Locked-in Retirement Income Fund (LRIF) and cannot currently be used to purchase a Registered Retirement Income Fund (RRIF). These restrictions are in place to ensure the funds provide a retirement income as originally intended by the pension plan that provided them.

### What is a spousal RRSP?

A spousal RRSP is an RRSP to which one spouse (usually the higher income earner) contributes for the other. Revenue Canada recognizes common-law relationships for the purposes of contributions to a spousal RRSP. Now a spouse is defined as "a person of the opposite sex to whom the individual is married or with whom the individual has cohabited in a conjugal relationship for a period of at least one year, or less than one year if the two individuals are the natural or adoptive parents of a child."

A spousal RRSP belongs to the individual in whose name the plan is registered, not to the contributor. You can contribute as much as you wish to a spousal RRSP, up to your annual RRSP deduction limit, and your contributions to a spousal RRSP do not affect your spouse's contribution to his or her own RRSP.

Spouses who are eligible to make RRSP contributions should not contribute to their own spousal RRSPs. Since there may be significant tax consequences for making withdrawals from a spousal RRSP, spouses who wish to make contributions to RRSPs should set up regular RRSPs for themselves.

Between the tax-deferred compounding return and the tax deferral on the investment (often referred to as your tax refund), an RRSP puts your savings way ahead of the game. And you can use your tax refund to help supplement the growth of your annual contribution. Let's say you can afford to save $50 a month in an RRSP. Go ahead, put it away. At the end of your first year you'll have contributed $600. Assuming a marginal tax rate of 30%, you'll receive a tax refund of $180. When you get your tax refund, stick it in your RRSP for next year. At the end of next year, you'll have contributed $780 (your $600 plus the $180 refund you received). Assuming your tax rate hasn't increased, you'll get a refund of $234. Roll that into your RRSP, and in year three you'll have a total contribution of $834, for a refund of $250. And so on, and so on. All that growth without taking another nickel out of your cash flow!

# 10

# Risk Management: Your Income and Your Life

*The value of money is that with it you can tell anyone to go to the devil.*
ATTRIBUTED TO W. SOMERSET MAUGHAM

To achieve financial peace of mind, we need to prepare for the risks of everyday life. To a certain extent, we are quite good about protecting our "stuff," spending buckets of money on property and contents insurance. The risks we tend to overlook, however, are those associated with our economic earning power. If you or your partner were to die or become disabled and unable to work, would your family have the resources to meet their day-to-day needs? It's a tough question to face, but the consequences of not facing it can be even tougher on your family.

Whether you're looking at disability insurance or life insurance, what you are really buying is cash when you need it most. You're buying replacement for the income you would have had if you had not become disabled or had not died. And you're shifting the risk to the insurance company instead of assuming the risk yourself.

It's not unlike what happens within the life insurance industry when one insurer turns to another — called a re-insurance company — so that it does not have to bear all the responsibility and financial risk of a policy payout, particularly for large policies. By purchasing insurance you're doing much the same thing — reducing the risk to your own financial plan. While your emergency fund may be able to replace your income for the first six months, past that point you know there's no way you can support yourself and your family. So you shift the risk to the insurer and you pay a premium for this.

That's the objective in a nutshell. If you have no form of income-replacement insurance, you're betting that you'll just keep chugging along until you're a ripe old age. Wake up! If you're 30 years old, there's a 23% likelihood that you'll die before you reach age 65. And there's a 52% probability that you'll be disabled for 90 days or more.

Unfortunately, people seem to be completely unaware of the impact of not having coverage, the right coverage, or enough coverage. When you consider the media exposure of investments such as mutual funds, or the deluge of promotion that accompanies the RRSP deadline, the area of disability insurance is one that is pathetically underrepresented. One reason may be people's unwillingness to look at the potential downsides of life. This can't happen to me, right? Yet I know six women who are about my age who have been diagnosed with debilitating diseases such as multiple sclerosis and lupus. The growth of an RRSP, the phenomenal performance of the stock market, these are happy stories. Thinking about getting sick or dying is a bummer — so we don't do it.

But we should. It's part of our responsibility to those we love, and it's part of a healthy financial life. Think of insurance, any kind of insurance, as protection against two things:

1. The financial loss resulting because of an event that has a high probability of occurring.
2. The financial loss resulting from an event that may not have a high probability of occurring, but which would be financially devastating if it did occur.

"Most people don't appreciate the assets that they have in the form of their future earnings," says insurance specialist and financial planner Leslie Macdonald Francis. "If someone is earning $60,000 with a very modest annual increase, over 30 years that's a multi-million-dollar asset. It sounds corny, but it's like the old fable: *We* are the goose that lays the golden eggs."

So, let's look at risk. What's the probability of your dying or becoming disabled: one in 100; one in 80; one in 50? Do you know? Regardless of that probability, how adversely affected financially would you and your family be if the unthought-of, unprepared-for happened?

You have fire insurance, right? You've insured your car, your possessions, your home. Yet if you don't insure your ability to keep those home fires burning by insuring your income, your goose will be cooked. Quit procrastinating. You can't assume that it won't happen to you. And if your significant other is the primary breadwinner, you can't assume his continued health is guaranteed. Men like to think of themselves as invincible. My husband refers to it as feeling "bulletproof." Like Superman, right? Yet every day we hear stories of men who keel over in the prime of their lives. You had better make sure he has enough insurance so that you can take care of him, and the family, while he recovers.

If you're not convinced yet, here's a statistic to blow your socks off: According to the Society of Actuaries and the National Centre of Health Statistics and Transactions, each year, one in eight people become disabled. One in eight! What would your family do if one of the people bringing home the bacon couldn't anymore? Could you live on your savings? How long would that last, and what would the cost be to the future? Could you borrow the money? Your lender is more likely to call your existing loans, including your mortgage, than to lend you more money. Put all the pressure on your spouse? That's a great way to get a divorce. Tap your RRSP? What will you do when retirement arrives? Rely on the government? Yeah, right!

*Leslie Macdonald Francis was awarded the Calgary Life Underwriter of the Year award in 1994. She's been the chairperson for the Canadian Institute of Chartered Life Underwriters and the president of the Calgary Life Underwriters Association. She played an integral role in the formation of the University of Calgary's insurance and risk management program in 1990. A founder of Francis McLachlan Financial Group in Calgary, she's also a member of the Estate Planning Council of Calgary, the Pastoral Institute of Calgary, and the Business and Professional Women's Club. Leslie has two stepdaughters and a stepson, with whom she shares her passion for anthropology.*

## DISABILITY INSURANCE

Leslie Macdonald Francis is absolutely passionate about women's needs for disability insurance, largely because, as she says, after more than 21 years in the biz, "I've dealt with lots of disability claims but I've only had one death claim."

According to the Society of Actuaries' Commissioner's Individual Disability Tables, for the top occupation class, at age 35 the claim incidence rate is three times greater for women than for men. After 40, the gap in incidence of claims begins to close, narrowing to six percent higher for women by age 60.

The other frightening issue for women is that the incidence of divorce seems to rise sharply for women who become disabled. "This is something I heard in an industry seminar that really had an impact on me," says Leslie. "The probability [of divorce] is far greater when a wife is disabled than when a husband is disabled." You could put this down to men not having been socialized to be nurturers. More important than the why — because there's little we can do about the fact — is the realization that disability puts a significant strain on marriages, so every woman needs to be prepared to cope financially with this devastating situation should it arise. *Do it!* You owe it to yourself so you don't end up poor and alone. You owe it to your spouse so your sweetheart has the means to get the help needed to make your life more comfortable. Your partner should not have to bear the full financial and emotional responsibility alone. And you owe it to your children too. Is it important to you that they see you deal with your setback with dignity? Being prepared can only help. And it will send them the right message: that they must take personal responsibility for their own lives.

Choose four female friends that you know well, that are all around the same age as you. Write their names on a sheet of paper along with your own. There's a 65% to 75% chance that one of the people on that list will die before she's 65. Worse still, there's a 92% to 98% chance that one person on your list will become disabled. How sure are you that it won't be you?

When Leslie was reviewing my material on disability insurance, she was struck by how appropriate this illustration was and offered her own story. "I belong to a study group of four women who are all financial planners," says Leslie. "I'm the one that's most into disability, but we all offer it to clients and we all think about it. One of those women — a dear friend of mine — was diagnosed with breast cancer recently. Now she's had a full mastectomy and has done her chemo treatments. Here I am a perfect example of the one-in-five statistics."

According to the Commissioner's Table on Disability, at most ages there's a one-in-three chance of becoming disabled for at least six months before age 65. When that disability occurs, if it lasts 90 days, then the average length will likely be about five years. According to the U.S. Housing and Home Finance Agency, 48% of all mortgage foreclosures on homes result from disability. With the right coverage, you can avoid this. You'll be able to continue making your mortgage payments without having to use up savings or liquidate investments. Being prepared means those assets are protected, so you, your family, and your long-term financial future are protected.

**What to look for in a disability plan**
There's no question that you need the help of a qualified insurance adviser when you go shopping for disability insurance. Why? Because there are so many sizes and styles out there, it's very easy to buy one that looks good on the hanger but just doesn't fit. There is a lot involved in arranging an individual disability contract. Using a generalist will get you in trouble. Remember, too, that with insurance, as with just about everything else, you get what you pay for.

Leslie says that you should make sure, above all, that your disability insurance policy is *non-cancellable* and *guaranteed renewable*. It would be useless to buy a policy if the insurance company could refuse to renew it after one or two years. "This is such a fundamental issue," says Leslie, "because you don't want your contract to be changed. The definition of disability might become more restrictive, premiums might increase, or entire benefits, such as cost-of-living increases, might be eliminated." You would have bought a pig in a poke because despite all your comparison shopping, you could end up with a policy that looks significantly different from the one you bought.

The *definition* of disability is also extremely important. "If you think about a life insurance policy," says Leslie, "no one needs to define death. But when it comes to disability, the variables are almost unlimited as to what is or is not a disability, and how you define it, and when it begins and ends."

Maria was playing field hockey with her daughter's team when she fell and shattered her left wrist, thumb, and index finger. After several operations it became clear she would never recover the full use of her hand. As a left-handed endodontist, Maria was no longer able to perform dentistry so she decided to take a position at the local university. How does the change of occupation affect her disability insurance? Is she still entitled to a monthly income benefit even if she is working at something other than what she was originally qualified to do? Well, that depends.

The insurance industry basically offers three definitions of total disability, and they come with different price tags. The narrowest definition, and the one that carries the steepest price, is "own occupation," which considers an individual totally disabled if she is unable to engage in her own occupation, even if she is working at something else. Next down the price scale is "regular occupation," which considers an individual totally disabled if she is unable to engage in her own occupation and is also not working at anything else. "Any occupation" is the least expensive, as well as the broadest and least likely to pay should something go wrong. It considers an individual totally disabled if she is unable to work in any occupation for which she is reasonably suited by education, training, or experience.

While Maria may be earning a substantial income, under an own-occupation definition of total disability, she would be entitled to full benefits for total disability regardless of the fact that she is gainfully working in another occupation. If she had taken out disability insurance with a regular-occupation definition, her university employment would preclude her from receiving monthly income benefits because even if she remained totally disabled from her own occupation as a dentist, she is gainfully employed. If she had disability insurance with an any-occupation definition of disability, she would not qualify for monthly income benefits, except during the initial acute treatment phase of her recovery because, by virtue of her training, education, and experience she would be considered suitably trained and educated to hold a variety of other jobs such as lecturing at a university, consulting for an insurance company, or working for a pharmaceutical company.

Disability is a grey area. It is a matter of degree and debate. Are a fractured wrist and fingers totally disabling? It depends on your job. Will you receive monthly income benefits? It depends on the definition. Make sure you know what your insurance does or does not cover.

So find out how your plan defines disability. Must it be total? Is the determination made by your doctor or the insurer's doctor? How long must you be disabled before you'll begin receiving benefits?

Equally important is the *residual disability* feature. While some people become totally disabled, it is much more likely that you will be able to do some work, but at a lower income. In the case of a slow recovery or a slow deterioration from a progressive disease, this becomes very important. "If you don't have residual disability insurance, it could take five or 10 years before your claim can begin because you must have total disability," says Leslie. "I have a friend with MS and she's far from totally disabled. Some days she can walk better than others. It fades in and out. She seems to get much more exhausted than the rest of us. And a flu bug seems to affect her much more severely. But she's not totally disabled. If you're in this situation and do not have residual or partial disability coverage, you have no claim until you reach the point where you are totally disabled." Think of it on a scale ranging from black to white. If your ability to work whole hog is white, and total disability is black, residual disability represents all the shades of grey in between. Since most group plans have limited or no benefits for residual disabilities, you can be up a creek even though you think you're covered.

Some individual policies require earnings loss only, without requiring any loss of time or duties, which is much more restrictive. "This is a very important point," says Leslie. "The question becomes, 'what is the definition of residual disability?' One company might say it requires a loss of time or duties plus income. Another might say it only requires a loss of income. Look for a contract in which the payout is based on a loss of your income." Leslie cites the example of a young dentist who injured her back. She was still practising, but because she was not as effective due to her pain, she was only seeing half the usual number of patients each day. She had a loss of earnings, but no loss of time or duties. "Whether you are a doctor who can see only half the patients or a realtor who can handle only half the number of clients, your reduction in income should be the qualifier. If you bought a policy several years ago which required both definitions at the time, as long as you're in good health you should try to have the definition changed to 'loss of income.' Most newer, better-quality policies now base payout on a loss of income."

Make sure you also understand the *qualification period* in the plan. This is the number of days of total disability required before the insurer will pay residual disability benefits. A policy with a zero-day qualification period is best and means there is no requirement of total disability. Multiple sclerosis is a good example of an illness that may take years to create total disability. However, as the disease progresses, this could cause significant loss of income. The requirement for, say, a 30-day period of total disability would prevent you from ever being eligible for residual benefits, making your policy almost useless.

We all know that inflation is an evil monster that eats away at our money's purchasing power. Having an *inflation rider* or a *cost-of-living rider* is a good way to increase your monthly benefits. While this is an expensive "addition" to a basic policy, it is critical when you look at the long-term cost to your purchasing power when inflation is taken into account. At an inflation rate of 5%, today's $1,000 will be worth only $613.90 in 10 years, $376.90 in 20 years, and $231.40 in 30 years. So what looks like a healthy payout today may seem paltry in a couple of decades.

"An inflation or cost-of-living rider is different from a policy which is indexed, although they sound much the same," says Leslie. The cost-of-living rider is meant to increase your claim cheques after you've been disabled. Indexing keeps the protection level of your coverage up to what it should be while you are healthy. Sometimes called an update benefit, it is a way of keeping your protection level current.

Another way benefits might increase is under a *future insurability rider*. With this option, the insurance company periodically allows you to increase your benefits by quite large sums without additional health questions. "This is important for the young healthy person who anticipates there will be significant increases in income in the future," says Leslie. "While there are no additional health questions, and you don't have to disclose that you've taken on a more dangerous hobby, the increases do have to be financially justified."

There are a lot of i's to dot and t's to cross when it comes to making sure you have the best policy for your needs. Here's a case in point. When Maya bought her disability plan in her early thirties, she checked on the definition, the residual disability feature, and the qualification period. About 10 years later, Maya went through a difficult divorce and sought counselling from a psychiatrist. She was prescribed antidepressants, and over time, everything fell back into place for her. In her mid-forties, Maya decided to increase her disability coverage to keep up with her increased income stream. She was in for a shock. The insurance company felt Maya was too high a risk because she had been treated for depression, so her request for increased benefits was declined. Maya couldn't understand it. She was well past that. It had been almost five years since she had taken any drugs. Why was this coming back to haunt her now?

Are there exclusions for *pre-existing conditions* on the policy? If you are a diabetic, how would that affect claims for disability arising from conditions that could be linked to your diabetes? In the case of individual disability coverage you must declare all your health issues and then you will be covered, if you are accepted for coverage, that is. Nearly all group policies have pre-existing condition clauses. If you have a disorder before buying a policy, usually you will not be covered for disabilities related to this disorder. It's just as important to know what you're not covered for as what you are.

Another thing to look for is an *integration clause*. Some policies deduct the amount of benefits paid by Employment Insurance, Canada Pension Plan, or car insurance from the amount they pay out in benefits. This has advantages and disadvantages. It can mean that the premiums are lower. However, low-income individuals might end up with no benefits at all from their insurance policy until Employment Insurance sick benefits run out. "Also look for the use of the terms 'payable' and 'paid,'" says Leslie. If the term "payable" is used in your policy, then the insurance company can hold back the portion they expect you to receive from other sources. If it turns out that you do not receive that other income, the company will pay, but you'll have been out-of-pocket for the six months it takes the government to come to a decision.

Another way to reduce the cost of your premiums is to eliminate short duration claims or claims for periods when you are covered by an employer or by government benefits. Know that if you choose this route, you will not be able to make a claim until the waiting period in your policy — usually three or six months — has expired.

Do you smoke? Quit and you'll pay 10% to 15% less in premiums. To qualify as a nonsmoker, you must not have used any tobacco products for 12 consecutive months prior to applying for coverage. Another good reason to give up the evil weed!

**I don't have to worry about this, I'm covered at work**
How much do you know about your company disability coverage? Can
you answer these questions?

- How much are you covered for? Will your income from disability
  be taxed? Group policies paid for by an employer generate income
  that is taxed. If you pay the premiums directly from your after-tax
  income, your benefits are tax-free. Is your coverage sufficient once
  tax is taken?
- Is there a maximum? Group plans usually cover a percentage of your
  salary, but some also have a specified maximum.
- For how long will your benefits be paid? Most plans cover you for
  only two years if you can't work in your own occupation, shutting
  off completely if you are deemed by the insurance company to be
  able to do any type of work at all.
- If you leave your company, will you be able to take the plan with
  you, or would you have to requalify at your new employer? If you
  developed a problem in the interim, would you qualify?
- Are your benefits indexed to inflation?
- What's your policy's definition of "disabled"? If you can't do the job
  you were hired to do, will you be paid your benefits regardless of
  what other work you find?
- Can the insurance company deny you your benefits because they see
  you as fit to do any other type of work? Let's say you're currently a
  salesperson who must drive as part of your duties. If you cannot
  drive because of a sight problem, can the insurance company deny
  you your claim on the basis that, according to them, you could do
  any other work? Will partial benefits be paid if you can only work
  for a few hours a day?
- Can the company raise the premiums for one group of insured
  people and not for another? How will you be affected?
- What are the exclusions on the policy? Travel outside Canada?
  Pre-existing conditions? Previously treated mental, nervous conditions? Alcoholism?

One of the biggest distractions from individual disability coverage is the
fact that many people who benefit from company coverage think that

they're fully covered. And they figure that since the coverage is free, it's fine. Remember, you get what you pay for. The question you should be asking yourself is, "Does this come anywhere close to meeting my needs?" If you find your group plan lacking, look to an individual policy to supplement it. "Then you have a non-cancellable, totally portable policy you can take with you regardless of where you work," says Leslie, "along with rates that are fixed."

**It can't happen to me**

According to Statistics Canada, one in seven Canadians today have a disability. If you think accidents are the primary cause of disability, think again! Accidents represented only 21% of claims for long-term disability of three years or longer, according to Aetna Canada. Bone, muscle, and back problems caused 21% of claims. Circulatory system problems caused 8% of claims. Nervous system disorders caused 7% of claims. And mental disorders resulted in a whopping 15% of claims. Then there's a miscellany of problems like digestive disorders, ulcers, and the like that make up another 27%. Of course, there are many more causes — don't worry, I won't list them all — but you get the picture. Anything that has the potential to keep you from earning a living is a threat to your family's financial health. And you don't have to live with the threat. You can protect yourself. *Do it!*

## CRITICAL ILLNESS INSURANCE

Ever heard of this one? Me neither. Not until I spoke with Leslie about disability insurance and she urged me to include this related topic. So what is it? Well, it's the insurance you take out just in case you become critically ill. "It started in South Africa," says Leslie, "then moved to Europe. There are only five or six companies that offer it, but what really brought it home for me was that my associate had clients who were insured — the man fully, the woman to a lesser degree. After the birth of their last child, she was diagnosed with breast cancer. And before the baby made it to kindergarten, she died. So while she was going for all her treatments, her husband was unable to work as much as he ordinarily would. And there were all the additional costs."

When one spouse doesn't work outside the home, people often

don't think about the cost to the family of replacing the efforts of that person. Should mom get sick, the kids still need child care. Mom may need nursing care. There may be additional transportation costs and other extras that could make life easier for the whole family. "Money really makes a difference, and it doesn't fit into either life insurance or disability," says Leslie. This is a category all to itself. "What's unique about critical illness," says Leslie, "is that it will pay on diagnosis. You could be diagnosed with a critical illness and not yet be disabled from it. Or you could be someone in a wheelchair who has lump-sum costs to renovate your home. There are a lot of different concerns."

Critical illness insurance is intended to reduce the financial impact of a critical illness. It provides a lump-sum payout to deal with expenses not covered by traditional health programs, such as the costs associated with lifestyle adaptation, transportation, in-home care, and the like. You are insured against the likelihood of being diagnosed with any one of a list of serious medical conditions ranging from cancer to AIDS to heart attacks. The insurance pays off when you are diagnosed, so it is not tied to your ability to work and benefits are tax-free.

## LIFE INSURANCE

The protection of your assets is one of the cornerstones of a healthy financial plan. That includes your ability to earn an income. But the hot button of RRSPs — the chance to reduce your annual taxable income — is something people identify with much more easily. When people have, let's say, $200 to put away toward their financial health, they will tend to contribute all of it to their RRSP because of the immediate gratification. According to Kathy Farrell, former director of the Women's Financial Planning Centre, those people do not have a well-rounded financial plan. Instead, she says, "They should be allocating a certain portion of it to good-quality protection." Protection of what? Protection of your future income.

The term "life insurance" is a misnomer. After all, you're not insuring your life, you're insuring the economic value of your life, or your ability to earn an income in the future. It's a matter of taking care of one of the most important details of your life: your responsibility to make sure that those who count on you have been wise in their judgment.

A survey conducted by the Life and Health Insurance Foundation for

Education showed that more than half of Canadians think they don't know enough about life insurance. Even more alarming is that one-third of those with life insurance don't know what kind of policy they have. This is a perfect example of being so afraid, resistant, unwilling to deal with a difficult issue that we'd rather just stick our heads in the sand.

People seem far more willing to spend a mint insuring their stuff than to spend a much smaller amount insuring their future economic stability. Look at car insurance as just one example. My young friend Judy pays approximately $300 a month for her car insurance. At just 23 years old, Judy could buy a universal life policy for $300,000 for a premium of just $50.50 monthly.[19] And by the time she reaches 60, Judy will have accumulated $235,350 in assets through her plan.

Kathy Farrell sees four main reasons for people's resistance to life insurance. First, she says, "people don't want to face their own mortality." It's the same story with wills. People don't want to make a will because superstitiously they believe that once they take care of the details, the hand of fate will strike them down.

The second reason is that life insurance is intangible. It's not like buying an investment, where you walk away with a share certificate or an investment statement that shows what you have. The idea of creating a source of income to replace your contribution to the family coffers should you die seems far less concrete for many people.

The third reason is that people are very suspicious of the product, of the industry, and of the people within the industry. There's an image

*As the former director of the Women's Financial Planning Centre, and with more than 20 years of broadcasting experience, Kathy Farrell is especially well qualified to communicate with women and show them how to make the most of their money. While working, Kathy added the rigours of an MBA program to her hectic schedule. She is past-president of the Fellow Life Management Institute and a former member of the board of the International Association of Business Communicators. Kathy is wild about gardening and fiction writing, and is now focused on the pursuit of her personal dreams, surrounded by her Siberian irises.*

---

19 Figures provided by Kathy Farrell as at May 1998.

that remains from years ago, where life insurance representatives hounded you. Since life insurance is difficult to sell, that very well could have been the case. In fact, there's a saying in the industry that "life insurance is never bought, it is sold." People are afraid to deal with insurance people because they are afraid they are going to be coerced into doing something they don't want to do. And while it's often sold on the fear factor, that's just the kind of tactic that has people running away from the product.

The fourth reason for people's resistance is the fact that life insurance seems complicated. Will you need to have a physical? What special terms and conditions do you have to watch for? Will the amount you buy now be enough for the future? How much should you buy?

In combination, these concerns prevent people from addressing this key component of their financial health. Everyone pretty well accepts the fact that the worst time to buy something is when you need it — when it is *always* more expensive, or worse, unavailable. Life insurance fits this truism to a T. The best time to buy life insurance is when you don't need it: when you're young, when you're healthy, and when it costs less. It will be an asset that you will much appreciate many years down the road.

The thing about insurance — whether it is life or disability insurance — that makes it different from any other financial instrument is that you can't always get it when you want it. With practically everything else you can go out and buy it if you're willing to spend the money. With life insurance, if your health should deteriorate, as it tends to do when you get older, you may not qualify. Health underwriting is also more rigorous for higher-value plans.

Kathy Farrell says the single most important part of buying insurance is sitting down with a financial adviser that you trust. Because life insurance is a fairly complicated product, you need someone who can explain the differences. According to Kathy, you should be suspicious of anyone who starts off with a set amount you should have: "You need $100,000." And you need someone who begins by trying to understand your needs and concerns. What are the risks you are trying to cover? What are your issues? This person should be both able and willing to guide you through the alternatives.

Kathy and her husband first bought insurance when they purchased their home and wanted mortgage insurance. Kathy says, "At the time, I wondered if I had been swindled because, in my mind, we only had a short-term need. Our insurance representative was considered to be one of the best in the industry and he said it would give long-term value and we would always have a need. I more or less just went along, always questioning it in my own mind. Now that we're at this point in our life, it has very significant cash value. What I like best about it is that if our best-laid plans are sideswiped because we end up with unexpected financial needs, we can always access that policy. It's something you can literally take to the bank and they will give you 90% of the cash value. Or you can borrow against the cash value."

If you take care of the details, you may not end up rich, but you will end up with more options to help minimize the stress in your life and increase your personal freedom. Kathy believes that no one vehicle is better than another. "In my opinion, this is the single largest problem today. Because mutual-fund companies do a lot of advertising, people are solely focused on asset accumulation and on returns. They want the single best. There is no one single best. It's like mix-and-match clothes. You want to have a nice collection of things that complement one another and can perform double duty. Using a holistic approach like that gives you the benefits of synergy." Kathy likens the concept of investment diversification to the issue of life insurance and its place in your whole financial picture. We know it makes sense to hold a variety of investment types within our portfolios so that the underperformance of any one asset type doesn't have too much impact on the entire portfolio. Kathy says, "Insurance is such an important part of the formula because you are protecting your most important asset: your ability to make a living."

Whether or not you need to buy life insurance depends on a lot of things, such as:

- how much you currently have in the way of assets
- how much debt you have
- how much your family will need to make ends meet
- whether you're concerned about minimizing the tax impact on your estate.

The first thing to consider is why you even need insurance. You may not. However, if your death would cause economic hardship to others, you probably do. As a quick test, read through the following questions. If you answer no to any, you'll likely need some insurance.

Will your estate have sufficient funds to:

- take care of your funeral expenses?
- pay your accounting, legal, and probate fees?
- pay taxes owing at death?
- provide sufficient income to meet your family's day-to-day needs?
- eliminate any debts you have at death?
- provide for other areas of priority, such as the education of your children/grandchildren?

**How much insurance will I need?**

Here's a quick formula you can use to calculate how much insurance you'll need:

$$A - (B + C + D + E) = \text{insurance needed}$$

A = your family's Assets and income
(including existing insurance, a spouse's income, government benefits, pension income, income from investments [e.g., GICs, CSBs, mutual funds], income that could be realized from the sale of assets, etc.)

B = your family's monthly Budget needs
(including shelter, food, and household supplies, clothing, utilities, car maintenance, insurance [home and car], child care, entertainment, etc.)

C = Costs associated with your death
(including funeral expenses, accounting and legal fees, probate costs, estate taxes, etc.)

D = Debts to be paid off
(including credit-card balances, mortgages, loans, etc.)

E = Exceptional expenses
(including educational costs, vacations, major purchases [e.g., new car, medical equipment], etc.)

Begin by calculating the income your family would have, based on the current income (from pension, spouse's employment, etc.). To that, add the income that would be generated from your assets. A $25,000 GIC at 10% would generate an annual income of $2,500. And if you have an existing insurance policy that would pay out $100,000, if that money is then invested, earning a return of, let's say, 12%, it would provide an annual income of $12,000.

Once you know how much income your family will have, you then have to calculate the expenses it will face. Some of those expenses are one-time costs, such as your funeral or the payoff of existing debt, while others are ongoing, such as monthly expenses and educational costs. The discrepancy between what your family has and what it will need must be covered in some way if you wish to minimize the financial impact of your death. That's where the insurance comes into play.

In deciding whether or not to buy insurance, or how much insurance you should buy, look at each of these areas to analyze its impact on your family.

### What type of insurance should I buy?

Whether you buy "term," "whole life," or "universal life" insurance will be dependent on two primary factors:

* the amount of insurance you need, and
* how long you need that insurance to be in place.

Term insurance provides protection for a predetermined period of time (perhaps five, 10, or 20 years) or until a certain age, such as 65, 70, or 75. Think carefully before you buy insurance with age cut-offs: statistics show that you can reasonably expect to live past the age of 75, so if you're looking for longer-term protection, term insurance may not be for you.

With term insurance, when the term of the contract expires your coverage ends unless you renew the term. Each time the term is renewed, the premium is adjusted, usually upward. For example, you may buy term insurance that covers you until you're 65. Your policy may dictate that the term must be renewed every five years, so in five, 10, 15 years (and so on), you will receive notice of your new, adjusted amount. If you renew, you're still covered until you turn 65. If you don't, your protection is gone. The benefit paid by term insurance can be level, increasing, or decreasing; however, in most cases the face value remains level while the premiums increase with the risk of death.

When it comes to insurance with decreasing benefits, there are a couple of ways to go. Sometimes people choose bank-offered mortgage life insurance, the benefit of which is full payment of the mortgage upon death of the insured mortgage-holder. With traditional mortgage life insurance, while the premium remains the same for the term of the insurance, the benefit goes down as the mortgage balance decreases. As well, since mortgage life insurance is always paid to the mortgagor (usually the bank), you give up the control of how the money will be used. (Kathy Farrell says mortgage life insurance should be called "group creditor insurance," since the creditor is the person who is protected by the policy.) If your spouse should die, wouldn't you rather have a lump sum of money that you can then use to either pay off the mortgage or do something else? Perhaps you'll continue to make the mortgage payments from the proceeds of the insurance. Perhaps you'll move to a smaller home, or to a home closer to family. The ability to have your options open to you should be factored into your decision.

If freedom of choice is important to you, a private "decreasing" or "declining" term insurance policy might suit you more than a mortgage life insurance policy. Decreasing term insurance is similar to mortgage life insurance in that the benefit declines over the life of the policy. However, when premiums are reevaluated at the end of each term, they typically decrease; and what's more, you or your family, and not the bank, are always the beneficiary.

Think of term insurance as an expense. While it will give you comfort and peace of mind, it accumulates no residual value. If you're only after peace of mind, term insurance may be the ticket. If you're looking at the longer term, if you want coverage to last your lifetime or want to use insurance to build assets, term insurance isn't the right choice. And with term insurance, the statistics are all in favour of the insurance company.

Whole life and universal life insurance are permanent, remaining in place until death. With whole life policies, the insurance company does the investing. With universal life, you have much more control over the types of investments the money is going into.

With both these types of policies, the premium is generally the same for the life of the policy, so the annual cost can be low if taken early in life (when the risk of death is low), or very high if taken late in life. Most whole life policies have a "reserve," which can be refunded if you cancel the policy before your death. This reserve is referred to as the cash value of the plan. You can also borrow against this cash value at an interest rate set in the policy. However, if you haven't paid it back, the money owed will be deducted from the death benefit.

At a certain point, both whole life and universal life can become self-funding: the assets built up in the policy can be used to pay for the policy so that the cost to you is eliminated. That was one of the reasons why I bought my whole life policy at 30. I wanted to set the rate before I got any older or any sicker, and I wanted the benefit of having a policy that would eventually pay for itself. Since I had no idea at the time that I would end up with two children eight years later, in retrospect, my decision was brilliant. But over the years I've taken a pile of flack for having bought a whole life policy. Mostly the criticisms have centred on how much more I am paying for my insurance than I would have if I had purchased a term policy. To see the realities of the situation, I asked Kathy to do a calculation for me.

Let's say that Jane and Suzie, nonsmoking twins aged 30, are evaluating the costs and benefits of a $200,000 life insurance policy. Jane is considering a 10-year-term renewable and convertible policy with premiums of $294 a year. Suzie is looking at a whole life policy with premiums of $2,710 a year. Both want their plans to remain in effect for their whole life. Suzie's whole life plan is projected to become self-funding after 12 years. Here's how the numbers look:

| AGE | INSURANCE COSTS | |
| --- | --- | --- |
| | **Term** | **Whole Life** |
| 30–39 | $ 2,940 | $27,100 |
| 40–49 | $ 4,400 | $ 5,420 |
| 50–59 | $ 8,720 | 0 |
| 60–65 | $13,236 | 0 |
| Total costs | $29,296 | $32,520 |

Since Jane will likely live well past 65, she will need to switch to a whole life policy to avoid the age cut-off. At age 65 it would cost her $11,754 a year to convert her term policy to a whole life policy. Assuming Jane's whole life policy becomes self-funding in 11 years, Jane will have paid a total of $158,050 for the same benefits Suzie got for $32,520.

When I purchased whole life insurance, like Suzie I chose a $200,000 policy which was projected to be self-funding after 12 years. When I purchased my policy back in 1989, the premiums were calculated at just under $1,200 a year (less than half the amount Suzie would pay today). So my policy is projected to cost me approximately $14,400 for coverage for life. Compare that with the quote given to a woman shopping for term insurance coverage for her husband because they have a new family (her first, his second): they would have to pay $4,800 a year. And if he renews the term at 62 (his children will then be just 15 and 18), his annual premium for the next 10 years would be approximately $14,000 a year.[20]

So, back to the question, "What kind of insurance should I buy?" The best place to start is with the amount of coverage you need. Let's say you'll need $125,000 to pay off your mortgage, $5,000 to cover your funeral expenses, $15,000 to cover legal and accounting bills, and an additional $100,000 to cover the capital gains your estate will be hit with. All told, you'll need about $245,000. Buying a policy with a lower payout clearly won't serve your needs.

The next thing to look at is how long you'll need the coverage. Some of your needs may be short term, in which case declining term insurance may be the most cost-effective way to cover yourself. On the other hand, the need to meet your funeral expenses and minimize the tax hit on your estate is permanent. Whole life insurance will be your best bet here, because you won't die after your coverage ends.

Remember, the premium on your whole life policy will remain the same, while the premium on most term insurance will rise each time the policy is renewed. So while the cost of term insurance will appear far less expensive in the early years of a policy (if taken at an early age), you have to look at the long-term costs. Have your insurance salesperson compare the lifetime cost of both types of policies (remember to compare similar features and benefits), and then make your decision.

Another interesting fact: With some policies, you can buy the right to convert your term policy to a whole life policy at a later date. So if you

---

20 TD Insurance, quoted May 1998.

decide to start off with term insurance to protect your young family, and then wish to convert to a whole life policy when your needs change and you have more money, your health won't be a factor in setting the premiums. However, your age *will* be considered: The older you are, the more your insurance will cost.

Many people don't shop around for individual life insurance plans because they are covered by "group insurance" offered by their employer. But don't assume the group plan gives you the type of insurance or coverage that you need. One of the critical differences between a group plan and an individually owned plan is that with a group plan, you don't own the plan (your company does) even though you're paying a taxable benefit on that policy. Since you don't own the plan, you can't take it with you, and you can't convert it. So while you're covered for as long as you remain with the company, if you're wholly dependent on your group policy, you may find yourself out in the cold if you are terminated from your job (unless your group plan has a provision that allows you to purchase your insurance privately upon termination).

With more than 150 insurance companies in Canada, you *must* shop around when looking for life insurance. Get several quotes, make sure you're comparing apples with apples, and buy the policy that best meets your needs. Resist the urge to overbuy, but don't sell yourself, and your family, short either. Evaluate your future earning potential and your family's ongoing needs realistically, take inflation into account, and then buy enough insurance to meet your requirements.

When deciding which options, or "riders," to add to your policy, remember that each option will increase the cost of your premiums. Here are a few you may be presented with:

- *Waiver of premium.* If you become disabled (sick or injured), this option will waive your premiums but keep your coverage in place. Often this option is of little value because the definition of "disabled" is extremely restrictive, so few people qualify. Before you buy this option, make sure the definition of disability suits you. Also, see how the option is priced; it's usually very expensive. Rather than purchasing this option, consider buying disability insurance coverage — which you should have anyway — that makes allowance for maintaining your life insurance premiums.

- *Accidental death benefit.* This is often referred to as "double indemnity," because it doubles the benefit if death is caused by an accident. However, since your family needs a certain level of insurance coverage regardless of how you die, double indemnity often creates a false sense of security. Don't be tempted to buy only half as much insurance as you need, relying on the fact that if you die it will be by accident. Fewer than 8% of deaths among people 25 to 65 are the result of an accident.

- *Guaranteed insurability.* This is a guarantee that in the future you will be able to buy more insurance at standard rates despite a change in your health. The amount you can buy, and when you can buy it, are spelled out in the policy. Your option to purchase additional insurance usually cannot exceed the original face value of the policy. Remember that while you have the option of buying more insurance, you should only do so if your circumstances have changed and you need more insurance.

- *Increasing face value.* This option allows you to increase the benefit of your policy by a set amount each year; your premium increases with each increase in the benefit. Since the increases are provided automatically, you will be assured that your coverage has some inflation protection. And since there is no need for proving your insurability, even if your health circumstances change, you can still benefit from an ever-increasing face value. As well, with a locked-in schedule of premium increases, you can take advantage if rates are competitive, or decline the option if you feel you can arrange separate, less expensive insurance. This rider usually has an annual administrative fee, so it's only economical on larger policies.

- *Insuring the cash value of your plan.* If you chose this option, the death benefit paid will also include the cash value of the plan. This means that the policy provides an increasing benefit over time — good for inflation protection.

**Who owns what?**
So you've decided that insurance is an important part of your basket of goods, but you just can't get your better half to move toward the purchase. What now? I asked Kathy Farrell if you can take out insurance on a spouse. (This sounds like the plot for a murder mystery, as opposed

to a financial book, doesn't it?) Kathy says that as long as your spouse is aware and is in agreement, you can take out the policy, name yourself the beneficiary, and pay the premiums. You'll own the policy so any cash value will accrue to you. It is simply his life that is insured.

If you haven't yet considered the importance of insuring your future earning potential from the rigours of disability or death, I hope you're convinced now. Find a professional to help you assess how much and what type of insurance is just right for you. Remember, you'll need a person who is knowledgeable and experienced in the type of insurance you are seeking. That person should be willing to provide you with quotes from more than one insurer, and should be willing to explain the ins and outs of the wide variety of features available.

Ultimately, we all hope to live long, healthy lives that are challenging and full of joy. When circumstances change in ways that threaten to rob us of that joy, or present us with challenges we never imagined, the last thing we need is to be financially challenged at the same time. If you haven't yet faced the possibility that you might become disabled or die, the time has come to take a long, hard look at the statistical realities. The cost of insurance is nothing compared with what your family will pay, both emotionally and financially, if you are not insured and your worst nightmare becomes a reality.

# 11

# Taxes, Taxes, Taxes

*Taxes are what we pay for civilized society.*

OLIVER WENDELL HOLMES, JR.

*Taxes are the sinews of the state.*

MARCUS TULLIUS CICERO

Everybody pays too much tax. It doesn't matter how much or how little you pay, it's too much. Since the introduction of personal income tax in 1917 as a temporary measure to pay for the expense of World War I, our income-tax burden has increased steadily. In 1992, we paid over $100 billion in taxes. But taxes, like a lot of other things in life, are a reality. Everyone in Canada who earns income above a certain level is taxed on their Canadian income, as well as any income received from outside the country. Knowing how to deal with taxes is the ticket to ensuring you keep more of your hard-earned money in your own pocket.

While Canadians report tax on a calendar-year basis, the deadline for filing a personal tax return is April 30 of the following year. Scads of people leave it to the very last minute. You shouldn't. Leave yourself some breathing space to make sure you've claimed everything to which you're entitled and to check your arithmetic. And if you owe money, you'll need to figure out where that money will come from. Minimizing your taxes isn't something you do on April 30. It takes planning. Tax planning should start in January, not April. While you'll have to deal with last year's taxes in a few months, you still have all of this year to plan for your next year's tax bill.

Canada uses a progressive tax rate system. As your income increases, the rate of tax you pay also increases. Your taxable income is calculated by adding up all your sources of income and then subtracting certain deductions to come up with your net income. So, if you earn $36,000 a year, you would pay 17%[21] in federal tax on the first $29,590 you earned, and 26% on the remainder up to $59,180. For those who earn even more, the tax rate is 29% for amounts over $59,180.

It's not only the feds who tax our income. After calculating your federal tax payable, you must then add the provincial tax. While British Columbia charges 51% of the federal tax, a surtax of 30% applies to amounts in excess of $5,300, and there is an additional surtax of 24.5% levied when your provincial tax exceeds $8,745. In Newfoundland, you'll pay 69% of your federal tax as your provincial tax. As you can see, the rates vary by province, so check with an accountant for the rates and special surtaxes applicable to your province.

There are a number of deductions and credits that can be claimed to reduce the amount of tax you have to pay; it is by taking advantage of these claims that you can avoid tax. *Avoid* is a very important word. While tax *avoidance* is a perfectly acceptable way to minimize tax, tax *evasion* is a violation of the law. Since the tax laws become increasingly more complex with each passing ruling, it is very important that you check and recheck to ensure you're reporting fully and accurately.

*A word of warning:* Just because you get advice from Revenue Canada doesn't mean that you can go ahead and follow that advice, assured that you're well within the rules. *Revenue Canada's representatives can't be held accountable for the information they provide.* The idea of seeking advice from those closest to the whole process seems like a logical one. If you aren't sure whether your deductions or your business setup are within the confines of the tax man's rigorous restrictions, it would seem natural to go straight to the horse's mouth for the answer. And you would assume, of course, that you could bet the farm on that answer. However, there is a

---

21 All figures given in the tax section are based on the 1997 tax year.

long-established principle of law that disallows taxpayers from seeking refuge from a negative assessment simply because they were guided by Revenue Canada's advice. Comments from officials are not binding. So, if you're not sure where you stand, you would be well advised to check with someone who really knows the answer: an accountant or a well-experienced tax lawyer.

The way to pay less tax is to keep more of your taxable income in the lower tiers, so you pay a lower percentage of tax and you don't get hit by the surtaxes. You do that by maximizing your deductions. One of the best ways is to contribute to an RRSP. If you're making $50,000 a year, you have an RRSP contribution limit of $9,000. If you contribute the full $9,000 to an RRSP, you'll essentially reduce your taxable income by that amount. Instead of paying over $16,500 in tax, you'll end up paying only $12,781.50 — a tax saving of $3,718.50 — and your $9,000 can remain on a tax-deferred basis inside your RRSP for when you need it. You'll also have an additional $3,718.50 that you've kept out of the tax man's hands to do with as you wish. You can take a well-deserved vacation, make a principal pre-payment on your mortgage, start an unregistered investment plan, or roll it right into next year's RRSP contribution. Whatever you decide, you'll have been smarter to keep the money for yourself than to send it to Revenue Canada. I bought my first car using the tax refund from two years' RRSP contributions. From my perspective, the government bought me the car. I paid cash. No finance charges. The cost to me: a little deferred gratification. The benefit: I still have the RRSP which provides a nice little nest egg for the future.

The most common mistakes people make when filing their returns are in not claiming all deductions and credits for which they are eligible. The information you need to make sure you pay as little tax as possible is laid out in Revenue Canada's tax guide. Take the time to read it, from cover to cover, highlighting those things that are applicable to you. If you don't read the whole thing, you won't know what you may be missing. It's not the most stimulating reading in the whole world, but you have lots of time if you start now. Keep a copy in the bathroom along with a highlighter pen, and when you get 10 minutes away from the kids, start highlighting. If you're not a bathroom reader, pick another place where you spend 10 minutes a day and work through the guide slowly. Having read it through at least once, you're more likely to identify opportunities for taking advantage of the credits and deductions that come up when you change jobs or make changes in your personal circumstances.

A deduction reduces your taxable income. A $200 deduction for moving expenses may be worth between $54 and $100 in tax savings depending on your marginal tax rate. A credit is a direct reduction of tax, so a $200 credit is worth exactly $200 to you. However, most credits are included in calculating your basic federal tax. Since provincial tax and surtax are calculated as percentages of your federal tax, credits end up being worth more than their face value because they reduce these "secondary" taxes as well. Now, some credits are refundable and some are non-refundable. If credits are refundable, they are always worth what they say they are. So even if you end up paying no tax and you have an outstanding credit, the tax man will send you some moolah. However, non-refundable credits work more like deductions because they become non-existent if it ends up that you pay no tax at all. Note, though, that some credits are transferable, so your spouse may be able to use them if you can't. (Also, in some cases, if a dependent child can't use a credit it may be transferred to a supporting parent.)

## File a Return Even If You Don't Owe Any Tax

People often think that because they don't have to pay any tax, they shouldn't bother to file a tax return. If you're one of those people, you may be losing out on an opportunity to build yourself some RRSP deduction room, which you can use to offset any tax you might have to pay in the future. To build RRSP contribution room, you must file a tax return to show earned income. It doesn't matter how small your income is, and it doesn't matter that there's no tax owed. As long as you have earned income, you will have eligible RRSP contribution room that you can carry forward, at this point, indefinitely. That can translate into a deduction when you do have sufficient income to pay tax. Making the contribution is even better. While there's little point in claiming the RRSP deduction when you owe little or no tax, you will benefit in two ways. First, any contribution can compound to produce what can seem like a magical amount. Second, the RRSP tax deduction can be carried forward and claimed when your tax bracket goes up so you get the biggest bang for your buck. Most young people who are just starting out at their first jobs have little extra income to make an RRSP contribution. It can be a challenge just making ends meet. But small amounts are all that are needed. An annual contribution of just $200 (from age 21 to 65) to an RRSP compounding at 12% will generate a tidy sum of over $300,000.

Suppose you did your return and then found out that there were credits or deductions you could have claimed but didn't. The first thing you should do is check your Notice of Assessment to see if the smart people at Revenue Canada caught your mistake. *You should always review your Notice of Assessment in case a mistake was made.* Remember, those guys are human too. Assuming your error wasn't caught, the next step is to call Revenue Canada and see if you can recover those deductions or credits. This may entail filing a Notice of Objection — a time limit of one year applies, so heads up. Ask the Revenue Canada people to guide you through the process, or consult a tax specialist for help.

### Waiver of interest and penalties

Believe it or not, there are times when the tax man leads with his heart instead of his hammer. Revenue Canada recognizes that there may be times when extraordinary circumstances prevent a person, despite his or her best efforts, from complying with the Tax Act. So, at his discretion, the Minister (and, of course, his representatives) may waive any interest or penalties that may have accrued. What qualifies as an extraordinary circumstance? Natural disasters, civil disturbances, disruptions in services — read postal strikes — and the like. Also included are more humanitarian issues such as a serious illness or accident or serious emotional or mental distress such as that caused by a death in the immediate family. It also applies to situations where the tax department messed up: processing delays, errors in publications, incorrect written information, departmental errors, or delays in providing information to taxpayers. It's also interesting that if the tax man thinks you won't be able to pay your back taxes because you just don't have the bucks, he may waive the penalties and interest as part of his collection efforts. And if you might be able to pay back the principal, but the penalties and interest are so big that they prevent you from even starting, voilà . . . they can be wiped away, providing you keep to the agreed-upon repayment schedule.

## INSTALLMENTS

Lots of folks don't realize that they may be required to remit tax in installments during the year. Since most people have their tax deducted at source, they figure they're always on the right side of the tax man and are astounded when they are charged interest on tax owing. After all, how do you know you're going to owe tax before you complete your return? Under the law, you have to remit installments if the difference between the amount of tax you owe and the amount of tax that's been withheld at source is more than $2,000 in both the current year and either of the two preceding years (the three-year rule). So if you have alternative sources of income from which no tax is deducted — let's say tips earned, a second job, income from self-employment or, in my case, royalties — it's your job to make sure the tax man has his fair share on time. And on time doesn't mean when you file the return. It means quarterly: on the 15th of March, June, September, and December.

To figure out how much your installments should be, calculate how much income you'll have from your other sources from which tax hasn't been withheld. Let's say you earn an additional $7,000 a year in tips and your marginal tax rate — the rate at which you pay tax on the last dollar you earned, or your highest rate — is 30%. Then you'd owe $2,100 for the year. Divide that by four, and you'll see that your quarterly remittances should be $525. Another alternative is to take the balance you had to pay last year, and pay that amount in four equal installments. Remember, no matter how it shakes out, if you owe, Revenue Canada collects. So if you guess wrong and still owe tax you'll have to pay interest on the difference between the amount you owed and the amount you paid, based on the three-year rule. The only time you won't owe interest is if you made installment payments according to the notices sent to you by Revenue Canada.

## VOLUNTARY DISCLOSURE OF UNFILED RETURNS

The tax department, in an attempt to encourage taxpayers to come forward and correct deficiencies in past tax filings, has a set of rules relating to voluntary disclosure. If you've never filed a tax return, and you do so voluntarily, you will only be required to pay tax owing on your reported income along with interest. In other words: you will incur no penalties and no prosecution. You'll have to pay the total amount of tax and interest owing according to an agreed-upon schedule.


## What to Do If You Are Audited

Could there be anything that strikes more fear in a taxpayer's heart than the word "audit"? Almost everyone has heard a horror story about a friend of a friend being reviewed with a fine-toothed comb. And, unfortunately, even people who have had advice directly from Revenue Canada can find that advice overruled when the tax man cometh.

Most people file their returns without anticipating that anything more will be said. In 1996, 214,519 people found out just how an audit feels. And 1.3 million people were subject to a variety of other verifications. Cumulatively, they had to pony up over $5 billion more in tax.

So, what exactly is an audit and should you be petrified? What we think of as an audit can be as simple as a request for additional documentation to support a deduction or as complex as a full-fledged review of your taxes for the previous five years. In fact, the audit can start long before you're contacted, such as when doctors' incomes are compared to provincial health plan payouts, or waiters' tips are compared to the average tips on credit-card slips in the restaurant where they work. If something looks suspicious to the tax man, an audit ensues.

If you're informed that your taxes are being reviewed, the first thing to do is ask for a letter of notification from the Audit Group so you can see what they want. If you have a tax adviser, get advice immediately. Respond promptly to your notification since Revenue Canada allows a specific number of days for your response. Need additional time? Ask for it. Whatever you do, don't ignore the request. It won't just go away. And if they think you're obfuscating, watch out.

If it comes down to a meeting with the auditor, your behaviour will be a critical factor in the outcome. Don't be confrontational. Co-operation and credible presentation of the facts will go a long way in your favour. Be frank and open in your responses but do not volunteer information. Give the tax man what he asks for and no more.

If it ends up that Revenue Canada disallows a deduction and sends you a notice of reassessment stipulating the amount you owe, you can challenge the reassessment by filing a notice of objection with the Appeals

Division. You must file your appeal within 90 days of the date on the notice of reassessment or within one year of the original filing date for your return, whichever is later. However, you'd be wise to pay the amount for which you've been assessed in the interim to avoid the accumulation of interest should things not go your way. Don't worry, paying up is not an admission of any sort so it won't prejudice your appeal.

Back to the question of how scared you should be. That depends on how honest you've been thus far. You're not likely to be prosecuted for tax evasion if your claim has been based on an honest difference in opinion on how the rules apply. But if the tax man concludes that you deliberately underreported your income or overstated your deductions, you're in for it. Tax evasion is punishable by a fine of up to twice the tax evaded — that's in addition to the tax you owe — and a prison sentence of up to two years.

# 12

# Wills and Powers of Attorney

*I loved you, so I drew these tides of men into my hands and wrote my will across the sky in stars.*

T. E. LAWRENCE

*A man's dying is more the survivors' affair than his own.*

THOMAS MANN

A lmost everyone should have a will. Unfortunately, many people think they don't need one. Research done by the Trust Companies Institute in 1992 showed that only half of Canadians have a will. Some people think their wishes will be carried out by a family member. Others feel they don't have sufficient assets to justify the cost of making a will. And some people simply avoid making a will because their personal circumstances — marriages, divorces, and accumulated children and stepchildren — just seem too complex to unravel. If you've delayed seeing a lawyer about a will because you believe it's not worth the expense, let me assure you that dying without a will is far more expensive than the cost of drawing one up.

Few people understand the estate rules set out by provincial governments, and the implications and costs associated with dying *intestate* (without a will). It is enough to say that if you die without a will, trying to figure out who gets what, and when, is often an unholy mess.

Consider making a will as soon as you begin to accumulate assets. This will ensure that your assets are distributed as you would wish. If you are married or in a non-traditional partnership, you and your spouse or partner may want to have your wills drawn up together so that they reflect an integrated estate plan. Your will may need to be amended or redrawn whenever there are changes in your personal or financial circumstances or if you wish to name new executors or beneficiaries. Review and update your will every three or four years or when:

- family circumstances change. Weddings, divorces, births, and deaths all result in changes in family structure.
- financial circumstances change. Increases or decreases in financial assets may necessitate changes to the will.
- new legislation is implemented. This may have a significant impact on the existing will.
- there are changes in residence. If you change your province of domicile, update your will to ensure compliance with the rules and regulations of your new province.

If you die intestate, your estate is distributed according to the laws of the province in which you were domiciled. (Your domicile refers to the location of your chief residence, where you intended to remain for the rest of your life.) Your probatable assets are frozen until the courts appoint an administrator to oversee the sale of the assets and distribution of the estate. Your funds can be frozen for months while the estate issues are being resolved; these delays can cause financial hardship for surviving family members, who would be deprived of the use of those funds during that time.

A will can minimize delays in the administration and distribution of your estate, since your executor can begin to take action immediately. You can specify who gets what and when. (In some cases, the provincial family law legislation can override provincial distribution formulas, or even override your will. In Ontario, the terms of a will can be frustrated by certain spousal rights under the Family Law Act.) You choose the best person or trust company to represent you as executor of your estate. You're in control, even from the grave.

Your executor or estate trustee is the person (or trust company) you appoint in your will to ensure your testamentary wishes are honoured and your instructions are followed. Your executor or estate trustee must be of sound mind and must have obtained the age of majority to act. Trust companies are the only organizations eligible to be named as executors. An executor can be a beneficiary or a witness. However, a beneficiary should not also be a witness because, while the will is still valid, any gift to the beneficiary will be void.

Through your will, you can also appoint guardians for children who are minors. While such an appointment is only temporary, without it the appropriate government agency may become the guardian of your children until an application to the court is made to appoint a relative or other person. This can be painful for the kids and a sure cause of fights within a family.

To make a will, you must have reached the age of majority — among the exceptions to this are people under the age of majority who are married or who have been married — and have "testamentary capacity." This means that you must have sound mind, memory, and understanding, and must clearly understand that you are making a will that is disposing of your assets. You must understand and recollect the nature and relative value of your assets and understand the claims of those you may be excluding from the will.

There are several circumstances that may affect the validity of your will. Your will may not be valid if:

- you made your will while under the influence of alcohol or drugs (so that you no longer have testamentary capacity)
- undue influence is exerted on you in making the will
- the will was executed under duress or coercion.

## WHO SHOULD DRAW UP THE WILL?

Although you can draw up your own will, or use a standard form, don't. While some may feel that lawyers are simply being protective of their industry when they say you need professional help, the fact is that estate law is a complex beast.

Hilary Laidlaw has seen many cases where home-executed wills have been invalidated because of the way they were executed. While a holograph will (one that is completely in your handwriting and signed by you) does not have to be witnessed, a formal will must be witnessed by at least two people. Hilary says, "I've seen cases where a preprinted will form has been filled in and signed, but has not been witnessed. It is neither a formal will, because it has not been witnessed, nor is it a holograph will because it is not wholly in your handwriting." Then there are the cases where people have typed and signed what they believe to be a holograph will so that everyone will be able to read it, totally invalidating it as a holograph will. Another common mistake: Nothing written after the signature forms part of any will, so a postscript doesn't count.

While the language of a will may seem opaque and redundant, Hilary says that it is used largely because much of it has been around for years and its effect is tried and true. However, there is a move afoot to put the language of wills into plain English. Until then, you're still better off letting a professional who is familiar with the technical rules and requirements draw up your will so you can be sure it is valid. An estate lawyer can also help you focus on the important issues, so that your real intentions are translated into the legal language required. "The mistake made most often," says Hilary, "is that the testator's wishes are not clearly expressed and the time it takes to sort them out can be interminable." Let's say I draw up my own will and indicate that I want my husband, Ken, to have all my money by writing, "I want all my money to go to my husband, Ken." Hilary asks, "What do you mean by 'money'? Do you mean your cash? Do you intend to include the money in your RRSP? Do you want to include any debts owing to you? If you mean all the money in your bank chequing account, what happens if you move banks?" As you can see, "money" can have myriad meanings. That's where the guidance of

*Hilary Laidlaw has focused her professional life as a lawyer on estates and trusts. A former partner at McCarthy Tétrault, where she practised for 10 years, Hilary now works with Canada Trust as managing director of estate and trust development. Motherhood has strengthened her commitment to educating both the public and her professional peers about the consequences of poor planning. She is a frequent lecturer, writer, and media guest, but it is with her husband and son — at home, travelling, or sailing — that she's the real star.*

someone who does this day in and day out can be invaluable.

Just as "money" can mean a dozen different things, so can the term "household contents." Do you mean to include your grandmother's antique pearl brooch? What about the collection of paintings hanging on your walls? Perhaps you don't mean to include the car in your garage as part of your household contents. "It is a matter of context," says Hilary, "including the testator's personal circumstances. One person's financial status may be such that those paintings are simply considered part of their household effects. For another, the collection may be their primary investment — in effect, their 'money.' Either way, intentions must be clearly stated to avoid ambiguity."

The naming of a beneficiary is another area where lack of clarity can cause problems. Imagine you haven't seen your sister Laura for 20 years. If you choose to leave a bequest to your sister Martha, but in your will you simply refer to your "sister" without using her name, guess what? You can't assume that it is implied that you are leaving the bequest to Martha just because Laura isn't really in your life anymore. But with an experienced estate lawyer at your side, you'll be able to avoid these ambiguities.

When you hire a lawyer to draw up your will, you are reducing the risk of misunderstandings and minimizing the delays and costs associated with sorting out those misunderstandings. Here's another example: Hilary warns that when you use a term like "children" or "issue" in your will, it applies not only to your children and remoter descendants born within marriage, but those born outside marriage as well, even if you don't know about them. And it applies to children who have not yet been born at the time of your will, unless you state otherwise.

A lawyer will also help you plan for how beneficiaries will respond to the will. If you have two children to whom you are leaving your family cottage, will one want to sell while the other wants to keep the property? How will you structure your will to eliminate the fighting over what should be done with the property? The same holds true for a business that is being passed on to children. If only one child has taken an active interest in the business, but you leave it to all the children equally without further clarification, who will decide if the business is to continue being run or be sold? How will the child who has invested time and energy in running the business feel if the business is sold "out from under her"?

Often a lawyer can help you in choosing your executor and in deciding the breadth of powers you wish your executor to have. If you've established a trust under your will, your trustee will need to be able to invest that money. However, there are restrictions on what trustees can do in terms of investing if you do not broaden the scope of their authority. For example, without clearly stating that mutual funds are permissible investments for your trustee to make, mutual funds may be forbidden for two reasons. First, most mutual funds are not exclusively invested in trustee-authorized investments (read bank-issued investments such as GICs). Second, by investing in mutual funds, the trustee is arguably delegating the authority for investing to the mutual-fund manager, working against the maxim of law that says, "A delegate cannot delegate further." While there is a bill before the legislature which would remove the legal list (which outlines what investment alternatives are legally allowed), replace it with "a prudent investor" standard, and specifically authorize investment in mutual funds, if you wish your executor to have this authority under current legislation, you should include explicit wording to this effect.

If you're well prepared for your meeting with a lawyer, the process should go smoothly and the cost should be quite manageable. Before you start, do a little research. Most large law firms have a will booklet that will guide you through the process. Trust companies, too, have similar materials you can use as a primer. These booklets often include a list of the information you need to bring with you so that you are well prepared. Call ahead and ask that one be mailed to you.

In preparing for your will meeting, you and your spouse should discuss your financial details together before you go to see a lawyer. You each have a right to know where you stand, and you should both have a say in how your joint assets will be distributed. Make a list of your personal information, including your full legal name, any other names by which you are known, your address, social insurance number, date and place of birth, name and date of birth of spouse and children, marriages (all of them), and existing wills, trusts, and powers of attorney. List your assets, estimating their value. Indicate assets for which a beneficiary designation has been made, or assets that are held in joint tenancy (since these will be distributed on your death independent of your will). If special bequests are to be made, prepare a list of items to be left to particular individuals or organizations. List your liabilities and any insurance provisions you've made to eliminate those liabilities.

## NAMING YOUR EXECUTOR

Before the meeting, think about who your executor should be. Your executor is the individual appointed to administer the terms of your will, and is responsible for assembling and protecting your assets, handling tax requirements and filings, and distributing your estate, among other things.

You can appoint a sole executor to act alone or two or more coexecutors. And you can make a contingent or alternate appointment in case the first appointed executor cannot act. Some people choose to name a friend or family member because these people are familiar with the personal details of their lives. Since Aunty Val knows and loves the kids, she's the perfect person. However, rather than being an honour, being named as executor can be quite an imposition. It can be an extremely time-consuming job. Without financial or investment knowledge, some executors feel out of their depth. If your executor is too emotionally involved, that can impede the whole process. Also, get the agreement of the person you plan to name before you do so, since an executor can give up the right to act at any time before the will is probated and before he or she begins administering the estate.

The person you select must be of sound mind and must have obtained age of majority in order to act (a minor may be appointed as an executor, but can only act after having attained the age of majority).

Here are some of the people you might consider as your executor:

- *Partner.* Your spouse or life partner may be a good choice if the assets being transferred under the will are relatively uncomplicated. An estate made up of bank accounts, term deposits, a house, an RRSP, and pension benefits would not be difficult to administer if it were going directly to the surviving spouse. With complex assets (unless your spouse has special skills), or if there are testamentary trusts involved (particularly a trust that will pass on to your children after your spouse dies), consider appointing a coexecutor with expertise in investments, accounting, and tax. Remember, too, that this will be a very stressful time for your partner. Think about how able he or she will be in dealing with the emotions while dealing with the legalities of managing your estate.

- *Children.* Appointing adult children, either alone or with the surviving spouse, can have some advantages. Mature children may be familiar with the assets. Keep in mind, however, that unless they have had specific training in a profession such as law or accounting, children may lack the expertise to complete the administration of the estate. As well, appointing one, but not all, could lead to friction, even if you have good reasons for the decision.

- *Friends and business associates.* Age is a factor in choosing friends and business associates. Inevitably, these individuals tend to be about your age and may find themselves acting as executor at a time when they themselves may require help to manage their own affairs. Older friends may die before you, leaving you to name a new executor — another trip to the lawyer. Worse still, your executor may die during the administration period, in which case his executor — someone you may not even know — would take on the administration of your estate if you have not made provision for an alternate.

- *Family lawyer/accountants.* The family lawyer is often seen as a logical choice to be either an executor or coexecutor. Lawyers may be an appropriate choice if they have the time to devote and have a sound knowledge of estate law. However, unless they are set up to carry out estate administration, these professionals may not be equipped to manage investments and run complex trust accounting systems. Moreover, some lawyers prefer not to act as executors.

- *Corporate executors.* For an institution to act as executor, it must be a corporation licensed to do fiduciary, or trust, business. One of the main advantages of a corporate executor is that these companies have the expertise to handle the obligations. They also have the neutrality to make objective decisions that affect beneficiaries. Company representatives are available 52 weeks of the year so the estate administration won't be delayed because of illness, vacation, or business commitments. As well, these professionals have a wealth of experience, having handled thousands of estates. However, unless you have a pre-existing relationship with a trust company, they won't know your family. You may feel that a friend or family member would offer a more personal touch. Where there's good reason for a corporate executor, don't let the lack of a relationship deter you. Instead, make it clear that you expect your corporate executor to devote the time and energy necessary to get to know you and your personal circumstances so that when the time comes, they can deal with your family on a very personal level.

Choosing an executor requires a high degree of trust. You must be sure in your own mind that your executor will carry out your wishes as you intended them. And you should regularly reevaluate your choice as your life progresses and things change. Choosing the wrong executor can have serious ramifications.

Sally was a successful actress who, like many other artists, had given over the management of her financial affairs to a financial adviser. She felt she had neither the time nor the expertise to be bothered with the money part of her life. Unfortunately, she later discovered that her trusted financial adviser had been neglecting her affairs. Worse still, Sally didn't have nearly as much invested as she thought. When confronted, the financial adviser disappeared with most of Sally's remaining savings. Not long after, Sally died unexpectedly. Her will named as executor none other than the same rogue who had stolen from her. She had been so busy trying to sort through her financial mess that she completely forgot her will. Her family was left with the stress and complication of having this man removed as executor and dealing with the countless debts and liabilities that had been ignored. The whole process took several years, during which time the estate was virtually in limbo.

Estate planning also means thinking about whom you feel would be most appropriate as a guardian for your children. A guardian is someone who assumes the responsibility for your child until he or she reaches the age of majority. Hopefully, the person you name will never need to do the job. But that's no reason to ignore this detail. While your children may be minors, this is anything but a minor consideration. If you are a single parent, or if you and your spouse were killed in a common disaster, who would care for your babies?

The guardian you name is granted temporary guardianship of your kids. To make the custody legally permanent, the guardian must apply to the court. While the court is not required to appoint the guardian you have named, it usually does so unless there is a challenge to the appointment or a valid reason not to. If your kids are old enough to express their opinions, the courts often ask them where they would like to go before a final decision is made. If you have strong feelings about whom you would want or would not want as guardian for your children, make them clear in your will. That may help the court reach a decision that more closely reflects your wishes. Make sure you check with your intended guardian before you write it into your will to be sure that person is willing to accept the responsibility. Think about the kind of home life this guardian would provide. Would your children want to live with this person? Can this person afford to raise your children, and will your estate provide sufficient financial support to ensure no stress on the guardian's own financial resources? Remember, raising your own children is tough enough. Raising someone else's is an act of supreme kindness. This is particularly true in cases where children are physically or mentally challenged. Check back from time to time to see if the person you have appointed remains willing and able to do the job.

Of course, you will spend most of your energy thinking about how your estate will be distributed. This used to be pretty straightforward. But with divorces and remarriages, half-siblings, stepchildren, and all the other family permutations that are now part of almost everyone's life, the question can be considerably more complicated. Who will be your heirs? When will they receive their bequests — immediately or in the future? How will the bequest be handled if your beneficiary predeceases you?

## PLAN YOUR FUNERAL

Just as making a will can be difficult for many people, so too can making funeral arrangements. But planning your funeral is part of estate planning. Funerals are a rite of passage. They bring conclusion to an episode of life. While you may not want an elaborate funeral that rivals a marriage or other significant ceremony in your life, think about the fact that there is little time to prepare for even a simple funeral — at most a few days. And this is a time when your family is most vulnerable both financially and emotionally. The last thing you should want is for them to be spending money in an emotional state, without direction. Better that you spend a couple of minutes thinking about it, and putting it on paper, so there's no debate about how fancy or simple the whole thing should be. If you want a party, plan the party. Some people even identify the guests with prepared invitations. They choose the music to be played, and the food to be served. Others want to keep the whole thing simple. I want to be cremated. It's fast, simple, and doesn't use up valuable land resources.

Your funeral instructions aren't binding, but they're likely to be followed in most cases and will ease the burden on your family members.

### WHAT ARE YOU WAITING FOR?

If you haven't thought about these things yet, now is the time. If you don't have a will, make arrangements to make one. If you haven't designated a guardian for your children, start thinking about who is worthy of the job. Don't allow your emotions to get in the way of your responsibility. Hilary talks about redoing her will when she was pregnant. "Just before John was born," she said, "I redid my will and had to think about issues like guardianship. I sat and cried. How could I be thinking about my own death when I was awaiting the birth of my baby? It gave me a whole new appreciation for how difficult it is to go through the exercise; but how absolutely necessary."

It all comes back to the responsibility issue. If you don't do the detail work, the financial and emotional repercussions can be dreadful for those you leave behind. The point of executing a well-thought-out, well-executed will is to make the whole process of tying up the ends as neat and painless as possible for those you love.

Now is also a good time to think about how your affairs should be handled if you become incapacitated physically and/or mentally.

### MORE POWER TO YOU

While lawyers and financial planners have been calling attention to the importance of having a Power of Attorney (PoA) for years, for many people the question remains, "Do *I* need a power of attorney?" *Everyone* should take the time to execute this relatively simple document.

A power of attorney is a legal document that authorizes another person to act on your behalf. The most common type of power of attorney deals with property and gives the person you choose the legal authority to deal with your assets. If you become mentally incapacitated, a "continuing" power of attorney would allow your representative to act for you. Note that it must be "continuing" to be binding if you become mentally incompetent. By executing a continuing power of attorney, you eliminate the likelihood of your family facing a cash-flow crisis because they cannot access your chequing or savings accounts, or liquidate investments in your name in the event that you cannot act on your own behalf. If you become incapacitated without a power of attorney, certain family members could obtain authority to act, but might have to post a security bond first and would also be required to file a management plan for your assets.

The person you choose to act for you can be your spouse, another family member, your lawyer, or a trust company. Since the person who has your power of attorney can do anything you can do (except make your will), you should have implicit trust in this person. If a relationship is shaky, don't test it by adding the burden of a power of attorney to it.

A power of attorney can be "general" or "restricted" in nature. With a general power of attorney, all your assets are covered. With a restricted power of attorney, you set out the specific conditions you want met.

Since a power of attorney is legally binding, consult your lawyer to have one prepared.

In the spring of 1995, Ontario introduced new legislation to allow you to also make your wishes known with regard to medical and non-medical care. While this had been the domain of the "living will" for some time, living wills were not legally binding. The new personal care power of attorneys executed under the Substitutes Decisions Act are. Ontario joins British Columbia, Manitoba, Quebec, and Nova Scotia in having legislation (either passed or pending) to give you the power to choose who speaks for you if you are unable to speak for yourself.

Within the power of attorney for personal care you can appoint someone to make decisions on your behalf and can establish in written form your instructions regarding medical treatment and non-medical personal care issues. You can also establish the specific medical treatments you do or do not want, including the specific circumstances in which you want medical treatment to cease. You don't have to include instructions — you can leave it up to your personal care attorney to make the appropriate care decisions based on your wishes and preferences.

# 13

# Building Financial Relationships

*If you don't know your jewels, know your jeweller.*

UNKNOWN

*Don't ask a barber if you need a haircut.*

DANIEL GREENBERG

One of the questions I'm asked most often is how to find someone to trust in helping with financial matters. Whether you're looking for a banker, a broker, a financial planner, an insurance agent, a lawyer, or an accountant, you must establish a *relationship*. Now, relationships don't just happen. You have to work at them. And if you have yet to establish a relationship with any one of these advisers, you're starting from ground zero.

The first place to look is in your own backyard. Speak with friends and family. Ask them what adviser they deal with. Do they trust him? Do they like her? Does the adviser give good feedback? If none of your friends or family members knows of anyone, ask the people at work. If your peers don't know of someone, your boss may. The fact that you're looking for an adviser will look good on you, so don't be bashful.

You've got a name at last. Now what do you do? You interview. The only way to get to know the person is to talk to them, preferably in person. And the only way to find out if they can do the job is to ask plenty of questions. Some of the questions you'll ask are basic service questions to see if the level of service the adviser gives matches your expectations:

- how many times a year will you meet?
- what kind of information will you receive on a regular basis?
- how quickly will your calls be returned?
- when can you reasonably expect to receive information that you've requested, or answers to questions you've asked?

You must also ask about the person's credentials and experience. While credentials will give you an educational overview, experience is far more important in terms of your day-to-day activities. If you are looking for an insurance agent to handle a disability insurance request, you need someone who has specialized in disability insurance. A life insurance agent who dabbles in disability insurance won't do the job well enough. The financial world is just too complex to expect one person to know it all. Of course, you may choose to use a financial planner as your quarter-back; he or she could then refer you to specialists as you need them.

I'm quite opinionated when it comes to choosing advisers. I believe in the specialist. After all, you wouldn't go to an ob/gyn to have bunions removed, and you wouldn't seek advice from a car mechanic about how your furnace is running. So why would you go to a commercial or real estate lawyer to draw up a will? Or a generalist financial planner for information on insurance? Or a banker for help with your investment portfolio? When you choose an adviser, you need one with lots of experience in the area for which you're seeking advice. If you need help with your current account, ask a banker. If you need help with invest-ments, ask an investment specialist such as a broker or an investment manager. Asking a mutual-fund seller about how the underlying invest-ments in the mutual fund work will likely leave you knowing a lot less than you should. It's not fair to those people, because they can't possibly keep up with the day-to-day activities in the market. And most don't understand how economic conditions will affect your portfolio. If you don't believe me, the next time you're in your branch, ask the mutual-fund specialist the question, "What factors do I need to think about when trying to decide which areas to focus on in broadening my foreign content?" and watch the eyes glaze over.

Another good question to ask is, "What types of investments do you hold, and why?" A financial adviser should be able to explain the rationale for her own investment portfolio, insurance coverage, or whatever instrument she specializes in so you can understand it. All too often, I read about advisers who suggest clients buy a product they would never consider for themselves. Then there are the advisers who use a strategy they would never suggest for their clients. You have to wonder why the disparity. If there's no good answer, find another adviser.

Next you should ask about fees. How will you be billed? By the hour? Will the person receive compensation from any other sources? Financial planners who are compensated by investment companies such as mutual-fund companies obviously have a vested interest in selling you a particular product. That's not bad if the product suits your needs. But you may find yourself questioning just how unbiased their financial advice is. If you're uncomfortable with such an arrangement, go for a relationship with a fee-only financial planner. They'll guide you financially, recommend the types of investments you should have, and offer advice on where to get those products.

Which brings us to the next thing you need to do when seeking financial advice: check references. Know that the adviser is only going to give you his or her happiest clients as references. But even knowing that, you can uncover interesting information about the adviser just by chatting with a couple of clients. Don't ask too many direct questions. Questions such as "Did she make you any money?" deserve a one-word answer. Instead, ask about the relationship. Talk about the kinds of expectations the client had and how they were met. Ask about areas where the adviser added value by delivering more — information, service, time commitment — than was expected.

If you and your spouse will be using the same adviser, get the ground rules straight right from the start. First, you must both feel comfortable talking to him intimately about your money. It's no good working with someone your spouse thinks is great if you have doubts. Second, make sure the adviser knows that you are two separate clients. Yes, you will have similar needs. But you should expect all your information to be kept confidential at all times, unless you say otherwise.

It is equally important that you feel comfortable with the kinds of investments your adviser recommends, and the way those recommendations are delivered. I met Ann Richards when I was publishing my financial magazine and she agreed to be a contributing writer. Working with her on the magazine gave me insight into her values and how she operated. When the magazine stint ended, I asked Ann to take over the management of my self-directed RRSP. I've not been disappointed. Ann not only takes the time to understand what I'm trying to accomplish, when she thinks I'm going off half-cocked, she says so. And if she doesn't know how to do something, such as when Ken and I decided to put our mortgage in our self-directed RRSPs, she finds out and gets back to me. She managed the resources on her end so that from my perspective the whole thing went smoothly. My husband uses Ann's services as well. And despite the fact that we are completely different in our investment and communication styles, Ann bridges the gaps. She makes it easy for us to deal with her. When my husband decided to do a little speculating, Ann requested that he complete a new "know your client" form. It's not only required, but it helped to bring home to Ken just how far he was stepping out of his original investment strategy.

That's what you want from a financial adviser. Whether the person is drawing up your will, helping you with your taxes, or arranging your mortgage, you should feel you are the most important person in that adviser's life at that point in time. You want someone who will watch your back, even if the enemy lies within!

Does everyone need a financial adviser? Probably. And at some point in your life you may need two or three at the same time, depending on what you're doing. The number of people on your financial roster depends on the circuit your life takes. Conceivably, you may need an accountant, an estate lawyer, a real estate lawyer for your home purchase, a banker, a broker for your investment advice, and a financial planner for your overall financial health. You might also seek specialized help in retirement planning, if your financial planner has chosen not to be an expert in this area.

# III

# ADAPTING YOUR PLAN AS YOUR LIFE CHANGES

*Even in slight things the experience
of the new is rarely without
some stirring of foreboding.*
ERIC HOFFER

*T*here is no greater constant in life than change. No matter how well you plan, how carefully you prepare, how tenaciously you hold on, at some point, everything nailed down comes loose. That's life.

Many years ago, I came across a beautiful saying that I've held close to my heart. I can't remember where I read it, or whom to attribute it to, but it goes like this: "To grow is to change and to change often is to have grown much." I really like the idea that I'm not fickle (as Virgil would have us believe), scatterbrained, vacillating, shifty, warped, flip-flopping, or bent. I'm much happier thinking of myself as growing, metamorphosing, remodelling, reorganizing, moving, improving, bettering. The bottom line: I'm changing. And a good thing too since my life continues to evolve and if I didn't keep up, it would sure be a funny picture. Or a sad one.

As my girlfriend Brownie says, the golden rule is "Get Up." No matter how often you're flattened, you can only move forward if you get up. Of course, it's easier to get up if you have some tools at your disposal. And it's easier to stay financially healthy if you have a road map of what to watch for as you move along life's glorious, muddy, winding, uphill, rocky path. That's what this section is all about. Change.

Since your priorities as a young adult will be different from your priorities as a parent or a retiree, it's important that you repaint your financial canvas to reflect the changes in your life. No one thinks about saving for their kid's education before they actually have a child. And few people can contemplate retirement at the sweet young age of 24. But as you progress, morph, move forward, you need to reorganize and remodel. If you don't take the time to reassess, you may waste a lot of time working to old plans.

# 14

# When You Partner

*Keep from your wives the actual amount of your income — because the management of the money should not be put into the wife's hands. It is a popular error which is the cause of many misunderstandings between married people.*

HONORÉ BALZAC

*When you're young, you think of marriage as a train you simply have to catch.*

ELIZABETH BOWEN

There are almost as many different ways to partner as there are people to partner with. When it comes to partnering, life's changed a lot in the past two or three decades. Fewer women marry. In 1992, there were only 5.8 marriages for every 1,000 people, down from 9.2 in 1972. Women are also marrying at older ages. In 1992, the average age for first marriage for brides was 26.5 years, up from 22.1 years in 1971. There's also been a substantial increase in the number of remarriages. In 1992, about 23% of the women who married had been married before. That's up from just 10% in the 1960s. And divorced women make up almost nine out of 10 women who remarried in 1992. Again, that's a significant shift from the 1960s when most women who remarried were widowed.

While the percentage of women who are spouses in the traditional sense has declined, the number living in common-law relationships has increased. In 1981, only 4% of women were in a common-law relationship. By 1991, that had risen to 7%. The net result is that while fewer women marry, the share of all women living with a partner has changed only marginally.

Each time I've partnered, I've done it differently and I've done it better. The only common factor was that in each case I lived with my partner before I married. Having been married three times, I can tell you from experience that no one way is the right way. It's a matter of where you are in your own personal development, and what is important to you at that particular point in your life.

When I partnered with my first spouse, I was very young. I left home abruptly and went to live with him in his flat. Then we moved into an apartment together. A few months later, we married. It was fast and short-lived. I made some significant mistakes — my choice of partner being just one of them.

Recently, I was interviewed by a journalist asking about the financial issues people should think about when they begin living together — married or not. My first response was, "No joint accounts, unless he puts in and you take out."

My first experience with a joint account was negative. I was the only one working. My husband planned to return to Australia, where he felt he would be in a better position to contribute to the family coffers. I was to join him shortly thereafter. Before he left, he emptied the joint account of the $600 we had managed to save and bought me a television to keep me company. I was aghast! Six hundred dollars may not seem like much money now, but in 1979 it was all the money we had in the world. And it had been hard to scrape together. My security was gone. I was going to end up alone, and without a safety net. From his perspective he was doing something nice for me. From my perspective, he had placed me in a horrible position. To him, money was for spending. To me, money was for saving in case something dreadful happened and you needed it. And in his mind, $600 wasn't a lot of money. In mine, it was a fortune.

The point of this story is that you have to talk about what you expect of your spouse, and what he expects of you if you plan to have a successful relationship. You have to talk about it all. How you will live together. How you will share responsibilities. How you will cope with challenges. How you will deal with financial issues. Things one partner does shouldn't come as a shock to the other. That's not to say that as you live together, you won't uncover new, wonderful, challenging aspects to your spouse's personality and ways of seeing things. That's natural. What's destructive is not to have an open line of communication so you can discuss the things that make you sad, mad, crazy, and over-the-top frustrated. While the early months of shared life can be very exciting, they can also bring some very interesting discoveries. You have to be able to talk about them.

If you or your partner are reluctant to talk in a straightforward way about money, you're in trouble. Since every family is faced with challenges, the ability to put the issues on the table, talk openly about them, and come to some resolution is absolutely crucial to your relationship.

As cynical as this may sound, the reality is that money and power have a very close relationship. The partner with the most money is far more likely to control most of the key decisions in the relationship — from which house you'll buy, to where the kids will go to school, to who will stay home with a sick child. In fact, conflicts about money prompt more divorces than any other single issue, regardless of income.[22]

Assuming you and your partner agree to communicate openly about money, your first task will be to set the ground rules. Set aside an hour or so when you will not be interrupted — no kids, no friends, no background distractions. Your first order of business should be to agree on the time and place for your next meeting. Some couples run these meetings like board meetings. Others use them as an excuse to get out of the house for a quiet dinner. Whatever your choice, start your meeting by setting the time, date, and place for the next meeting so no matter what the outcome of this one, you will have already agreed to continue the process.

Begin by talking about the things you agree on so you set a positive tone. Decide how you are going to arrange your money matters: who will pay the bills, who will save toward the downpayment on the home, who will make the contributions to the kids' educational fund, and who will make the investment decisions. If you've already identified a habit your spouse has that makes you nuts, put it on the table. Ask your spouse to do the same. The rule should be that anything is up for discussion providing it is being handled without acrimony. Your discussion should

22 Victoria Felton-Collins with Suzanne Blair Brown, *Couples and Money* (Bantam, 1990).

also bring clearly into focus the things that are very important, somewhat important, and a little important to each of you. This may take some thought and may be deferred to your next meeting, but don't skip this step. If making sure you maintain a $500 safety cushion in your chequing account is important to one spouse, and the other runs the account to within a hair's breadth of zero every month, you'll drive each other nuts. Knowing the rules will help you not to break them.

One reason many couples fight about money is that each person has different priorities. One wants to save madly, the other is a shopper; one wants to pay down debt, the other continues to charge purchases and take out loans; one wants to own a home, the other wants to invest the money in the market. And as time goes by, each position becomes more polarized as the individuals attempt to balance the other's "wrong."

Another reason couples fight is because their expectations are not met. Implied promises are hard to escape. A new mother may feel she was implicitly promised time to stay home and take care of her baby, but her spouse may insist she return to work. A husband may believe his wife should stay within the household budget, while she continues to use her already stressed credit card to buy clothing and toys for the kids. One spouse may be disappointed that the other doesn't make more. The other may feel embarrassed, ashamed, or angry at not being able to live up to expectations.

## YOUR SPENDING PLAN

Consolidating your spending plans will be one of the first challenges you face when you begin living together. Will you pool your money, or will you manage separate accounts? Who will pay which bills? Who will be in charge of saving? Who will maintain the emergency fund?

The most challenging part of your early conversations about money management may be coming to terms with the fact that you have different money personalities. Your partner may be a charge-ahead spender. You may be a careful saver. Your partner may be illiterate when it comes to investing. You may be well read and enthusiastic. Both you and your partner may be take-charge money managers who struggle over the power to make decisions. Whatever the case, you'd better get to know each other and come to some agreement about how you will handle this aspect of your relationship. The worst thing you could do is simply settle into a financial relationship that pleases neither of you. In the end, fights, tears, and, ultimately, resentment will be the dividend of your unwillingness to talk it out.

So, today, it's time for a chat. Talk about your attitudes. Talk about your expectations. And disclose. I know this isn't easy for everyone, but if you can't trust the person with whom you are partnering, think twice about this life-changing decision. Begin by talking about what you own and what you owe. It may be difficult admitting debt and listening to someone else's asset-building saga, but you have to know each other's circumstances fully to start off right. And don't assume you know your partner simply because you've been acquainted for years. You don't know anything about anybody until they choose to tell you. So there may be some significant gaps you aren't aware of. Talk about your goals. Do you want to buy a house? When? Do you want to have children? How will you share the care, nurture, and rearing of your babies? How much will you put away for the future? How will you decide where that money will be invested? If you and your partner have different expectations as you start out, it would be a good idea to come to an understanding of each person's position. Talk through your financial arrangements so that for each, the process and the outcome are fair.

Barb Godin says that when she and her husband started out together, they didn't have much money. "We had jars labelled 'food money,' 'gas money,' et cetera. On payday, we put the cash in the jars and when the cash was gone we stopped spending. If the food money jar was empty, that was too bad, unless there was anything in the entertainment jar, which almost always went unfilled."

Once upon a time, men brought home the bacon and women fried it up in the pan. But the times, they are a-changin'. One of the most dramatic changes in Canadian society has been the increase in the number of women who are employed. In 1994, 52% of all women 15 and over had jobs — up from 42% in 1976. In 1994, women represented 45% of all paid workers in Canada, up from 37% in 1976.

So there are more women working now than ever before. In *Money: Who Has How Much and Why*, Andrew Hacker charts the wives' share of combined income in dual-income marriages.[23] At the lowest income levels, wives contribute the most. At an income level of $10,000 to $20,000,

---

23 Andrew Hacker, *Money: Who Has How Much and Why* (Scribner, 1997), p. 174.

wives contribute 47.7% — almost half — of the family income. As the family's income increases, wives' contributions represent a smaller share. At the $20,000 to $30,000 level, wives' income represents 38.9% of the family pool. And at $30,000 to $40,000, wives' incomes make up 34.3% of the family's income.

For many women the question of whether or not to work isn't really a question. They have to work to help their family attain or maintain a certain standard of living. For women who are now better educated than ever before, the choice to work is also a personal one. Women want the option of being able to contribute to the world at large in a meaningful and productive way.

When it comes time to set up a joint household, the fact that many women come into the relationship already financially responsible for themselves is something both they and their significant others have to deal with. For many partners, this is a welcome change. For others, it is a challenge to their ability to take care of the family ("Don't I make enough to support us?") and to maintain their primary-breadwinner status.

The tack you take in consolidating your households will be a reflection of how similar or different your circumstances, attitudes, values, and objectives are. Here are five approaches that can work.

- *Pool your resources.* All your income would go into a joint account, and all bills and spending money would be paid out of this pool. The remainder would be invested in both names. This works best when both people earn approximately the same income, have the same goals, and can agree to merge everything. One downside to this approach is that it's unclear what happens when one person's income significantly outstretches the other's. Will that person, at some point, feel they are unfairly carrying too much of the burden?
- *Contribute proportionately.* Each person puts part of his or her income into the common pot. If both choose to contribute 50%, the actual dollar amounts can be quite different. If you earn $60,000 a year after taxes and your partner earns $35,000 after taxes, your share of the pool would be $30,000 a year, while your partner would contribute $17,500 a year.
- *Split expenses 50/50.* Let's say you determine that your joint living expenses will be $50,000 a year and you decide to split that 50/50.

Assuming the same incomes as in the previous example, you would end up paying $25,000 a year, leaving you with $35,000 a year to do with as you wished. Your partner would end up with only $10,000 in his or her pocket.

This is the way my husband and I did it while I was working full-time. We each contributed a set dollar amount to a joint house-account every month, from which all the joint bills were paid: mortgage, utilities, insurance, children's educational savings. What remained of our money was ours to do with as we pleased. One year, I'd pay for the vacation, another he would. We each did our investing separately. When I stopped working full-time so I could spend time with my babies, we tried to maintain this for as long as possible. Some months would be fine. Others I'd come up short and he'd make up the difference.

- *Split the bills.* You would decide who pays what bills. Perhaps you'll pay the mortgage, while your spouse pays the utilities and entertainment costs. Often, people choose this route to split the financial responsibility, as well as the responsibility for getting things done. (There's nothing more aggravating than this conversation: "Did you pay the phone bill?" "No, I thought it was your turn to pay the phone bill.")
- *Go month by month.* If you particularly enjoy keeping the records or are an absolute control freak, this method may be for you. You would pay all the bills each month, total them up, and then give your partner the total of his or her share.

The fact that women are marrying later also means they may bring assets — sometimes considerable assets — to the family. The question of how those assets should be identified in the event of a relationship breakdown is becoming more of an issue. The same is true for people who are remarrying and integrating their families and their family assets.

Everyone has an opinion about marriage contracts. Some people wouldn't dream of visiting the minister before visiting their lawyer. Others see a marriage contract as an act of pessimistic fatalism. A marriage contract is simply an agreement on how assets will be divided should the marriage break down. Unfortunately, those people who have signed marriage contracts without being aware of their rights, or what they were giving up, have made the concept seem more like a negative than a positive. But think for a moment. If you were entering a second marriage, after your previous husband had died, and you had children from that first marriage, wouldn't you want to protect your children's interests in those assets you had prior to remarrying, just in case?

Even if you are both entering the relationship with no significant assets, think about how you want to keep your records straight as you accumulate joint assets. After all, if you pay the rent every month, and your partner buys the furniture, will your spouse want all the furniture if the worst should happen and the relationship fails? How will you decide who gets that beautiful antique armoire that your partner bought at an auction and you lovingly and painstakingly refinished?

### KEEPING A ROOF OVER YOUR HEAD

Where will you live? Your place? His place? A new place? In my mother-in-law's early married years, couples often lived in apartments, flats, or rental units for years as they accumulated a downpayment for a home of their own. It wasn't unusual for people to buy their first home in their forties. Now, everyone wants a house, a bigger house, more stuff. But taking on a big mortgage can be daunting for young couples. And it is often done at the expense of other parts of their financial lives: emergency fund, insurance, pay-yourself-first investment plan, retirement savings. The thing about having a healthy financial life — and a balanced life overall — is to have reasonable expectations that are in sync with your overall objectives. That's not to say you shouldn't buy a house. But it should be part of the equation — not the sum.

### REVIEWING YOUR GOALS

If this hasn't happened as part of your financial discussions, it still needs to be done. When you partner, you have a whole new set of inputs — financial and otherwise — that need to be accommodated. While one would hope that you have similar goals toward which you're jointly working, that doesn't mean giving up your own dreams. Perhaps you'd like to go into business for yourself one day. How will marriage affect that? Will you move toward your goal more quickly or more slowly? Perhaps your goal is as simple as getting away for a couple of weeks every winter. Will you go together? Will you go with friends? Maybe your goal is to move to the country. Does your partner share your love of nature? Will your partner still work in your present locale? What about the commute?

Partnering requires a series of compromises to work. But that doesn't mean compromising yourself. Your personal goals are important. What you want to achieve is important. If you give up your lifelong dreams to make the marriage work, you'll only end up feeling resentful. When my second marriage ended — he is a lovely man, but our different objectives were too much to overcome — I realized that I had compromised my way right out of our relationship. To make him happy and keep him happy, I kept changing who I was. There was a significant difference in our ages and I had to compensate so people would stop referring to me as his daughter. I wore different clothes. I always wore makeup. I gave in, and gave in, and gave in, until I had nowhere to move. I had compromised myself right into a corner: I didn't like who I wasn't, and I didn't like where I was. When it suddenly occurred to me that we were on different paths — I was just getting started with a wonderful career, while he was beginning to wind down and wanted to spend more time out of the city — I realized we weren't going to end up in the same spot.

I'm not the only person with a story like this. I've met scads of people who suddenly realized they had to change. They were losing themselves. It comes as a huge shock to the partner. It seems like a betrayal. The only way to avoid the you-don't-know-who-I-am-or-what-I-want outcome is to talk. Talk about your dreams: what you want from life; what's important to you; how you feel and what you would like to change. And keep talking about your dreams and goals until you feel they are being recognized and accommodated. You have them, whether or not you realize it now. And if you don't share them, they'll overtake you. It's a matter of riding the wave, or being completely washed away by it.

## CASH-MANAGEMENT STRATEGIES

Having established a new spending plan, how you will deal with day-to-day transactions should be part of your discussions. If you've decided to set up a joint account, might I suggest you use it only for your joint expenses. When couples pool their money and things go wrong, inevitably one spouse is shocked when the other empties the joint account. You shouldn't be shocked. Anger, bitterness, and resentment make people do things they would never do when they are happy. The first rule of coexistence is to maintain your personal identity. That means having your own accounts, your own investments, and your own credit card. It also means not losing touch with the financial world.

I hear from couples in which one does all the money management and the other hasn't a clue about what's going on. This was often reported of women, particularly women of a certain age. But I've also met women who worry about their husbands' lack of attention. They worry that if something should happen to them, their hubbies would be lost. So it's not strictly a gender thing. And I've met young people who were shocked to find that when their partner left they had no idea of where anything was, or how much they had. So it isn't an age thing. It's a matter of taking personal responsibility for your own financial well-being.

Naturally, there are some things you can benefit from as you consolidate your lives. Throwing double your weight around could get you a lower rate on a loan. Even more significantly, if one of you doesn't have a credit rating, you're more likely to qualify as combined borrowers, but you'll both be on the hook for repayment. Joint bank accounts will let you keep a higher balance on a single account to avoid service charges. The flip side of this is that if your spouse bounces cheques on your joint account, the NSF will be reported in both names, and will affect your credit record. If this seems to be a routine event, then separate your accounts to protect your credit history.

## KEEPING A HEALTHY CREDIT IDENTITY

Even thought there are two to a couple, you may be perceived as one as far as your credit identity is concerned unless you do something about it. I recently read a story on an Internet bulletin board entitled "Married Women Beware." I was intrigued. The story was from a young woman who had asked her mother to co-sign a loan for her. She chose to ask her mother, because since her mom made more than her dad she figured she stood a better chance of getting the loan. Imagine their surprise when they found out that mom had no credit history whatsoever. Even though she had been using credit cards and paying them off promptly for years, all her credit history was under her husband's name because her cards were secondary cards on his account.

"Married Women Beware" indeed. If you do not apply for your own credit cards, loans, or personal lines of credit, you're not building your own credit history. And no matter how well you manage your money, it won't be reflected anywhere. In essence, you won't exist from a credit perspective. Don't let this happen to you. You have to take care of yourself and your credit identity now so that you can take care of yourself in the future should you end up on your own. Your best bet is to have your own credit card, in your name alone. Remember Barb Godin's advice: When you borrow money, make sure you borrow it in your own name. If you borrow with your husband, insist that the credit granter report the information to the credit bureau in your name. Better yet, be the first one to sign on the application so the reporting is done automatically to your file.

Call your credit-card company and make sure that *your* accounts are set up in your name only. You're not Mrs. Edward Johnston. You're Jane Johnston. Make sure you keep your nose clean so your credit bureau report is a shining example of good financial management. And check your credit report every year or so to make sure no mistakes have been made that might tarnish your credit glow.

"I can't tell you how many women I've dealt with who have signed unlimited guarantees for their husband's business," says divorce lawyer Sandy Morris (see her bio on page 297). A smarter approach would be to limit your exposure to half of the debt, or to a specific time period. Get independent legal advice — your own lawyer telling you the implications and ramifications — so that you can make unbiased, informed decisions. The bank should require this as part of the process. If no one has told you to get independent legal advice, consider yourself informed as of today.

Getting the advice is only half the equation. The other half is taking it seriously. If you don't understand what an unlimited guarantee is, ask. And keep asking questions until you're quite sure you do understand. After all, you should not be finding out for the first time that you are primarily liable for your husband's debt on the day he declares bankruptcy.

## YOUR PAY-YOURSELF-FIRST INVESTMENT PLAN

As you start out together, keep your eye firmly on the future. Without kids, your living expenses are probably on the low side. You're young, healthy, and, very likely, focused on your career. With two incomes, you have more disposable income now than you will once you start a family. While you can enjoy that discretionary spending power to travel, accumulate your stuff, and have fun, you should also be using a part of it to establish an asset base. Invest in your future.

If you plan to have children, you will experience significant shortfalls in income, and a considerable drop in your disposable income, once the babies start arriving. Your early years are the perfect time to establish a savings plan that will help bridge this gap. Whether or not you intend to become a full-time mother, those savings will come in handy. They can also cushion the financial shock when, having held your warm, cuddly bundle, you decide you can't leave her to go back to work — at least for a year, two years, six years. Invested wisely, those savings can protect your family's standard of living, create more peace of mind, and offer you options for how to live your life.

## YOUR EMERGENCY FUND

Once you get married, you only need to cover one person's income so you can cut back on your emergency fund. True or False? FALSE. If you think that your spouse's income is your safety net, might I remind you that there are many couples who have found themselves both out of work at the same time in our new economy. Might I also remind you that with most people living to the edge each month, it's unlikely that any one salary would be able to take care of all the costs associated with your joint lifestyle. Marriage should not be your excuse for giving up your financial responsibility.

Both members of a partnership should have emergency funds established to ensure that should the worst happen, they'll be covered. Trying to accumulate an emergency fund during a divorce, when your spouse is laid off and has exhausted his, or when the world has come crashing down on both of you is next to impossible. If you haven't already done so, start today, putting a little away each week. You'll sleep better for it.

## REVIEWING YOUR INSURANCE

If either you or your spouse has health, life, or other insurance benefits at work, partnering is a good time to take another look at the plan. Most people have no idea what their company plans cover. Remember your first day of work? Remember receiving that little handbook of benefits? Where did you put it? Most people never bother to look at it until something comes up that they need to check. But not knowing what you're covered for may mean you're missing several things you could be claiming. And if your partner is paying for coverage, adding him or her as a beneficiary of your plan is one way to save some money.

Under an employer's benefit plan, a spouse usually receives all the health-related coverage that the employee receives. In some cases, same-sex couples are also covered — you can expect to see more equality in this area as time goes by. Even if they are not covered formally, benefit administrators may turn a blind eye when the forms are being filled out. However, currently pension benefits do not apply to same-sex couples because of income-tax regulations.

If both you and your spouse have benefits, pick the best plan and opt out of the other to save money. Since most plans only allow you to claim the portion not covered under another plan, dual coverage often means you're paying more than you should.

A common perk for most employees is life insurance. If you have no children, the minimum may be enough. However, remember that if you plan to have children, or one spouse will be dependent on the other, trying to get insurance when you need it could be harder than you anticipate, since even a small change in health may disqualify you. And it will definitely cost more as you get older. If your company plan offers you the ability to buy more insurance at the group rate, take the time to compare the rate with insurance you can buy on your own. And make sure that before you buy insurance through your company plan, you can take that insurance with you when you leave your employer.

The same rules apply to disability insurance. While many companies offer disability insurance as part of their package, you may want to consider topping it up with a private plan to ensure you are covered even if you are laid off. If your employer allows you to opt out of the company plan, consider buying your own plan with your after-tax dollars so that your disability income will be tax-free. If you are self-employed, disability insurance is absolutely, positively, without question *a must*. It's unlikely that your business can survive a long-term disability, which means you'll have no source of funds with which to support yourself through the disability. Premiums are expensive, but disability insurance must be a priority. If you don't believe it can happen to you, remember the statistics: One in eight people become disabled each year.

## TAX IMPLICATIONS

Before 1993, common-law couples received different tax treatment than married couples. That has changed so that under the Income Tax Act, unmarried couples of the opposite sex are treated exactly the same as those who have signed the licence. As far as Revenue Canada is concerned, you are considered married if you have lived together in a conjugal relationship for at least 12 months, or are the natural or adoptive parents of a child. Now, even if you haven't taken a trip down the aisle, you can contribute to an RRSP for your spouse, claim the married credit, lump your medical and charitable donations together, and transfer credits between your returns. You can also leave assets to a common-law spouse without capital-gains attribution.

Here's a question just about everybody in financial planning hears: "How do I minimize my taxes?" Now that you're partnered, you have some more options. You can maximize your tax savings by combining the claim for medical expenses (including your premiums for health and dental insurance) incurred by you, your spouse, and your eligible dependents, for any 12-month period. The lower-income spouse should make the claim. You can also maximize your tax credit for charitable donations by combining your claim on one return.

### Income Splitting

Income-splitting strategies aim to reduce the amount of tax you have to pay and increase your family's cash flow. The objective is to have two equal incomes for tax purposes. Many of us can only work to narrow the gap as much as possible.

One way to minimize taxes and keep more money is by rigging the system so that all the family's investments are held in the name of the lower-income earner. When income (interest, dividends, or capital gains) is generated there it will be taxed at a lower rate. Revenue Canada's response to income splitting and the tax reduction it brings was the introduction of attribution rules. So, if you *give* your spouse money for investment, Revenue Canada will tax you on the interest, dividends, or capital gains earned. In other words, they attribute the return earned on the gifted money back to the person who gave it. The one small loophole: "second generation" return — or the income earned on income — is taxed in the hands of the person holding the investment. So, if you give your partner a $50,000 bond earning $5,000 interest income (10%), the $5,000 will be taxed in your hands. However, the $5,000 payment becomes your partner's property, and any subsequent income generated will be taxed in his name. Over five years he will have accumulated $25,000 (5 x $5,000), which may also generate $2,500 (10%) a year, taxable at his lower rate.

One way to avoid the attribution rules is to have the higher-income earner pay for all household and operating expenses. Then the lower-income earner can invest some or all of his or her net income directly. Revenue Canada doesn't have a problem with that. And interestingly enough, it also doesn't have a problem with one spouse paying the other's taxes. So if the lower-income spouse owes money, the higher-income spouse should pay the taxes, and the lower-income spouse should invest.

One of the best options for income splitting is available to people who own their own business. You can hire your spouse to work for you and pay a regular salary. The only condition is that the amount you pay must be a reasonable salary for the work being done. If you need a family income of $4,000 a month, and you split the income between you and your honey, you'll pay much less tax overall. This will also give a stay-at-home parent the CPP contribution credits, and the ability to build RRSP assets, which will allow you to split your income when you retire.

Attribution ceases for years when you become a non-resident for tax purposes, when there is a marriage breakdown, or when you die.

Lending money to a spouse and charging Revenue Canada's prescribed interest rate is yet another effective way of income splitting. At the time of writing, the prescribed rate was 5%. Let's look at an example to see how this would work. Let's say Mark's been working on a novel for the last two years, during which time he's made about $15,000 a year as a part-time handyman. His wife, Laticia, who works as a dental hygienist, makes $65,000 and has accumulated a nifty little nest egg of unregistered investments. Now, let's say Laticia lent $25,000 to Mark, who in turn invested those funds and earned a return of 12%. Here's how the income-splitting strategy would work.

Laticia would have to charge Mark the prescribed rate of 5% on the loan to keep everything kosher with the tax man. Yes, the money would actually have to change hands and be reported on the tax return of everyone involved. So Laticia would have to pay tax on the $1,250 in interest income from the loan at her marginal tax rate of 50% for a total of $625 in tax. Mark would earn $3,000 on his investment, and have an interest expense deduction of $1,250, on which he would pay tax at his lower rate of 27% ($473). In the end, after all was said and done, the couple would pay $402 less by taking this route than by earning all the return in Laticia's hands and paying the $1,500 in tax at her higher marginal rate.

Another popular way to income split is to use a spousal RRSP to accumulate retirement assets. A spousal RRSP makes oodles of sense for income splitting if your projected retirement income will be significantly higher or lower than your spouse's. It is a good way to get more income into the lower-income spouse's hands where the tax paid will be at a lower marginal rate.

A spousal RRSP works like a regular RRSP except for one difference: One spouse contributes for the other. The spousal RRSP belongs to the individual in whose name the plan is registered, but the contributor receives the tax deduction for having made the contribution. You can contribute as much as you wish to a spousal RRSP, up to your annual RRSP deduction limit. So, if you are allowed to contribute $7,500 to an RRSP, your total contributions to your own RRSP and the spousal RRSP cannot exceed $7,500. How you split the contributions is up to you. If you decide to contribute $4,000 to a spousal RRSP, then you will be able to contribute only $3,500 to your own RRSP.

While your contributions to a spousal RRSP do not affect your spouse's contribution to his or her own RRSP, spouses who are eligible to make their own RRSP contributions should not contribute to the spousal plan. Keep the non-spousal RRSP contributions in a separate plan so that the attribution rules that apply to a withdrawal from a spousal plan don't affect the non-spousal contributions. What "attribution" rules, you might ask?

Revenue Canada has very specific rules for the withdrawal of funds from a spousal RRSP. When funds are withdrawn from a spousal RRSP, they will be taxed in one of two ways:

1. If no contribution has been made to any spousal RRSP in the year of withdrawal or the two preceding calendar years, the funds will be taxed as the plan holder's (the spouse's) income. The word "any" is particularly important. It doesn't matter which spousal RRSP account a withdrawal is taken from, the attribution still applies. Trying to take the money from a spousal RRSP set up five or six years ago at one institution doesn't work if you contributed to a spousal RRSP at another institution at some later point.
2. If a contribution has been made at any time during the year of withdrawal or the two preceding calendar years to any spousal RRSP, all or part of the money withdrawn will be taxed as part of the contributor's income, depending on how much is withdrawn.

Let's say your spousal RRSP is worth $20,000 and that in each of the years 1997, 1996, and 1995, your spouse contributed $2,000 to the plan for you. If you were to withdraw $8,000 from the plan in 1997, $6,000 of the withdrawal would be taxed as part of the contributor's income since those contributions were made "in the year of withdrawal" (1997) and "two preceding years" (1996 and 1995). The remaining $2,000, which represents contributions made before 1995, will be taxed as part of your income.

Again, as with everything else in the tax legislation, the wording is very specific and the use of the term "calendar year" is important. If you made a contribution in January 1996, your spouse would have to wait until January of 1999 before a withdrawal would not have any tax impact on you. However, if you made the contribution in December 1995, your spouse could withdraw without attribution as early as January 1998.

To ensure that withdrawals do not inadvertently work against your income-splitting objectives, it is extremely important to consider the impact of this three-year period before making any withdrawals from a spousal RRSP.

The three-year rule does not apply if the spouses are living apart due to relationship breakdown or if the contributing spouse died in the year of the withdrawal. Other circumstances where there is no attribution include: if either spouse becomes a non-resident of Canada; if the plan holder transfers money directly from the RRSP to an annuity or Registered Pension Plan that cannot be commuted for at least three years; or if the plan holder transfers money to a registered retirement income fund (RRIF) and does not withdraw more than the minimum amount.

When it comes to income splitting, retirement planning specialist Ann Eynon says that people often overlook their company pensions as one factor in the calculation. She says, "People often don't see the relationship between the RRSP and the pension income. The name of the game is to have equal income, including the pension. Spousal contributions may be appropriate by the spouse with a pension even if that means the non-pension spouse ends up with more RRSP assets." It's one way of evening the playing field. Rather than one individual having a huge retirement income with the other partner getting little or nothing, a spousal RRSP can be used to redistribute income evenly between both. That means less tax for the family.

On a total income of $70,000 earned in only one person's hands, there would be a tax liability of about $25,000. However, split that income equally between a couple, and the family tax bill drops to about $20,500. That's a savings of almost 20% for simply having chosen to use a spousal RRSP.

By income splitting, you will also make your spouse eligible for the non-refundable tax credit upon reaching 65 if your spouse receives income from a RRIF or annuity purchased with the proceeds from the spousal RRSP. And it may help you avoid the Old Age Security (OAS) and Age Tax Credit clawbacks. (See Chapter 16 for details on clawbacks.)

Consider, too, the fact that a spousal RRSP is the only way to continue benefiting from an RRSP's tax-deferred growth once you've passed the age of contribution. If your spouse is younger than you and you have earned income or unused contributions carried forward from previous years, you can continue deferring tax by contributing to a plan in your spouse's name even after you are required to stop contributing to your own RRSP.

Too often people are reluctant to use a spousal RRSP because they are concerned about marital breakdown. What they don't realize is that under family law each spouse owns half of the other's RRSP anyway. So just because your name is on the plan doesn't mean it won't be divided when you divorce. Scarlett Ungurean, a chartered accountant and financial planner with William M. Mercer Limited, warns that these same laws don't apply to common-law spouses. "If you're in a common-law relationship, the provincial family law act may not provide for property rights and equalization."

Insurance specialist Leslie Macdonald Francis suggests that people who have been once bitten and are twice shy consider using an RRSP with an irrevocable beneficiary clause from an insurance company. "You can make spousal contributions and have your spouse name you as the irrevocable beneficiary. Your spouse won't be able to make a withdrawal without your signature because you are the irrevocable beneficiary." An additional benefit: You won't unknowingly be removed as beneficiary of the RRSP even in the event of a divorce.

## YOUR ESTATE PLAN AND OTHER LEGAL ISSUES

"When you marry," says estate specialist Hilary Laidlaw, "Your will is automatically revoked, unless you made the will in contemplation of marriage." So whether you are marrying for the first time, or for the fourth, you will need to make a new will.

Common-law relationships are recognized as legal marriages for certain purposes but not for others. So, if you wish to contribute to a spousal RRSP, you can, as long as you have "cohabited in a conjugal relationship for a period of at least one year, or less than one year if the two individuals are the natural or adoptive parents of a child." However, according to Hilary, under estate law, if you're in a common-law relationship — no matter how long-standing it is — your partner has no rights on intestacy. So if you die without a will, your 20-year partner

*Scarlett Ungurean is a consultant with William M. Mercer Limited. She has 16 years of experience advising individuals on personal tax, personal financial planning, estate and investment planning, and general business matters. A member of the Canadian Tax Foundation, she's a chartered accountant with a degree in mathematics. Scarlett is a Registered Financial Planner, the former vice-president of the Canadian Association of Women Executives and Entrepreneurs, and former treasurer of the Toronto Symphony Women's Committee. With her wry sense of humour and eclectic training and experience, she's proof that accountants aren't all boring and women aren't all mathematically challenged.*

would have no rights under the succession laws. "In this situation, the common-law spouse's only course of action," says Hilary, "is to make a claim against the estate for support as a dependent, providing they have been in a common-law relationship for not less than three years or for a lesser period if there is a child of that relationship." So the common-law spouse would have to go through the process — and the cost — of making a claim against the estate through a formal proceeding in the court. That's a rough road to walk emotionally, but particularly so when you're also dealing with a family from a first marriage. To protect your spouse, or to ensure you are protected, a will with specific designations must clearly state who gets what and when.

In terms of property rights, legally married spouses can opt into the elective regime so if they don't like what they are getting under the will, they can say, "Forget it, I'll elect for an equalization," which is a 50/50 split of the property amassed during the marriage. Common-law spouses don't have this option. Nor do same-sex spouses.

When it comes to estate planning for same-sex couples, says Bernadette Dietrich, a lawyer with McCarthy Tétrault in Toronto, "There's so little law that it's easy to fall into traps." Because same-sex couples are not spouses under the Income Tax Act, they have certain advantages when it comes to tax planning. "They can have two principal residences for tax purposes," says Bernadette. "But the downside is they can't transfer property back and forth between them without triggering capital gains." The same holds true on death. While heterosexual couples can roll over significant portions of their assets to their spouses — things such as stocks, RRSPs, and the like — same-sex couples don't have that option.

"It's also important to look around and see who survives the same-sex spouse at death," says Bernadette. "There may be a legally married spouse who comes forward as a dependent or as a claimant under the Family Law Act if they were never divorced." People often don't think of this because once the relationship is history and there are no present support obligations they just don't think of the future implications. They never get around to a divorce. Bernadette warns, "But that can then mean that the legally married spouse is the first person who is technically entitled to apply to be the administrator of the estate."

There is no precedent for a same-sex spouse to make a claim for support due to dependency (as can be done by a common-law spouse) upon death. "What we have seen is one case that basically said that same-sex spouses ought to be entitled to support in the same way as common-law spouses on relationship breakdown," says Bernadette. "It would be hard to imagine that if it is found acceptable on marriage breakdown that it won't be at death."

There is a move to have same-sex couples recognized under the Family Law Act, where same-sex couples could list themselves as "registered domestic partners" so they would be entitled to the same rights as spouses. "But that's been out there for a long time," says Bernadette, "and nothing much has happened with it."

Under the Estates Act, there's no provision for same-sex spouses to be appointed as an estate trustee without a will. "That can be a real problem because there's often conflict between the same-sex spouse and the deceased's family. The family has a prior right, leaving the same-sex spouse in a very weak position." So if you are in a same-sex relationship, you have a responsibility to have a will that protects your partner, since there are so many areas in which she simply has no rights.

"It's unfortunate that our society just hasn't evolved to the point where everybody accepts same-sex couples. We tell clients that when we're taking instructions for the will, we don't want the same-sex spouse in the room, which

*Bernadette Dietrich is a partner at McCarthy Tétrault, where she specializes in personal tax, estate planning and succession, trusts, estate litigation, and charitable organizations. For a number of years, she taught estate administration courses for the Institute of Law Clerks of Ontario and for the Law Society of Upper Canada Bar Admission Course. She is also the secretary and an executive member of the Trusts and Estates section of the Canadian Bar Association (Ontario). Former editor of the publication* Deadbeat, *Bernadette is a frequent speaker and writer on estate-planning issues. She enjoys spinning, cycling, running, and skiing and is an avid reader and movie devotee.*

we don't do with heterosexual couples," says Bernadette. She admits it takes a bit of explaining before this is usually agreed on. The purpose: to ensure that no claim can be made down the road that undue influence was placed on the person whose will is being made. "If we know that the person is HIV-positive or suffering from any kind of illness including depression, we get a letter from a doctor stating that 'these are the drugs being taken and the effect of those drugs, and in my opinion they don't affect testamentary capacity,' because that's something the family likes to bring up." That letter guards against a challenge based on testamentary capacity.

Another way to help protect a will from successful challenge is to make sure that everyone who should be taken care of is mentioned in the will. "A will leaving everything to a same-sex spouse will be vulnerable to challenge. If there are children or a former spouse, they should be taken care of." You can designate your same-sex spouse as beneficiary of your insurance and RRSPs, name her as a joint tenant on property, and hold bank accounts jointly to have assets pass directly to a partner without having to be probated. According to Bernadette, "Sometimes it's just a question of optics. If the family can look at a will and it says, 'the residue of my estate to my mom and my dad or to my brothers and sisters,' even if there is no residue they feel better. It's the publicity they don't like. They know wills are public documents and they don't want their neighbours and friends to know that this kind of relationship existed."

While you don't need independent legal advice to sign a power of attorney, don't do so without (a) knowing what you're signing, and (b) keeping a copy for your records. "You wouldn't believe the number of women who come in to talk about divorce and have absolutely no idea what they've signed," says Sandy Morris. You trust your partner, right? You love him or her. Why wouldn't you do it if asked? There's no reason not to, as long as you know what you're signing and you keep a copy. If you don't, then you're asking for big trouble.

## PARTNERING AGAIN

You know the saying, "Love is better the second time around"? I can attest to that. And the third time, it's even better. But the fact is, remarriage brings its own complications. There may be one or two ex-spouses. Perhaps you have children, or he has children. Maybe you plan to have children together. Then there are all the habits you've established that you want to keep, but that drive your partner nuts.

Combining families brings additional complications to a new relationship. Older children can feel resentful that their parent's assets are now going to be used to support someone else, or someone else's children. New babies may increase that sense of resentment. Parents or siblings may feel angry at being denied what they feel is rightfully theirs.

Dying intestate is just about the worst thing you can do to your family at this point. Let's say your husband has children by a previous marriage. You have no children. Now let's say you have a terrible car accident. You die first. He dies shortly after. If you don't have a will, your spouse will have been deemed to have survived you. All your assets will pass first to your spouse, and then to his family, leaving your siblings and parents completely out of the loop.

If you have children from a previous marriage, it is important that you safeguard their interests, and you have to talk about this in a calm and rational way. It may be difficult at first but you have to work through it. Just as important is protecting children of the new relationship. You have to weigh the responsibilities you have to the older children against the responsibilities you have to the younger children and come up with a fair deal. This can be particularly difficult if only one spouse has children from a previous marriage.

In complicated family situations, the best thing to do is seek professional advice. A professional will be close enough to the law and have enough experience to help you muddle through your options. And don't choose a generalist. For complicated issues you need someone with a wealth of experience, a specialist. It may cost more, but it will save you time and aggravation, and it will give you peace of mind. What's the going rate on peace of mind these days anyway?

# 15

# When You Have a Baby

*When the first baby laughed for the first time, the laugh broke into a thousand pieces and they all went skipping about, and that was the beginning of fairies.*

SIR JAMES BARRIE

Perhaps the single largest source of conflict for women is in reconciling their roles as caretakers and nurturers with the need to do everything else: keep a job, further their careers, achieve financial independence, just to name a few. I know that until my children were born, I had no trouble deciding what my first priority should be: Me! While a lot has been written about women's innate need to nurture — to put others at the centre of their lives and before themselves — little can prepare us for the impact of a baby. The best description I've ever found was a story by Dale Hanson Bourke in *Chicken Soup for the Woman's Soul*:

I look at her carefully manicured nails and stylish suit and think that no matter how sophisticated she is, becoming a mother will reduce her to the primitive level of a bear protecting her cub. That urgent call of "Mom!" will cause her to drop a soufflé or her best crystal without a moment's hesitation. I feel I should warn her that no matter how many years she has invested in her career, she will be professionally derailed by motherhood. She might arrange for child care, but one day she will be going into an important business meeting and she will think about her baby's sweet smell. She will have to use every ounce of discipline to keep from running home, just to make sure her child is all right . . . I want to assure her that eventually, she will shed the pounds of pregnancy, but she will never feel the same about herself. That her life, now so important, will be of less value to her once she has a child.[24]

When Alexandra was born, I was broadsided on my career track. Until then, I could work 17 hours a day, seven days a week when the situation demanded it. With a sweet angel waiting for mommy upstairs, I was loath to make those kinds of commitments anymore. When Malcolm came along, I was hit by a two-by-four, never to be the same again. My shift in priorities was final and, without question, the kids came first.

That's not to say that I didn't continue to want a career. I did. But now I was going to have to fight with myself each time I contemplated a job of any size. It was no longer a question of, "What do I do to get this job?" Now it was, "How badly do I want this job and what am I willing to give up to do it?" Often what I was willing to give up was sleep. I've spent hundreds of 3:00-to-7:00 mornings (just as I am today) trying to get a decent amount of work done before the kids get up. Thank goodness those early months of motherhood and the accompanying lack of sleep prepared me so well for the rest of my life.

## YOUR SPENDING PLAN: INCORPORATING THE COSTS OF RAISING A KID

Kids are expensive. There are diapers, the crib, bum-cream, and child care, the "big bed," breakage, and the footprints on the furniture. Try taking a holiday with two children and suddenly your travel costs have doubled. Go out for a meal and, wham, there's another bill that just went up. Then there are the medical and dental costs. There's the cost of sheltering their wee bodies, summer and winter. The birthdays, the

---

24 Karen Wheeler in Dale Hanson Bourke, *Chicken Soup for the Woman's Soul* (Health Communications, Inc., 1996), p. 164.

holiday season, the parties they'll attend for which you have to supply a gift. If you opt for enrichment lessons such as music or gymnastics, or sports such as hockey, skiing, or anything of a competitive nature that requires travel, you're looking at a whopping bill. And when they become susceptible to the triple whammy of advertising, brand power, and peer pressure, watch out.

While the costs of raising kids can be daunting if looked at all together, it's surprising how you manage to get by with a little less of this or that so Molly can have that new Beanie Baby. And there are strategies you can use to minimize the cost of things such as toys and clothing.

When you get pregnant, you'll be overwhelmed with the desire to provide the best of everything for your new lassie or laddie. The first thing to do is hunt up all your old friends who have had kids and ask them what you'll need. Make a list. Check a baby book to see what's missing. Then start shopping, slowly. Put the word out and you'll be amazed at the number of people who will offer things you'll find useful. Mommies are the most sharing of all creatures.

If you want an idea of what it will cost to raise your child, talk to your friends. Do up a budget for your new expenses and then confirm your figures with those who are in the know. One useful resource is a fact sheet study put out by the home economics section of Manitoba's agriculture ministry. Each fall, they compile a list of basic goods and services used to keep kids healthy and happy. Then they go to popular stores and price the list. The figures they come up with may be slightly lower or higher than in your area, but they're a good starting point. Call the ministry or hit their website (www.gov.mb.ca) for the most recent numbers.

When it comes to shaving dollars off your kid budget, buying second-hand can save you scads of money. Hunt up the secondhand stores in your neighbourhood, or ask friends for the names of good stores. Shop the garage sales. When Alexandra was about 18 months old, I was an avid garage sale shopper. It got me out of the house on my own and for just a few dollars I participated in a great shopping experience. I got an enormous bucket of Lego for $30. My husband and I bought a $200 climber for the backyard for $65. I bought toy cars, books (one of my favourites came from a garage sale), clothes, and dress-up supplies such as beads, necklaces, and scarves at a fraction of the store price.

Secondhand stores are also great places to recycle stuff you want to get rid of if you don't know of anyone who can use it. After Malcolm outgrew his bassinet, I took it to a secondhand store and got 60% of what I paid for it. That's not bad. And I used the money from his crib to pay part of the cost for his new big-boy bed.

My greatest savings have probably been in clothing my daughter. Her cousins who live in Florida are two and four years older than Alex. The timing couldn't be better. Twice a year, my cousin boxes up her girls' out-growns and sends them to me. Alex wears the most beautiful dresses. I have to do winter, but summer is taken care of each year. Until now, I've never had to buy my daughter a bathing suit because Vanessa sends two or three every year. And Malcolm benefits too from the tee-shirts, shorts, and other non-girlie stuff.

## MAKING SPACE FOR BABY

One decision most new parents face is that of making room for a new baby. If you're already in a house or a large apartment, chances are you can just clear out that room you've been using for storage. But if you're out of space or starting to consider things such as school locations and recreational facilities, you'll be planning to move. If it's your first home purchase, you'll have to start thinking about downpayments and mortgages. If you're considering upgrading to a new house, you'll have to figure out what to do with your existing mortgage. See Chapter 7, "Putting a Roof Over Your Head," for details.

## REVIEWING YOUR GOALS

Now that you have a new dependent, this is a natural time to review your goals. Things like retirement planning and vacations tend to take a back-seat to raising a baby. But it's not always a good idea to put your own financial goals on hold completely. After all, raising kids is an 18-year proposition.

Let's say you can currently contribute $7,500 to an RRSP. You decide to forgo the RRSP for the next 18 years. At just 8%, that'll cost you $296,000 — and a whopping $161,000 in growth (translation: money you didn't have to contribute). Okay, so you can't contribute $7,500 a year. We'll drop the figures and see the result. If you could contribute $5,000 a year, you'd be out of RRSP-pocket $182,251. If you could contribute $2,000, you'd be out of RRSP-pocket $72,900.

While you will have to trim expenses in some places, and your RRSP may be one of them, it's worthwhile to continue contributing as much as you can because of the magic of compounding return.


## Saving for Your Child's Education

If you think raising kids is expensive now, wait until you see what it's going to cost to send them to university. According to Statistics Canada, between 1985 and 1995, university tuition increased by 134%. If costs continue to rise at the same rate — and there's no reason to doubt they will, given recent government spending cuts — the 1996 cost of about $9,000 a year is expected to spiral to a whopping $16,000 a year by 2006. That's almost $65,000 for a four-year degree. The average debt load for students who graduated in 1996 was $22,000. While you may believe it is at least partly your child's responsibility to pay for their education, no one likes to think about their children graduating from school with an albatross of debt around their necks. So what can you do to ensure your little ones have all the educational advantages you think they should? Start planning, and start now!


### RESPs

One of the most popular ways to save for future educational costs is with a Registered Education Savings Plan or RESP. An RESP is a savings plan, registered with the federal government, that allows money to be saved for a beneficiary's postsecondary education. Like an RRSP, all income earned within the plan is tax-deferred. Unlike an RRSP, there is no deduction for money going into an RESP. You can set up a single family plan, in anticipation of educating more than one child from the same fund, or individual plans for each child.

You can invest up to $4,000 a year in an RESP for each beneficiary (regardless of whether the beneficiary has an individual plan or is named as one beneficiary of a family plan), to a lifetime maximum of $42,000. Contributions can be made for up to 21 years and the plan must be collapsed within 25 years of the starting date; otherwise you will lose the income earned on the plan. That expiry date is sometimes a bummer for parents with kids who are far apart in age, or who are part of a family plan. If the parents wish to pass on their older child's unused RESP savings to a much younger child, timing could become a tricky issue.

If you want to get around the 25-year limit, open up a new RESP every five years or so. With several RESPs you won't have all your money in one plan. If there is a delay in using your RESP because your daughter decides to take time to travel or work before entering university, you won't have to forgo all the income earned because the 25-year time limit has expired. You'll still have two or three other plans to draw on.

Overcontributions to an RESP are subject to a penalty tax of 1% per month. Penalty tax is charged proportionally against all contributors. While overcontributions may be withdrawn at any time, the overcontribution amount will be included in the calculation of the lifetime limit of $42,000, so don't do it.

To use the total accumulated in an RESP, beneficiaries must attend an accredited postsecondary institution on a full-time basis. The program must be no shorter than three consecutive weeks, with at least 10 course hours per week. Correspondence courses qualify, as do universities, community colleges, junior vocational and technical colleges, as well as many universities outside Canada. If an alternate beneficiary is named (another child, or anyone else related by blood, adoption, or marriage), the RESP money must still be used within the original 25-year time frame.

Should your child decide not to pursue a postsecondary education and no other beneficiary will be named, you can withdraw the full amount contributed to an RESP without tax ramifications. As long as the plan has been in existence for at least 10 years, up to $50,000 of the income earned in an RESP to which you have contributed can be transferred to your own RRSP, or to a spousal RRSP, providing you have sufficient contribution room to claim a deduction for the contribution. If you do not have sufficient contribution room, or you wish to withdraw more than the allowable $50,000, the withdrawal will be subject to tax at your marginal tax rate, and the excess above $50,000 will be subject to an additional penalty tax of 20%. Ouch!

If you do withdraw the RESP savings yourself, note that an RESP must be terminated before March 1 of the year following the year in which you make your first withdrawal. You'd be wise to spread the withdrawals over two calendar years so you can take advantage of accumulated RRSP contribution room and avoid penalty tax. Another benefit: Canada's graduated marginal tax rates may mean less in tax since the income is taken over two years instead of in a single year.

Whether or not the child ends up using the income earned on the RESP for school, the principal contributed to an RESP can be withdrawn at any time without penalty, since there was no tax deduction for having made that contribution. Having been a diligent parent and saved, saved, saved, once you're comfortable that your child will have enough, you can take back what you've given without tax consequence. The RESP will have cost you nothing at all. You can put a downpayment on a nice condo in Florida while your child uses the earned income (taxed in his or her hands, not yours) to investigate the halls of higher learning.

Personally, RESPs are not my favourite education savings tool. Even though there are provisions to allow you to withdraw the funds if your child does not end up using them, these plans are far too restrictive. This is particularly true of pooled or group plans where you have no say in how your money is being invested. All investments are made by the plan administrator and tend to be conservative. I get very cranky when I see brochures for these "scholarship trusts" in places they don't belong, such as the doctor's office, the dentist's office, medical labs, hospitals, and the like — places that offer no competitive information or advice and that lend them an air of authority that I don't think they deserve.

The most recent change made to RESPs was the proposed Canada Education Savings Grant (CESG), which will assist parents by adding 20% of the annual amount contributed to an RESP up to a maximum of $400 a year. To get the maximum grant, you'd have to contribute at least $2,000 to an RESP. These grants only apply to contributions made after 1997, and only to children under 18. And there is a maximum total: $7,200. Children who turn 16 or 17 in a year a contribution is made to an RESP on their behalf will only get the grant if there have been contributions of $300 or more for at least four years prior to the year the child turned 16 or if there was a total of $4,000 contributed on behalf of that child prior to the year he or she turned 16.

Unused grant eligibility can be carried forward until the age 17 cut-off, so if you can't make the annual contribution of $2,000 to receive the full $400 grant in a single year, any amount not claimed can be claimed with a later contribution. Let's say that this year I made a contribution of $1,500 on behalf of my son, Malcolm. The maximum grant I'd receive is $300, representing 20%. Since the maximum grant in any given year is $400, it means I can carry forward $100 of the grant to next year, for a total eligibility amount of $500. As long as I made a contribution of $2,500 or more, I'd be able to claim a grant of $500. While grant room accumulates from year to year and can be carried forward, the maximum grant that can be *earned* in any one year is $400. In other words, if you contribute more than $2,000 to an RESP, you do not earn additional grant room that can be carried forward, so keep your flow of contributions even.

Grants must be repaid if beneficiaries do not attend an eligible post-secondary institution or if RESP contributions are withdrawn before a beneficiary is eligible to receive the payments from the RESP (which are called Educational Assistance Payments, or EAPs). Grants cannot be transferred to beneficiaries other than a sibling or blood relative (including adoptive relatives) under the age of 21, and cannot be transferred to another RESP, except if there is no change in beneficiary under the new plan. If a CESG balance remains in an RESP after all eligible beneficiaries have received their lifetime maximum, as may occur with a family plan where all beneficiaries earned CESGs but not all pursued qualifying postsecondary education, that balance must be repaid. Grants must also be repaid if a contribution is removed from the plan. Whenever a withdrawal is made for non-educational purposes, an amount equal to 20% of the withdrawal must be repaid to the government, up to the total of the CESGs that were received. As well, if more than $200 of non-CESG-eligible contributions are withdrawn, RESP beneficiaries under that plan will not qualify for the grant for the remainder of the year or the two subsequent years. And, they will not accumulate grant room for those years.

The upside to an RESP — aside from that enticing grant — is that the income generated, regardless of whether that income is interest, dividends, or capital gains, grows on a tax-sheltered basis. Some people aren't aware of this, and continue to choose traditional interest-bearing investments such as CSBs, savings accounts, or GICs to save for their children's or grandchildren's education, in the mistaken belief that they, as contributors, won't be taxed on anything that accumulates. In fact, whenever an investment earns its return in the form of interest, the person who buys the investment has to pay the tax on the interest earned at their marginal tax rate. So for every $1,000 in interest earned, assuming a marginal tax rate of 45%, you would have to pay $450 in tax. The tax man is earning almost as much as your child! Only the second-generation interest — the interest earned on the interest through compounding — is taxable in your child's hands. The exception to this is an investment bought with funds solely provided from Family Allowance and Child Tax Benefit payments or an inheritance; this money is already classified for tax purposes as your child's money, so tax on *all* income earned must be paid by your child. Take care to keep these investments separate from any you may buy your child with your own funds.

If you're only comfortable with interest-bearing investments as the option for your child's educational savings, an RESP is a good idea because the interest earned within the RESP is tax-deferred. Remember, though, during periods of low interest rates, the plan will struggle to earn a return. If you're willing to step outside the realm of the tried-and-true interest-bearing investment, then take a look at mutual funds. With thousands of mutual funds now available in Canada, you have many options, ranging from the relative security of a money-market fund, through to the income-producing mortgage and bond funds, ending with the most aggressive of all: equity funds.

**In-trust accounts**

If RESPs are not for you, consider establishing an in-trust account. An in-trust account is set up with a financial institution to invest funds for a minor. The account is set up in trust because kids aren't allowed to enter into binding financial contracts, so an adult has to be responsible for providing the investment instructions and signing the contract on the child's behalf. Most in-trust accounts are informal since setting up a formal trust is expensive. To make the fees for setting up and managing a formal trust worthwhile, you need a minimum of $100,000. Most of us just don't have that kind of change in our pockets. For us, there's the informal in-trust account.

Creating an informal in-trust account that keeps Revenue Canada happy isn't difficult, but it does require you to take some specific steps. First, make sure the account is set up as "Gail Prue in trust for Alex Prue" as opposed to "Alex Prue in trust." This clearly states who the trustee is

(Gail Prue) and who the beneficiary is (Alex). Next, write out the terms of your trust and make sure you clearly spell out:

- who is giving the money (whether that is a father, mother, grand-parent, aunt, or other relative), referred to as the "donor"
- who is controlling the trust, referred to as the "trustee"; this cannot be the person who is giving the money
- that the property is "irrevocable," which means that the person who gave it cannot get it back, and has no control over how it is invested or used.

In the case of a couple, decide ahead of time who will be providing the money to the trust and who will be managing the investments, since this cannot be the same person.

Having set up the informal trust, you now have to decide what to invest in. While the attribution rule we saw in the context of earned interest (which dictated that the donor must pay tax on first-generation income, while the account holder pays tax on any second-generation income) also applies to dividend income, it doesn't apply to capital gains. A very important benefit of investing in equities is that there is no income-tax attribution on capital gains earned in an in-trust mutual-fund account, so every dollar earned by way of a capital gain is taxable in your child's hands. And by declaring some capital gains each year, you reduce the gain that will be recorded when the funds are withdrawn, so little or no tax will have to be paid at that time.

If you're choosing a mutual-fund investment for the in-trust account, don't be enticed by enormously high rates of return for the last year or two. Look at the long-term results. And don't look simply at the average rate of return — great years can mask the losses suffered in rotten years. Instead, check out the year-over-year returns. Since it's important not to stick all your raisins in one cookie, choose a good fund family. If you decide to switch from one fund to another as performance and economic conditions change, being in a family of funds will minimize the cost of switching from one type of fund to another. Also consider holding some foreign equities in your child's portfolio. Since Canada accounts for less than 3% of the world's stock market capitalization, diversifying globally will let you take advantage of the economies in other regions around the world. And as your child closes in on graduation, and you decide to get a little more conservative with the portfolio, you'll be able to switch from one fund type to another without incurring additional commissions.

The closer your child is to using the money, the more conservative you'll have to be with how you invest. If you start on your child's savings soon after she's born, you'll have plenty of time to ride out the highs and lows of the equity market to come up with a decent average return, so you can afford to be more aggressive. However, if your child is only five years away from university, you'll have to be more cautious. Fixed-income funds may be the ticket.

The closer your child is to needing the money, the more likely you will be to choose interest-bearing investments. So this might be a good time to catch up on all those CESGs you've not yet gathered by contributing future savings to an RESP.

There's no question that saving for your child's education is important. The trick is to use the option that creates the best possible return while offering the most flexibility. Your child's education savings program shouldn't penalize you for decisions that won't be made for many years yet. The idea of forfeiting income earned should be repulsive, as should the idea of paying a 20% penalty tax. Let's face it, the next best thing to an education is probably a downpayment on a home or the money to set up a new business. Whatever your child decides in the future, your decision now boils down to this: Who would you rather have the money? The RESP administrator, the tax man, or your child? Rhetorical question, right?

### PREPARING FOR THE INTERRUPTION IN YOUR INCOME

If you're planning to have a baby, there are steps to take to assure your financial health, just as you take steps to ensure your physical health. Women who want to get pregnant often change their own life patterns in anticipation of creating a new life. They change the way they eat, how much sleep they get, take extra vitamins, stop smoking — lots of stuff to prepare themselves for the blessed event. However, fewer people take into account the cash-flow crunch they'll experience during their maternity leave. Fewer still are prepared for the strong desire to remain at home caring for that sweet little bundle of joy, even after the maternity leave period has expired.

If you want your maternity leave to go smoothly, if you want to be able to focus on the baby without having to worry too much about money, then you have to do some planning. It's like everything else in life. Look ahead, see what has to be done, and just do it.

You'll have to start by guestimating how long you'll be off. EI pays benefits for 26 weeks, so the standard mat-leave is considered to be six months. But some women take longer, because they can't bear to be parted from their wee ones, while others go back to work earlier because they need to return to their regular cash flow to survive. Check with your benefits department at work to find out how much you'll receive from EI as well as what benefits you'll be covered for during your maternity leave. If EI will pay only a small portion of the money you'll need to meet your commitments, you'll have to save aggressively before your income is reduced.

Lots of women think of maternity leave as the prime time to dip into their RRSPs to support themselves while they aren't earning a regular income. If you've contributed to your RRSP with this in mind, then you've been using your RRSP as a savings account with a special tax advantage. You haven't been planning for retirement (which you'll still have to do), so don't fool yourself. Every cent you take out of your RRSP is out for good. There's no way to get that money back into the plan. And the long-term growth . . . poof, that's gone, if there's no money in the plan to grow.

I received an e-mail one day from a woman who was in a panic. She was about five months from her maternity leave, her husband was not working, and she had no idea how much income she'd have while she was off work. She hadn't checked to see what her EI benefits would be, but she was already sure they wouldn't be enough to cover her rent, never mind her food and everything else that comes with a new baby.

Okay, so she didn't plan. It's not unusual to see a woman surprised by the fact that the strip turned pink, or blue, or whatever the going colour is. The thing is, panicking won't help. It'll add stress to your life, not to mention your partner's life. It'll stress the baby. But it won't solve anything. It's time to sit down, have a talk about how you're going to cope — what are you going to *do* — so that you can move from panic to planning. Remember *telesis*. A little creativity will go a long way toward getting you through the tight spots. Remember, too, that women aren't the only caregivers in the world. If a child has two parents, both are equally capable of nurturing, cuddling, and caring for that child. And no, he doesn't have to do it the way you'd do it, he just has to do it well.

Here's another tip to consider when planning your maternity income. Just because you make an RRSP contribution doesn't mean you have to claim the deduction in the same year. You can claim that deduction when it suits you most. That's usually when you're in the highest tax bracket because that's when you'll get the biggest refund. Choosing the right time to claim is particularly important for people who are planning on having a family, or anyone who has left the workforce for a period of time or who has income that rises and falls from year to year. Let's take the example of Sue who worked all through 1995 and had an income of $55,000. In 1996, Sue was eligible to make a contribution of $9,900. Smart Sue was on a periodic investment plan, and had socked away all her eligible contribution. In June of 1996, Sue gave birth to Michaela and did not work for the rest of the year so she only earned $25,000 that year. If she claimed her full deduction, she'd get a deduction at her current marginal tax rate of only 25%, so her refund would be $2,475. But let's say Sue held on to the deduction for another year. When she returned to work in 1997, she'd be back to her $55,000 income so she could claim the deduction at a much higher marginal tax rate of 38%: that's $3,762 in tax back. Planning when to take the deduction is an important part of using an RRSP as a tax-reduction strategy. Plan carefully, and you'll get a bigger bang for your buck!

### KEEPING A HEALTHY CREDIT IDENTITY

Since having babies is very expensive, rest assured your cash flow will be tested. And since the income interruption associated with having kids is almost a guarantee, you might decide to fill those shortfalls in your cash flow by utilizing some of that wonderful credit you've been granted. According to a study done by Ernst & Young on credit use in Canada (1996), 46% of people aged 18 to 34 have an outstanding balance on at least one of their credit cards. And half of Canadians who had outstanding balances said their balances were higher than they had been three years previously.

In the best of all worlds, you'll have enough set aside to stay in the black while you're off work having and caring for your kids. But most people don't live in that world, and credit becomes one tool for helping to make ends meet. I have a girlfriend who is a single mom. She's chosen to work only part-time so that she can be at home with her little one as much as possible. Working only three days a week, she has seen her income plummet and her debt rise. She's frustrated. She's worried. She's sometimes even angry. And she's always looking for ways to get to the end of the month without getting any further into debt. But there's always something. When she came to me with the problem, she was $12,000 in debt, including her car loan and several credit-card balances. We talked about what she could do to ease the pain. She was carrying a lot of money on a credit card that charged 17% in interest. The first thing I told her to do was apply for a cheaper card and transfer the balance. "You can do that?" she said. Like many people, she didn't realize credit-card companies allowed this kind of transfer. Last year when she was hit with a tax bill, she chose to take an advance on her credit card to pay the government. She didn't ask me first. I would have told her that the government is very happy to accept postdated cheques for taxes, and the interest rate they charge is lower than she's paying on her credit cards.

Sometimes when people get into debt, they can see no way out and everything they do gets them in deeper and deeper. They don't know the rules so they don't know how to play the game to their advantage. They start to bounce cheques. The miss their minimum monthly payments on their credit cards. They skip mortgage payments or car payments, figuring it won't have any long-term impact or that they'll catch up later. Out the window goes the emergency fund, followed closely by the spending plan. Unfortunately, the long-term impact can be quite severe since our credit history tends to show all our financial indiscretions. And it can take a long time to repair the damage done.

It's important when you hit any financial crunch that you keep your credit picture in mind. Credit mistakes aren't quickly erased so you must be careful about what you do and how it will be perceived by a lender in the future. Bouncing cheques may only carry a small penalty now, but the black mark on your record can have significant consequences when it becomes really important to qualify for a loan.

In my girlfriend's case, her car died. She needed her car to do her job. When she went to the bank to get a loan for a new car she was astounded to find that she was denied the loan. It wasn't a huge loan, but her credit history was blotchy and she was already in debt to the tune of about $20,000. She felt trapped. Thankfully, her wonderful parents stepped in and co-signed for her, so she could get a car and get back on her feet. But she felt ashamed and embarrassed in having to turn to them.

Don't do this to yourself. Remember, money is a tool that can be used well or not. So is credit. Learn the rules. Play the game to your advantage. Don't assume little mistakes will be overlooked — they often won't be. Keep your credit record clean so that each time you need it, it will serve you well.

## YOUR EMERGENCY FUND

Now that you have a baby, your emergency fund is even more important. You're not just responsible for yourself anymore. You've got a baby to feed, clothes to buy, and a roof to keep over his head. If your husband were to die, if you were to become unemployed, if you were to become disabled, you would need your emergency fund. If your roof were damaged in a storm, if your furnace were red-tagged, if you separated from your spouse, you would need your emergency fund. This is no time to give up your safety net.

If you've established an emergency fund already, you may have to top it up to cover the additional expenses associated with your kids. Major changes in lifestyle such as divorce, widowhood, and illness have their own traumas. You and your children do not need the additional worry about where the groceries will come from next week, or how you'll pay the phone bill.

## INSURING YOUR DEPENDENTS' SECURITY

The arrival of a little one brings many added responsibilities, not the least of which is your need to make sure that child can be cared for in the event you are no longer around, or are unable to earn a living because of disability.

Babies are beautiful, aren't they? They are the most innocent of creatures. And it takes longer for a human baby to reach maturity than for any other animal on earth. That means our roles as parents and providers are extended far beyond the other animals. Thank goodness we have the good sense to take steps to protect them.

Or do we? Ask yourself this question: If you or your spouse were to die tomorrow, would there be enough money available to raise your sweet innocent to maturity? Would there be enough for food, clothing, a roof over her head? Would he be able to take piano lessons, travel, get a university education? Or are you depending on the kindness of family and friends, and the hope that if the worst happened, your little angel would be taken care of?

If you don't have enough protection for your children, *now* is the time to do something about it. It would be bad enough having to deal with the loss of a mom or dad — or even worse, both parents. But no child should have to deal with the repercussions of not having any money. It's too much for a single spouse to have to deal with too. Imagine the stress of suddenly being forced back into the workforce to put food on the table, or of finding the additional income to hire a caregiver for the children whose stay-at-home parent has died.

Money doesn't solve all the world's problems. But having sufficient insurance to protect the family gives your loved ones the breathing room and financial resources to cope, adapt, and move forward. And it takes the jeopardy out of the future. Joseph Heller says it perfectly in *Catch-22*:

> Mrs. Daneeka had been widowed cruelly again, but this time her grief was mitigated somewhat by a notification from Washington that she was sole beneficiary of her husband's $10,000 GI insurance policy, which amount was obtainable by her on demand. The realization that she and the children were not faced immediately with starvation brought a brave smile to her face and marked the turning point in her distress.[25]

How much life insurance should you have? That's a good question that has a couple of answers. The most straightforward approach is to ensure you have sufficient insurance coverage to provide the level of income your family will need until your dependents are on their own.

Many people worry about how they'll work the premiums into their cash flow. Don't start there. If you look at the barriers first, you'll never

---

25 Joseph Heller, *Catch-22* (Simon and Schuster, 1996), p. 353.

see the end. Look instead at the opportunities. If you are young, you have an opportunity to establish an insurance policy at a premium rate that will cost less and less, as a proportion of your cash flow, as your income increases. If you're healthy, you'll find it easier to get coverage. The later you leave it, the greater the risk that you won't be covered, and the higher the cost of the insurance.

Now, more than ever, you must insure your ability to create an income stream. By the time you're 40, there's a 21% chance you'll die and a 48% probability that you'll be disabled for at least 90 days before you turn 65. Think of the impact of losing your income for even just five years. If you make $30,000 a year, that's $150,000. Clearly, the risk to you and your family is huge. Besides the mounting debt as you watch bills go unpaid month after month, there are also all the increased costs associated with being treated for your condition. With the appropriate disability coverage, not only will you be able to meet your financial commitments, you'll be protecting your assets.

## TAX IMPLICATIONS

According to Manitoba's Agriculture Ministry, it can cost upwards of $150,000 to raise a kid today. So claim all the deductions and credits you can to help make ends meet each year.

Claim all your child-care costs. Child-care expenses include everything from a nanny to occasional baby-sitting. Regardless of your baby-sitter's age, as long as you get a receipt you can claim the expense. And child-care expenses can be claimed for children up to the age of 15. While you don't have to submit those receipts with your return, you must keep them in case they are requested by Revenue Canada for verification. Make sure that all your payments for the year will be made by December 31.

Want to income split with your kids? Do you have older kids to whom you're paying an allowance? Well, get them to give you a receipt each time they spend an evening looking after the younger children. They'll be building up RRSP contribution room, while you get to claim the allowance as a child-care expense. Children and RRSPs? What am I talking about?

Anyone with earned income in Canada can contribute to an RRSP, regardless of age. Whether your baby is a model or your 12-year-old is shovelling snow or baby-sitting, as long as your child files a tax return, and has qualifying earned income, she can begin to contribute to an RRSP. And when you look at the numbers, the story can be quite compelling. A single RRSP contribution of $300 at age 12, compounding at an average return of just 9%, will grow to over $28,800 by the time the child turns 65. Have your child make those $300 contributions every year until age 19, and the figure jumps to over $159,700. While overcontributions can't be made for children under 19, if your child adds the overcontribution amount of $2,000 at 19, the RRSP will grow to over $273,800 by age 65. Any way you cut it, an investment of $4,400 that grows to over a quarter of a million dollars is a good idea.

To be eligible for an RRSP contribution, your child must file a tax return to show earned income. He'll need a social insurance number to do that. And he'll need to keep all his financial information — receipts from baby-sitting or snow-shovelling, and tax slips from part-time jobs and summer employment — as proof of income. While there's little point in claiming the deduction since your child will likely owe little or no tax, the benefits of contributing to an RRSP are two-fold. First, any contribution can compound to produce what can seem a magical amount. Second, the RRSP tax deduction that most people make in the year of contribution can be carried forward indefinitely so that when your child does start working, he will have deductions he can use to offset the tax on his income.

Most young people who are just starting out at their first jobs have little extra income to make an RRSP contribution in their first few years of working. It can be a challenge just making ends meet. But a habit started at age 12 can be one that lasts a lifetime. And small amounts are all that are needed. If children don't start out enthusiastic about putting their hard-earned dollars away for the future, don't be surprised. It's difficult for children to see benefit in such long-term savings. You can help them get started with an RRSP by offering to buy the dress or pay for the ski trip if your child contributes the equivalent amount to her RRSP.

Part of your child's financial education will come when you discuss what types of investments to hold in the RRSP. Younger individuals have time on their side and time gives you the most flexibility over your investment choices.

Keep in mind that the RRSP must be set up in the minor's name. Some institutions won't even accept an RRSP for a child. But some will. They'll likely ask for a letter indicating who has the authorization to make investment decisions since minors aren't allowed to trade.

What about kids who want to cash in their plans? It's their money, so that's their prerogative. The best you can do is show them the long-term cost of making the withdrawal in terms of both the lost growth and the tax that will have to be paid. Remember, even if the deduction hasn't been claimed, the withdrawal is still considered income and, therefore, taxable.

So why don't more parents and children do this? From my experience as a writer trying to find experts to comment on it, the reason is simple. Few people have thought about it. Once you do the math, it's hard to deny the benefits. You don't have to be wealthy to make an RRSP work for you. Putting time on your side — along with the magic of compounding return — and a healthy discipline of long-term savings can do the trick.

If you have children in university, make sure they file their own returns. According to Scarlett Ungurean, "If your children do not need all their tuition fees to reduce their federal tax payable to zero, those fees may then be transferred to you. But this is only possible if your children file returns." If you have kids in private school, check with the school to see if part of the tuition is eligible for the tuition fee credit. It will be if there are courses that apply to the postsecondary school level. If your spouse or child has tuition fees of more than $5,000, income splitting may create enough income to allow him or her to use any non-transferable tuition and education credit.

Remember that money you receive through the Child Tax Benefit is considered your child's for tax purposes. By depositing that money into a bank account in your child's name, the income earned will be taxed in your child's hands.

## REVIEWING YOUR ESTATE PLAN

At any point in your life after you've accumulated assets it's important to have a will. At no point is it more important than when you have children. If you don't have one yet, go and get one today. The peace of mind is well worth the money.

I remember the first trip I planned to take away from the children. My girlfriend Leslie asked me how I was feeling about going. I answered that the only thing I was worrying about was the flight (I'm not a frightened flyer, just a dumb mom) and what would happen to my children if both my husband and I were to drop from the sky. Leslie smiled. "Do you have a will?" she asked. "Yes," I replied. "Then nothing can happen," said Leslie with a huge grin. "You only die without a will. Once you get a will, you'll live forever!" I laughed myself silly and felt much better. The point: If you take the right steps to protect your family, you have much less to worry about.

## TEACHING KIDS ABOUT MONEY

I've written a whole book on this topic entitled *The Money Tree Myth: A Parents' Guide to Helping Kids Unravel the Mysteries of Money*. I wrote the book because I believe strongly that educating children about money — what it is, how it works, its value, and its place in our lives — is a vital part of raising healthy and responsible children. Without your guidance, how will your children learn to do it right? Where will they learn to do it at all?

There's no safer place to learn about money than at home. And there's no one better equipped to teach it than you. Never mind that you're not a financial expert. You can learn too. What's important is that you know your child. You know how she learns best. You understand what motivates her. And you know what won't work. *You* are her best teacher.

You taught him to walk, to talk, to use the toilet (though you may have thought yourself a little out in left field on that one). You taught him to read, to sing, and to dance. You helped him shape his view of himself. Now help him shape his view of money so he learns where it fits in his life, that it is a tool, that it is manageable.

Barb Godin works hard to help her kids see money as an "enabler." Like Barb, I believe that kids have to learn that the money itself shouldn't be the issue. It's what you do with that money, and for that money, that defines how good you are at managing this tool. Barb and her family roll coins together and when they have enough, they take a vacation — once every four or five years. "My kids know that a vacation isn't something that you're due," she says. "You have to work hard for it."

And apparently the lessons are well learned.

Barb tells the sweetest story about her son's special gift to her for Mother's Day. "Matthew gave me a gift I'll never in my life forget. He knows that I like model classic cars." She reached behind her and took from her bookshelf a small blue car. "I was looking at this in a store one day, and Matthew said, 'Mommy, aren't you going to buy it?' and I said, 'No, Mommy doesn't have the money right now, it's not something I really need. It's pretty and I like to look at it.' We left it at that. Well, for Mother's Day, he went through his room and said to his father, 'I really want to get Mom that car, I really do. I've got some toys I don't use a lot. Would it be okay if I sold them?' He took toys I knew he liked to school, sold them, and used the money to buy me this car. That is the sweetest, nicest thing. When he gave it to me he was bursting with pride. I was bursting with pride."

Learning about money prepares children for the future. By teaching your children about what money is, how it works, and how it enables you to do what you really want, you're giving your kids one of the most useful lessons of all. And it's a lesson that will serve them for a lifetime. Learning about money doesn't steal the magic from childhood. It gives children an opportunity to make their own magic.

# 16

# As You Approach Retirement

*I like work; it fascinates me. I can sit and look at it for hours. I love to keep it by me: the idea of getting rid of it nearly breaks my heart.*

JEROME K. JEROME

Retirement is just around the corner and you can hardly believe it. With five years or less left working full-time, you've got to start thinking about a lot of the issues you thought you'd have plenty of time to contemplate. Where will you live? What will you do with your time? How will you structure your finances so you don't have to spend the next 30 years worrying about money?

Thirty years? That's right. One little-known reality of retirement is that the majority of Canadians retire before 65 — the age we traditionally associate with retirement. In fact, according to the General Social Survey (GSS) conducted by Statistics Canada in 1994, 67% of people who retired did so prior to age 65, with as many as 14% retiring prior to age 55. Add to that the fact that life expectancies are increasing. A woman aged 50 today can expect to live to about age 82, while her male counterpart can expect to live another 26.5 years.[26] When you combine earlier retirements and longer life spans, the result for most people is more time

26 Roger Sauvé, *Canadian People Patterns* (Western Producer Prairie Books), 1990.

to fill, more inflationary pressure on fixed incomes, and more concern about how to make the money last at least as long as they do.

But retirement shouldn't be a time of stress and worry. Put your mind at rest by planning for the financial and sociological impacts of retirement. What will you do with your time? How will you maintain your friendships? Where will you live? Look at the big picture as well as the individual pieces of the puzzle. By developing new skills as a rehearsal for retirement, you can set the stage for a more orderly transition. And, if you happen to be forced into retirement before you're ready, you'll be better able to deal effectively with your change in circumstances.

While many people look forward to escaping the rat race well before age 65, retiring early requires some careful planning. You'll be retired for a longer period of time, so your savings will have to last longer. But leaving the workforce early will also mean that you'll have less time to accumulate your asset base. By looking ahead, you can adapt your plan while there's still time to accumulate and organize assets, and plan the transition to the next phase in your life.

In order to retire when you want and live the way you want, take a good look at what retirement will cost. One rule of thumb, according to retirement specialist Ann Eynon, is to estimate that you will need approximately 70% of your income just prior to retirement. "But this is just a starting point," she warns. "You actually have to live in retirement for a couple of years to see what your needs and desires are before you can come up with a fixed amount." She says money is as much an emotional issue as it is a financial issue. "When you retire, some of your emotional needs — that you may have set aside for many years — come to the forefront."

Another way to figure your expenses is to do a budget for what you're spending now, and then project what it will cost when you retire. Some costs will go down. You'll probably spend less on clothing and transportation. And if you've planned carefully, you'll have made all your major purchases (such as a new car, new appliances, etc.) and you may also have eliminated most, if not all, of your debt. But some of your expenses will increase. Premiums on life and health insurance, costs for medical and dental care, and travel and entertainment costs may rise. Don't worry about being too precise in your projections. The point of the exercise is to gain some insight into what your retirement lifestyle will cost, compared with your current costs.

Next you need to add up how much income you'll receive. Your retirement income will come from a combination of sources, including government pensions, employer pension, RRSP savings, and your unregistered assets.

Finally, determine if there is a gap between income and expenses. If you have a positive gap (i.e., your expenses are less than your income), you're in great shape and can let your RRSPs continue to grow tax-sheltered. If there is a shortfall, you'll have to look to your unregistered assets and retirement savings to supplement your income. If you're unsure of all your holdings, do a net-worth statement. It will help you see how healthy you are financially and it will help when the time comes to decide where income will be drawn from, and how investments must be structured to maximize your cash flow, minimize your taxes, and protect your estate.

Whether or not you think you have enough will partially depend on your money personality. Ann says she sees three distinct types of retirees: those who are fearful of not having enough and spend little or nothing; those who want to maintain their capital and strive to live on the return their investments generate; and those who plan to draw on their capital to enjoy their retirement. How much you need will depend on how willing you are to spend your money.

*Ann Eynon is an associate of The Rogers Group in Vancouver and has been working in financial services for over 20 years. She offers clients comprehensive and pragmatic advice on retirement planning, investing, and estate planning. She's an active member of both the Canadian Association of Insurance and Financial Advisors and the Canadian Association of Financial Planners, and also belongs to the Women's Insurance Network. She's been a single mom for 20 years, raising two children to share her love of Hawaiian holidays.*

## YOUR SPENDING PLAN

Developing a spending plan for retirement begins before you retire. As with most things in life, a little planning goes a long way toward making the transition easier to manage. Not thinking about it will only leave you grappling to pull the threads together on the final day. Planning will let you determine when exactly that day should be.

You have to be prepared to make the important decisions that come with such a major life change. That means knowing where you are right now, and where you need to be in the coming months. Review your current spending plan to ensure your expenses are nicely in hand, and that you are on target with your savings goals. If you're not, you'll need to do some belt-tightening while you accumulate the extra savings you need. Better now than later. One of the best ways to see how you'll likely do is by preparing an estimated spending plan for your retirement years.

Review your current expenses and look for ways to eliminate little costs here and there. Brown bagging it, eating out two times a week instead of three, and taking the bus instead of parking the car are all ways of taking money out of your cash flow so you can put it into your retirement nest egg. You might also decide to delay your retirement. The later you retire, the more time you have to save, the higher your company and government pensions will be, and the more time your money has to grow before you have to start pulling on it. And if you also plan to work during retirement, you'll stretch your retirement savings even further. Do you have an interest or hobby you could turn into a moneymaker? Would you consider working part-time in a completely new field? Be creative. Don't underestimate the value of your skills. If you're in a position to take an extra job, you can boost your savings by increasing the money currently coming in.

Use your equity. Whether you decide to sell and rent, or use a reverse mortgage (more on that in the next chapter), your home equity is a good source of additional retirement income.

Remember that your retirement savings are made up of both your principal and the income earned on your savings. Does this sound obvious? Many people resist drawing on their principal during retirement for fear that they will outlive their money. If necessary, take your figures to a financial adviser who can show you exactly how long your principal will last. And for those of you who deny yourself even the smallest of pleasures because you are hell-bent on leaving an estate for your children, who was *your* benefactor?

When it comes to figuring out what your income will be in retirement, the key is to gather lots of information. While we often take for granted our entitlement to government pensions, neither CPP (Canada Pension Plan) nor OAS (Old Age Security) benefits are automatic. You have to apply for them. You'd be wise to send in your application about six months before you wish to receive income (age 65 for OAS and as early as age 60 for CPP), so you're sure to begin receiving your benefits when you need them. Get CPP to determine what your benefits would be if you were to decide to take them early or late. If your CPP benefits are lower than your spouse's, consider splitting your benefits so you will receive more income. This may help to eliminate or reduce the OAS clawback for your spouse. And it may also put each of you in a lower tax bracket so you'll lower your total family bill.

Next, look to your corporate pension plan, if you have one. Find out exactly how it works. If your spouse has a plan, make sure you understand the benefits of that plan too, especially the death benefits. Often pension plans pay out more when a woman signs away her survivor benefits. You may think that makes sense in the early years. But how will you cope if your husband dies before you do — which statistics show he very well might — and your income is drastically reduced? Don't just sign away your rights. Do the math. Understand the implications. Stay in control.

Check to see if your company plan or that of your spouse is integrated. This is important because an integrated plan means the corporate pension is reduced when government pension benefits kick in. This can affect your decision to take CPP early or late. And it can throw a real spanner in your budgetary works if you have not made allowance for it. If the plan promises to provide $1,200 monthly and is integrated with CPP and your monthly benefit from CPP is $650, you'll end up receiving one cheque for $650 from the government and another from the pension plan for $550, for a total of $1,200. For integrated plans, when you get pension income estimates from your employer, make sure these are the "integrated" amounts, so that you don't double-count your CPP benefits. If your integrated-plan benefits are reduced once you start receiving OAS, make sure that if your OAS is clawed back you will not lose out twice. Have a chat with the plan administrator to check the likelihood of this and then discuss how to avoid the problem with your employer. Find out if your pension is indexed to provide protection against inflation. While most pension plans have eliminated this feature, there are still some people who will benefit from indexing. Also check to see if your existing benefit programs continue into retirement. Will your health and life insurance remain intact? Do your benefits include a dental plan? Extended health care? Know where you stand, then make provision for these items yourself if you are not covered when you retire.

Ann also suggests that you ask your corporate pension plan administrator for quotes at a variety of ages. "Do your homework," she says. "Find out year by year what your pension will be approximately so you can decide when it's the right time to retire."

The role your RRSP savings play will be dependent on your other sources of income during retirement. If you'll be depending on your RRSP throughout your retirement, you'll want a steady stream of monthly income that will last at least as long as you do (and perhaps as long as your spouse as well). But you'll also need flexibility so that as your needs change, you can adjust the amount you take or how often you receive your income. Since this will be your primary source of income, inflation protection will be important. Choose investments that will help you preserve your capital (to protect your future income) while maximizing your yield (to cover inflation).

For some people, RRSP assets will be supplemental to the income they'll receive from other sources such as a company pension plan or rental property. If you are one of these fortunates, wait until you're 69 to convert your RRSP so you aren't forced to take income before you need it. The next chapter provides more detail on your options when it comes time to make decisions on RRIFs, annuities, and other strategies.

### KEEPING A ROOF OVER YOUR HEAD

It's time to set the date for your mortgage-burning party. If you eliminate this single largest debt from your cash flow, you'll find yourself with a substantial increase in disposable income. But just getting rid of the debt isn't the only thing to look at. Since your income will likely be reduced during retirement, you'll need to do any repairs that may be required while you still have a strong income. Look at your house objectively. Does it need painting? A new roof? How's the furnace?

Look at the expenses associated with running your home so you can get a clear picture of your fixed expenses during retirement. What does it cost to maintain your home? What are your costs for taxes, heating, electricity? Think about the amount of space you'll be using when you retire. If your home is larger than you will need, consider converting the basement to a separate apartment to provide some additional income during retirement — or to provide a home for wayward children as they return to the once-empty nest.

If you plan to stay in the home long term, make sure that you take care of anything that will become difficult to manage as you age. Large lawns are tough to cut. Slippery floors, long driveways that have to be shovelled in the winter, and too many stairs can become real encumbrances, draining the pleasure from staying in your home.

Also think about how much of your time will be spent at home, in the neighbourhood, or out of town. If you plan to spend lots of time at the cottage, do you really want to keep two houses going? If all your friends are in Florida in the winter, how will you feel? How many of your interests and activities take place close to your home? How close do you live to other family members?

## Reviewing Your Goals

For now, you'll mainly be focused on preparing for that all-important and fast-approaching retirement date. You'll want to have most, if not all, of your debt paid off. You'll want to make sure you're maximizing your RRSP contributions and growth so you can accumulate as much as possible before you stop working. But those shouldn't be your only goals. After all, you'll likely live as long in retirement as you spent working.

One of the biggest mistakes people make is thinking that at retirement everything becomes fixed in time and space. There's a real sense that the accumulation of assets will end (what about investment income?) and that inflation will cease (what about the inflation that will erode your income throughout the 20 or 30 years that you are retired?). It's a mistake to see your retirement date as the end. It isn't. It's the beginning of a whole new stage of life. And it brings its ups and downs just as in every other stage of your life.

Since retirement is a new beginning, think about how you will restyle your life. In my *Retirement Answer Book*, I offer suggestions on how people can mentally prepare for the shift from working to retirement. Many people skip this important step. Once you've spent some time on the psychological stuff, and you've made plans for what you'll do during retirement, you have to make sure you'll have enough money to fund your excursion into a new lifestyle. And remember, since that new lifestyle will probably last almost as long as the old one did, you had better be prepared for some long-term financial planning.

## CASH-MANAGEMENT STRATEGIES

Holding bank accounts jointly is one of the first things you should consider as you move closer to retirement. It's one way to simplify your life and your estate plan. Another way to simplify is to consolidate all those savings and chequing accounts into a single account. "Bring it under one or two roofs," says Ann Eynon, "so you don't have to worry about what your money is doing." Ann says that for people who have moved into retirement, "a common mantra is 'I cannot be bothered with watching the money anymore. I am retired. I have other interests. I need this to be as simple as possible.' Other people see themselves spending more time charting their money's growth, monitoring their portfolios on their computers. But eventually, even these people find the whole thing overwhelming and move to simplify."

One of your primary objectives in planning for retirement should be to do so debt-free. Ongoing credit-card or loan payments can create a real strain on a fixed income. And if interest rates should rise, you could find more and more of your food money going to interest costs. If you have outstanding debt that is not tax-deductible, make sure you're working to pay off that debt as quickly as possible. Your investment strategy should balance your need to reduce your debt with your need to grow your assets. If you have a low-return investment (say, a GIC earning 5%) and a high-cost credit balance (your Sears card has a balance and you're paying exorbitant interest), you'll be way better off cashing in your pre-tax GIC to pay off your post-tax Sears card. Another good strategy is to use your tax refund from an RRSP contribution to pay off a part of your debt.

## KEEPING A HEALTHY CREDIT IDENTITY

You're likely to be well past your major borrowing needs at this point in your life. Now you're looking to get rid of all your debt. But the fact remains that a healthy credit history and the ability to borrow money when you need it are part of a sound financial plan. You just never know when you might need a bridge for your cash flow. If the car suddenly needs major repairs and your GIC doesn't mature for six months, being able to access credit could make the difference. Since one of the only sure things in life is change — and the most significant changes are seldom predictable — having the flexibility to adapt will give you a greater sense of control.

Keeping a healthy credit history as you approach retirement means continuing to borrow money and pay it off to maintain your credit history. Use your credits cards to make purchases, and pay them off every month on time. With each payment, you'll keep your credit history current. If you have a line of credit, draw on it from time to time, as the need arises, and pay it off quickly. That'll keep it in good standing.


## YOUR PAY-YOURSELF-FIRST INVESTMENT PLAN

Your registered assets will likely be one of the mainstays of your investment portfolio, so it's very important that you stay on top of them. Monitor the overall rate of return you're getting, and take a little time each year to evaluate your plan to ensure it's achieving your objectives. A small increase in annual return can mean a significant increase in your portfolio's growth over the long term. Two percent may not sound like much, but it is. Over time, even a small difference in your rate of return can have a tremendous impact on how long your retirement nest egg lasts. The following chart shows the difference in growth for $10,000 invested at various rates of return. As you can see, the differences are significant.

| | RATE OF RETURN | | | |
|---|---|---|---|---|
| **YEARS** | **2%** | **4%** | **7%** | **11%** |
| 5 | $11,040 | $12,161 | $14,025 | $16,851 |
| 10 | 12,189 | 14,802 | 19,672 | 28,394 |
| 15 | 13,459 | 18,009 | 27,590 | 47,846 |
| 20 | 14,859 | 21,911 | 38,679 | 80,623 |
| 25 | 16,406 | 26,658 | 54,274 | 135,855 |
| 30 | 18,114 | 32,434 | 76,123 | 228,923 |

Assuming you choose a portfolio of investments that gives you only a 2% higher rate of return, over 30 years your investments would have earned an extra 78%.

If you think these differences are only applicable when you are building your assets, here's more good news. Once you retire and begin to make withdrawals, even a small difference in return can extend the life of your retirement portfolio. A portfolio of $100,000 invested at 7% with an annual payout of $12,000 would last approximately 14 years, for a total payout of approximately $167,000. By increasing your return just 2%, the same portfolio would last just over 17 years, for a total payout of approximately $205,000. With a return of 11%, the $100,000 portfolio would last almost 25 years, for a total payout of approximately $298,000.

There's no better way to get a big-picture perspective of your financial position than by completing a net-worth statement. Start by listing your assets. Be realistic about their value. Assets will include your cash on hand, in accounts, and on deposit. Check the value of investments such as stocks, bonds, and mutual funds in the financial section of the newspaper or with a broker. The cash-surrender value of your insurance should be stated in your policy. To estimate cars, boats, and trailers, refer to comparables in the classifieds. And remember, while you paid the retail price for many of your possessions, you'll likely only receive the wholesale value if you decide to sell them. Now add up everything you owe. This will include your mortgage, outstanding balances on your line of credit and credit cards, and any loans you may have. It'll also include yet-to-be-paid bills (referred to as your "accounts payable"), as well as taxes owing. Subtract your total liabilities from your total assets and you have your net worth.

Once you've completed your net-worth statement, take some time to look over your assets. Are you satisfied with their quality? Are they earning the return you expected? Are you satisfied with your total asset base? Perhaps you have a large amount of cash in a savings account. By moving that money to a term deposit or money-market fund you'll very likely earn a higher rate of return. Next, have a look at your liabilities. Are you paying the lowest possible interest? Can you renegotiate? How quickly can you eliminate these debts? Perhaps you have an underperforming investment that you could sell to eliminate all or part of your debt. Even a small payment toward your mortgage principal will move you closer to freedom from a mortgage during retirement.

## YOUR EMERGENCY FUND

Don't forget your emergency fund. An unexpected big bill can put a serious crimp in your spending plan. The size of your emergency fund will depend on your financial commitments and the amount of income you have regularly flowing in. If it looks like things may be tight during retirement, establish a fairly significant emergency fund before you retire. If you know for certain that you will have more income than you'll need, your emergency fund can be smaller. Also consider the source of your income. A pension that is indexed is more reliable than income from interest-bearing investments, since a decline in interest rates could mean significantly less income.

## REVIEWING YOUR INSURANCE

At the very least, have enough insurance to cover your funeral expenses. However, you may also need to have enough insurance to protect a dependent or two. With family structures changing, it's no longer fair to assume that all your dependents will be self-sufficient before you take leave of this world.

I tease my lovely husband quite often about the fact that he'll have to mature his RRSP assets before his youngest son reaches 21. Just because Ken decides to retire at 60, 65, or 70 doesn't mean that Malcolm's needs for support will have disappeared. And with university costs set to explode, it's unlikely he'll be able to put himself through under his own steam. We'll have to help.

Another important consideration that will have an impact on the amount of insurance you'll need is how your retirement income cash flow will change after the death of one partner. Let's say your spouse has a great pension and after he dies, you'll receive 60% of the pension income. That's the typical survivor's benefit. Have you thought about whether or not this will be enough? I know that you'll have fewer expenses with only one person to feed, clothe, and the like. But inflation will have done its dirty work in terms of reducing the purchasing power of your money. The question to ask yourself then is, "If my spouse dies 20 years after we retire, will there be sufficient cash flow from all sources to allow me to live comfortably?" If the answer is no, speak to an insurance agent about getting extra life coverage. At this point, you'll probably only want to look at term insurance. And prepare yourself for some pretty stiff premiums.

The alternative, of course, would be to put yourself on a savings plan — perhaps investing the amount you would have spent in premiums. Over the long term, you might end up ahead. You'll have to feel fairly secure in terms of how long you and your spouse will live. An unexpected death would cramp the plan.

## TAX IMPLICATIONS

Your income-splitting strategies should be well established at this point. But this is a good time to check how much retirement income you and your spouse will be receiving to make sure you're on the mark. If you find that one of you has significantly more projected pension income than the other, you can make all future contributions to a spousal RRSP to even the playing field. Registered assets will be taxed as they are withdrawn from an RRSP or RRIF. If you also plan to use unregistered assets, or to liquidate investments for cash flow, consider how these will be taxed. Remember, the trick is for each of you to pay the same amount of tax so that, as a couple, you pay the lowest amount of tax possible. You also need a strategy to maximize your government benefits.

When the feds announced in 1989 that people with annual incomes over $50,000 must repay part or all of their Old Age Security (OAS), there was an uproar. Despite the hullabaloo, no one did anything about it, so now if your income exceeds the threshold (which was $53,215 in 1998 because it was partially indexed for inflation) you'll be assessed a tax on any income above that threshold, at a rate of 15%, up to the total of all the OAS you've received. In plain English: For every $100 in income you receive above the threshold amount, you have to pay back $15 of your OAS benefits.

One way to reduce the impact of the clawback is to split your income as evenly as possible between you and your spouse. As a couple, you could have a joint income of over $100,000 and not be affected by the clawback. Another is to delay receiving your CPP/QPP benefits until you absolutely need them to meet your expenses.

If you are subject to the OAS clawback, proactively manage your income to claim at least some benefits. A particularly high income in one year and a lower income the next may allow you to keep your OAS

benefits at least every other year. How so, you say? Try this. If you plan
to draw income from your registered investments, withdraw the amount
you need from your RRIFs, above and beyond any minimum withdrawal
amounts required by law (see the next chapter for details), for two years
at once. You will be taxed on the full amount in the present year. Then
the next year, you won't need to withdraw any income beyond the minimum amount. Ta da! Your income won't surpass the clawback threshold,
so you'll keep your OAS for that year. By making a larger-than-normal
withdrawal in one year and a smaller withdrawal the next, you'll be able
to take advantage of OAS every other year.

One of the things many people are concerned about as they approach
retirement is how their estate will be taxed. My mother-in-law is a perfect
example. She wants to make sure that she passes as much of her remaining assets on to her kids as she can and so, inevitably, the following
question came up: "Does it make more sense to use my registered assets
first, leaving my unregistered assets to my children, or should I do it the
other way?" Good question. And not an easy one to answer. Advisers
often say you should leave your registered assets within the plan as long
as possible so they can continue to compound on a tax-deferred basis.
However, as soon as you die, providing you do not have a spouse to whom
to pass those assets, the full amount of the registered assets will be
included in your income for the year of your death and you'll likely pay
a whopping amount of tax. The other option is to draw down on your
registered assets first so you're paying a lower rate of tax over a longer
term, while leaving your unregistered (previously taxed) assets intact for
passing on.

So what should you do? As with most things about money, it all depends.
It depends on your specific circumstances: how much you have, how long
you think you'll live, what the mix is between registered and unregistered
assets. If the amount you draw from your registered assets moves you into
the highest marginal tax rate so you'll be paying the maximum tax anyway,
it makes sense to leave the registered assets intact and have your estate
pay the tax at the end when you no longer need the money. If you want to
mitigate the loss to your beneficiaries, you can always use a portion of
the money you pull each year from the registered pool to purchase a life
insurance policy to help offset the loss to the tax man. For the average
Canadian, however, life insurance at age 60 or 70 is very, very expensive and

the cost often outweighs the benefit. Ann Eynon suggests that you "look at your RRSPs and RRIFs as your money, and use it."

## ESTATE PLANNING

It's time to review and, perhaps, update your will and get all the legal and financial information in order. If you haven't already done so, put your powers of attorney in place. If you're still hesitating about making a will, might I suggest a small shift in perspective. While estate planning is often seen as a discussion about death, it really isn't. It is a way to make the lives of the people you leave behind less stressful. It's also the only way to ensure your assets are distributed as you would want them to be.

Don't fall into the trap of thinking that your estate isn't big enough to warrant the time and money of bothering with an estate plan. And don't think that your lawyer, accountant, or financial planner will be able to step in and deal with the issues. Once you leave this beautiful earth, everything financial stops until your estate is probated. If you die without a will, you just prolong the agony.

Immediately upon your death, the government will deem that your capital property has been disposed of (watch for the term "deemed disposition" in this context.) Any increase in value on a stock, bond, your cottage, or any other asset that can increase in value will be subject to tax at the current capital-gains rate. There are some exceptions. You can transfer capital property to a spouse without paying tax. This defers the tax until your spouse dies. If you have U.S. assets such as stocks, bonds, a business interest, or a condo in Florida, you might also have to pay estate tax on these assets. The problem that arises from deemed disposition is that while tax may be payable, it may not be the best time to sell the asset because to do so would be to get less than fair value. Or perhaps you don't want to sell the asset at all. It may break your heart to think about your art collection, painstakingly acquired over the years, being sold off to pay the taxes on your family cottage. Whatever your feelings, your estate will have to deal with the legalities of your move from this world to the next.

There is an excellent booklet available from Royal Trust entitled "The Cottage: Keeping it in the Family and Away from the Tax Man" that I recommend for anyone with cottage property they wish to pass on.

If you don't have a will, you've effectively given up control over your hard-earned money to the government. You wouldn't do that in life, so why would you do it in death? I know you won't be here, but your spouse, your children, and your grandchildren will. Don't put them through that discomfort and aggravation. If you don't have a will, put down the book, go to the telephone, and call your lawyer. If you don't know whom to call, ask the Law Society for a recommendation. If that doesn't sit well with you, e-mail me at getgvo@interlog.com or write me care of my publisher and I'll try to help. It doesn't matter what it takes. *You need a will.* Get moving!

# 17

# When You Retire

*Money can't buy happiness, 'tis true, but it certainly quiets the nerves.*

IRISH PROVERB

*An aged man is but a paltry thing.*
*A tattered coat upon a stick, unless*
*Soul clap its hands and sing, and louder sing*
*For every tatter in its mortal dress.*

W. B. YEATS

Oh, joyous retirement! They've presented you with the gold watch, feted you with wine and cheese, and packed you off home. Now what? It's a question lots of people have as they watch the hands on their newly acquired timepiece slowly count off the seconds, minutes, and hours.

Hello! Now you get to do all the things you've always dreamed of but never had time to do. If you've planned for this first day of the rest of your life, that's great — your date book is jammed, and you have the money you need to pay for all your activities. If you haven't, it's time to get moving.

## Your Spending Plan

Your retirement income will come from a variety of sources: government pensions, employer-sponsored pensions, personal retirement savings, unregistered investments, and the sale of assets. You and your spouse should keep your figures separate so that you'll be ready when you get into a discussion of how much either one of you will have individually. You'll also need separate figures to calculate your income tax. Check with Revenue Canada to see what the most current income-tax brackets are for your province.

To retire when you want, and to live the way you want during retirement, you have to know just what it will cost to live. Costs will go up or down depending on what stage of retirement you're in. If you are still working part-time or if you are travelling extensively, your expenses will be higher than they will be when you choose to sit on the porch watching the sunset.

You'll also have to make a decision about what to do with your RRSP money. You must mature your RRSP assets by the end of the year in which you turn 69. You can do so earlier if you find you need additional retirement income.

If you think your RRSP savings will be your primary source of retirement income, ensure the retirement income option you choose provides a steady stream of monthly income that will last at least as long as you do (and perhaps as long as your spouse as well). Registered Retirement Income Funds (RRIFs) are usually my first recommendation because they provide the flexibility to design an income stream that meets your specific needs — in terms of both amounts and frequency — as well as the ability to increase or decrease your income as your needs change. More about RRIFs shortly.

If you benefit from a nice company pension plan or you'll be using your unregistered assets to provide an income stream, delay converting your RRSP to keep the tax-deferred growth going for as long as possible. Converting before absolutely necessary means you'll be forced to take income when you don't need it. If you find that you do need some of your retirement savings to make ends meet, you can always make a withdrawal from your RRSP. If you have no other source of pension income (which you need to claim the $1,000 pension-income tax credit), then roll only as much as you will need each year to a RRIF (it'll be the $1,000 plus the applicable withholding taxes if the $1,000 is above your minimum annual payout amount) and take the full year's amount as a lump-sum withdrawal.

With sufficient income from your company and government pension plans to meet your basic needs, allocate your RRSP money to special needs: to travel, to supplement your family's income when pension benefits are reduced due to death of the primary pensioner, or to offset the impact of inflation on your purchasing power. If you don't need to draw on your RRSP savings at all, focus on minimizing the income you need to withdraw and, by extension, the tax you must pay. As we'll see below, you can mitigate your tax liabilities by using your younger spouse's age to determine how much you are required to withdraw or by taking the income annually at the end of the year.

### ANNUITIES AND RRIFs

Okay, so now it's time to mature your RRSP. You could simply withdraw the money in cash. Careful, though. What may seem like the easiest option can have negative tax ramifications. When you take cash from your RRSP, that money is included in your income. This can push you into a higher tax bracket and result in your having to pay considerably more tax. The best way to minimize the tax implications is to convert your retirement savings to a regular stream of income using either an annuity or a RRIF.

When you buy an annuity, you give an insurance company, bank, or trust company your money in exchange for a promise of a specific amount of income each month. There are two basic types of life annuities: a straight life annuity provides a regular income payout over your entire life; a joint-and-last-survivor annuity provides income over your life and/or that of your spouse. The amount you receive depends on several factors, including how much money you have, your life expectancy, your sex, and the interest rate in effect when you buy the annuity. Low interest rates mean low monthly incomes, which is one reason why annuities are less popular when interest rates are low. Assuming you buy a $100,000 joint-and-last-survivor annuity with a 60% residual for your spouse and no other guarantees, a 65-year-old man would receive $8,787.68 a year for life. A woman purchasing the exact same annuity would receive $8,500 a year.

There's a potential downside to an annuity: you'll be living on a fixed income, since the monthly payments remain the same. What seems a princely sum at the outset may feel like a pauper's allowance in 20 years. An annual income of $8,500 would have a purchasing power of only $4,700 in 20 years. Remember, too, that surviving spouses will receive less income. The death of the first spouse usually means a 40% drop-off, so the survivor receives only 60% of the original income amount. While you may find $8,787 a year to work for you as a couple, the question you have to ask yourself is, "How comfortable would my spouse be on only $5,272?"

The retirement income alternative that has become most popular with Canadians is conversion of RRSP savings into a RRIF, to create a flow of income during retirement. Your money remains tax-sheltered as long as it remains in the plan, and you pay tax only on the money you take out each year. Basically, a RRIF is a continuation of your RRSP so you can hold the same investments. You can open a RRIF at any age and roll over as much or as little of your RRSP dollars as you wish. You can choose from a variety of investment types so you can use an investment strategy that will help you preserve your capital (to protect your future income) while maximizing your yield (to cover inflation).

A legislated minimum annual payout (MAP) must be paid from the RRIF each year, with one exception: it is not necessary to take a minimum amount in the year the RRIF is opened. In the year in which the plan is set up, the MAP is considered to be zero.

The MAP is calculated using one of two rules: the minimum-amount formula and the minimum-amount schedule of percentages. The formula calculation applies when you open a RRIF before you reach 71, and stays in effect until you turn 79. The formula is: the value of the RRIF at the beginning of the year, divided by 90 less the age of the planholder at the beginning of the year. You can also use your spouse's age for this calculation, provided you make that decision before the first payment is made. So, if on January 1 your RRIF was worth $165,000 and you were 64, your calculation would look like this: $165,000 ÷ (90 − 64) = $6,346.15.

The schedule-of-percentages calculation applies in all other circumstances. The difference is that you need to consult a table of values for the calculation (see the next page). To determine your minimum amount using this schedule of percentages, choose the percentage that corresponds with your age at the beginning of the year. Multiply that percentage by the value

| SCHEDULE OF PERCENTAGES | |
| --- | --- |
| Existing Age | Percentage of RRIF |
| 71 | 7.38 |
| 72 | 7.48 |
| 73 | 7.59 |
| 74 | 7.71 |
| 75 | 7.85 |
| 76 | 7.99 |
| 77 | 8.15 |
| 78 | 8.33 |
| 79 | 8.53 |
| 80 | 8.75 |
| 81 | 8.99 |
| 82 | 9.27 |
| 83 | 9.58 |
| 84 | 9.93 |
| 85 | 10.33 |
| 86 | 10.79 |
| 87 | 11.33 |
| 88 | 11.96 |
| 89 | 12.71 |
| 90 | 13.62 |
| 91 | 14.73 |
| 92 | 16.12 |
| 93 | 17.92 |
| 94+ | 20.00 |

of your RRIF at the beginning of the year. So, if on January 1 your RRIF was worth $45,000 and you were 81, your calculation would look like this: $45,000 x 8.99% = $4,045.50.

Be sure to structure the assets in your portfolio so that you will have enough cash available each year for the withdrawal.

The main advantage to a RRIF is flexibility. As Ann Eynon puts it, "With a RRIF, you have not made a lifelong decision. You've made a decision that can be changed at almost any time, depending on the underlying investments you're holding." You can change your asset mix at any time and, if desired, you can take out more than the minimum amount. And, as you get older, if you decide an annuity suits you more because you no longer want to be concerned with the management of your investments, you can buy one using your RRIF assets. Alternatively, if you want to lock in interest rates because they have risen dramatically, buying strip bonds is another option that guarantees the rate for the term you choose, while giving you the flexibility to sell the investment should you need the cash.

So, a RRIF gives you the flexibility to receive more income in years when you need it and less in years when you don't. It gives you the flexibility to change your mind and change your investment strategy. And if you decide to take only the MAP each year, your RRIF is guaranteed to last a lifetime (the size of the fund may get very small as years go on, but it will never be completely depleted). Ultimately, it gives you more control over your money.

Besides your RRSP investments, you may also have a portfolio of investments that are unregistered. Perhaps you have been buying CSBs through a payroll deduction plan. Maybe you've been investing in mutual funds. Or perhaps you have GICs, or a rental property or two, which can provide a regular income. Having established an investment portfolio to supplement your retirement income needs, you may now be looking for ways to manage the income from those investments to supplement your cash flow in retirement.

Consider a GIC that pays monthly interest. Each month, you'll receive a steady flow of interest income that you can use to supplement your other retirement income. And since the interest rate is guaranteed for the term of the GIC, you'll know exactly how much you're going to get. "Taking monthly interest from your GIC," says Ann, "gives more of a sense of steady cash flow so you can plan your expenses and life." You'll lose about 0.25% (or 25 basis points, if you're talking bankese) by choosing a monthly payout, but your financial life will be more predictable.

In setting up your GICs, stagger your maturities. Instead of buying a single five-year GIC, split your money between a one-, two-, three-, four-, and five-year investment. Referred to as "laddering," this will help to protect against fluctuations in interest rates at renewal time. Also consider investing a portion of your nest egg in a redeemable GIC. This will provide you with the flexibility to get extra cash, should you need it. While the interest rate on the redeemable GIC is a little lower, it's often worth it to have access to cash — just in case.

If most of your investments have been in mutual funds and you need some way of taking a steady income to supplement your other retirement income, ask about a systematic withdrawal plan. Each month you can redeem a specific dollar amount in mutual-fund units, with the cash being deposited directly to your account. This strategy also allows you to use a dollar-cost averaging strategy, but instead of buying regularly, you'll be selling regularly. This will even out the ups and downs in the market so you'll end up with an average selling price. "This often gives tax-preferred income," says Ann, "because the withdrawals are a combination of dividend and capital gain, both of which receive special tax treatment."

Anyone over 60 should also take full advantage of the special rates offered by most banks. For GIC investors, it usually means an extra 0.25% in interest on GICs. And it can mean lower account fees. Once you've retired, you know how important it is to take care of those pennies. Start by figuring out what you want, and then go shopping for the products and services that will help you meet your needs. That's the way to make your investments pay for retirement.

## KEEPING A ROOF OVER YOUR HEAD

Where do you plan to live? In the same house or apartment, or will you sell and move to a smaller home? For most people, the bulk of their financial assets is tied up in their homes. Folks figure that when they retire, they'll sell, buy a smaller place, and have lots of money left over. But do you really want to move away from your family, your neighbours, and everything that's familiar?

For some people the decision to move is easy. Perhaps they're attracted by warmer climes. For some the lure of a small town or being part of a retirement community is very attractive. Or maybe the house is just too big or inappropriate for their needs. How much more income would you have if you sold your house, eliminated your maintenance/tax costs, and rented? Here's a calculation that may help.

| | |
|---|---|
| Approximate value of home | $ _____ |
| Less sales-related costs | $ _____ |
| Balance to invest | $ _____ |
| | |
| Return expected at ____% | $ _____ |
| Tax payable on return | $ _____ |
| Net return | $ _____ |
| | |
| Net return | $ _____ |
| Plus savings on maintenance• | $ _____ |
| Less estimated cost of rental•• | $ _____ |
| Balance | $ _____ |

• When you sell your home, you'll likely eliminate many of your expenses, such as property tax, snow removal, house maintenance, heating, and hydro. Remember, though, that you may still have to pay utility costs if you rent.
•• Make sure you choose a comparable home, one you'll be happy to live in. Check the newspaper for the prices of rentals in areas where you'd feel comfortable living. Investigate subsidized-housing alternatives. Don't underestimate your space requirements. Often people who move from houses to apartments feel "squeezed."

You also have the option of living in your home while using the equity to finance your retirement. This is done with a reverse mortgage, which draws on the equity in your home to generate a monthly income. No interest or principal is due until the home is sold, the reverse mortgage comes due, or the homeowner dies. At this point, if the appreciated value of the property is greater than the amount of the accrued reverse mortgage, the excess goes to the estate. If the value of the property is less than the amount owed, the financial institution that gave you the mortgage has to eat the difference. This is one reason financial institutions don't allow you to use the full value of your home for a reverse mortgage. They limit the amount they will "reverse mortgage" to protect themselves from a decline in the value of your property.

There are two basic types of reverse mortgages: a straight reverse mortgage and a reverse annuity mortgage. A straight reverse mortgage provides a monthly amount for a specified term while building a mortgage against your home. When the agreed-upon term has expired (that is, the mortgage comes due), you must repay the mortgage, usually through the sale of the home. If the property has increased in value, you may be able to finance another loan. If the property has decreased in value, this can leave you with no equity and no place to live.

With a reverse annuity mortgage, a portion of your equity is used to purchase an annuity with a term that matches the mortgage's. The income you receive (as with any annuity) is based on your life expectancy, sex, marital status, and the prevailing interest rates. When your home is sold, or at your death, you or your estate will receive the difference between the sale price of the home and the income you received from the reverse mortgage. If you live longer than the insurance company expected, you'll continue to receive payments for life. The repayment to the insurance company will come from the proceeds of the sale of the home. Your estate will not be liable for more than that.

A reverse mortgage is a "rising debt" loan. This means that the total amount you owe grows over time. Let's say you have a house that is currently worth $189,000. You decide to use a reverse mortgage for $30,000 over 10 years at 11% to supplement your income. You receive $250 a month, or $3,000 a year. At the end of 10 years you will have been paid $30,000, and you will owe the lender $30,000 plus the accumulated interest ($23,970), for a total of $53,970.

In trying to decide if a reverse mortgage is for you, think about whether housing prices in your neighbourhood will likely appreciate or depreciate. Consider, too, interest rates and the various fees (legal, administration, and so on) associated with a reverse mortgage.

If you want to generate some extra income on a temporary basis, a reverse mortgage may be just the ticket. But be prepared to sell your home or be certain that you'll be coming into a whack of money that will allow you to repay the debt you've built up. If you're looking for long-term income, know that at your death there may be no residual value from the home payable to your estate. If you can live with these facts, then a reverse mortgage may give you the financial flexibility to ensure a comfortable retirement.

Many lower-cost housing alternatives exist that you may wish to look into. Subsidized dwellings are not limited to public housing; non-profit housing and co-operative housing developments also offer alternatives geared to a retiree's income. Canada Mortgage and Housing Corporation (CMHC) has information that may help you decide how you want to live in retirement. Contact your local CMHC office for copies of *Housing Choices for Older Canadians* and start learning about your alternatives. You can also get information on subsidized housing from non-profit and co-operative housing agencies.

If you decide your present home isn't suitable for retirement, you'll have to decide whether you will move within your community, divide your time between two communities (perhaps your cottage in the summer and autumn, and a warm climate in the winter and spring), or move to a whole new area. Keep in mind that there are special considerations that must be given to moving to a whole new community and to spending all or part of your time in another country. These are covered in more detail in my *Retirement Answer Book*.

## CASH-MANAGEMENT STRATEGIES

The key to keeping your cash flow working during retirement is to know when the money is coming in and when it has to go out. This is something of an adjustment for people who have been on the payroll for years and have received their salary every month on the second Friday or on the 15th and the 30th. During retirement, it may take a little more planning.

You may receive income quarterly, if you'll be earning dividends, or annually, if you're earning interest. And depending on how you structure your RRSP or RRIF payouts, your cash may flow in monthly, semi-annually, or even annually. You need to know specifically when the money will come in and when money will flow out. Some expenses such as your tax bill will come up quarterly. Others, such as insurance, may be on an annual basis. The whole idea of setting up a cash flow is to have the income when you need it.

A cash flow typically lists all the sources of income and expenses down the left side of the page. Each month has a column of its own going across the top. For each month, the sources of income and the expected expenses are written in so that you know exactly when the money is arriving and when it is departing. It gives a clear picture of what you can expect, and shows you where the potential holes may be so you can adjust your income stream to meet your needs. If you know you'll have an insurance bill in December, you could arrange to take extra from your RRIF in November to cover the cost. Similarly, if you're concerned about meeting your quarterly tax payments, even if you're receiving a monthly income from your pension or annuity, you can arrange to have extra income — perhaps from dividends or from GIC interest — paid to you to cover your tax bill.

## KEEPING A HEALTHY CREDIT IDENTITY

The same rules that apply just prior to retirement carry through to retirement. Keeping a healthy credit identity is one part of a sound financial plan. Without it, you could find yourself in trouble. You may not ever need it, but if you do, it'll be there.

## YOUR PAY-YOURSELF-FIRST INVESTMENT PLAN

You'll likely spend as long in retirement as you did working. And since retirement means different things to different people, and has its own series of stages, you need to keep planning for the next stage. You may begin by semiretiring. Stage One could include working part-time, starting a new business, or working as a consultant. In Stage Two of your retirement, you may plan to stop working completely while you remain very active in other areas. Your active retirement might include extensive travel, activities such as golfing, skiing, or cycling, or active volunteering. Stage Three would be your less active years — the years when you plan to remain in your home, with or without help from others. Stage Four may be the years when you choose to move to a retirement home that provides you with the help you need in managing day-to-day activities, as well as specialized medical attention.

Since your RRSP contribution limit is based on your previous year's earned income, you can make an RRSP contribution during your first year of retirement based on your last year of working (providing you and/or your spouse are under the age of 69). Make sure you adjust your income during your first year of retirement to take advantage of this tax-deferral opportunity.

If you receive a retiring allowance (a kind of lump-sum bonus payment) when you retire from work, you can transfer a large portion of it to an RRSP in order to shelter it from tax. The eligible amount is limited to $2,000 for each year of employment plus an additional $1,500 for each year of employment prior to 1989 for which employer contributions were not made to the company pension plan or were not vested (or made a permanent, unrescindable part of the pension). For the purpose of calculating retirement allowance rollovers to an RRSP, any part of a calendar year is considered a full year.

Your employer will determine the amount that qualifies for the rollover, and if you have the transfer done directly (using a TD2 form, or NRTA1 form if you are a non-resident), no tax will be withheld at source on the funds that have been rolled over. If you receive your retiring allowance directly, you have until 60 days after the end of the year in which the payment is received to contribute the amount allowed to your RRSP.

Accumulated vacation pay and pension benefits are not eligible for this rollover. Your retiring allowance can be transferred only to your own RRSP, not to a spousal plan.

Even after you retire, you can continue to contribute to an RRSP, providing you or your spouse is under 69 and has a source of earned income. Rental income and income stemming from employment, such as disability payments, are forms of earned income.

Another way to maximize your RRSP investments' growth is to allow them to grow in their tax-sheltered environment for as long as possible. Even if you retire before 69, you can continue to maximize your retirement assets by leaving the money invested in the RRSP for as long as possible. Use your unregistered investments as a source of income first. Then, when necessary, take only as much as you need from your plan each year, leaving the remaining amount to continue to grow on a tax-deferred basis.

A lot has been said about the importance of diversifyng your investment portfolio. Since different types of investments earn varying rates of return depending on economic conditions, by holding a mix of investments you can reduce your exposure to the poor performance of any one type of investment to produce a steady rate of growth. That steady rate of growth, in turn, helps to keep the impact of inflation in check. As you move into retirement, you may be asking yourself, "Should I change my asset mix?" Rules of thumb abound in the financial world, and a common one for asset mix is that it should be adjusted based on your age: The percentage of equities in your portfolio should be equal to 100 minus your age. That would mean that at age 60, you'd hold 40% of your investments in equities.

Ann Eynon has a different philosophy. She says, "I don't think any rule of thumb can be used for adjusting the basket of investments since money personality is number one." It's a difficult thing to explain, this idea of money personality, because feelings come into it. "On the day you retire, if you have a good asset mix and it's been working for you, if you can sleep and if your tummy says it's okay, stick with it. After all, every single person has their own comfort level or sleep factor. Some people want to be so cautious that they will only invest in term deposits and Canada Savings Bonds, and that's absolutely correct for them. They shouldn't be criticized for doing that." She stresses, however, that it is important that you regularly review your investment mix to ensure that as your life and priorities change, your asset allocation continues to satisfy your needs. If you find there are significant changes to your lifestyle, at that point, "you may want to make changes to your financial picture."

## YOUR EMERGENCY FUND

By this time you probably feel you no longer need an emergency fund. You may be right. It really depends on how often you receive your retirement income, how accessible your assets are, and how likely you are to hit an emergency at this point in your life. You know you won't be laid off. But what would happen if interest rates took a significant downturn for a few months and you were forced to start dipping further into your capital to make ends meet? Or what if a sudden illness required you to lay out money for a nurse? How would you and your cash flow cope? As one person said to me as we sat together in a hospital, waiting for our children to be diagnosed, "Life is an emergency."

At this point in your life, make sure every dollar is working as hard as possible for you — since you're not doing any work yourself! Having the equivalent of three or six months' income set aside for an emergency may be too much of a burden on your overall investment portfolio. Instead, look to other ways of coping. If you have your credit cards, you could use them in the short term. A line of credit would be better because the cost is usually lower. Or you could use investments that can be easily liquidated. Canada Savings Bonds come to mind. One of the nice things about CSBs is that the rate is guaranteed not to decline during the year. However, if interest rates are increasing, the government generally increases the rate on the bonds to discourage people from cashing in their bonds. In this respect, they beat short-term GICs hands down.

## REVIEWING YOUR INSURANCE

One reason for having insurance at this point in your life is to provide enough money to meet the tax liability your estate will incur at your death. Since market or economic conditions may make it an inopportune time to sell assets immediately after your death — and since some assets, such as the family cottage, have a lot of sentimental value — having a lump-sum benefit from an insurance policy would provide the flexibility needed.

Let's take the example of a couple who have RRSP assets. When the first spouse dies, the assets can be transferred to the surviving spouse on a tax-deferred basis. In two words: No Tax. But when the second spouse dies, guess what? Tax — and big-time! Let's say you and your spouse each have $100,000 in RRIF assets. Your spouse dies, and so his $100,000 rolls into your plan. Now you have $200,000. Assuming you live on air and die with $200,000 remaining, and the highest marginal tax rate in your province is 48%, your estate will have to pay $96,000 in tax to the government. Ouch! If you have three children to whom you would leave this money equally, they'll each get just under $35,000. Now let's say you had an insurance policy that covered those taxes owed, along with any other taxes calculated on your estate. Instead, each of your three children would be able to split the full $200,000, receiving almost $67,000 a piece. The question to think about is, How much estate protection will you need to cover your assets? If you feel you'll have sufficient cash to pay the taxes directly from your estate, that's cool. You won't need insurance. But if your estate will be eaten away by taxes, leaving far less than you imagined for your heirs, insurance could be the solution.

## TAX IMPLICATIONS

Here are 16 tips to help ensure that when you retire, you're not paying more tax than is absolutely necessary. I've taken them from my *Retirement Answer Book*.

1. Once you are 65, make sure you have enough pension income to take advantage of the $1,000 pension-income tax credit, which allows you to earn the first $1,000 in pension income tax-free (see pages 267–68).
2. People 65 and older also qualify for the age credit. If one spouse can't use this tax credit fully, the unused portion can be transferred to the other spouse's return.
3. The government has broadened its definition of disability, so more people now qualify for the disability credit. If you think you may, have your doctor complete the Disability Credit Certificate (Form 2201). For more information, check the rules in the General Tax Guide. If you find that either you or your spouse can't claim all the tax credits available to you because you don't have enough income, you can transfer some of these credits to the other spouse. The pension income, age, and disability credits all qualify to be transferred. Since this can save you a lot on your taxes, be careful not to overlook it.
4. Claim the GST tax credit. Since your income in retirement will probably be less than when you were working, you may be eligible for this. In 1998, you were entitled to a GST rebate if your family's net income was less than $25,921. Don't assume you won't get it; check it out.

5. Maximize your medical expense credit by having the lower-income spouse claim all medical costs. Private insurance premiums for coverage both inside and outside Canada qualify for the medical tax credit. The expenses you claim may be for any 12-month period ending in the tax year for which you're filing, so choose the time frame that gives you the largest claim. And since the credit is based on when expenses are paid (as opposed to when the service is rendered), it may make sense to prepay an upcoming expense to maximize your tax benefit.

6. If you receive a retiring allowance, you can transfer a portion (or perhaps all) of that to your RRSP to maximize the tax deferral on those funds.

7. When you retire, you can still make at least one more contribution to an RRSP (based on your previous year's earned income). Take advantage of this. If you have eligible earned income and you and/or your spouse are under 69, you can continue making RRSP contributions.

8. If you have any unused deduction room (that is, if you have not claimed all your allowable RRSP deductions), don't let it go unclaimed.

9. If one spouse has dividend income but has little or no other income and therefore cannot claim the dividend tax credit, the dividends can be reported on the other spouse's return. This transfer is particularly beneficial when it reduces the lower-income spouse's income enough to allow the higher-income spouse to claim the spousal tax credit. Partial claims are not allowed. In most circumstances, whenever there is any opportunity to claim the spousal tax credit, all the lower-income spouse's dividends should be claimed by the upper-income spouse.

10. Take advantage of the tax benefits of income splitting by using a spousal RRSP and, if appropriate, by splitting CPP benefits.

11. Defer tax for as long as possible by first using your unregistered assets to produce an income. Leave your RRSPs intact for as long as possible so they can continue to grow on a tax-sheltered basis.

12. If you have investment income, you can claim a number of expenses against it, including the expense of a safety deposit box and the interest on money borrowed for investment purposes.

13. Let one spouse claim all charitable donations. You get the biggest break when donations exceed $200, as long as both of you have an income. Revenue Canada doesn't care who makes the claim. Just remember that your claims are limited to a maximum of 20% of your net income. By claiming all donations made over several years in one year, you'll increase your tax benefit. When you make a donation to a registered charity, you'll receive a federal tax credit of 17% on the first $200 and 29% for all donations over that. So if you normally make donations of $100 a year, by combining three or more years of contributions, you'll qualify for a larger tax credit.

14. Remit your installment payments on time. You're responsible for getting tax to Revenue Canada. And there can be heavy penalties for failing to do so. Contact Revenue Canada for the information you need to stay on their good side.

15. If you have a high retirement income (even after income splitting), manage your income to benefit from OAS at least once every two years. (See pages 262–63.)

16. If you plan to help educate a grandchild or help children buy a home, you may want to consider using an inter vivos trust. You would be giving a certain amount of money to a beneficiary (while you are still alive), and the return on that money would be earned, and taxed, in the beneficiary's hands.

## Reviewing Your Estate Plan

You can do a lot of estate planning outside a will to bypass the probate and executor fees. Assets that are not probatable bypass your will and go directly to the joint owner or beneficiary. As well, assets that pass through the estate are liable to the estate's creditors, but those that don't cannot be touched. Ann Eynon suggests that "anything that can be held jointly, such as GICs and bank accounts, should be held in joint names."

Once you've decided what you want to do with your estate, the next step is to make or update your will. Minimize the work for your executor by having complete documentation on where everything is. Minimize the stress on your family by planning your funeral. Make sure you have enough income to maintain your current lifestyle; then you can arrange your affairs to maximize the estate for your heirs and make things easier for your executor. If you have assets you do not need to maintain your lifestyle, consider gifting them to children. As long as the person is over 18 there's no attribution. You can also make loans that are forgivable on death.

As your life progresses, you will move through stages that require specific strategies. But it's hard to think about the implications of a stage that seems so far away. Witness the number of grasshoppers who delay planning for retirement despite the foresight and warnings of a great many ants. The best we seem to be able to do is to cope with the stage we're at. The big downside, of course, is that we often miss things, important things, that we could be, should be, would be doing if we just had the benefit of hindsight. But with these chapters on the most common steps and stages — the "highly likelies" — of life, you can consider yourself well equipped to cope financially. Part IV will help you deal with the true "what-ifs."

# IV

# JUST
# IN CASE

*There was only one catch and that was
Catch-22, which specified that a concern
for one's own safety in the face of dangers
that were real and immediate was the
process of a rational mind.*

JOSEPH HELLER

*N*o matter how well you plan, life has a way of throwing a punch that can knock you flat. If you want to survive, you've got to keep getting up. Life is about being resilient. This section of the book deals with those knockout punches. I wish we all could lay out a plan and then peacefully follow through. That never happens. No matter how it looks from the outside, everyone is dealing with something difficult in her life. There's no such thing as perfect. But there is a zone.

In the zone, you have things in perspective. In the zone, things are neither bigger nor smaller than they should be. It's a fairly quiet place. From time to time things intrude, but you find it relatively easy to rise above them. Changes don't bring panic. Uncertainty doesn't bring sleeplessness. Life seems to flow around you with a certain symmetry and serenity. I've been in the zone and I can tell you it is wonderful. Unfortunately, I can't tell you how to get there. You have to find your own way.

I can tell you that I found my way by being true to myself and to others. I said what I thought, without being mean. I did what I wanted, without being irresponsible. I never said "yes" when I really meant "no." Perhaps most importantly, I knew what I wanted, and focused on that.

Now, this may seem odd coming from a woman writing about money, but I got into the zone when money became less important to me. Once I realized that I had taken care of the details, I let go of the worry and started living every minute of the day. It came right in the middle of writing this book. Interestingly, all the research I did, all the lessons I learned about how money affects us emotionally, came home in a grand sweep and I entered the zone. It wasn't always perfect — I'm not talking about perfect. I'm talking about happy. Some days I still felt frustrated. Some days, I still felt bogged down. But most of the time I felt alive, sunny, and able to share myself with others. I'm telling you, the zone is a great place to be.

Does this seem like a strange place to be talking about the zone? Well, I mention it here because I believe that being in the zone helps you to get through any of the events discussed in the following chapters with grace and a sense of completeness. And it doesn't matter how it looks from the outside. It's how it feels on the inside that counts.

I have found, throughout my life, that the people furthest from the zone are *the ones most concerned about how things look to other people. They are very secretive. Who cares what you make? Money doesn't define who you are. Who cares how much debt you have right now? Money is not a measurement of your worth. Who cares how much you've accumulated? A pile of money doesn't make you smarter. Remember, money is a tool that gets us what we need and want so we can get on with our lives. Break the barriers of silence and secrecy and move into the zone. Figure out what you want and move into the zone. Be true to yourself and move into the zone.*

*When I was a girl, my Aunty Angie told me something that has stayed with me my whole life. She quoted Shakespeare in my autograph book: "To thine own self be true, and it must follow, as the night the day, thou canst not then be false to any man." Will was right. Thanks, Aunty Angie.*

# 18

# Just in Case You Become the Sole Breadwinner

*You are rich when you can meet the demands of your imagination.*

HENRY JOYCE

**B**eing the sole provider for your family is an extremely stressful position to be in. You are responsible for it all: the roof, the food, the emergencies. Without your income, the family would founder. Without your attendance at work every day, day in and day out, your family wouldn't survive. If something went wrong and you became ill, or your income were interrupted for some other reason — well, the consequences are almost too alarming to imagine.

## LIVING THROUGH IT

Of all Canadian working women, 55% provide half or more of the household income.[27] So it's not as though we aren't used to bringing home the bacon. But the shock of being the only one on whom the family counts when it hasn't always been so can knock even the most even-minded person off-kilter. And it's not the same as being self-sufficient — suddenly becoming totally responsible for the family is a different story altogether.

---

27 Dun & Bradstreet, 1995.

Several years ago, when my husband was laid off, I was faced with being the sole breadwinner. While I had taken care of myself all my life, the added responsibility of the family sent my face into spasms. I twitched. My husband said it was stress. I denied it. What stress? I could do this. I would just work harder, do more, spend less. I remember thinking to myself, "This is a changing point in my life. I have to look at things differently from now on." It helped me to be more aware of my guy's burdens when we later changed roles again, and he became the primary income-earner while I spent more time with the kids.

More and more women face the stress of being the sole breadwinner each year. Whether it is through divorce, widowhood, or because your partner is suddenly out of work, the strain can compromise your health, your financial life, and your relationships.

Barb Godin has been the sole provider in her family since 1989, when her husband was laid off and decided to stay home and look after the kids. "I worry constantly," she says. "I worry about providing for the family. If I need credit, will I be able to get enough?" Funny coming from a deacon of credit, right?

Traditionally, men have borne this particular burden, and they haven't talked about the stress. They might get snippy, but they rarely say, "I am just so tired of being solely responsible for this." Now that we women are finding ourselves in the role of primary breadwinner, we too are bearing up bravely, dying earlier of stress-related diseases, and snapping at our children.

Recognizing that the stress is there is the first step in dealing with it. You'll have to acknowledge any changes in status. There is a great deal of literature out there about the relationship between money and power. Don't add this demon to the stresses you're already dealing with. Talk about what the change in circumstances will mean to you as a couple, as a family, and as individuals. Continue to talk all the way through it. If you share your worry with your friend, the burden will immediately lighten. If your partner is not behaving like your friend, find someone to listen to your worries until your partner steadies.

You'll need to keep your financial house in order so you don't exacerbate the stress. Reconciling yourself to living on less money is one of the hardest things to do — particularly when the decision is forced. Intellectually, you make all the compromises. Emotionally, you're way behind. Old habits die hard, especially the ones that let you have what you want, when you want. But die they must, because if you try to maintain the status quo, if you behave as though nothing has changed, you will drown in a credit quagmire.

Time to revisit and adjust your spending plan. The rent or mortgage has to be paid. You need to put food on the table. But there may be several areas where you can cut back, cut down, or cut out to get by on a single income. People do it all the time and survive. The challenge is to do it and be happy. Take a copy of your spending plan and work through it to determine which costs will go down. Here are some things to consider:

- Can you eliminate child-care costs for as long as there is only one income? If your partner is actively looking for work, shared day care would be less expensive than the full-time day care used while you were both working.
- Have you reduced the budget for things like transportation, lunches, and ordering in dinner? Add it up and you may find that the savings are substantial. So are the savings on work clothes, after-work entertainment, and income taxes.
- Could part-time employment supplement the family income in the interim? Does your partner have skills that could be used on a free-lance or consulting basis?
- Would a lifestyle change help? Do you still need the second car? Think of what you'd save on maintenance and insurance, never mind the boost to your savings when you sell the car.

Keeping a roof over your head will be one of your top priorities. It is a somewhat simple decision, really. Can you afford to continue living in your home on the income you are making? For how long can you afford to do this? How long do you expect to have to do it on your own? Is there anything you can do to reduce your mortgage expenses, such as renego-tiate your mortgage if rates have fallen, or rent a part of your home in the interim? There's no way you will have the answers to all these questions at your fingertips. So this is where a woman's intuition comes into play, along with some good ol' common sense.

If you've been living well within your means as a family, if you've got your emergency fund set up along with a pretty clean credit situation, you're much more likely to make it through intact — home and all — than if you've been living way beyond your means and have run up thousands in credit-card debt. To see just how you'll cope, you'll need to do a new spending plan, one that's a lot leaner.

I can't remember where I first read the phrase "involuntary simplicity," but it applies to all those circumstances in which you are forced to simplify the way you live because of less money. Lately, there has been a wide-sweeping trend toward simplification. The media is full of stories about how people are reducing their consumption and honouring frugality as a way of life. The words "tightwad," "cheapskate," and "miser" used to have very negative connotations, but that's changing; in fact, stories abound about people who were forced into simplicity only to find that they loved it. They move to the country, grow their own food, and try to live on as little money as possible. They reuse and recycle. They share ideas, coupons, and the inside scoop on bargains. While they may be poor of pocketbook, they are rich of spirit.

Now, this may all seem too cloud-with-a-silver-lining-ish to you if your buddy has just been cast to the wolves by his former employer. But don't discount it completely. Yes, you'll have to spend the next few days, weeks, and months managing the bruise to your pocketbook as well as the bruise to his ego. But you will come through it. This is not the time to pick at each other's shortcomings. If you have children at home, this is not the time to scare them to death with threats of never again having two brass farthings. This is a time to take it slowly on the emotional front while moving quickly to shore up your financial situation.

Having reviewed your spending plan and identified areas where you can cut back, next you must ensure that your cash-management strategies continue to work for you. While you may have had two or more accounts before you became a single-income family, having a single account will probably make more sense now, at least for the short term. Consolidate the money you may have in several accounts to see if you can minimize the cost of doing business with the bank. Look hard at the services you will be using. Now is not the time for services you may only use once in a blue moon. Little things like choosing a passbook option (rather than receiving a statement) can save you money. Remember, too, that the banking world is constantly changing and the banks are very competitive.

Shop around to see who has the best "package" for your specific needs. Many banks offer no-charge chequing and no-charge ABM use if you maintain a specific minimum balance. By consolidating your accounts you may be able to take advantage of these features.

If maintaining a monthly balance is a problem, which it very well may be while you learn to live on less income, then you'll have to compare individual service charges — costs for cheques and withdrawals, for statements, and for ABM transactions. Choose the least expensive account for your purposes. If you're attracted to the packaged accounts, compare the individual fees with the package costs to see if you come out ahead. And compare the interest you're earning with the cost of the account. There's no point in earning minimal interest if the service charges on that account are more than you pay on another non-interest-bearing account.

The easiest thing to do when you have a shortfall in your cash flow is to use your credit cards or personal line of credit to fill the gap. For those people who intended to use their PLC as their emergency fund, a word of caution: Don't get complacent about the fact that you are accumulating debt that will eventually have to be repaid. For those who plan to use their credit cards to get over the hump, make sure you're using the cheapest credit card you can find. If you add a 17% interest rate to your existing burdens, you're dooming yourself. Get a cheapie card and if you're already carrying a balance on an expensive one, transfer your balance.

While I don't often advocate overdraft protection because it is so expensive — and because using it is such an easy habit to get into and such a hard habit to get out of — it may be a good idea while you're adjusting to your new cash flow. You won't need it if you are determined to stay within your means and are meticulous about your record keeping. However, if you tend to let things slide a bit, having overdraft protection to avoid NSF cheques will keep your creditors happy and avoid the negative long-term implications of a rotten credit history.

Don't forget to pay yourself first. Yeah, like you really think I'm going to be able to save *anything* while living on one income? Get real!

If you're divorced, widowed, or any other form of single, you must try. It may not happen immediately. You may need time to adjust to your new lifestyle. But if you don't get yourself back on track and start saving, you're asking for trouble. Everyone has to save. That doesn't mean you have to save your maximum RRSP amount, or the amount your sister saves, or the amount the media advocate. But you do have to set something aside for the future. It's your responsibility.

Your current circumstances are the reason you need an emergency fund. If you have one, you're going to feel a lot safer moving through this trying time. As soon as you can, you'll need to start rebuilding it. It may take longer this time, but at least now you're convinced you need one.

As the primary breadwinner, you are now solely responsible for your family's continued peace of mind. And for your own peace of mind, you had better make sure you have enough insurance. If you had been counting on your spouse's work plan for life, disability, or health benefits, these need to be replaced. If you think that this isn't the time to make a cash-flow commitment to new expenses (like insurance, which nobody ever really uses anyway, right?), think again. What would your family do if you became disabled while you were the only one with a job? How would your spouse cope if you died? How will you cover those medical bills when they arrive? Insurance is not the place to skimp.

Some good news: You will end up paying less tax as a family, and if your spouse has no income at all, you'll get a tax break there. Since you're now living on one income, you'll be claiming all the deductions and credits, so make sure you take advantage of everything you can to minimize your tax liability. If your partner has little or no income, remember to take advantage of the spousal or equivalent-to-spousal tax credit. If you have no spouse, you can claim the equivalent-to-spousal credit for any qualifying dependent, including a child or parent.

While a tax refund may seem like a gift from the government, getting one means you aren't planning particularly well. The idea is to keep money in your hands for your own use, not to provide the government with an interest-free loan. Using the tax man as a forced-savings system may work for some, but the alternative makes more sense financially.


## PREPARING FOR IT

Sometimes it comes as a surprise when you find yourself the sole breadwinner in the family. Other times it doesn't. If you and your partner have decided that one of you should stay home to be with the children, and it makes more sense that you keep working, then you may have time to plan this change in lifestyle. One of the best ways to see how it will work is to live on only your paycheque for several months leading up to the change. You can use the other paycheque to actively pay down debt or to build a sturdy emergency fund for those unforeseen financial crises.

Remember to check your insurance benefits to be sure you've got enough coverage for life, disability, and health. Redo your spending plan, incorporating the changes necessary for you to live on a single income. If you plan to eliminate your child-care expenses, remember to leave some money in the plan for baby-sitters while your partner attends doctors' appointments or takes some "sanity time." Set some goals for eliminating or significantly reducing your debt before you make the switch to one income. Talk about the money/power shift that may take place, and the warning signals you'll use to cue each other when that shift begins to manifest itself.

# 19

# Just in Case
# You Divorce

*Money is always there but the pockets change.*

GERTRUDE STEIN

*Note*: All the provincial legislation referred to in this chapter is based on Ontario's Family Law Act. While the Divorce Act is federal and deals with the grounds for divorce, custody, and child and spousal support, each province has separate legislation that deals with property (which is a provincial matter) as well as custody and child and spousal support. People who do not wish to get divorced (for religious or other reasons) but who separate and need the issues of support settled use the provincial legislation to achieve that end. Please seek advice from a lawyer within your jurisdiction for the legislation that applies to your situation.

## LIVING THROUGH IT

According to Statistics Canada, people who are currently married and are 20 or younger have a 40% chance of divorce. At age 25, the chance of divorce drops to approximately 35%. At 30, a man's chance of divorce runs at about 33%, at 40 it's about 20%, and at 50 it's about 10%. The probability of divorce is lower for women at all ages because they are more likely to be widowed. Either way, we're going to end up alone and in charge of the money. So we'd better figure out how it works.

Another disconcerting statistic courtesy of StatsCan: after divorce, a woman's economic status generally falls by about 45% (the guy's goes up by about 72%). All sorts of factors come into play: the oft-bewailed discrepancies in income; the fact that more women leave the workforce than do men to look after family, resulting in a loss of skills and financial security for women; women's naiveté in handling their separation and divorce. If women have in fact been socialized to believe money is a man thing, it's time for some new socialization. Women *must* learn how to handle money if they want to be sure they can have a secure future. And we must teach our daughters that marriage is a noble institution, but that they *must* be capable of doing what is needed to survive, take care of their babies, and get on with their lives.

But before we get into the money part of this, I'd like to talk a little about where your head goes when your love (or whatever it is that's been holding you together) walks out the door. As with just about everything else in life, it depends. It depends on whether you are the person leaving, whom I'll refer to as the "leaver," or the person being left — the "leavee."

If you are the leaver, you have time to plan. You can make an appointment with a lawyer, get advice, and ready yourself for the storm. You can learn the rules of the game and practise your moves and countermoves ahead of the starter's gun. That's not to say that you'll be protected from the emotional upheaval and sadness that comes with a marriage breakdown. You will still grieve — dealing with divorce is not unlike dealing with death — but you'll do it at a different pace than the person you are leaving.

If you are the leavee, you have no opportunity to prepare. The starter's gun is a shot to your gut. Your mind careens from one disastrous scenario to another. A very close friend of mine describes her divorce as shaking her foundation. "Suddenly I felt all the societal taboos: a divorcée, oooh, a single mother, ugh. I felt I had lost my position in society. The security issues had to do with a lot more than just money. It was my emotional sense of self that left. It took me a long time to accept and deal with that. For a time, whenever I was in public with my daughter, I wore a fake wedding ring because I couldn't deal with people thinking I was an unwed mother. You have crazy thoughts. Things come into your mind that would never occur to you if you were feeling safe and secure."

Whereas the leaver has had time to prepare herself, the leavee must make time — slow the whole thing down — so she can catch up emotionally. Whereas the leaver has planned carefully, the leavee must put together a plan. If you do it on the fly, it won't be your best plan. Since this divorce will affect you, and perhaps your children, for a long time to come, don't rush, or be rushed, into decisions. Time makes the difference. And the very first thing you should do is see a very good lawyer.

Family lawyer Sandy Morris says that one mistake women make (and she qualifies this as a generalization) is that they have no knowledge of the family's financial affairs. Leavees panic not only because "He's leaving," but also because they realize they don't have access to the bank accounts, or they don't know how and when to make the mortgage payments.

"When they come into my office looking for me to say everything's going to be okay, I can't always say that," says Sandy. "When I try to get the financial picture, it becomes so apparent that they know nothing. The whole divorce procedure is so much more difficult."

Take the case of Paula R. She had a wonderful life. At 54, she drove a very nice car. Every year she went on a vacation. Her son was working and living at home, and her daughter was finishing her last year of university. Paula was well educated, well turned out, and ill prepared for divorce. When the credit check was done on Paula's husband, the results were abysmal. Paula was guarantor on several of her husband's loans. "Oh, yes," she said, "I signed something, but I don't remember much about it." With his high level of debt, Paula's husband fit the definition of bankrupt. His idea of negotiation was to say, "Look honey, if you're not prepared to accept what I'm going to give you, I'll just make an assignment [meaning he would hand over all his assets to a bankruptcy trustee] and I'm done." Since the bankruptcy would extinguish her claim to property division, that would leave Paula holding an empty bag. Paula's lack of knowledge — and lack of interest — in anything financial left her vulnerable to her ex-husband's tactics.

Danita B. is another case in point. Before marrying, she was an independent career woman. After she had her second child, she decided to stay home full time, at least until the last baby was in school full-time. Over the years, her husband Harry encouraged her not to worry about the financial stuff and she lost touch with what was going on. Since Danita came from a traditional family, it seemed natural to hand Harry the reins of their financial lives while she concentrated on nurturing the children and making sure everything ran smoothly at home. Danita was stunned when Harry walked out. He came home one night, packed his bags, and left saying, "You'll be hearing from my lawyer." With her fourth child still in diapers, she felt abandoned. The fact that Harry left for another woman didn't help Danita's self-image. She was furious and wanted revenge. And she'd use any tactic to make him pay.

Madelaine T. is at the other end of the scale. A child of divorce, Madelaine always maintained control over her own money. Hypersensitive to her parents' messy divorce, Madelaine stayed on top of everything. She admitted to even being slightly secretive about her finances. "I don't think Mathew should know everything," she said. "It's just not his business. I don't expect him to tell me everything." Madelaine was shocked to find out that while she had been very successful at wealth accumulation, Mathew hadn't been quite so prudent. "You mean I'm going to have to give him part of my assets? But he's the man. Why would I have to give him money?" she asked, astounded at the prospect. "But I've been the responsible one. He's been the gadfly. Why should he get half?" That's equality, girls!

Another mistake women make is to let emotion carry them away, as in Danita's case. "Many situations can be resolved without the need for protracted litigation if cooler heads prevail," says Sandy, "so that the parties walk out financially intact."

If you've managed to get this far without a spending plan, you'll need one now. And if you're not familiar with how the money flows in and out of the family pocketbook because the other guy's always taken care of it,

*Sandy Morris is a partner with the Toronto firm Torkin Manes Cohen & Arbus, where she specializes in family law. She is co-author of the family law section of the Law Society's Bar Admissions Course material and has written articles for the Canadian Bar Association (CBA) Continuing Legal Education programs. She is a regular speaker at New Directions, a branch of the Toronto Women's League, and serves on myriad committees, including the Appeal Committee and the Executive Committee of the CBA. Married with a daughter, Sandy is a fan of the Brontë sisters, loves Greek food, and makes a great case for women to know exactly what's going on in their marriages.*

it's time to become familiar. Whether you are litigating or negotiating your divorce settlement, you'll have to complete the standard financial statement provided by your lawyer. One section includes a budget with 69 different types of expenditures to help figure out the family's spending pattern and what that spending pattern will likely look like in the future. Of course, if you've never had a spending plan, you probably have no idea what the numbers are. Refer to Chapter 4, where I explain what a spending plan is, how it works, and how to build one.

The budget section of the financial statement you prepare is, in large measure, what the judge looks at to determine your future needs for support. If you can't complete this properly — if you don't know what you're paying for taxes, entertainment, vacations, food, rent, and medical expenses — you won't be able to paint a clear enough picture for the judge. For example, Sandy says that many people don't know how much they spend on medical expenses. "People will say, my husband has a plan. When I ask if it has 100% coverage, a co-payment, whatever, they have no idea. They don't know if there are any limitations on the plan, or how long the plan lasts after divorce." Many people also think that because they have a drug plan, they don't need a drug budget. But what about those items that aren't covered by the plan: headache, cold, and allergy medicine, antibiotic cream and Band-Aids, potions for diarrhea, stomach upset, and nausea? Anything purchased without a prescription is not covered so everyone needs a drug budget. "Your lawyer should give you a document that shows you how to complete the financial statement," says Sandy. That explanation should draw your attention to each of the expenditures, including those you are likely to overlook. Remember, your financial statement is considered evidence under the rules of the court; so if you don't give complete evidence, the judge has less to work with, and that might be reflected in his or her decision.

"If a woman comes to me before she's actually left her husband, I tell her that her mission is to go home and find every scrap of paper that she can and photocopy it. Unless there is physical abuse or serious verbal abuse, even if she has to stay with her spouse for another month, my view is she should stay there because she has to prepare for this next step," says Sandy. That may include scouring the house for his tax returns, investment information, insurance details, everything that may be pertinent to your settlement.

If you're saying to yourself that this feels scummy, that it's an invasion of his privacy, that you're above such behaviour, give your head a shake. It is your right as a member of that family to know everything. If your spouse hasn't shared information with you, or if you haven't been paying attention, it's time to become informed. You must rectify your lack of knowledge to protect yourself, and perhaps your children. "Quite frankly," says Sandy, "you're saving yourself a lot of money because you won't have all the back-and-forthing that comes with a lack of disclosure. The financial statement is supposed to be a complete disclosure." If your spouse has purposely or inadvertently left something out, and you know about it because you have informed yourself, then it's a relatively easy situation to fix. If you don't know what's going on, you don't know when you're being had. It is healthy to be informed.

Don't forget to budget in your legal costs. The first thing you'll have to do is provide your lawyer with a retainer. People often look suspiciously at lawyers when they ask for a retainer, but the reality is that the exchange of that money — even if it is only one dollar — is what establishes the client-lawyer relationship. "Technically speaking," says Sandy, "in order for there to be that solicitor-client privilege, you need money to change hands."

In order to create a realistic budget for your divorce, ask what your lawyer's hourly rate is at the office and in court, since they are often different. If your lawyer uses a law clerk, find out how that person's time is billed. And remember, everything costs money. Your lawyer's time is the commodity you're paying for, so expect to be billed for telephone calls and letters, as well as face-to-face meetings. Remember, too, that the more prepared you are, the better use you can make of your lawyer's time.

Also check on your lawyer's billing procedures. The last thing you need is to go merrily along fighting your ex-spouse, only to find a bill for $20,000 at the end of it all. "I bill every month," says Sandy, "to give clients an ongoing appreciation for what the procedure will cost." If you'll be counting on a settlement to make good on your legal fees, make sure you gain your lawyer's agreement to a payment plan, and ascertain what the interest rate will be on the outstanding balance.

Since there may be interruptions in your income as you go through the divorce, particularly if your husband is ticked off at the amount of spousal or child support granted to you, you need to have a stash at the ready to fill the gaps. That may mean taking money from a joint account, pulling on a joint line of credit, or, in extreme circumstances, taking advances against a supplemental credit card. Yes, I am advocating getting the money from whatever source is available. The road to divorce can be long and bumpy and you may have to lay out a lot of cash along the way. Document all your withdrawals and advances and give the list to your lawyer (and your ex's lawyer), indicating that you know these amounts will be incorporated in the accounting and final division of assets. If you're in the house with the kids, you can't risk missing mortgage payments. Nor can you miss tuition payments for school or other activities. If the furnace goes, the car dies, or some other unforeseen event occurs, you need a way to cope financially. Remember, when it comes to separation or divorce, you rarely know what you're getting into. You can't afford to be left without money while your husband, the lawyers, and the courts try to decide how much it costs for you and your children to live.

Do you think this is extreme? It only seems so because you haven't yet had to live from week to week without money. I had a girlfriend who was left stranded by her ex when he left. For several months, she barely made ends meet while she continued to pay the mortgage (on an asset that was half his), buy the food (for herself and *their* daughter), and meet every other financial commitment. The stress was unbearable and she came within a straw of breaking. You must protect yourself. And that means having a healthy emergency fund *just in case!*

On separation, each party is equally entitled to live in a matrimonial home (that's possession, not ownership), until there's a court order saying one must get out or there's a separation agreement in which one party gives up the right. "I often tell people not to leave the home until they've seen a lawyer," says Sandy, "because there may be strategic reasons why you don't want to leave." Even if your husband tells you to get out and says he owns the house because only his name is on title, you don't have to leave. And if your husband comes home and tells you he's leaving you but not quite yet, you can't toss his stuff onto the lawn and lock him out, because changing the locks bars him from his right to possession of the matrimonial home.

"The matrimonial home," says Sandy Morris, "is any residence in which either party has a legal interest [so that applies to the home you own or rent] and which is ordinarily occupied by the spouses as their family residence at separation or immediately before separation." If you have a city house that you ordinarily occupy, that's a matrimonial home. You don't need a document saying that. If you have a cottage that you ordinarily occupy for a few weeks each year, that's a matrimonial home. You can have as many matrimonial homes as you live in. Investment properties don't count. You have to live on the property at some point in the year.

"Living separate and apart" for the purposes of being "separated" does not mean you have to be living physically apart. There are situations where people cannot immediately find alternative living space. "So living separate and apart can mean living in the same house," says Sandy. "It can even mean sharing the same bed." The objective test for "living separate and apart" is this: Would a third party looking in determine that these people are holding themselves out to the world as husband and wife? The judge looks for evidence to support the separation: not going out socially together, not doing the husband-and-wife things. "In one of my cases," said Sandy, "technically the woman had been separated for about eight years before she came to see me. I explained that to her. When we got to court, her husband claimed that she couldn't apply for equalization of net family property because the limitation period had passed. [You must make your claim within six years of your date of separation.] His claim was that they had been separated for eight years. We're still working to get to the bottom of this.

"Lots of people who grow apart simply carry on together as man and wife while leading totally separate lives," says Sandy. "I have clients who tell me that people are shocked to find out they were even married because those people never saw them with their spouses socially."

To prepare for your visit to the lawyer, make a list of all the real property you own and indicate whose name appears on the title for each. That way your lawyer will be able to register a "matrimonial home designation." This document is registered on title and has no legal effect other than to flag to would-be lenders that the property is a matrimonial home requiring spousal consent for any changes. That means you're protected if your spouse tries to take out a mortgage without your knowledge.

If you're dealing with a violent spouse, while you're not allowed to change the locks, here's at least one good reason to have him charged for assault. One of the terms of the bail order will be to restrict your husband from coming within a certain distance of your home. With this kind of criminal order in place, keeping him away from your doors, judges are likely to overlook it if you changed the locks (which would be a violation of civil law). You could also change the code on the alarm system so that if he enters the house, the police would be notified immediately. You could also change the frequency on your garage door so he can't get in through the garage.

No matter what your husband promises you as he exits stage left, take it with a grain of salt. Emotions and attitudes swing from one extreme to another during marriage breakdown, and today's guilt-induced promise can be easily rescinded tomorrow. Protect yourself. Get to work finding everything you can to take to the lawyer. Remove your name from all forms of joint credit. Fill up your emergency fund, and batten down the hatches.

Regardless of how lost, negative, abandoned, and rudderless you feel when you're going through a divorce, you will have goals to work toward. Or perhaps you're excited at the prospect of setting out on your own journey — one where you read your own map (and get a lot less lost). Whatever the case, *do not make any significant decisions for the first six to 12 months.* This probably isn't the right time to deal with the stress of a new job, start a business, buy a new house, change your investment portfolio significantly, or remarry. It is perfectly fine to dream. Dreaming is good. Imagine all the possibilities. Work through all the scenarios in your mind. Just don't *do* anything drastic. You need time to adjust emotionally as well as financially, and that means cutting yourself some slack. Don't listen to those who try to impose a time frame on you by telling you to "just get on with it." This is a huge change in your life and you have to take some time to get used to it.

If you have someone to whom you can turn for financial advice, great. But you should already have a relationship with this person. Otherwise, deal with someone who comes very, very highly recommended. Follow your instincts. You should feel comfortable and secure. You should like the person. You should feel that person is helping you to understand your options, not pushing you to make a decision.

You shouldn't be in a hurry to make financial decisions that will affect you or your children for the long haul. Instead, take notes, get second opinions, study up on what's what. Create your personal plan of action.

Don't worry if the stock market skyrockets while you're on the sidelines; you'll get another opportunity. What you'll lose by jumping in is sleep, and right now, girl, whether you are the leaver or the leavee, you need all the rest you can get to recover from your wounds.

While you may end up with half the family assets as part of the divorce, you may very well end up with less cash flow and see your standard of living drop. Since women usually earn less than their male counterparts, moving from a dual income to a lower single one means you may not be able to maintain your lifestyle. If you've been an at-home wife who is now dependent on alimony and child support for income, you, too, may find it difficult because you are not able to meet your previous expectations.

As part of your new independent state of being, if you have not already done so, you'll have to establish a financial identity for yourself. That means setting up a chequing account in your own name, applying for credit cards, and the like. If you've never managed money before, let me reassure you that it isn't hard, but it takes some practice.

Start by talking to a girlfriend or female family member who seems to be doing well on her own. Join a support group in your community. Groups like New Directions in Toronto provide a wealth of information to help women make successful transitions and rebuild their lives. New Directions offers workshops on topics ranging from how to make the legal system work for you if you are separating, to how to manage the effects of divorce on young children, to mending your heart and healing your body through meditation. Ask at community centres, look in the Yellow Pages under "Divorce," and ask friends and family.

Part of what you want to find out is how to manage your money efficiently on a day-to-day basis. If you have a relationship with people at your bank, ask them for help. Since they are closest to the subject, they'll have the most expertise. Don't worry about looking foolish. All that matters is getting informed and learning how to take care of yourself.

Do you have a credit card in your own name? Get one. (By the way, why isn't this ever an issue for men?) Supplemental cards — or the credit cards you use that are tied to your husband's cards — do absolutely Jack Squat to build you a credit history. It doesn't matter who pays the bill. If the card is in his name, the reporting is in his name and *you don't exist.*

What would you do if your husband cut off your supplemental card and you were in Zellers buying your kids new boots when your card was declined? First you would be mortified. Then you'd be angry. Save yourself the trouble. Get your own card.

When Janet divorced several years ago, she discovered that all her credit cards were held jointly with her husband. While she had made payments consistently on the cards she had used, he had not been quite so punctual. The result: Her credit history was far less pristine than she had imagined. Janet hadn't written the credit-card companies to have her name removed from the cards her ex was using, so when he was lackadaisical about making payments during the months they were separated, he was also tarnishing her credit history. When she tried applying for her own credit, she found several banks unwilling to extend her credit because she was now living on substantially less income and her credit bureau report showed a shoddy payment record. She was furious. Take a lesson from Janet's case. If you're holding cards on which you are jointly liable with your spouse, call and have those cards cancelled and new cards issued solely in your name. The fact that you're deep in the throes of a nasty divorce is of no interest to your creditors.

If you and your husband had a joint line of credit at the bank, go and have your signature removed, if you can. If you can't, then hand-deliver to the bank a letter that says, "As of today's date, no cheque can be drawn against this line of credit without both signatures." That way, no one is doing anything without the other's knowledge.

Change your PIN number. Remember that Tuesday last year when you asked him to take some money out of the machine for you? He has your PIN number. If you don't change it, you're allowing him the opportunity to mess with your accounts. While you're at it, change all your PIN numbers and passwords. And don't change them to something obvious like your children's names. Use something obscure like the name of the first man who nibbled your ear or your great-aunt Lucy's birth date.

Since you're completely dependent on yourself, if you're not taking care of your future, no one is. If you have earned income, you should be contributing to an RRSP. Get on a periodic investment plan. You can start with as little as $25 a month.

If you think you can't afford to be investing for your future because your present costs so much, ask yourself this question: If I don't save for my future, what will I live on when my future becomes my present? If you think you have plenty of time to catch up, ask yourself what you did with the last five years of your life and how much you would have today if you had started back then. If you think the government is going to take care of your future, a gentle reminder: You thought your husband was going to do that too. You can't depend on anyone but yourself.

The other thing to think about when reviewing your investment strategy is how the divorce has affected your retirement plan. When RRSP assets are divided as part of a divorce settlement, this can significantly alter your retirement plans and colour how you will invest those dollars for the future. The most important question for many people is how to balance their risk tolerance with the need to grow their RRSP assets now that they are on their own. When you're negotiating who gets what in the divorce, women who have stayed out of the workforce to raise a family or have lower-paying jobs should choose to hold on to RRSP assets, particularly if your spouse has a company pension plan to rely on. With little or no RRSP room to catch up, you'll be starting from ground zero if you relinquish RRSP assets totally; this is of greatest concern if you are in your late forties or fifties and have less time to build a strong retirement asset base.

Often women choose to keep the family home, giving up retirement assets in exchange. But this isn't always a smart move. With expensive upkeep and slow increases in real estate values, a home can become an albatross, inhibiting women from building the investment reserves they need to take care of themselves in later years.

Other areas to watch for:

- A 50/50 split of assets may seem fair, but if your spouse also has a company pension plan, that has to be taken into consideration.
- If you won't be entering the workforce immediately, you'll need to negotiate extra income for investment purposes so you don't spend several years contributing zilch to your retirement plan.
- If your spouse has significant unused RRSP contribution room — if he could have made contributions but chose not to — those catch-up contributions aren't divisible after the settlement. Negotiate for a portion of those contributions to be made in your name (as a spousal contribution) prior to the division of assets, and that the spousal RRSP will not be equalized. That way you'll have assets that can continue to grow on a tax-deferred basis.

Keep in mind that once you are living separately, the RRSP rules for withdrawals from a spousal plan change. The money will be taxed in the hands of the planholder — the "spouse" — so if that's you, don't go grabbing money out of your spousal plan thinking your old buddy will get stuck with the tax bill. You'll end up paying the piper.

If you considered your partner to be your disability plan, it's time to get a new one . . . no, not a new partner, a real disability plan; one that will be with you, regardless. You're the only one you can truly count on should you be unable to work. If you have kids, it's even more important. You don't really want to hear your ex say, "Well, since I'm supporting the children completely now, I think they should live with me and my new wife. After all, you have enough on your plate."

Life insurance is just as important. If your ex isn't in the picture a whole lot — some husbands do move away and start new lives, as though their previous lives and families never existed — then you must have life insurance to protect your children.

Another good use of life insurance is to protect the stream of child-support payments you may be receiving from your ex. Any good lawyer will advise you to have it stipulated in your separation agreement that your husband will take out and pay for an insurance policy that will guarantee your children support until a specific age. While the separation agreement and support order are binding on your ex-spouse's estate, if the estate doesn't have enough to fund the support, you're out of luck. And, of course, if your ex agrees, you can insure his life, pay the premiums yourself, and know your kids will be protected should he depart this earth.

If your partner just can't get insurance, don't give up. Insist that you (if you are being paid spousal support) and your children be named as irrevocable beneficiaries on his RRSPs. "While you won't be able to roll the money over on a tax-free basis because you're no longer spouses, you can set up certain types of trusts to minimize the tax consequences," says Sandy. "Every court order or separation agreement should contain some form of risk mitigation." Of course, there's absolutely no point in arguing for these types of provisions unless you are going to follow up to make sure they are in place. Each year you should receive proof that the premiums have been paid and that your interests and those of your children are protected.

Also keep in mind that if your spouse belongs to a group health plan, your joint dependent children should still be covered under that plan. If you just can't get on with your ex, include in your separation agreement the specifics for when you'll receive payment for submitted claims, so the procedure doesn't turn into a power struggle. And since you probably won't be covered under his medical plan, make sure you get a medical plan of your own.

Even if you're the person initiating the separation, there are some things that aren't top of mind: the tax man, for instance. But he should be. After all, how you structure the financial side of your divorce will have an impact on your money management for years to come. Tax planning for divorce starts before you draw up your separation agreement, especially where support is being paid. Spousal support is deductible for the payer, and is included in the income of the payee (and therefore subject to tax), as long as the payee is receiving support as directed by a written separation agreement or court order, and those payments are made on a periodic basis. This only applies to people who have been legally married. If you've just lived in sin, the payer will need a court order to have support payments deemed deductible by the tax man. Revenue Canada will recognize payments made on a periodic basis one calendar year prior to the year your separation agreement is signed. So if you sign a separation agreement in 1998, the payer can claim any periodic payments made as far back as January 1, 1997.

When you're filing your income tax return for the year of separation you can choose between claiming payments made or the spousal credit. So if you legally separated in December, it might be worth more to claim the spousal credit than a single month's support payment. Do the math before you make the choice. Also note that the same flexibility applies if you pull a Liz Taylor; should you and your spouse get back together, you can make either of these claims for the year the reconciliation takes place.

Under new legislation, child support is no longer deductible for the payer or included in the income of the recipient. This applies to support orders made or orders renegotiated after May 1, 1997. For support orders made prior to that date, the old rules still apply: child support is a deductible expense for the payer, and taxable income for the payee. If you're thinking of renegotiating your child support so you don't have to pay tax on the income, be careful. There are new guidelines for child support and some people think the amounts being awarded are abysmally low. For example, if the supporting parent is making $100,000 a year, the base amount for one child is just $773 per month. Amounts payable above this base amount are awarded at the discretion of the judge — and that's not always a good thing.

Remember, too, that if you choose to renegotiate your support and it becomes non-taxable in your hands and non-deductible in your spouse's, your RRSP contribution limit will be affected, since you'll have reduced your earned income. And if you are the payer, and you used to claim a deduction for support but have stopped, make sure you tell your employer so sufficient tax can be withheld from your paycheque.

Divorce gives you a rare opportunity to fiddle with your RRSP or registered pension plan without tax consequence. If RPP or RRSP assets are being split between spouses, the rollover from one spouse's plan to the other's can take place on a tax-free basis using form T2220 for RRSP or RRIF rollovers, and form T2151 for RPPs.

Do either you or your spouse have any unused RRSP contribution room you could catch up on prior to your split of matrimonial assets? Since registered assets can be rolled between spouses on a tax-free basis, you'd do well to maximize those assets ahead of time, perhaps by liquidating some of your unregistered funds, which *would* be taxed on transfer from one spouse to another.

Most people don't even know what "contingent liabilities" are, let alone how to take them into account when splitting their assets. Take for example a situation where registered and unregistered assets are being equalized separately — let's say one person's taking the RRSP and the other is taking the house. There has to be some recognition that the party holding the RRSP will be taxed when those funds are withdrawn, so the RRSP holder will negotiate for those assets to be discounted for the tax that will later be paid on them. The same kind of negotiation would protect the spouse who took the house as settlement if that house had to be sold sometime in the near future. So the true value of the house — and the settlement — is determined by factoring in the reduction in the asset for legal fees, real estate commissions, GST, and incidental expenses.

By the same token, if your settlement does not include an asset that might appreciate and attract capital gains, you don't want to pay the taxes that come with those gains. To make sure you aren't taxed, you must indicate your intent to Revenue Canada by filing the appropriate forms (referred to as filing an election) at the next tax filing after the split of assets. Imagine Jane takes over an asset such as a painting that is subject to capital-gains tax, and the painting goes up in value. If it's sold within the next year, the tax man would want to tax her ex-husband, John. If John filed an election, the asset would be taxed in Jane's hands.

Of course, most decisions involve more than just money. Many people have a stronger emotional attachment to their homes than to their partner's RRSP. And other issues, such as not wanting to uproot children, come into play.

Once you're divorced and filing your tax return, take full advantage of all credits and deductions. If you are a single parent with children, claim the equivalent-to-married amount and you'll save about $1,400 in tax. Which parent gets to claim? The custodial parent. And a parent required to make support payments is not entitled to claim. If parents have joint custody, and no money is changing hands, only one can claim this deduction. And if you can't come to an agreement as to who should claim, you'll be cutting off your nose to spite your face, since Revenue Canada will simply rule that no one gets the deduction.

Don't overlook the GST and child tax credit. Since they are based on family income, you may not have qualified as a family unit. However, if you are a single income earner supporting a child or you are thinking of skipping filing because you don't have much income, think again. The only way to qualify for these credits is to file, so sharpen your pencil.

Remember, too, to claim all your child-care expenses. You'll need receipts that include the caregiver's social insurance number or day-care address, but you don't have to file them. Hang on to them in case your return is questioned.

Legal fees may be tax deductible if incurred to enforce a support order. So if you have a separation agreement or support order and you had to incur legal fees to get those payments, you can deduct your legal fees. If you had to sue your spouse to get a court order for support payments, you can deduct those expenses too.

Divorce is never easy, but a little planning can make it less painful financially, especially when it comes to paying tax. Working together to resolve many of these issues may be the furthest thing from your mind, so get yourself a good lawyer and tax accountant, and let them do the job for you. The last person you should want to make money from your divorce is the tax man!

Don't forget about your will. "When you divorce," says estate specialist Hilary Laidlaw, "the law provides that any benefit to your former spouse in your will is revoked. However, that automatic revocation does not apply to designations made with respect to your spouse. So if your spouse has been named beneficiary of an insurance policy or of your RRSP, you have to take steps to remove him as a designated beneficiary."

If you've executed powers of attorney in which you've named your ex to act on your behalf, remember to have them revoked immediately. There's no way I'd leave the decision on whether or not to pull the plug in my ex's hands, would you? The same holds true for a financial PoA. This applies to brokerage accounts where your husband may have been making most of the calls, and you executed a PoA to give him the right to trade on your behalf. "I can't for the life of me understand why a woman would ever do that," says Sandy Morris, "but if you've done it, revoke it immediately."

A reminder about documentation: If you've been married for a long time to a really, really nice guy and have signed lots and lots of paperwork that you have not kept copies of, you have to get to work to collect it all back. "Women come in to see me and have no idea what they've signed," says Sandy. "When you get to litigation, the husband is giving you all these documents and it becomes apparent that she owned this or executed that. But she has no copies and perhaps no recollection."

A final word on keeping the paperwork. When I was divorcing my second husband, I had to come up with the Decree Absolute (final divorce papers) from my first marriage. One would think that once divorced and remarried, there would be no need to hold on to the evidence of your bad judgment. But marriages, like wrinkles, can only be denied, not abolished. And so, since I had gleefully tossed all my pre-husband-number-two stuff when I was post-husband-number-two, my lawyer had to get another copy of my Decree Absolute — at a cost, of course.

# 20

# Just in Case
# You Are Widowed

*All weddings are similar but every marriage is different. Death comes to
everyone but one mourns alone.*

JOHN BERGER

I remember being surprised as a child to learn that there was a word for
a man whose wife had died: widower. I knew the word widow; I knew
widows. I had never met a widower. That's not surprising when you
look at the statistics. At every age, women are more likely than men to be
widowed. And as we get older, we're even more likely to be left alone.
At some point in their lives, nine out of 10 Canadian women will be
responsible for the family finances. Since women live longer than men do
— 81.1 years compared to 75.1 years, according to Statistics Canada —
even if you marry a younger man, chances are you'll end up on your own
at some point.

It's not unusual for women to report lapses in memory after the death
of a spouse. All the key things seem to get done, but they have little
recollection of how. As with other life-changing losses, such as divorce,
widowhood demands time to cope. And yet in those early days it
seems there is no time at all because there are so many things to take
care of: making the funeral arrangements, contacting family and friends,
calling the lawyer, finding the will, keeping the house running.

Coping with the financial aspects of widowhood requires that you wear two hats. First, you must close your partner's financial books and deal with what has been left. Second, you have to continue (or start) dealing with your own financial books as you move through the next stage of your life.

In the first instance, there are several financial items you must attend to:

1. You must find your partner's will, if one exists. Ideally, you've both made wills and you are aware of the contents and location of your partner's will.
2. If you are not the sole executrix, you will have to notify the executor. You should also contact an experienced estates lawyer for legal help if the estate isn't absolutely straightforward.
3. You will need to make funeral arrangements. If your partner left specific instructions in his will, you'll probably want to follow those instructions, though you're not legally bound to do so. If there are no instructions, then you'll have to decide how to handle the ceremony and his remains. Although this is technically the job of the executor, if you have not been named executor, the person who has will usually defer to your wishes as long as the cost of the arrangements is reasonable.
4. Get at least eight copies of the death certificate from the funeral home. This will save having to apply for more when you learn you need copies for just about everything.
5. Make sure your immediate cash needs will be met. If you had a joint account at the bank, the assets immediately become yours. You should transfer the funds in that account to an account solely in your name. Wait a few days to do so in case payments to your spouse or automatic deposits in your partner's name are owing and will be made shortly. If your spouse had an account solely in his name into which his income was automatically deposited, you won't be able to get to the money until the estate is settled, since his account will be frozen. You can, however, access his account to pay for his funeral.
6. Contact your husband's employer to find out what final payment (salary, bonuses, vacation pay) will be coming to you. Ask for a summary of his income for tax purposes. Find out which of his benefits you will be entitled to, and for how long. In all likelihood, you

will no longer be covered under his group benefits, which means you'll have to get your own. Since many companies have insurance in place providing death benefits for widows of employees, check this out.

7. If your partner was receiving a pension at the time of his death, you may receive all, part, or none of it. If your sweetheart was not yet retired, you may receive a lump sum from the plan; this sum can be transferred tax-free to an RRSP in your name. The plan administrator can provide you with information on all your options.

8. If you're not up to date with what your husband had and where he kept it, you'll have to start tracking down what might be out there. If your partner belonged to associations or clubs, check with them to see if there was any insurance in place. Ask the credit-card company if the card balance was insured.

Most of the activities related to tying up your partner's estate will be handled by his executor. If you are the executrix of your partner's estate and feel out of your depth handling the legalities, consider either renouncing this role and hiring a substitute (an estates lawyer or a trust company), or retaining a lawyer or trust company to act as an agent to help you through the details.

While your financial circumstances may necessitate your making some important decisions about where and how you'll live, you should resist making any life-changing decisions during the first six to 12 months. There are significant stages through which you will have to pass emotionally. Making big decisions during that first year can be tough not only on you, because of the responsibility of coming to the decision, but also on your family, because you all have to live with the consequences. You want to move as slowly as you can to maintain your own peace of mind and comfort level.

Please, please, give yourself the time to grieve. It's okay to feel sorry for yourself. Whether you've been married for five years or 50, you will feel lonely. Ask for help when you need it. Plan your days. Keep lists (a journal might also be a good idea), since you may find it hard to remember things. You are distracted by your pain, so compensate. Don't give yourself hell for being weak, wussy, or simpering. Be kind to yourself. And don't let someone else try to set the timeline for your "recovery." This is your grief and you must work through it at your own pace in your own way. Finally, don't let anyone push you into a decision with which you are not comfortable. Sadly, there are people who may try to take advantage of your confusion or distraction to satisfy their own ends. If you feel you are being pushed, push back. If you can't, tell a dear friend and let her do the pushing for you. If it is your dear friend giving the unsolicited advice, smile and nod, turn a deaf ear, and let it slip quietly past you.

Use your friends to get the nurturing you need during this difficult time. There are also support groups to which you can turn that will be able to help you pick up the pieces. Meeting other women at various stages of the grieving process will help. So will having someone to listen as you babble on about what you feel, fear, and worry about. You also need to be careful about your health and well-being. Make sure you eat. It's easy to forget, and you might think you could stand to go a few days without eating, but this isn't the time. You need physical strength to deal with your emotional hurt. If friends offer to make you a meal, accept. Don't say, "Oh, no, I don't want to be a bother." I hate that! I wouldn't offer if I didn't mean it, but I don't want to have to fight you in order to help you. Your friends probably feel exactly the same way. Let them help. Try to get some regular exercise and find a way to release the tension that will build up as you cope. Walking while focusing on your breathing can be great, and you can do it at your own pace. Try to avoid too much alcohol, caffeine, sugar, and tobacco. I know my first instinct would be to immediately light a cigarette (I quit smoking years ago) and eat a box of chocolate cookies. But this probably wouldn't help.

## Living Through It

While the emotional part of widowhood is never easy, plenty of money makes the financial part of widowhood a lot less scary. Unfortunately, few of us are so fortunate. We may end up with a home, with or without a mortgage, some investments, some debts, and, perhaps, some insurance. But we will also likely end up with a significantly lower income. If you did not work outside the home, the death of a working partner could bring your regular income stream to a complete halt. If your spouse was retired, death could mean that the pension income you were both receiving will be cut back severely. The likelihood is that you will be cash-flow constrained, even if you are asset-rich.

The first thing you need to do is review your spending plan. With a reduced income stream, you may have to liquidate investments as a buffer to your reduced cash flow. Don't forget to apply for death benefits provided by government programs such as Canada Pension Plan, Old Age Security, and Workers' Compensation. You or your partner's executor should file the paperwork for CPP benefits as soon as possible after the death, since there is a one-year limit on the payment of retroactive benefits. It's your job to find everything that is due to you. Look everywhere for hints and clues. Talk to your partner's stockbroker, insurance agent, accountant, lawyer, and employer. Look at his old tax returns to see if capital gains were declared on investments that might now belong to you. Look in the safety deposit box, in his desk at work, in his computer files — everywhere.

On the expenses side, what can you cut? Typical things include cancelling subscriptions and memberships in clubs or organizations, and asking for a prorated rebate. Cancel disability and medical coverage you no longer need. Look at your bank statement. What's being automatically debited that should be stopped? With less regular income coming in, you may have to make some other changes to accommodate your reduced cash flow. While there are some areas in which your expenses will likely go down — now that your family is smaller, you will likely spend less on food, clothing, health, and myriad other items — some costs just don't go away. It'll cost the same to heat, light, and maintain the home.

You may have to sell your home if you find that the costs of keeping it are too high. Unfortunately, many people die without sufficient insurance to cover their outstanding debts, forcing the sale of assets to settle the estate. While a home held jointly will immediately pass to you, if the mortgage is too high for you to manage on your own, and there's not enough in the estate to pay it down, you could wind up selling and moving to a more manageable home.

When? When is the right time to tell the children, put up the sign, and start looking for the new place? That depends. It depends on how long you can maintain the status quo without digging yourself a huge hole of debt. It depends on how long you've been in the home and how attached you and your children are to the house and your neighbourhood. It depends on how willing you are to try other alternatives. Could you rent a part of the house to help carry the mortgage? Would you be willing to share with a friend in a similar position? What are your other options?

There's never an easy, black-and-white answer to any question that involves feelings and money. It's a matter of balancing the need to live within your spending plan with your emotional needs. What's important to remember is that your feelings will be in turmoil, so you should ask someone who doesn't have a vested interest in the decision to help you work through the pros and cons. That's not necessarily your grown children who would love it if you would move closer, or your sister who would love it if you would let her live with you because she loves your cooking, or your best girlfriend who is a real estate agent and knows she can get you a terrific price right now. By definition, this impartial, unbiased other party shouldn't have anything to gain by any decision you make.

If you have not already done so, you'll have to establish a financial identity for yourself. That means setting up a chequing account in your own name, applying for credit cards, and the like. Women who have never had to manage money before sometimes panic at the thought of all they have to do. I remember seeing Joan Rivers being interviewed after the death of her husband. She said she didn't even know the name of her bank. Imagine. She's no dumb bunny, yet she left so much up to her husband that she didn't even know where to begin.

First thing: don't panic. It may take time to figure everything out, but you'll do it. Take it one step at a time. Breathe deeply, and then go through every piece of paper on his desk, in his drawers, in his pockets. Piece the puzzle together so that you have the full picture.

What if you don't like the picture? The accounts are overdrawn. There are bills that haven't been paid in months. The life insurance policy lapsed because the premiums weren't paid. I'm so sorry if you have to live through this, but live through it you will. You will be brave. You must let your friends help if they can. You must come to terms with the fact that you are now in complete control of your destiny.

You have to start somewhere, and somewhere is the bank. Go in and speak with the bank manager with whom your partner was dealing. If you feel that relationship is in the dumpster because of how far in the hole your husband was, then it's time to search for a new, friendly banker. Ask a friend for a referral and a personal introduction. The more sway your friend has, the more willing the new banker will be to accommodate your needs. Be honest. Tell the banker what's happened and what your plans are.

When Rhonda's husband died, leaving her high and dry with no way to meet her expenses (she had a job, but it wasn't enough), Rhonda went to her banker. She described her predicament and explained that she would be selling her house within the next six months. Because she had a good relationship with her banker, she was approved for a loan to get her through the crunch. She made it through, sold the house, repaid the loan, and is completely loyal to her banker.

If you've never written a cheque before, don't know a PIN from an ABM, and can't imagine how you're going to get by, ask for help. Your banker can help. Your best friend can help. Even your children may be able to help. Don't be embarrassed. The fact that you don't know is nothing to be embarrassed about. The only thing you should be embarrassed about is if you are unwilling to learn. It's time to move ahead. Ask for help.

If you think you may be faced with shortages in your cash flow, consider applying for overdraft protection as a way of avoiding NSF cheques. Of course, you won't need overdraft protection if you spend only what you have available. Hah! In a perfect world. The fact is that from time to time people find themselves in a cash-flow squeeze. You can use overdraft protection to ensure that squeeze doesn't have a long-term negative impact on your credit rating. Remember, however, that overdrafts charge significantly higher rates of interest than other forms of credit.

If you've never had to manage money before, you need to establish a credit identity for yourself, and you must keep it healthy. Having a whole bunch of credit cards that you never use doesn't win you brownie points. The only way your credit identity will shine is if you use your credit and repay it on time. And if you use the right kind of credit — credit cards, for example — building a credit history doesn't have to cost you a cent.

Since credit cards only charge interest when your balance has not been paid off in full, if you pay off your balance each month, you pay no interest. You will have used the bank's money for anywhere from 30 days to 60 days — and it will have cost you absolutely nothing. What a deal!

If you don't have any credit history, it may not be easy to qualify for your first card. One way is to use a secured credit card. With a secured credit card, the issuer has to assume no risk — which is why they're willing to give you the card — because you provide the credit-card company with enough cash to cover your balance. Financial institutions typically want twice the amount of credit you're asking for. So if you want a credit card with a $500 balance, you must put up $1,000 in cash. After you've made regular payments for about a year or so, the financial institution will drop the security requirement and return your deposit. And once you've had one credit card and established a good credit rating, you will always be able to get another or have your limit raised.

Remember to cancel your partner's credit cards. While you're at it, check to see if your spouse had creditor life insurance to take care of outstanding balances. If not, the estate will have to settle up.

If you are widowed while you are still working and building that nest egg for the future, you may face one of three scenarios. You may find everything taken care of financially by a smart, well-prepared partner who was insured to the eyeteeth and had dotted all the i's and crossed all the t's. You may find yourself with little or nothing, struggling just to make ends meet. Or you may be somewhere in the middle.

If you are left in sound shape financially, you'll still have to make some decisions about how to invest the money you've been left. If it's in a trust and there's no thinking involved, carry on! Chances are, if you're an in-charge kind of person, you'll want even a modicum of say in how your money works for you. Get educated about investing even as you take the advice of trusted lawyers, financial planners, accountants, and the like. Remember, this is *your* money we're talking about. Don't be passive about it.

If you are struggling to make ends meet, I'm sorry you have to be dealing with your grief and a financial nightmare at the same time. It shouldn't happen that way, but it often does. It is important to do whatever is necessary to get yourself back on track, and then take care of the future.

If you're somewhere in the middle — you have no horrendous debts, but you'll have to continue working for a living — once you've dealt with the pain, anger, and despair of being left, you can get back on track. You, too, will need to take care of your future, one day at a time.

If you always figured you didn't really need an emergency fund because you had your partner, it's time to get an emergency fund. Depending on whether you are working or retired, you will need more or less. If you are retired and have a regular flow of retirement income, the emergency fund will help if something untoward happens. If you are still working, you not only need to protect yourself from unusual expenses, you need to protect yourself from interruptions in your income (due to illness or layoff), so you need a very healthy emergency fund. Failing that, make sure you have a line of credit.

If you have children, parents, or anyone else who is now dependent on your income, you may need life insurance. If you don't have dependents, in most cases, life insurance shouldn't be a consideration. However, if you receive a number of assets from your partner on which no tax had to be paid but on which a whopping amount of tax may be owed at your death, life insurance could help offset the tax bite for your heirs. You'll have to weigh the cost of the insurance against the need to protect your children from the tax man.

If you were covered for health benefits under your spouse's plan, you will probably have to go shopping for coverage for yourself and your kids. You might also consider upping the amount of disability coverage you have, depending on your other financial resources.

Remember to change the beneficiary designations on your own insurance, RRSPs, RRIFs, or anything else on which your partner was your beneficiary.

As a widow, you will inherit your husband's assets without tax consequence. Usually, at death, a person is deemed for tax purposes to have disposed of all their assets at fair market price. So if someone owned 200 shares of a stock bought at $20, and at the time of death the stock was worth $40 a share, the estate would have to declare a capital gain of $20 a share and pay tax on that gain. However, since you, as the widow, may inherit the shares at their original cost, there is no capital gain, so no tax is payable until you sell the shares or die, whichever comes first.

Your spouse's RRSPs or RRIFs can also be rolled to you on a tax-deferred basis. You won't have to pay any tax on the money, provided you roll the funds, referred to as a "refund of premiums," directly to your own RRSP or RRIF. Or you could use the funds to buy a life annuity or a fixed-term annuity to age 90.

A financially dependent child or grandchild under the age of 18 can also be named as the beneficiary of an RRSP or RRIF. To be "financially dependent," the child's income must be less than the basic personal exemption and no one else must have claimed a tax credit on the child's behalf. The assets are then passed to the child, but they must be used to purchase an annuity for a fixed number of years; that number cannot exceed 18 minus the minor's age at the time the annuity is purchased.

In terms of benefits you may receive from government programs, while the CPP widow's benefit is taxable in your hands, the monthly orphan's benefit (paid for children under 25 as long as they are in school) is considered to be your child's income and taxable in his or her hands. If you plan to invest that money for your child, take care to keep it separate and apart from other money so that it is easily identified by Revenue Canada as the child's money. Insurance proceeds are also free of tax.

You'll need to visit your estates lawyer to change your will, powers of attorney, and any other documents in which your spouse was named. As well, decreases or increases in assets resulting from the death of a spouse mean you should review your own estate plan thoroughly.

## PREPARING FOR IT

Regardless of whether your partner suffered a terminal illness or the death of your spouse came as a complete shock, the finality will be staggering. If you know you will be widowed — that your partner's passing is only a matter of time — then there are some things you can do to prepare. The obvious ones include things like making sure that all your insurance is paid up, that you have cash readily available so you aren't cash-flow poor while the estate is being probated — this would be a good time to consider a joint account — and that you know where everything is so you're not scrambling to come up with the documentation you may need. You should also begin to assume some, if not all, of the responsibility for the financial side of your family's life so you are well equipped to continue on your own.

However, there are many less obvious things you may need to consider. In some cases, you may find yourself facing huge debt as you also come to terms with your aloneness. If there is no way around this — if it is a matter of care for your beloved — then get yourself emotionally ready for accepting this debt all on your own. Another less obvious issue: Will you remain in your current home on your own? Will you feel secure? How will you cope with the memories? While it is never a good idea to make big decisions so close to an emotionally traumatic event, if you are given time to prepare, this could be one of the things you seriously think about.

The other thing you can do to prepare is get in touch with organizations you may need to use as support. Widows' groups and grief-counselling workshops, for example, will make things easier. You may not feel you need them now, and that's okay. After all, friends are friends no matter where you meet them. Consider too that you may not want to meet new people as you initially work through your grief. By forming those alliances sooner rather than later, however, you eliminate the stress of meeting new people at an already stressful time.

Finally, buy yourself a good book on grief and have a read. Elisabeth Kübler-Ross wrote *On Death and Dying* in 1969 and it is still considered the definitive guide to coping with grief.

# 21

# Just in Case
# You Inherit

*Men possessed of money, like men earlier favored by noble birth and great
title, have infallibly imagined that the awe and admiration which money
inspires were really owing to their own wisdom or personality.*

JOHN KENNETH GALBRAITH

If you've had to deal with the loss of someone very close to you, then give
yourself time before you do anything with your inheritance. Six months
to a year is the time frame most often mentioned when we talk about
getting over the stress of the loss, and dealing with your head and heart
in the same place. For those who inherit without a huge sense of loss, it's
still a good idea to let the money rest for 30 to 90 days so you can think
clearly and make plans. A money-market fund would be just the ticket.
Don't invest in anything you haven't researched, like a new business or
unfamiliar investment option. And don't take investment advice from
people you don't know or who don't have the expertise.

## LIVING THROUGH IT

Of course, part of the fun of getting a windfall is dreaming about what you'll
do with it. It's okay to go a little crazy. That's part of the fun of life. But
before you blow your stash, remember that this could be a turning point.

Don't forget to have some fun. We have to be so practical most of the time that it's easy to forget that money is simply a tool to help us get the things we need and want. An unexpected windfall is a great excuse to treat yourself and someone you love to something special.

This would be a good time to review your spending plan. If there have been areas where you've been skimping, you may be able to flesh them out now. However, heed this warning: it doesn't take long to get used to a less restrained spending plan, so it will be hard to pull back later. Sure, you can undo the belt a few notches — just don't be tempted to replace it with an elastic waistband.

You have *no* excuse for not establishing or beefing up your emergency fund. No ifs, ands, or buts. *Do it!*

Been hankering for a home of your own? Here's the perfect opportunity to get into your own place. If you have enough to buy outright, good for you. Don't be a fool about how much you spend. Negotiate hard. Every nickel you save today is a nickel you'll have tomorrow (and we all know that life has a way of changing). If your inheritance is sufficient to give you a downpayment on your home, be careful that you don't buy too much simply because you have a decent downpayment. Remember, the smaller your mortgage, the easier it is on your cash flow and the less you'll spend in interest.

Remember to consult your spouse before you go off on a spending spree. When Alice inherited money from her aunt, she decided to surprise her husband, Mark. She knew Mark had always wanted a house with a large porch and a huge garden, so she bought him one. She couldn't understand why he was so angry. He couldn't believe she had made such an important purchase without his input. She thought he was ungrateful. He thought she was being unreasonable.

My husband's always wanted a house with, in his words, "a large footprint." He means he wants lots and lots and lots and lots of space. I just know that if he ever laid his hands on enough money all at once, we'd be moving to a bigger (more to clean) house. I, on the other hand, just want to be mortgage-free. We've talked about this a lot. I told him I'd love a house with a bigger footprint, as long as it didn't have a mortgage. We've agreed on that as a future strategy. Of course, we've never had to put it into practice since no one's dumped a barrel of money in our laps. The important thing is that we've talked about it.

Make a list of the things that are important to you. Then decide which you can affect with your inheritance. Perhaps you want to invest in the future. Use a portion of your cash to do something to enhance your career options. Have you been thinking about upgrading your skills? Want to try your hand at working for yourself? Use part of your stash to get you going or help with your cash flow as you move to the next stage of your career. Retirement is also in your future. You're likely to be retired for more than 30 years, so consider contributing to an RRSP. You may have unused room you can catch up. That'll make for a tidy nest egg and a handsome tax refund.

If you want to invest for your children, use part of your windfall to jump-start an educational fund. With university costs expected to soar in coming years, that's another solid investment in the future. Ten thousand dollars invested in an educational fund at 12% will equal $60,000 in 15 years, just when junior is getting ready to head off to university.

Shopping for the right chequing or investment account is always important, but now that you've got more financial clout, it's time to throw your weight around. Years ago I sold a piece of property my company owned. My broker, Ann Richards, talked me into opening up a Triple A account at Wood Gundy. She convinced me that the fee (a hefty $200 a year) would be offset by the benefits. Well, she was right. The account paid substantially more interest than I was earning on my old Bank of Montreal corporate account. In fact, in just two months, the entire annual fee was covered. After that, it was gravy. And the statements are so detailed and well designed that reconciling has never been easier. I would never have known about this account if Ann had not introduced me to it. And this raises an interesting question: If a brokerage house can afford to pay me substantially more interest than can a bank account, what's wrong with the bank's approach to business?

Ultimately, it is your responsibility to find yourself the best deal going. It helps to have a relationship with someone in the know, but if you don't you aren't stymied. You simply have to do more legwork. Call around. Ask for brochures. Negotiate fees and rates. Demand more and you'll get more.

You may want to use your inheritance to rectify some of your past mistakes. A lump-sum cash influx can help to eliminate or minimize past lapses in judgment or unfortunate financial circumstances. Get rid of as much of your debt as you can. Start with the debt that's costing you the most in interest. Getting rid of your high-cost debt gets you back into the black faster and can save you a whack of interest. Paying off a $5,000 balance on a credit card that charges 17% in interest can mean savings of up to $850 in interest in just one year.

If you have an outstanding RRSP loan or a balance on your personal line of credit, or if you have used expensive financing to buy household items, pay it off. Then use the money you would have made in monthly payments to save for that special purchase or holiday. With a little patience and some planning, you'll still be able to go to Disney World while saving a ton of interest.

Have a mortgage? While interest rates are relatively low right now, over the life of your mortgage you could pay up to double the original cost of your home because of that interest. A one-time pre-payment of $10,000 on a $100,000 mortgage amortized for 25 years at 10% will save up to $52,223 in interest and get you to the mortgage-burning party 6.25 years sooner.

Trying to decide between your mortgage and your RRSP? Most financial institutions have computer programs that can help you see the relative value of each option. Let them do the math for you so you can choose the option that gives the best return. Of course, you could follow a balanced approach and do both. If your marginal tax rate is 40% and you contribute $10,000 to an RRSP (as a regular contribution or to catch up past unused contributions), you'll get a tax refund of $4,000. Use that as a mortgage pre-payment.

To decide what you'll do with the money you have left over for investment, answer the following questions:

- How much do I want to keep easily available just for the fun of spending it (or helping to pay the bills)?
- Do I need an income from my inheritance to make my life more comfortable?
- Do I want my capital to grow to provide for retirement or for an estate for my children?

These questions lead you to the three considerations for investing, aside from your investment personality, which we talked about in Part II. They are your need for liquidity, your need for a regular stream of income, and your desire for growth. If you're an experienced investor, you may feel comfortable figuring this all out on your own. Chances are if you've come into a bundle of cash for the first time in your life, you'll need help figuring out what to do with it. Get yourself an excellent financial adviser before you do much about your money (see Chapter 13).

Do you still need insurance? That depends. You need enough capital so that if you should die, your family would have enough money to pay off all its debts, provide for your children's education, pay your final taxes, and generate enough income to support the family comfortably. If your estate will do that without insurance, scrap your plan. If you plan to invest your inheritance in a business or in some other endeavour where there is a chance the money won't be there if you die prematurely, keep your insurance. You may be able to scale back, but totally eliminating it may mean you would have to buy it again, at more expensive rates, if your financial picture changes.

The same holds true for your disability insurance. If your inheritance provides enough income to support you (and cover your medical expenses) whether you're working or not, then you may no longer need to carry hefty disability premiums. But be quite sure before you cancel your policy that you will no longer need it. With all that money, you can probably afford to maintain the premiums and protect yourself and your family's future, *just in case!*

Several years ago, a young woman in Ontario won an obscene amount of money in the lottery, and the media kept asking me (and several other financial people) the same question: "What should she invest that money in?" Over and over I said the same thing. "She doesn't have to worry about investing, she has $21 million. Now she has to worry about taxes and estate planning."

While an inheritance is usually delivered net of taxes, once it's yours, any income earned on the capital (or any appreciation realized by the sale of the asset) is taxable in your hands. Make sure you have a good tax accountant.

If you plan to pass any of your inheritance on to your children, then you'll need to do some estate planning to protect your newfound wealth. Get thee to an estates lawyer for advice.

# 22

# Just in Case You Lose Your Job

*Work is the price you pay for money.*

ANONYMOUS

One of the life events that can shake a girl to her very foundation is losing her job. Not only do you have to consider the financial implications — how are you ever going to make the next rent payment? — but significant social and psychological issues come into play. There's the loss of self-esteem associated with being terminated, regardless of the reason for termination. There's the sense of not knowing what to do next. And there's the loss of relationships; all those people with whom you worked will soon forget who you are as they move on with their lives and you with yours. It can seem pretty dismal, but you will live through it. You've got to grit your teeth, believe you will be fine, and keep moving.

## LIVING THROUGH IT

Before you can move ahead, you'll have to deal with the personal anxiety of having joined the ranks of the unemployed. First comes the immediate sense of panic. How will you tell your partner? the kids? your mother? While you may find it hard to believe right now, these very people whom you fear telling will provide you with enormous support to help you deal with the trauma and get back on your feet.

If you're feeling a sense of guilt or your self-esteem is lower than the belly of a snake, take a deep breath. There is no point in blaming yourself. You likely had little control over what happened. Today's economic reality is very different from the past, so we can't use the old rules and standards to make judgments about our worth and accountability. Shake loose the feelings that try to invade and focus on the future. Yes, you will get another job. No, you haven't let your family down. Yes, you will be fine, and so will they.

If you're furious at the world, know that this is a part of your response to the situation. You must get past this stage so you can make a convincing show when you go knocking on doors. Don't deny the anger; that will just delay your recovery. Do what you must to get past it. Meditate. Kickbox. Talk, talk, talk.

Perhaps the most important thing you will have to learn to do is ask for help. For many people, this is the most difficult of all. It shouldn't be. People love to help; just ask. And since you're far more likely to get another job because someone you know knows someone else than from the traditional route, tell everyone you know when you're ready to go back to work.

So often, the shock of the announcement throws people into a tailspin and the last thing they feel like doing is sitting down to make a plan. But if you want to be successful in dealing with your unemployment, you'll need a plan. First you'll have to come to terms with your significantly reduced cash flow — forced simplicity, right? Then there's the prospect of going job hunting. You'll need an up-to-date résumé, a good idea of the work you want to do next, and lots of contacts to get you that next job. Will you need to upgrade your skills? This could be the perfect time to do it. Ever considered self-employment? Don't rush into anything, but starting your own business may be the answer to your joblessness. Finally, there are the things you must do to keep yourself healthy as you deal with the stress of the termination and the job hunt. Some turn automatically to exercise routines. Others feed their emptiness with food. What will you use as your outlet?

Typically, when individuals are terminated due to economic factors (i.e., not a performance-related termination), the dark cloud is often accompanied by a silver lining: a severance. Mandatory only in Ontario and in federally regulated industries, severances have become nationally accepted based on legal precedent set in courts across the country. So one of your first questions should be: "How much do I get?"

Severance can be given as either a lump sum or as salary continuance. It's all a matter of whether you want to take the full amount into income in one fell swoop, or use the salary continuance option to provide a regular flow of income that would extend over a longer period of time.

If you decide to take your severance all at once, consider using the retiring allowance provision of an RRSP to shelter some or all of the money. "Retiring allowance" is a misnomer, since it is money received both on retirement and at termination and includes unused sick leave (but not accrued vacation pay). The portion of your severance that you can roll over to your RRSP includes $2,000 for each year of employment up to and including 1995 plus an additional $1,500 for each year of employment, prior to 1989, for which employer contributions to a pension plan or deferred profit-sharing plan on your behalf were not made or have not vested.

If your severance exceeds your rollover room, the next place to look is your unused RRSP contribution room. Now that you have the money, this would be the time to catch up all those contributions not made.

Concerned about rolling money to an RRSP that you might very well need to live on while you look for a job? Don't be. As long as you choose an investment that leaves you the flexibility to pull money from your plan should you need it, you're set. A money-market mutual fund would be perfect. Monthly or quarterly, you can pull the amount you need to cover your living expenses while unemployed. You may have to pay a fee for withdrawals, so check with your financial institution before you decide how often to dip in. Once you get a job, you can deploy the money remaining to more aggressive investment alternatives.

When you cash in all or part of an RRSP, you'll pay withholding tax (a pre-payment of income tax) at the time of withdrawal. Outside Quebec, the rate is 10% on the first $5,000, 20% on withdrawal amounts between $5,000 and $15,000, and 30% for amounts over $15,000. Then when you file your tax return for the year you made the withdrawal, you'll have to include any amounts withdrawn in your income, and your true taxes owing are calculated based on your marginal tax rate. So consider yourself warned: It may turn out that your withholding tax was insufficient to cover the tax you really owe on the withdrawn income, and you'll have to dish out some more.

While you may pay significantly less tax on RRSP withdrawals because your income while unemployed is considerably lower, try to make your withdrawals in denominations of $5,000 or less. You'll pay less withholding tax, and you won't end up with extra money outside the RRSP should the perfect job suddenly appear on the horizon. More on RRSP withdrawals a little later.

Having figured out how much you'll receive from your employer, the next step is to take stock of what you have accumulated. If you set up an emergency fund, and you have the required three to six months' expenses covered, you now have proof that *telesis* works.

Make a list of all the assets you've accumulated: cash in the bank, money in money-market funds, CSBs, GICs, term deposits, investments in mutual funds, stocks, or bonds, as well as any other sources of income you may have.

Unless you're one of the filthy rich (why does the language of money always sound as though it could use a good bath?), you're going to have to cut back. Review your spending plan to see which expenses can be reduced and which can be eliminated. Do you need to keep the kids in full-time day care? Could you make arrangements with friends and family to spell you off when you need to go for an interview? This could save big bucks. What about your transportation and lunch costs? Those will go down. So, too, will your ordering-in and eating-out costs, since you'll have the time to make dinner at home now that you're not running in the door at 7:30 p.m.

Think about the kinds of things you could do on a freelance or part-time basis while you are looking for a full-time job. Would your former employer consider using your services as a freelancer or consultant? What other employers might? Who have you met through your work who has expressed appreciation for or satisfaction with your efforts on their behalf? Offer to buy lunch, tell them what you want to do next, and ask them to help. Network, network, network.

Finally, make a new spending plan incorporating both the reduced income and reduced expenses you've worked through. How much of a shortfall is there? How will you cover it? Will you use your line of credit and hope you get back to work before you're in debt for the rest of your life? Or will you liquidate assets to fill the hole in your plan?

If you're considering tapping your RRSPs, think carefully. Money you take out can never be replaced, so it's gone for good. If the mortgage has to be paid and food put on the table, and the RRSP is the only resource you have, then the answer is self-evident.

If you can delay making the RRSP withdrawal until the calendar year following your layoff and severance (depending on when in the year you got the old heave-ho), you'll be taking that income in a year when you have yet to earn any other income. That may mean a lower marginal tax rate, depending on when you return to work. Think about the timing carefully before you start pulling money out of your RRSP.

By the way, don't be so proud that you forget to apply for EI benefits, and when those run out, any other benefits to which you may be entitled. You've helped to support the system with your taxes and premiums. Now it's your turn to use the benefits. Taking care of yourself and your family means taking advantage of every option available to stay afloat during the storm.

Assuming you don't have an emergency fund, or it has run out, and you are scrambling to come up with enough money to get by each month, here are some things to consider:

- Can you skip a mortgage payment? Some mortgage agreements allow you to skip a payment and have the amount added to your principal. While this increases your loan, it keeps your credit history from becoming tarnished.
- Do you have a line of credit that you can use to help make ends meet? People often don't think about using a line of credit for emergencies until an emergency arises. But you need a job to qualify for the line. If you're a responsible borrower and don't have a history of using your credit to the limit, getting a line of credit before you need it may be a good idea.
- Are there assets you could sell to help make ends meet? This would be the time to sell assets that have appreciated, or to reap the benefits of long-term compounding interest. What's the point of having assets if you can't bring yourself to sell them when you need the money?
- Can you borrow against your life insurance policy? If your life

insurance has a cash-value component, you may be able to borrow
against it to supplement your cash flow in the short term.

Okay, so you have no way of paying the mortgage and you're sure you'll
end up losing the house. If you rent, you may already be looking for
cheaper digs. Relax. Don't allow your emotions to make your decisions
for you. Money, as much as we insist on making it an emotional issue, is
really best dealt with logically. So before you stick that sign up on the
lawn or pack your life's belongings to move, think about what you could
do to cope. There are always alternatives.

Perhaps you could convert part of your home and rent it to supplement
your current cash flow. Whether you own or rent, a roommate may be
one way of reducing your expenses. While the initial idea of having
roomers and boarders may be offensive, vile, intrusive, if it means you
can stay where you are, if it means you can limit the disruption to your
family's life, isn't it worth considering?

After some deliberation, you might decide that selling your home is
the best option. It is most likely to work to your advantage if you have
built up considerable equity and can use it to get yourself reestablished.
If you're swapping a $1,200-a-month mortgage payment for a $1,200-a-
month rental payment (yes, there are people who have done this), you
may not be seeing the picture clearly. Ask friends for advice, consult a
trusted real estate agent, check with your mother. Ultimately, you'll end
up doing what feels right for you. But with enough input, you will have
considered all the angles and can follow your instincts.

Are there areas you've wanted to explore previously that you've never
had time to delve into? Now you have time. But it won't last forever, and
there will always be something that could take priority over your dream.
If you really want to try something new, *do it!*

Financial advisers often say that you should think carefully before you
decide to go into business for yourself. That's true. But if you don't have
a job anyway, and you have a good idea for employing yourself, why not
go through the process of putting a plan together? What have you got to
lose but time, and you've got plenty of that, right?

Make sure you don't get mired in your own misery and stop dreaming.
If it's taking longer than you thought to get back into the swim, don't
spend the time you have sitting on the couch watching *One Life to Live.*

Remember, one life is all you have, so don't waste it. Volunteer. Get involved with your local school, church, hospital, shelter, library, whatever. Stay busy. Meet people. Give of yourself. And keep telling people what you want. Believe, and you will get what you want.

You probably should consolidate all your money in one place for a couple of reasons. First, it will help you see what you have. Second, it will likely cost less in service charges and fees. You may even earn some interest. If you have a partner, talk about how you're going to handle the day-to-day money management. If you've always done it and you're feeling a little overwhelmed, this might be the time for your partner to spell you off, at least until you feel less shaky. If your partner has been in charge, now that you've got some extra time on your hands, maybe you should take a run at managing the spending plan. Whatever the outcome, the only way you're going to get through this crisis intact as a couple is to talk. Talk, talk, talk, talk, talk. If you're in the unhappy circumstance of not being able to talk to your partner, find a friend with whom you can bounce ideas around. It's important that you not stay bottled up. Some of the worst decisions are made when an issue is seen from only one perspective.

Now is not the time to make large expenditures. If you have committed to buying a new car, investing in your best friend's business, or going on a vacation, back out. If there is a penalty to pay, so be it. You are going to need every red cent you can lay your hands on to get you through the next little while.

So, should you tell your creditors you don't have a job, or should you hold back for fear they may revoke your only source of cash flow? Good question. Like almost everything else in life, it depends. Don't tell creditors who can call the loan, because ten-to-one they will. This is one good reason why it makes sense not to have all your financial business in one place. (Everyone always talks about the benefits of consolidation. Here's a case where it may not be to your advantage.) If you have your mortgage at ABC Bank and your personal line of credit at XYZ Bank, you can call your mortgage company and negotiate a deal without running the risk that your PLC will be revoked. If you're carrying credit-card debt, you should call and work out a payment option. If you owe taxes, you should call Revenue Canada and work out a payment program.

No matter who's holding the paper on you, consider negotiating a reduction of interest and/or principal. In the first case, there's no point in the lender putting you into bankruptcy with astronomically high interest rates. In the second case, if you can pay off three-quarters of the entire balance, the lender may be willing to settle for that rather than losing the whole shebang to bankruptcy. Negotiate. Smile. Be very sweet. Since you are the fairer, more delicate sex, you might as well play it for all it's worth. This is not the time to be argumentative, authoritarian, or sly. You can be firm without sounding like a bully. You can negotiate without threats. Be upfront, honest, and sincere about wanting to work something out. Remember, your circumstances have changed, not your character.

While it may initially seem like a smart thing to do, reducing or eliminating your insurance to save on the premiums while you are unemployed can have long-term negative consequences. Applying for new coverage later may require a medical checkup and a new policy may exclude pre-existing conditions. Never mind the increased cost of premiums based on your new and improved age! Bottom line: don't cancel your insurance.

Check with your benefits coordinator at work to see if you can take on the premiums of your existing insurance benefits in order to continue being covered. If you've had difficulty qualifying for life insurance because of age or health, converting your group policy to an individual policy is one way to start building your insurance portfolio.

Also keep in mind that employment insurance benefits may be clawed back if your net income exceeds a specific amount ($58,500 in 1997). The total amount clawed back will never exceed 30% of the benefits, but the remaining 70% will be taxable in the normal way. While employment insurance benefits may help with cash flow initially, you may find that almost all your benefits are grabbed back when you file your next tax return. Just a warning so it doesn't come as a complete shock.

### PREPARING FOR IT

You've just been given notice. You have three weeks, three months, or something in the middle to adjust to the idea that you are going to be out of work shortly. Perhaps it is only the rumour of massive layoffs that has you worried. If you think the axe might fall, and it may be your head that rolls, it's time to start planning.

Start your job search immediately. Get that résumé up to date and put the word out that you're exploring your options.

Prepare a spending plan for surviving should your worst fears be realized. Your spending plan should cover at least six months. Eliminate all discretionary spending for items such as clothing, meals in restaurants, and entertainment. Beef up your emergency fund. Start paying off your debt with vigour. Charge nothing more on your credit cards. Pay cash for everything, or use your debit card, and make sure you keep meticulous records so you stay on track financially. If you have several loans or many credit cards with outstanding balances, this may be the time to consolidate so you have a single payment and are paying lower interest. When the lender asks why you want the loan, say that you want to reduce your interest costs and have the convenience of a single payment. Do not indicate that your job is at risk.

Review your investments to see what may be liquidated easily, and what should be restructured to provide you with some income during your sabbatical.

# 23

# Just in Case You Have to Relocate

*I will arise and go now, and go to Innisfree,*
*And a small cabin build there, of clay and wattles made:*
*Nine bean-rows will I have there, a hive for the honey-bee,*
*And live alone in the bee-loud glade.*

W. B. YEATS

You've been transferred. Or, perhaps, you've decided that new scenery would be just the ticket for a fresh start. Maybe you're taking a new job that requires a move halfway across the country. Whatever your specific circumstances, it's important to realize that relocating has significant stresses associated with it, many of them financial.

## LIVING THROUGH IT

Depending on how far you move and how different your new environment is, you should take stock of what may change in your spending plan. Some expenses seem obvious: the cost of housing may be more or less expensive, as may the cost of things such as food, clothes, and other consumables. Other less obvious expenses: utilities, transportation, and insurance. Is the new neighbourhood school to your liking or will you have to spend extra on private schooling? How far away is the local community centre — a walk or a drive? What about the costs for child care? Since you don't have a neighbour network yet and you may have left your entire support system behind, even getting out for routine tasks may be challenging.

Then, of course, there are all the costs associated with the move itself: the cost to sell and buy a new home or to get out of a lease; the movers; transportation for you, your partner, your kids, and your pets, including meals and lodging. All the little things will add up to a substantial kick to your spending plan. This might be a great time to hold the mother of all garage sales and get rid of unopened wedding presents, baby clothes, school mementos, and all the other paraphernalia you've accumulated.

If you haven't yet considered making a spending plan for moving, consider it now. It's not that things won't come up. They sure will. (Will you ship the car, or sell here and buy a new one there? Will you feed the cat the tranquillizer, or take it yourself?) But you're much more likely to get through it unscathed if you have thought through those what-ifs and created a pool of funds for dealing with the unexpected.

Get copies of the local newspapers for several weeks before the move so you can start to mentally acclimatize to your new area. You'll be able to uncover scads of information if you make like Sherlock and snoop. What are the local prices in the new area compared with those of your current stores? Who are the major retailers? What types of events are held in your neighbourhood? What types of social, community, or religious supports are there? Will there be a climate change that warrants a different wardrobe in your new location? What are houses going for?

If you're moving to a part of the country of which you know little, it can be stressful trying to decide where to live. And if you're working with a fixed budget, as most people are, then your wishes and realities may seem miles apart. Take heart. There are things you can do to make the whole process a little easier.

Enlist the services of a real estate agent who specializes in the areas where you would like to live. That means contacting a national organization that can refer you to a local broker, or asking friends or work acquaintances who live in that area for help. (Remember, people like to help, you just have to ask.) Ask the agent for copies of listings for the area, as well as for specifics relating to schools, health care, child care, transportation, and social facilities (closest supermarket, closest hockey rink, etc.). Visit your new neighbourhood before you buy and scout it out for yourself. Do you like the feel? Does it provide everything you must have or would like to have?

Test your new location before you make the final leap. Perhaps you can sublet an apartment for a few months to see what the area will be like to live in. I stress live, because often people make their decision to move based on their holiday experiences. Visiting a place for weeks can be very different from living there for months. Before you sink money into a permanent place, try it on and see how it feels first.

Don't try setting new goals for a few months. You need time to settle in and get your bearings. There's no point in trying to plot a new course until you've had a good look at the terrain, mapped the stars, and looked at the opportunities. But don't delay doing this forever either. It's easy to get wrapped up in the day-to-day excitement, frustration, and stress of living in a new place and completely lose track of your goals. Allow yourself about six months to settle. You might decide then that you need a little more time. If you've hit a year and you're still working with the old map, time to do some surveying. There's little chance, with all the changes that have taken place over the past year, that you're still perfectly on course.

Depending on where you bank, whether you move across town or across the country you may be able to maintain your existing accounts and simply carry on as usual. Our network of national banks offers us easy access to our money through branches, banking machines, computers, and the telephone. That sounds really great, doesn't it? And it's what our banks would have you believe. When our Aunty Jackie moved from the big city to a small town, she discovered the only branch of her bank in town was completely automated. She was some ticked off, I'll tell you. She didn't want to deal with a machine. She wanted a person.

It can be good to deal with a big bank, because you will likely be able to maintain all your services with little fuss. All you'll have to do is put in notices of address change and keep on trucking. Of course, if you deal with a smaller financial institution and there's no branch convenient to your new location, you'll have to go shopping.

The ultimate test of your worth to any bank will be how willing the branch people are to build a relationship with you when you move to town. After all, as a stranger to the area, you'll need help. If you're what banks refer to as "high value" you may get references to all sorts of resources you can use. If you're further down the value scale, you may find yourself with little attention and fewer services. The smaller your bank balance or use of credit, the more likely you are to need the care and attention of a smaller institution such as a credit union.

Earlier I used the word "shopping" to describe the process of choosing a new bank. You see, when I talk about your relationship with a bank — or whatever type of financial institution — I see you as the client, customer, or buyer and I see the other guy as the service provider or seller. You're spending your money (service charges and interest) to buy products and services, and the other guy is making a big profit. So, as a customer, client, or buyer, you have the right to choices. And if the other guy isn't treating you with the care and respect you deserve, one of the choices you should execute is walking across the street to the competition.

Now, you may think this would be an exercise in frustration since all banks are the same, and each one is as bad as the next. Not so, I say. They are if you paint them with the same big brush and call them by their corporate names. But if you look at the individual branches instead of the Big Name Bank, you'll see some significant differences. Every branch is made up of the people who work in it. Yes, there are corporate rules. Yes, they may even look exactly the same. But they aren't, so don't be fooled. Since no two people on earth are exactly the same, a group of people working in one branch cannot be the same as another group of people working in a different branch. All you have to do is find the right group of people.

When I moved into my current home several years ago, it was the perfect time to go shopping for a new financial institution. I interviewed five branch managers with a simple request. I wanted to pay the least in interest and service charges, earn the most return, and be treated like a queen. All but one manager told me why I could not have what I wanted. I was being unrealistic. One branch manager laughed at me. Mr. Cocky didn't get the biz. Only one manager had the wherewithal to say, "Let me show you what we *can* do for you." He got the biz.

The point of my story: You can have what you want even if four out of five dopes tell you that you can't. Just keep going until you find the one bright person who acknowledges that you are the customer, that it is your contribution to the company's bottom line that pays his wages, and that you deserve to have your needs met.

According to an Ernst & Young survey conducted in 1996, relocation is one of the most common reasons why people have difficulty making monthly credit-card payments. I have to admit I was a little surprised at first. It would make perfect sense if job loss led to missed monthly payments, as would marriage breakup. I had grossly underestimated the stress relocating places on cash flow. There might be an interruption in income. There will certainly be increased costs. The more I thought about it, the more sense it made. Have you thought about it yet?

Our first tendency when our cash flow is squeezed is to jump to the most convenient form of credit to fill the gap: credit cards. And the excitement and uncertainty of a move can create some needs that wouldn't be considered needs under normal circumstances. After all, if you've been driving for the last six hours and the kids are driving you crazy, will you really care if the next bed costs $75 a night or $125 a night? And if everyone is starving, it's a lot more likely that you'll stop at a restaurant than go shopping at a local grocery store for sandwich fixin's. Little costs add up. The king-size bed won't fit up the narrow stairway, so you'll have to buy a smaller bed. Your daughter's carpet is too big for her new room but too small to use in the basement. The coffee machine was broken in the move, and you need your coffee.

The single best way to stay on track with your credit usage is to keep a running log of what you're charging. A spending log is one way of making sure you know where your money is going and that you don't go off track. Don't add the stress of unexpected credit-card bills to the stress of your relocation. Know what you're charging and what it's going to cost you emotionally and financially.

If your expenses go up in your new location, it's a lot easier to save less than to live without, right? And if your expenses go down, it'll be better to have some extra money to spend than to have some extra money to save, right? If you agree with either of these statements, you're probably in the majority. It takes a certain discipline to look at expenses that have grown and commit to not changing the long-term investment plan. It would mean cutting back in some areas to keep 10% going to investments. It may mean giving up some of the things you previously enjoyed. On the flip side, it's a lot easier to spend money than to save it. After all, if your new lifestyle gives you more disposable income, you and your family deserve to be able to enjoy it. But it's also the perfect time to boost your savings. Split the difference. Take advantage of your extra disposable income. Put some extra money to work in investments too. After all, life is about balance.

Relocating may seem like the emergency you've been waiting for. Your expenses may have gone up. Your spending plan may have been blown. Your income may have been interrupted as you changed jobs. Yes, this may have had some emergency elements. Just remember, whatever you take out, you're going to have to put back to top up the emergency fund. It's fine to use it when you need it. After all, that's what it's there for. Just remember, tomorrow is another day, and you may need it again. Remember to restock your just-in-case larder, just in case.

Does your homeowner's insurance policy cover your contents while they are in transit? Do you need extra insurance as protection against the hazards of moving? Call your broker and find out *before* something breaks.

There are tax benefits associated with relocating to take a new job. If you move to a new home that is 40 km closer to your new work location — even if it is your own business — than was your old home, you can deduct substantial amounts for tax purposes. So, if you're planning to move, see if you can arrange to meet the tests for deducting your moving expenses.

Except where you are reimbursed by your employer, you'll be able to deduct:

- reasonable travelling costs to move all members of your household, so keep your receipts
- the moving costs for your stuff, including any storage costs, so keep your receipts
- the costs of meals and lodging near either the old or new home for up to 15 days, so keep your receipts
- the cost of cancelling a lease
- commissions and other sales costs associated with selling your old home, and legal fees and land transfer tax to buy a new home.

# 24

# Just in Case You Have to Declare Personal Bankruptcy

*O money, money, how blindly thou hast been worshipped, and how stupidly abused!*

CHARLES LAMB

You're broke. After years of university, getting up for work at the crack of dawn, working until late at night, and giving up weekends and holidays, you're flat broke. You tried to save, but everything was so expensive. Or maybe your partner left with the money and you got stuck with the mortgage and all the credit-card bills. Or perhaps you were laid off seven months ago and you've been doing everything possible to make ends meet since then.

No one plans for financial disaster, but it happens. And even if you have been scrupulous with your finances, economic circumstances, family tragedy, and deception can conspire to knock down even the most well-built financial house like a pile of toothpicks. "Unemployment has been a big issue for people who come to us," says Laurie Campbell of Credit Counselling in Toronto. "Often they have been using credit to help them through their circumstances. There are people who may have had a $60,000-a-year job and are now working for $30,000. But they have not adjusted their lifestyle to fit within their new income. They fill the gap with credit."

Another big contributor to financial distress: student loans. Laurie says, "For people between 20 and 30 years of age, student loans are becoming a primary problem. Their debt loads are so high and the interest is accumulating at such a phenomenal rate that by the time they come in to see us they are at the point of insolvency."

So, what do you do now?

A good place to start is at your local credit counselling service. Arrange an appointment with a counsellor to go over your situation and help you unravel the knots. The counsellor may be able to help negotiate a repayment plan with your creditors. But if your income and assets are insufficient to enable you to dig yourself out of debt, the idea of a fresh start may be more to your liking. Keep in mind that the road there isn't easy, but it is doable. Here are some of the most frequently asked questions about bankruptcy, and their answers.

*What is bankruptcy?* Bankruptcy is a legal proceeding to help individuals cope with financial crisis so they can move ahead financially without being burdened by past problems. To go into bankruptcy, you must be insolvent; that is, you must owe at least $1,000 and be unable to meet your debts as they are due. You can choose to go into bankruptcy, or you can be petitioned into bankruptcy by a creditor.

You must file for bankruptcy using a trustee in bankruptcy — a licensed professional — who will act as an agent for all of your creditors while assuring your rights. At the initial meeting, your trustee will review your financial situation and advise you of your options. Usually there is no fee for this meeting. To file for bankruptcy, you must complete and sign two main documents. The *assignment* gives your trustee all your assets (other than those that are provincially exempt), which will then be sold and used to repay your debts. The *statement of affairs* shows all your assets and liabilities (like a net-worth statement). It also includes basic personal information. Your trustee will file these two documents and then notify creditors of the "meeting of creditors." You must attend this meeting, since creditors may wish to ask questions and get information about your situation. Your trustee will come up with what he or she considers a manageable repayment plan; over the course of your bankruptcy, you must make the agreed-upon monthly payments to the trustee and provide any information necessary to file your tax returns. You will be completely discharged of your debts, if all goes well, at the end of the bankruptcy.

344 A Woman of Independent Means

*Who will know I've gone bankrupt?* If you have significant assets, a notice is placed in the "legals" section of the newspaper, notifying creditors of the date of the meeting of creditors; at the meeting, they will decide whether to accept or reject your proposal for repayment. If there are minimal assets, creditors are notified by mail. A legal filing of a bankruptcy is a public document. The bankruptcy is also recorded on your credit bureau record, and remains part of your credit history for seven years.

*Are there assets I can keep?* This varies from province to province. In Alberta, you are allowed to retain up to $40,000 in equity in your home. In Ontario, all home equity is assignable (i.e., given over to your trustee) to be used in repaying your debts. Depending on the province in which you go bankrupt, different allowances are available for clothing and personal effects, household furniture, tools of trade, and automobiles. An insurance contract where the designated beneficiary is a spouse, parent, child, or grandchild may be protected from seizure. This includes an RRSP or RRIF with an irrevocable designation. If you make your mortgage payments on time, the mortgagor must allow you to continue to own and live in your home. However, any equity may be assignable.

*Are there debts that are not discharged?* Yes. You will not be released from debts secured by an asset such as your car or your home (although those debts are limited to the value of the secured assets at the time you declare bankruptcy); nor will you be released from paying alimony, child-support payments, parking tickets, court fines, and debts obtained by fraud. Assets obtained during bankruptcy (an inheritance or lottery winning) will be taken and used to pay creditors. Your bankruptcy will not erase the liability of someone who has co-signed a loan for you. If the bankruptcy occurs while you're still a student, or within 10 years of having been one, debts or obligations for student loans are also not discharged.

*When will the bankruptcy be over?* For first-time bankruptcies, a discharge is automatic after nine months, if no one opposes and you have received counselling. If creditors do object, or if this is not the first time you have been bankrupt, the discharge must be heard before a judge or registrar. The discharge will usually be granted if you are earning just enough income to reasonably provide for yourself and your dependents, and so have nothing more to offer creditors.

*Must I take counselling?* Yes, if you wish to be eligible for an automatic nine-month discharge. Your typical cost for this is $85 per session and a minimum of two sessions is required.

*What does it cost to go bankrupt?* The trustee is usually paid out of the money realized from the sale of your assets. If no assets are available, a retainer is required or the trustee may allow the fees to be paid over time. The minimum cost is approximately $1,025 plus GST.

Alternatives to bankruptcy:

- Contact your creditors. Explain why you cannot make your payments and suggest an arrangement that could work for both of you. Suggest a reduced amount that you can afford to pay, or an extension of the repayment period to give you more time to make good on your debt. You may be surprised at a creditor's willingness to negotiate.
- Apply for a debt-consolidation loan. Pay off your debts with the loan advance. Not only will you then have one single monthly payment to make, but you will likely save interest because this bank loan may carry a much lower rate of interest than, say, your credit cards. Shop around carefully, since interest rates will vary.
- File a proposal. If you want to try to pay off the debts because you don't relish the idea of watching everything you've worked for sold out from under you, consider filing a proposal to your creditors. In it you would indicate how much of your debts you could afford to repay, requesting that creditors cut you some slack on interest, fees, or even principal. You decide who to include in the proposal with the help of an administrator, a person authorized to accept and manage proposals. Since all trustees are also administrators — though not all administrators are trustees — you would most likely use the same shop you would if you went bankrupt.

If you have debts of $75,000 or less, not including your home mortgage, you can make a *consumer* proposal. This is most often used by salaried employees. Credit counselling is mandatory. If creditors reject your proposal, they may resume collection activities. Only one consumer proposal may be filed, so it should be your best offer since the alternative is usually bankruptcy. An *ordinary* proposal, usually used by those who are self-employed, has no restriction on the amount owed. Counselling is not required, but a rejection of your proposal results in immediate bankruptcy.

## LIVING THROUGH IT

When you declare bankruptcy, you will have to prepare a spending plan of your monthly income and expenses. The trustee will review it and decide how much you should pay directly to him or her each month on behalf of your creditors. Trustees use a schedule provided by the superintendent of bankruptcy as a guideline in making their decision. But your trustee has the final say and can adjust your payment based on your actual income and reasonable living expenses.

Since you're going to have to live with the spending plan for at least nine months, this is a good opportunity to learn new habits. You may have already tried a budget (a masochist's word for a spending plan). If the last one didn't work, you'll have to ask yourself why. If you've never used a spending plan before, it'll take some practice, but you have to do it so *do it!*

They can't take your house. They can take all the equity you've built up, but you get to keep the mortgage payments. And as long as you continue to make the payments on time, you get to stay in your home. And you'll start rebuilding equity once your bankruptcy is discharged.

*Goals, who has time for goals? I just want to get out of this mess and get my life back.* That's a goal. And you have a timeline because your trustee has already explained how long the whole process will take. Now you have to live through it. But what will you do when you get to the end of the nine months and, heaven willing and you able, the bankruptcy is discharged? Now what? Go shopping to celebrate? Throw a party to declare unbankruptcy? What you should do (and I don't mean to sound preachy, but it may not be top of mind for you, and you really should do it) is set yourself some new goals. You may feel whipped. You may feel broken. So you've got to start dreaming again.

Time to make friends with your banker. In all likelihood, when you declared bankruptcy, you became persona non grata at your local branch. This would be a good time to create a relationship with a bank that was not a creditor in your bankruptcy or proposal proceedings. After all, you went through hell and back, so it's time for a fresh start. Spend some time developing the relationship with your banker by explaining what happened, how your circumstances have changed, and how much you are depending on this person to help you reestablish your credit identity.

Set up a chequing account as soon as possible and make sure you keep your nose clean. No NSF cheques. You've already been through the wringer once, don't do it to yourself again. Stick to your spending plan.

When you file for bankruptcy, you have to give up all your existing credit cards — even the ones you've paid faithfully and on which there is no credit balance. Having fulfilled your obligations, you next should visit your local credit bureau. Provide them with a copy of your certificate of discharge or full performance and ensure this is noted on your credit records. All your previous financial dealings should be expunged, and you may even want to put a short note on your own record to explain what has happened.

Once you've managed to accumulate a small amount of savings, take a loan using your investment as collateral and repay the loan over six months. This will create a record of borrowing and repayment — a new credit history.

You might also apply for a store credit card that you could use to reestablish your credit history. Use it for small amounts and repay it promptly when you receive your statement. After six months or so, apply for another card and keep it going. Eventually you will qualify for an Visa or MasterCard, at which point you should dump the store cards to avoid the ongoing temptation to spend. Remember, the more cards you have, the more likely you are to carry debt.

It may take several years to reestablish your credit history, so don't put off getting started.

Start putting aside some money each month using a periodic investment plan. It's not important how much you save each month. What is important is that you get on the bandwagon. It would be a good idea to establish an RRSP as well. Twenty-five dollars a month each to an unregistered mutual-fund portfolio and to an RRSP will create the right impression with your banker and start you back on the road to financial health.

When you declare bankruptcy, your trustee will prepare and file income-tax returns on your behalf. If the previous year's return hasn't yet been filed, that comes first. Then the year in which you go bankrupt is split in two: from January 1 to the date of your bankruptcy (referred

# 25

# Just in Case You Have to Move Back Home

*Home is the place where, when you have to go there, they have to take you in.*

ROBERT FROST

Thousands of 20- and 30-somethings are boomeranging back home for all sorts of reasons, many of them economic. No matter how independent you may be, circumstances may conspire to send you home to momma. If you are between jobs, spouses, or cities, you may need a place to bunk while you set yourself free of the past and noodle on the future.

If you're thinking of going home, the likelihood is that you'll be welcomed. Research done at Simon Fraser University shows that more than three-quarters of cohabiting parents and adult children surveyed were very satisfied with their situation. Of course, the extent of the satisfaction will be directly related to how well everyone is getting on. And there are some basic rules you can follow to help ensure mom and dad don't up and sell the house and move without telling you where they are going.

Don't expect things to be the way they were when you were a child, unless you want to be treated like a child. You're a grown-up now, so behave like one. That means you won't encourage your mom to do your laundry or your dad to hand over an allowance. And, even before moving in, you will have set your departure date, if at all possible.

Living harmoniously with your folks will be contingent on talking about your expectations of each other. It will be tough to redefine yourself to your parents when they maintain a firm image of you as a freckled, pigtailed 12-year-old. And they'll have a tough time getting used to the new limitations on their privacy. You'll need to be considerate of each other and honest in communicating. After all, if you can't talk to your parents about sex, then you probably shouldn't be having it under their roof.

## Living Through It

Assuming you moved home for economic reasons, whether you've lost your job, lost your apartment, or lost your spouse, you'll need to make a new spending plan. While you should insist on paying room and board if you are working, if you are unemployed you could substitute additional housework, run errands, and generally be Helpful Hattie around the house. Chip in to keep yourself on equal footing as an adult in the house. You don't want to be considered a charity case, right? This is a temporary setback, right?

Initially, your parents may be unwilling to accept money. Tell them how important it is to you to maintain your financial independence. While the amount may not be large at first, particularly if you have debt you need to get rid of, even a token amount helps pave the way for future increases.

Your spending plan should include money for your own phone line, entertainment costs when friends come over (why should your folks buy your beer?), as well as small treats for the family as a whole. If you'll be using the family car, budget for things like gas and insurance. If you have children living with you at your parents' home, you'll have to cover all their costs and keep a budget for child care. Don't assume your parents are there to baby-sit. They may be willing, but each opportunity should be presented in a way that gives them the option to say no if it's not convenient. You could say, "Mom, I'm going to catch a movie tonight, so I'm planning to call Sarah to baby-sit, okay?" Mom can then decide to take the job if she chooses, but has an easy out if she wants the night to herself.

Moving home probably means you didn't get to where you wanted when you wanted. You may perceive the move home as a temporary measure, or you may feel that you have completely failed. Whatever you feel, work through those emotions so you can get on with living. I'd give the same advice to you as I give to people going through bankruptcy: Set yourself some new goals. Remember, a goal is a dream with a deadline, and a dream is a gift we give ourselves. You deserve the gift of a dream, and you're worth the time it takes to turn that dream into a goal that you can accomplish and be proud of achieving. It's up to you.

Often people move home when things become unmanageable elsewhere. Divorce, unemployment, and high levels of debt all contribute to the feeling that things are out of control. And if you're carrying a huge debt burden, they may be. Moving home may cut you the slack you need to get back into the black. Of course, you're never going to get there if you keep spending more than you make. If you're unemployed and make nothing, that's just what you can afford to spend.

When Donna P.'s husband left, things got way out of control. To fill the gap between what she was making and what she was spending, she called upon trusty Mr. Credit Card. Within two years her credit cards were playing the tune and she was dancing as fast as she could. As a single mother, Donna wasn't finding it easy to make ends meet. "It was costing me about $5,000 a year more to live than I was making," says Donna. "It had to come from somewhere."

Getting off the credit treadmill isn't easy but it can be done. Good money management is simply a matter of doing what you very likely already know you *should* do. Read the section on using credit wisely on pages 122–23.

Whether it is to reestablish your emergency fund or to launch or relaunch your pay-yourself-first investment plan, you have to start saving. Why? Because you're supposed to. Because if you don't, your parents may have to install a revolving front door. Because goodwill only goes so far, and then it runs out. Because you're a grown-up now and it's *your* responsibility to take care of your future.

Because although you love your parents, you don't want to live with them forever; nor do you want them to have to install a revolving front door. The more you contribute to your nest egg, the sooner you'll be out of their hair and back enjoying the independence you've temporarily left behind.

# 26

# Just in Case Your Kids Move Home

*Home again, home again, jiggarty-jig.*

CHILDHOOD RHYME

D on't think this won't happen to you. Kids are more likely to move back home with you than you are to move in with them. If it happens in your family, there are some things you should consider.

Probably the most important part of this phenomenon is dealing with the emotional side of the change. If your child has been forced to move home because of a lost job, divorce, or illness, his or her self-esteem has been damaged, and your help is badly needed. Don't think you will be immune to heated moments as you redefine your roles within the new family structure. Your children may at once love you for being there to help and hate you for reminding them of their need — even if you don't say a word. And you may feel compassion for your children even while you resent being put back on duty as caregiver, financial supporter, grown-up.

## LIVING THROUGH IT

While it may not be reasonable or even possible to expect a financial contribution initially, there are other solutions. Talk about how your child will help to compensate for the additional financial stress on you. Yes, you are a mommy, but that doesn't negate your child's responsibility to pull his or her load. It may mean contributing to the household in the form of rent, or cooking and cleaning in exchange for room and board — whatever works for your family. But it is important that some compensation be given for three reasons:

1. The last thing you need right now is to create a situation where your child becomes so dependent on you that he can't get his life back on track. Washing his clothes, cooking his meals, paying his way will all diminish his sense of worth as a contributor to the family. You need to have some expectations of him, just as he has some of you.

2. You'll get angry if you see your child sitting on the couch all day eating bonbons and reading magazines while you're off slaving to bring home the bacon. It's human nature. And it's hard to change the rules once they have been established. So set the rules right from the start. Yes, those rules will evolve, but establishing guidelines at the outset creates the sense that everyone has an expectation — not just your kid.

3. Fair is fair. You want to help your child, but she must want to help herself and return your kindness. Parenting may be a lifelong commitment, but financial support isn't part of that. When you choose to (or have to) support adult children, it is going above and beyond the call of duty, and that should be acknowledged.

Several years ago when I was doing a television phone-in show, an elderly lady called in to say that her son was pressuring her to lend him money for a business venture. She wanted to know what I thought about her mortgaging her house to give him a leg up. I asked her this: "Who gave you a leg up when you got started?" There was a long pause — not a good thing on television. I filled it with, "Who helped you get started?"

She said, "No one. I had to do it myself."

I responded, "Give your son the same opportunity. Let him do it for himself so he can experience all the pleasure and pride of having done it on his own."

No child should expect an elderly parent to go into debt to help him or her get started. No parent should allow a child to do that. Yet children's expectations often exceed a parent's ability or willingness. I've heard dozens of stories of children who assumed their parents' home, cottage, or other assets would be theirs some day. Why? Just 'cos! I've never believed that my parents' house, money, or anything else was mine. My retirement plan does not consist of an inheritance from my parents. I fully expect them to spend every cent before they die. It's their money. And my children will know that the same rules apply. What are your rules?

If you own your home or have a place big enough to easily accommodate your returning child (and perhaps a brood of grandchildren), none of this may seem like a big deal to you. But if you have to get a bigger place, your finances will be squeezed, particularly if your child is unable to contribute financially in the short term. Make sure you both understand the ramifications of a change of address. This should be a long-term decision (i.e., you'll be living together forever and ever), not a months-long experiment. You might decide that you and your child will share the purchase of a new home. You could use your assets to provide the down-payment while you and your child split the mortgage 75/25, with your child paying the larger share. Or you might decide to do all the supporting while your child gets back on her feet, in exchange for her doing all the supporting at some other point while you catch up your retirement savings. Talk about what will work. Bounce the plan off a good friend to ensure you're not being too hard or too soft on the kid.

If your expenses go up substantially because of a change of address, you'll need to go back and revisit your spending plan and your goals to see how they are affected. If you stop making contributions to your retirement plan because your expenses have gone up, you'll need to think about how this will affect your long-term strategy. At some point you'll have to decide whether you should change your expectations for retirement, or catch up the unsaved portion of the plan. Visit your banker and plug the figures into the latest retirement software to see the long-term ramifications.

# 27

# Just in Case You Must Care for Your Aging Parents

*If one is not going to take the necessary precautions to avoid having parents, one must undertake to bring them up.*

QUENTIN CRISP

One of the most damaging myths surrounding aging is that getting old automatically means a decline in mental facilities. Our youth-oriented society makes older individuals feel less vital, less important, less significant because they are less youthful. As the baby-boomer generation ages, this attitude may change; no doubt boomers will continue to rock-and-roll through life in their nonconformist way. For now, though, we must battle our own stereotypical views of aging.

Perhaps it is human nature to be pessimistic, and it is our fear of the worst that drives us to push aside the elderly — to hide them from view so we won't have to deal with our own aging. When we see someone who's had a stroke, suffers from dementia, or is in a wheelchair, we tell ourselves, "That's what it's like to be old." We lump all older people into one demographic group. That approach is neither fair nor realistic. Older Canadians are a diverse group. As we grow older and are seasoned by life's milestones, we become more different from each other and age becomes the only common denominator.

Then there's the myth of mental decline. At 39 I forget things, as I will at 45 and 53. Women blame it on the brain cells we lose during pregnancy, and we laugh. We blame it on the fact that we must hold 17 thoughts at once, and we laugh. It's easy when we're young to dismiss it as just having too much on our minds at any given time. But when we're old and forget things, we automatically blame age. Just because a person can't balance a chequebook doesn't mean she can't handle her own financial decision making. Many young people can't balance a chequebook but would be aghast if a parent attempted to take over their financial management.

Unfortunately, when we project a limiting myth onto our aging parent, it becomes self-perpetuating. If you say anything often enough, you can make it so. Stereotypes rob people of their opportunity to participate and be independent. Ageism is insidious. You can see it in action in indicators like unemployment rates among seniors and in resource allocation decisions such as cutbacks to long-term care facilities.


## LIVING THROUGH IT

Studies have shown that children are reluctant to talk to parents about financial topics. A study conducted for Trimark in 1997 showed that 35% of people agreed to the statement, "I avoid discussions about money matters with my family." When presented with the idea that adults may need to assist their aging parents in managing their financial affairs, 31% said they'd never discussed their parents' finances. Tackling the what-if questions with parents can be especially hard. But you must.

There's real danger in not knowing about a parent's financial situation. If you don't know your parents' financial status, it's hard to know what type of care would be affordable if they were to have an accident or get ill. If you don't know how your parents would want matters handled if they couldn't do it themselves, you may find yourself making important decisions in the dark. If you don't know where all the important stuff is — the money, the investments, the insurance, the safety deposit box, the will, the powers of attorney — you'll be scrambling to find them just when you're scrambling to cope with a parent's death or disability.

There are some prevailing attitudes to watch for if you find yourself in the role of caregiver. First, there's the I'll-do-the-thinking-around-here approach that involves taking total control and negating the parents' responsibility for their own lives. If this sounds like you, when did you get so smart? It's the question your mom or dad would ask if they felt up to it. And it's a good question. After all, just because your notion of what should be done is different from your parents' doesn't mean you're right and they're wrong. If you find yourself being very bossy because you're worrying about every little thing, take a deep breath. If there is no evidence that a problem exists with your parent, relax. It may be your own anxiety and guilt that drives you to make decisions for your parents that they are fully capable of making for themselves.

Then there's the it's-your-life-do-whatever-you-want approach that, through frustration or lack of serious concern, leaves parents on their own to cope. This is also sometimes a symptom of denial: Children don't want to see any changes in their parents, so they write off a parent's inability to cope as "just part of getting old," when these things are problems that could be mitigated with proper attention. It would be irresponsible to walk away from issues simply because dealing with them brings conflict or consternation. Ultimately, when you watch your parents flounder, you'll be heartbroken that you didn't step in sooner. And if they will not let you help — if they push you away to maintain their privacy, protect you from their angst, keep their identities separate — that brings its own heartbreak too. The best you can do is be at the ready with information and time when it becomes apparent that you must step in.

A 1995 guide to elder care published by North Carolina State University recommends that the person you're caring for should always be given as much control and involvement in financial decisions as possible. If you must assume full responsibility for a relative's finances, the guide recommends that you continue to share information about your decisions with other family members to reduce the possibility of later recriminations." You may even consider family meetings to discuss finances, just to keep everyone current on spending and income. It's also wise to keep good notes about significant discussions you have with family members and the actions taken as a result.

Consider sharing duties with family and friends. While some regular responsibilities, such as bill paying or deposit making, might be done most efficiently by one person, don't be bashful about asking family, neighbours, and old friends to step in. Those with legal, health-care, or financial training can be particularly helpful with certain tasks.

As life expectancy has increased, so too have the responsibilities adult children must assume in caring for aging parents. In the old days, you were finished taking care of your children by the time your parents needed attention in their final years. But couples are having children at later stages, whether because they delayed starting their families while they focused on their careers, or because they're in second marriages where babies are part of the new union. The result: More people are being crushed between child- and elder-care responsibilities.

According to the Ontario Women's Directorate and Ministry of Community and Social Services publication *Work and Family: The Crucial Balance*, women spend 17 years caring for their children and 18 years helping an elderly parent. Chances are if you're a baby-boomer, you're also a member of the *sandwich generation*. This is Faith Popcorn's term for adults who are caught between caring for their children and caring for their parents. And it only begins to suggest how overwhelming it can be trying to do it right, do it better, do it all.

It's hard to give parents advice. Sometimes it's difficult because parents continue to see their offspring as the wee ones they once cradled on their laps, and are unable to acknowledge their expertise and experience in dealing with life's issues. At other times the adult children have integrated a great deal of knowledge that has escaped their parents, and it seems they come from different worlds. Personality clashes can arise as the child attempts to become mother to the woman.

One way to approach a parent who's unwilling to reveal financial particulars would be to present several options and ask the parent which one she or he would like to pursue. You might choose to use a friend's death as a place to start talking about the what-ifs. Or the death of a celebrity may provide an opening. You might also use your own financial review to ask for parental advice and begin the discussion.

You need to know where to find your parents' personal and financial documents in the event of an emergency. Find out:

- where they bank
- where their investments (RRSPs, RRIFs, mutual funds, etc.) are held
- the names of their accountant, lawyer, broker, financial planner, and so on

- where the will is kept and who they've named as the executor
- where they keep other legal documents, such as powers of attorney
- the names of their insurance agents, companies, and advisers

You're not prying. You don't need to know what's in the will, just where it is. You don't need to know how much insurance, just where it's kept. You simply want to know what documents to look for, and where to find them in an emergency. Being aware of your parent's financial situation may also help you to ensure dividends and interest are received, insurance is paid on time, pensions are administered appropriately, and so on. Approach your parent practically and non-confrontationally in a friendly environment. Having a family meeting where several family members gang up on an aging parent won't make your mom, dad, aunt, or grandmother any more open to your suggestions. And be prepared for the fact that you may have to suggest a discussion several times, or take small steps toward getting them to fully disclose their affairs. If your parents are reluctant to talk to you specifically, offer to help in finding a professional adviser, assuring them you'll back out once they're in good hands.

Once you've got your hands on the goods, you may find stuff you just weren't prepared for: unpaid bills, misplaced documents, unfiled tax returns. Don't panic. Begin by making a list of all the things that must be remedied, write to the people who have been offended, and start cleaning up the mess. There is no point in getting angry. Yes, you will be frustrated, but the job at hand is to fix the problems, and blaming your parents won't fix them any faster.

The other thing to avoid: judging your parents' choices. So what if your mother has a million dollars sitting in a savings account earning 0.25% in interest? That's her choice. Remember, it's her money. You might make suggestions for changes, but the decision should still be hers, at least until you assume full financial responsibility. Remember, older people are often more concerned about keeping their money accessible than about earning a big return.

Cash flow will become an issue for you when your parent or parents can no longer handle the routine transactions themselves. And there are a whole bunch of concerns that you'll have to address, ranging from who will pay the bills to how long the money will last. There may be plenty of expenses too, depending on the parent's health. Consider the costs of a stair lift or bath bench, or a scooter, walker, or cane. It's important that you check with your doctor or tax adviser before you purchase items for a dependent relative, since many items can be deducted only if prescribed by a medical practitioner. More on taxes a little later.

Be prepared for out-of-pocket expenses. Caregivers don't get paid, often don't get thanked, and frequently don't get reimbursed for long-distance phone calls, travel, groceries, medications, personal care items, or other purchases. A recent survey by the National Alliance for Caregiving and the American Association of Retired Persons found that families caring for an elderly relative spend a monthly average of U.S. $171 of their own money on elder care. This doesn't include "hidden" costs, such as unpaid leave from work. Keep your receipts for everything. You may need to produce them at some point to prove a claim.

You've read all those headlines about the trillion-dollar inheritance the baby-boomers can look forward to. That must mean their folks are pretty well heeled, right? The reality for many "wealthy seniors" is that while they quite often have a home and live mortgage-free, they need income for upkeep of the house, food, clothing, and the like. The majority of women living alone have incomes below Statistics Canada's designated "low-income cut-off" (currently $17,000 for one person). Overall, 19% of all seniors aged 65 and over had incomes below the cut-off. In 1994, people aged 65 and over had an average income (from all sources) of just over $19,000.

For many people, a home is their primary capital investment. However, it can be frustrating to be house-rich and cash-flow poor. Parents may need extra cash to take care of health bills, or to modify their home to make it more comfortable. However, they may not want to sell their home just yet, choosing instead to remain in a familiar neighbourhood. The answer to this conundrum may be a reverse mortgage (see pages 273–75 for more on this topic).

If you're worried about the little things falling through the cracks, but want to see your elder remain independent, here are some small steps you can take. Arrange for the automatic payment of important and recurring bills — water, hydro, and other utility bills, along with health insurance, mortgage, and other regular commitments. Pre-authorized and electronic transactions prevent hassles and interruptions in service that arise from late payments. You might also arrange to be notified if your relative misses a payment. Also arrange for the direct deposit of pension and benefit cheques into bank and brokerage accounts. That way there are no delays in getting funds deposited, no cheques are lost in the mail or forgotten at home, and notices about each payment and deposit can be obtained. And if you set up a joint account with telephone banking privileges, you can do a quick check every now and then to make sure everything in the account is going smoothly (no overdrafts!). Caring for an elderly parent will add so many additional thoughts to your already overloaded circuits that you should look for ways to eliminate routine tasks.

A word of warning: If you and your parent both have deposits at the same bank, and your parent adds your name to his or her account, you may find that you're personally exceeding the $60,000 limit for Canada Deposit Insurance Corporation (CDIC) protection. The solution: Since CDIC limits are based on balances within any single financial institution, move your personal accounts to a financial institution that is different from the one that holds your parent's account.

Beware the financial scam! Targeting the sick or the elderly has become a way of life. Since elderly people are often lonely, they may be willing to trust strangers who call on them. They become the ideal prospects for telemarketing fraud, trumped-up home repairs, and other cons. If you discover a problem, don't be critical. Try not to embarrass your parent. Yes, it can make you angry, but don't take it out on mom or dad. Report the potential con man to the authorities. At home, calmly explain that the friendly person supposedly offering great deals may be a crook.

When it comes to taxes, many health- and age-related expenses can be claimed as medical expenses; these can range from a truss for a hernia to a stair lift, bath bench, dentures, and air or water filters or purifiers. You'll need the advice of a tax specialist when dealing with complex medical expense claims. Don't wait until you've incurred the expense, since certain items can only be claimed if prescribed by a medical practitioner. The definition of medical practitioner is not limited to medical doctors but includes dentists, naturopaths, and a whole slew of other practitioners.

The medical expense claim on your parent's tax form may not include the portion of medical expenses that is covered by any medical plan. However, the health insurance premiums will qualify as medical expenses.

You must file original receipts with your income-tax return to support all medical expenses claimed.

There are also several tax credits a child may claim for a parent:

- The equivalent-to-spouse credit is available to a single child who supports a parent.
- In some cases, the child may claim a personal tax credit for an infirm parent. The disability tax credit requires a medical doctor complete a special form certifying that the parent is "disabled," and any portion of this credit not used by the parent may be transferred to the child. There are other rules and restrictions for claiming these credits.
- A child may claim the medical expenses paid for a dependent parent. Revenue Canada publishes an Interpretation Bulletin that lists in detail what types of expenses qualify as "medical expenses" and which of these items must be prescribed by a medical practitioner. This extensive list changes from time to time. Please consult Revenue Canada or a tax specialist. A medical expense claim for a dependent parent will be reduced if the parent had net income for tax purposes above the basic personal tax credit amount ($6,456 for 1998). This reduction may be greater than the value of the medical expenses of the parent and may even reduce the medical expenses that the child is claiming for herself.

If your dependent is in a nursing home, you can claim medical- and attendant-care costs as part of his or her medical expenses. Attendant-care expenses can include the cost of a companion or health-care aide. There are detailed rules concerning the deductibility of attendant-care expenses, including whether the care is on a part-time or full-time basis, the amount paid for an attendant, and whether the parent meets the government's definition of "disability." However, medical and attendant care are the most expensive costs associated with a nursing home, so a well-supported claim can result in a significant tax credit. Most nursing homes identify the portion that is eligible for the credit on their bills. You'll need form T2201 to claim this credit so Revenue Canada can verify that your dependent is under attendant care.

It is very important that your parent execute a will and powers of attorney, if they have not already done so. Since even beginning this discussion means facing difficult issues such as death or incapacitation, people are hugely resistant to talking openly about them. Superstitiously, people may feel they are tempting fate. But there is a very real danger in not having these documents completed.

Parents who are suddenly incapacitated, and have not executed powers of attorney, will have lost their ability to name a trusted representative to be in control of their affairs. And since there's a time lag before an attorney is appointed by the public trustee, during that time, no one has control or authority over things like paying bills or the mortgage, filing tax returns, and the like. Even if you have joint ownership of a home with your parent, you won't be able to make changes until someone is appointed to represent your parent's interest. And if your father has always controlled the finances and your mom has no independent means, should he become incapacitated, she would become totally dependent on your resources while the province appoints an attorney.

Parents who are reluctant to sign a document that they feel reduces their personal control over their finances, and even their lives, should consider naming two children (or a child and lawyer or accountant) to act on their behalf. The two parties named then act as a check on each other. And the power of attorney can be left with a third party, who is given specific instructions as to its release. As well, it can be limited in terms of the specific time period — such as when a parent is hospitalized — or specific acts.

When it comes to preparing the will or power of attorney, it's up to the lawyer to establish mental competence. He or she might ask your mother questions about her estate, her understanding of her assets, and her reason for visiting the lawyer at that particular time. As long as these questions are answered satisfactorily, the individual is usually deemed competent. If the lawyer has concerns about competency, a medical assessment will be done. This can be tough for an aging client to hear, but it may be necessary to ensure the legal documentation is valid.

# 28

# Just in Case You Become Disabled

*Illness is the night-side of life, a more onerous citizenship. Everyone who is born holds dual citizenship, in the kingdom of the well and in the kingdom of the sick. Although we all prefer to use only the good passport, sooner or later each of us is obliged, at least for a spell, to identify ourselves as citizens of that other place.*

SUSAN SONTAG

My husband often says, of the difference between men and women, that "men die. Women get sick." He's right. And the thought of getting sick and not being able to take care of myself, of being a burden to my husband or my children, of not being able to do what I wanted when I wanted kept me away from this chapter for a long time. Finally I worked up the courage, and here's what I have for you.

Women between the ages of 25 and 55 are far more likely to become disabled than to die. While we have a lower mortality rate than our male contemporaries, our likelihood of disability is higher. Statistics show that if someone becomes disabled for more than three months, that person will likely be disabled five years later. Pricing structures for disability insurance show that women are more often claimants, as reflected in their significantly higher premiums.

## Living Through It

I know a woman named Heather who has the fortitude of a brigade. Heather has multiple sclerosis. As a strong, career-oriented woman, Heather refuses to give up. Once when we met at a children's movie — our daughters are about the same age — she was in a walker and expressing frustration at her latest setback. That week she had awoken to find that she would no longer be able to drive. Her concern: How was she going to get to work?

I have to admit that Heather takes my breath away. I can hardly imagine wanting to go to work knowing that my body could no longer direct my car. Heather didn't just want to go. She went. Her husband now drives her to and from work each day. It's just one of the concessions they have had to make to her disease and the disability it has brought to their lives.

Heather's story isn't meant to set a standard to which we must all strive. On the contrary. Heather's story is a prime example of how we must all cope in our own way to make the journey worthwhile. Why didn't she just stay home and rest? She couldn't. That, more than the disease, would have killed her spirit. Each person facing trying circumstances must find her own way. We must each seek the road that suits our step. We must walk gingerly alongside all those other women who are trying their best to make life work. And, wherever we can, we must lend a hand to help.

Regardless of how well insured you are, you will have to make adjustments to your cash flow. And if you have arrived at this spot with little or no disability insurance, how you manage what you do have will have great bearing on how you will live your life.

The first thing you need to do if you have a disability plan is to find out when you will get your first cheque. This may seem quite straightforward. It can be. It can also be a nightmare. A girlfriend of mine was without disability income for well over a year because the company carrying the plan refused to accept that she was at least 60% disabled. Once her employment insurance (EI) benefits ran out, she ran out of money. She had to cash in her RRSPs just to keep the roof over her head. A few weeks, even a few days, spent gathering paperwork for the insurance company can mean the difference between meeting your financial commitments on time and struggling to put food on the table. In a state of general vulnerability, it's easy to let things slide. But you can't.

You must follow up, insist, push to get what you need. If you don't have the strength, get an advocate working on your behalf.

Your insurance company may have very specific wording for how it wants your disability described and your inability to work proven. Before your doctor starts writing letters and making phone calls, find out everything you can to make your case as strong as it can be the first time. Yes, there is usually an appeal process, and you can always add more information. But each delay, each change in your circumstances that must be documented, adds time to the approval process and leaves you without an income for even longer. If your doctor has had no experience dealing with insurance companies, or with claims like yours, ask for a referral to a specialist who will be better able to create a convincing argument on your behalf.

If you think your disability insurance is your right once you make a claim, you're like most people. We figure that since we've paid our premiums in a timely fashion for five, 10, 20 years, we're entitled to our disability payments when we need them. The insurance company sees things a little differently. Since the disability claim can be huge over the life of the disability, they want proof that you're disabled. Medical science's progress in documenting and naming new diseases means insurance companies are being faced with claims for illnesses they never imagined would exist when early policies were written. They are keeping a careful eye on what documentation should be required to support a claim for these new conditions.

If you are not covered by a private disability plan or a group plan through work, you will have to seek social assistance. The Canada Pension Plan (CPP) has a disability program that is applicable for long-term (more than one year) disabilities. The benefits paid are based on the amount of contributions you and your employers have made over the years. If you have made contributions for at least two of the last three years (or four out of the last six, pending legislative approval at the time of writing), you may qualify to receive payments. Benefits may also be paid to your children who are under the age of 18 (or up to age 25 if they are attending school on a full-time basis). This income is taxable in the child's hands. Remember, too, that this amount qualifies for RRSP purposes as earned income, creating RRSP deduction room for you and your children. CPP benefits kick in after a four-month waiting period.

Insurance disability benefits usually kick in after a waiting period too, during which time EI benefits, if you are entitled, may pick up the slack. It won't be as much as you were earning, and you may very well have some additional medical expenses you must meet, so the next step is to review your spending plan:

- Are there expenses you could minimize or eliminate completely — things like transportation, lunches, and ordering in dinner? Shared day care would be less expensive than full-time day care. Do you still need the second car?
- Are there areas in which your expenses will increase? Medical coverage used to be a given in Canada, but with the social safety net slowly unravelling, you may find yourself with more costs to bear, just at the time when you can least cope financially and emotionally.
- If you had a medical plan at work, will it remain in effect while you are disabled? If not, how will you replace the coverage of those medical costs?
- Are there assets you could sell to help make ends meet? Resist the urge to attack your RRSPs. You're going to need that money down the line, since most disability benefits end at age 65.

You're walking a fine line when you're on a reduced income and trying to manage your credit effectively. It's all very well and good to have scads of credit available on cards and to use that credit to make ends meet when you must, but if you have no hope of repayment, it's a fool's game.

There's no question that from time to time emergencies arise that force you to look to credit as the answer. The most important question to ask yourself before you decide to do the swipe is, "When will I pay this off?" If the answer is "Later," then you may be setting yourself up for a future of juggling one card against the other until the bankruptcy police catch up with you. Not a pretty sight. And not the kind of stress you need in your life. If you don't know when you'll be able to pay off your credit card, don't charge it. Pay cash. If you don't have the cash, do without. If you can't do without, you'll have to find another way.

Some forms of credit offer disability insurance in the event that you cannot work and, therefore, cannot pay your bills. I don't recommend this feature since, for the most part, the insurance doesn't pay off your debt; it simply takes care of the interest portion so the financial institution isn't out of pocket and trying to collect from a vulnerable client. It just keeps them from looking bad. It would be better to apply for disability insurance and have personal coverage that paid you directly so you could then redirect the money in the way that would do you and your family the most good.

If you find that you've become disabled while carrying a significant debt load, it's time to get on the phone and make some telephone calls. You're going to have to explain to your creditors that you may be unable to meet your commitments in the short term. Try to work out a payment plan that minimizes the crunch to your cash flow. Negotiate to make a reduced single payment in lieu of taking 10 years to pay the whole thing off.

When Alison became disabled, she had being flying full-force through life, charging up a storm and wreaking havoc at the mall. Suddenly she came to a full stop and found herself with a mountain of debt she could not handle. "I was doing fine," she said. "Then this thing with my hands started and now I can't work. I can't type or input data. Some days I can't hold a pencil or brush my daughter's hair." Alison still had a personal line of credit that was in good shape — she had only used $1,200 of her $5,000 line. But she was maxed out on her credit cards and department store cards, for a total of $7,500 in debt. And she owed Revenue Canada tax from two previous years. "What a mess," she said, as she looked at the papers on the dining-room table. I suggested Alison call the department stores' credit divisions first, since those cards carried the heftiest rate of interest. After several calls, a letter from her doctor, and proof of her reduced income, Alison managed to negotiate a deal where she would pay two-thirds of the outstanding balance all at once and that would clear her bills. Using her line of credit, she wrote cheques for a total of $3,000 and cleared away $5,000 in debt. The next call was to Revenue Canada.

Alison explained her situation and the tax man listened sympathetically. Most people don't realize just how thoughtful the tax man can be when he believes that you are honestly in a bind, particularly when the circumstances are beyond your control. Revenue Canada agreed to waive all interest and penalties, and they worked out a very gentle repayment plan of just $45 a month for the principal tax owed. Finally, she came to the charge cards. More heavy negotiating. More indications that if forced to she would have to declare personal bankruptcy. Finally, Alison won their acceptance of a repayment plan that fit with her cash flow. In the end, the amount of her monthly income that went to servicing her debt dropped from $750 a month to just $325. "I can do this," she sighed with relief. Of course she can!

For women with partners, the prospect of becoming homeless is less overwhelming. For women who are dealing with their disability on their own, it can be a constant worry. And if a woman has children, the stress is even greater. To deal with this situation, you need some unbiased advice. I'm referring to the kind of advice a good friend can give by asking you a bunch of questions you may not yet have thought to ask yourself. And it doesn't hurt if that friend knows how the financial world operates.

The decision to sell or not sell, move and rent elsewhere, or stay where you are is a purely black-and-white decision. Or, at least, it should be. We often let emotion get in the way of logic. Or we react too quickly, not considering all the options, and let opportunities slip past us. Here's an example of what I mean.

When Emma came to me asking for advice on whether or not to sell her home — she was disabled with a drastic reduction in her income — I asked why she wanted to. "I can't afford this house any longer," she said, as she wept into her hands. "I have my daughter to care for and I've little or nothing to live on."

"Where will you go?" I asked.

"I don't know."

"What are you paying for your mortgage and upkeep right now?"

"Just under $900 a month for my mortgage, so I'd estimate about $1,200 a month with taxes, insurance, and the like."

"And how much longer do you have on your mortgage term and at what rate?"

"It was originally a five-year mortgage at 9%, and I've got a year and a half left on it."

"Have you considered renegotiating the mortgage?"

"I'd have to pay an interest penalty, and I have no money."

"Actually," I said, "there's a thing called a 'blend and extend' mortgage, which I have to admit very few people know about or understand. With a blend and extend, in effect, you would continue to pay 9% for the next 18 months, and then the current rate of 6% for the remaining term — I'd suggest you go long, long at these rates. In reality, the two interest rates would be averaged out based on the terms applicable so you'd end up paying less than 9% now, but more than 6% for the rest of the term. Get my drift?"

"I understand that, but how would it help?"

"Cash flow, girl. Let's say you end up with a 7.25% mortgage. Your payments would go from about $900 to about $700 a month. That knocks $200 a month off your housing costs."

"Okay, but that's still too expensive."

"Didn't you tell me earlier that your basement is rentable?"

"Yes, but the house is so small and that's my daughter's playroom."

"Not if you have to move, it won't be. How much could you rent it for, reasonably?"

"About $400 a month."

"So your housing costs would drop another $400 to about $300 a month, right?"

"Yeah," Emma's face brightened, "I see what you mean."

"Okay, so tomorrow, you call the bank and find out the figures for the blend and extend and then you can make some decisions based on the real financial facts. And start putting feelers out for someone for that basement apartment."

Emma could see her way clear for the first time in a long time. And all it took was one conversation, a little application of black and white, and a sense of being able to do something.

What about your investments? Depending on the type of disability you are living with, this may be more or less important. Disability brought on by terminal illness may negate, in your mind and in the minds of most others, your need to build assets for the future. And if you are struggling to make ends meet now, the argument is moot. However, if your disability is one that will not affect your life expectancy, then you will need to make plans for the long-term future. Even a little put away regularly will make a huge difference in terms of the amount of money you will have when you finally reach 65 and your insurance benefits end. If you do not put something away for the future, you may very well find yourself in an awful place at some point down the road. It is important that you save and that you invest. If you are not taking care of you, who will?

You've probably had to use your emergency fund very recently, so you now know the value of this financial tool. If you're living on a much lower income, it's easy to say that you can't afford to rebuild the fund you've exhausted. But the fact is, with less cash flow available, you need one now more than ever. After all, on a restricted cash flow, even the smallest of emergencies can put a severe crimp in your spending plan. It may take longer to rebuild your emergency fund, but you've got to start. Five dollars this month, 10 dollars next; each little step will take you closer to your goal. Without the emergency fund you will constantly have to worry about the what-ifs. Do what you can to protect yourself so you have the money available, *just in case!*

Think you can't afford to maintain your life insurance on your reduced cash flow? You can't afford not to, since a new policy would be prohibitively expensive. Ideally, you had a disability rider for your insurance. The only way to know is to read your policies or check with your broker.

You may be able to get some breaks from Revenue Canada on your current and future taxes. People who suffer from a severe and prolonged mental or physical impairment — one that has or is expected to last for at least a year — that markedly restricts their ability to perform a basic activity of daily life are entitled to a federal tax credit ($720 in 1998). Look at the rules on Revenue Canada's Form T2201, which is the disability credit certificate.

There is also a substantial non-refundable tax credit ($4,233 in 1998) that can be claimed by a disabled taxpayer *or* supporting individual for a disabled spouse or other dependents. This credit is for individuals who are considered to be markedly restricted in their activities due to severe and prolonged impairment, including blindness, or who are unable to perform basic functions such as thinking and remembering, speaking in a way that can be understood, hearing, bowel or bladder functions, walking, feeding and dressing themselves. The credit can be claimed regardless of whether the individual is working or not, since working, social and recreational activities, and housekeeping are not considered a basic activity of daily life. This credit is available only if no other claim is being made for this or any other non-refundable tax credit.

Attendant-care expenses can also be claimed but may have an impact on whether or how you can claim the disability amount on the same return. Check with a tax specialist on the best way to ensure you get maximum benefit without forfeiting any disability amounts.

For people who are terminally ill, you must review your estate plan. It is surprising just how long you can delay something that you feel may be an unpleasant experience. But, it will continue to remain an unpleasant must-do for as long as it remains undone. Yes, it will be difficult for you, and it will be difficult for the loved ones with whom you must consult. But to do nothing, to die without a will, can create even more confusion and heartache.

If you are severely ill when you make your will, you must seek the best possible estate-planning advice to ensure that your wishes are acted upon, and not posthumously discredited due to your illness. If there are people you wish to protect, individuals you feel a responsibility toward, friends, lovers, or children you must care for, then you must have a will.

In terms of your wishes while alive, there may come a time when you cannot make decisions — be they financial or personal-care decisions — on your own behalf. You must have a legally executed power of attorney naming a trusted individual to act on your behalf so you can be sure your wishes will be respected.


## PREPARING FOR IT

I don't know if you can ever be prepared for disability. That's probably one of the reasons why I waited until D-Day to write this chapter. After all, just the idea of becoming disabled was stomach-wrenching enough. It was excruciating to watch a close friend deal with her own debilitating case of MS, to watch her relationship disintegrate, to watch as she swung from the highs of being able to cope one day to the lows of believing she would never be able to cope again.

The best advice I can give in preparing for a disability — assuming you can prepare because your condition is progressive and you still have time — is to surround yourself with your friends and ask them for help. Get yourself involved in an association that deals with your malady — there are hundreds of associations in Canada dealing with a variety of disabilities — and start to connect with like-minded individuals who can help you understand where you're going. A great place to start is on the Internet. Search by the name of your illness, or simply by the word "disability," and you'll come up with a world of information. You may also want to pick up a copy of *What's Stopping You?: Living Successfully with*

*Disability*, by Mark Nagler and Adam Nagler (Stoddart, 1999), at your local bookstore or library.

My only other advice (and it comes from observing what has worked for my friends): Try to spend at least a part of each week being "other-focused" or, in other words, helping someone else cope. Your disability and its impact on your life can be all-consuming, and financial clouds may seem so thick that they block out the very things we should be focused on: family, love, and enjoyment of the here-and-now. If you can take just a moment from your life to help someone else get over his or her hurdles, your spirit will be enriched and your burden lightened, at least for a little while.

# Conclusion

It isn't often that you get to work on a project that can actually change people's lives by helping them see things in a new light. With this book, I hope that I, and my comrades in money, have helped you change how you feel about the green stuff and what you'll do with it as you move through your life.

Good money management isn't magic. And it doesn't require you to be some sort of financial wizard. It's all about doing the right things consistently. It's about being deliberate in the steps you take to attain your particular goals. That means saving some money, investing smartly for your specific needs, and taking care of the what-ifs. It also means understanding who you are with money, and why, so you can shed your emotional baggage. If you face the money demons that inhabit both your soul and your wallet, you can move on from there.

Remember, *telesis* is about making progress. And no matter what comes along to throw you off track, you are the only person who can control what you do next. Sinking into a quagmire of misery and self-pity won't get you into that house, or out of debt, or back to school to build new skills. Now, I'm not saying there aren't some times when a nice thick blanket and a huge box of chocolates can't be your best friends. But if you stay in that place, you can't move forward. Inertia will keep you bogged down. The only way to get out is to make it happen. And you can.

Whether you're a little in debt or a lot, recently widowed or living through a divorce-from-hell, movin' on up or in a job that feels like the same-old, same-old, you can change your life. You need a plan. You must know the rules of smart money management. And you must follow them.

Today, pick one thing you'll do differently. You might choose to stash your cards behind the refrigerator and shop with cash. (If you have to dig through all that gunk under the fridge to get your cards out, you'll think twice about how much you actually *need* those new shoes.) Or perhaps you'll call your insurance agent and find out what it would cost to protect your family should you or your honey meet your Maker. Maybe you'll put yourself on a monthly investment plan. With as little as $25 a month you can start forming a habit that will hold you in good stead forever.

If you're one of those people who believe they're too deep in debt to ever get out, give yourself a good kick. You can if you want to. If you don't really want to, quit whingeing; if you do, ask for some help. There are all kinds of people out there ready and willing to come to your aid. For a start, check out the resources section on the next few pages.

Finally, after spending this much time reading my book, you know enough about me to know that I wouldn't kid you. You can take control. You can be financially at peace, if you want to be. But only *you* can make it happen, so . . . do it!

# Resources

The following is a list of books and organizations you may wish to consult when you have questions about money and specific aspects of financial planning.

**Banking**

Canadian Bankers Association
   199 Bay Street, Suite 3000, P.O. Box 348, Commerce Court West, Toronto, ON  M5L 1G2
   Tel: 416-362-6092

Canada Deposit Insurance Corporation
   50 O'Connor Street, 17th Floor, P.O. Box 2340, Station D, Ottawa, ON  K1P 5W5
   Toll-Free: 1-800-461-2342

**Credit**

Staats, William F., and E. D. Sledge. *How Chuck Taylor Got What He Wanted* (Canadian edition), Credit Counselling Service of Toronto, 1998.

Kisluk, Frank. *Life After Debt*, Doubleday Canada, 1996.

Vaz-Oxlade, Gail. *Shopping for Money*, Stoddart Publishing, 1998.

Access Nova Scotia
Department of Business and Consumer Services
Toll-Free: 1-800-670-4357 (only in Nova Scotia)  Fax: 902-424-0720
B.C. Ministry of the Attorney General
Debtors Assistance Branch
Toll-free: 1-800-663-7867 (only in B.C.)
Victoria: 250-387-1747  Fax: 250-953-4783
Burnaby: 604-660-3550  Fax: 604-660-8472
Kamloops: 250-828-4511  Fax: 250-371-3822
Consumer Services Officer (New Brunswick)
Consumer Affairs Branch, Department of Justice
Tel: 506-453-2659  Fax: 506-444-4494
Credit Counselling Service of Toronto
45 Sheppard Avenue East, Suite 810, Toronto, ON  M2N 5W9
Tel: 416-228-3328
Credit Counselling Services of Alberta
Toll-free: 1-888-294-0076 (only in Alberta)
Calgary: 403-265-2201  Fax: 403-265-2240
Edmonton: 403-423-5265  Fax: 403-423-2791
Credit Counselling Services of Atlantic Canada, Inc.
Toll-free: 1-800-539-2227 (only in New Brunswick)
Tel: 506-652-1613  Fax: 506-633-6057
Credit Counselling Society of British Columbia
Toll-free: 1-888-527-8999 (only in B.C.)
Tel: 604-527-8999  Fax: 604-527-8008
Equifax Canada Inc.
Box 190, Jean-Talon Station, Montreal, PQ  H1S 2Z2
Tel: 514-493-2470
Family Services of Fredericton, Inc.
Tel: 506-458-8211  Fax: 506-451-9437
Fédération des associations coopératives d'économie familiale du Québec
Tel: 514-271-7004  Fax: 514-271-1036
Manitoba Community Financial Counselling Services
Tel: 204-989-1900  Fax: 204-989-1908
Newfoundland and Labrador Personal Credit Counselling Service
Tel: 709-753-5812  Fax: 709-753-3390

N.W.T. Consumer Services
  Municipal and Community Affairs
  Tel: 867-873-7125  Fax: 867-920-6343
Ontario Association of Credit Counselling Services
  Tel: 1-888-7IN-DEBT (746-3328)  Fax: 905-945-4680
Option-consommateurs
  Tel: 514-598-7288  Fax: 514-598-8511
P.E.I. Department of Community Affairs
  Consumer, Corporate and Insurance Services
  Tel: 902-368-4580  Fax: 902-368-5355
Port Cities Debt Counselling Society
  Tel: 902-453-6510
Saskatchewan Department of Justice
  Provincial Mediation Board
  Regina: 306-787-5387  Fax: 306-787-5574
  Saskatoon: 306-933-6520  Fax: 306-933-7030
Trans Union of Canada
  P.O. Box 338–LCD1, Hamilton, ON  L8L 7W2

## Estate Planning
Foster, Sandra E. *You Can't Take It With You*, John Wiley & Sons, 1998.

## Financial Planning and Specialty Areas
Cohen, Bruce. *The Money Adviser*, Stoddart Publishing, 1999.
Flynn, Donald. *The Truth About Funerals*, Funeral Consultants International Inc., 1993.
Kerr, Margaret, and JoAnn Kuirtz. *Buying, Owning and Selling a Home in Canada*, John Wiley & Sons, 1997.
McNicol, Barry. *The Severance Package Strategy Book*, Stoddart Publishing, 1996.
Nagler, Mark, and Adam Nagler. *What's Stopping You?: Living Successfully with Disability*, Stoddart Publishing, 1999.
Orman, Suze. *The 9 Steps to Financial Freedom*, Random House, Inc., 1997.
Rhodes, Ann. *The Eldercare Sourcebook*, Key Porter Books, 1993.
Vaz-Oxlade, Gail. *The Money Tree Myth: A Parents' Guide to Helping Kids Unravel the Mysteries of Money*, Stoddart Publishing, 1996.

Vaz-Oxlade, Gail. *The Retirement Answer Book*, Stoddart Publishing, 1997.
Wylie, Betty Jane. *Enough*, Northstone Publishing, Inc., 1998.

Financial Planners Standards Council of Canada (FPSC)
   505 University Avenue, Suite 1600, Toronto, ON  M5G 1X3
   Tel: 416-593-8587
Canadian Association of Financial Planners
   60 St. Clair Avenue East, Suite 510, Toronto, ON  M4T 1N5
   Tel: 416-966-9928

## Insurance

Bullock, James, and George Brett. *Insure Sensibly: A Guide to Life and Disability Insurance*, Penguin Books, 1991.

Insurance Bureau of Canada
   181 University Avenue, Toronto, ON  M5H 3M7
   Tel: 416-362-9528
Independent Life Insurance Brokers of Canada
   2175 Sheppard Avenue East, Suite 310, Willowdale, ON  M2J 1W8
   Tel: 416-491-9747
The Insurance Institute of Canada
   18 King Street East, Toronto, ON  M5C 1C4
   Tel: 416-362-8586
Canadian Life and Health Insurance Association
   1 Queen Street East, Suite 1700, Toronto, ON  M5C 2X9
   Tel: 416-777-2221

## The Internet as a Resource

Carroll, Jim, and Rick Broadhead. *1999 Mutual Funds and RRSPs Online*, Prentice-Hall, Inc., 1998. (Make sure you get the most recent edition.)

## Investing

Canadian Securities Institute. *How to Invest in Canadian Securities*, 1997.
Canadian Securities Institute. *How to Start and Run an Investment Club*, 1998.
Edey, David. *Smart Money Strategies for the Canadian Mutual Fund Investor*, Regine Communications, 1998.

Hartman, George. *Risk Is a Four Letter Word*, Stoddart Publishing, 1994.

Moynes, Riley. *The Money Coach*, Addison Wesley, 1997.

Newsome, Mark, and Jeffrey Zahn. *Taking Control: Your Blueprint for Financial Success*, Key Porter Books, 1993.


Canadian Shareowners Association
    1090 University Avenue West, P.O. Box 7337, Windsor, ON  N9C 4E9
    Tel: 519-252-1555

Investment Dealers Association of Canada
    121 King Street West, Suite 1600, Toronto, ON  M5H 3T9
    Tel: 416-364-6133

The Investment Funds Institute of Canada
    151 Yonge Street, 5th Floor, Toronto, ON  M5C 2W7
    Tel: 416-363-2158

Investor Learning Centre of Canada
    Toronto: 121 King Street West, 15th Floor, Toronto, ON  M5H 3T9
    Tel: 416-364-6666
    Montreal: 1 Place Ville Marie, Suite 2840, Montreal, PQ  H3B 4R4
    Tel: 514-878-3591
    Calgary: 355–4th Avenue SW, Suite 2330, Calgary, AB  T2P 0J1
    Tel: 403-269-9923
    Vancouver: P.O. Box 11574, 650 West Georgia Street, Suite 1350,
    Vancouver, BC  V6B 4N8
    Tel: 604-683-1338

## Psychology of Money

Boundy, Donna. *When Money Is the Drug*, HarperCollins Publishers, 1993.

Dominguez, Joe, and Vicki Robin. *Your Money or Your Life*, Penguin Books, 1992.

Mellan, Olivia. *Money Harmony*, Walker and Company, 1994.

## Sociology of Money

Galbraith, John Kenneth. *A Journey Through Economic Time: A Firsthand View*, Houghton Mifflin Company, 1994.

Hacker, Andrew. *Money: Who Has How Much and Why*, Scribner, 1997.

## Taxes

Cestnick, Tim. *Winning the Tax Game*, Prentice-Hall, Inc., 1998.

Jacks, Evelyn. *Jacks on Tax*, McGraw-Hill Ryerson, 1998.

Rosentreter, Kurt. *50 Tax-Smart Investing Strategies*, Stoddart Publishing, 1999.

Canadian Tax Foundation
  1 Queen Street East, Suite 1800, Toronto, ON  M5C 2Y2
  Tel: 416-863-9784
Chartered Accountants of Canada
  277 Wellington Street West, Toronto, ON  M5V 3H2
  Tel: 416-977-3222

# Index